D0872355

The Angel Makers

GORDON
RATTRAY TAYLOR

The Angel Makers

A STUDY IN THE
PSYCHOLOGICAL ORIGINS
OF HISTORICAL CHANGE
1750–1850

E. P. DUTTON & CO., INC.
NEW YORK
1974

CONTENTS

CONTENTS

PART FOUR: *Interpretations*

PART FIVE: *Conclusion*

To Jane and Ian Phillips

IN APPRECIATION

ACKNOWLEDGMENTS

I HAVE RECEIVED generous help from many quarters. At the outset, I received help from Mr. Angus Wilson, who discussed problems with me and suggested clues to follow. Dr. Eric Dingwall kindly permitted me to consult his files of source material; and Dr. Réné Spitz of New York made available his researches into the bibliography of masturbation.

The application of my theory to the history of æsthetics would have been an impossible task without the continuous help and advice of Mr. Ian Phillips, who most generously made both his knowledge of the period and his library available. In this connection, I must also tender my thanks to Mr. Trevor Dannatt, for permission to use material originally gathered for an article in the *Architect's Yearbook*; to Mr. Roland Penrose, for permission to use material originally gathered for a lecture at the Institute of Contemporary Arts; and to Dr. E. H. Gombrich, for advice and facilities at the Warburg Institute.

To all these I am deeply indebted.

I should also like to make acknowledgment to Mr. Beswick, who allowed me to consult manuscripts of the Beswick Diary; to Mary Settle, for various references. In addition, I am obliged to the City Librarian of Bristol Public Libraries, for the opportunity to consult material from the archives; to the Hon. Librarian of the Royal College of Surgeons; and to the library staffs of the Bodleian, the British Museum, and the London Library, whose courtesy and efficiency are too well known to need my endorsement.

To my wife, who has lived with this book for two and a half years, I am particularly grateful.

1958

NOTE

In footnotes, the abbreviation op. cit. has been used when the title of the work referred to has been given in the passage annotated; the abbreviation ib. when the work referred to is the same as in the immediately preceding note. Titles of works cited are given in abbreviated form, and the date is supplied only where relevant to the argument. The full title, date and place of publication will be found in the list of sources on pp. 358–372. Where no author is indicated, the work is anonymous.

INTRODUCTION

"STUDY PROBLEMS in preference to periods," urged Lord Acton. In this book I attempt to study a specific problem: how, in Britain, did the eighteenth century turn into the nineteenth century? How, within a single lifetime, did a period renowned for its immorality turn into a period so strait-laced that the word 'Victorian' has become a symbol for extreme rectitude?

We live in a permissive period to-day, and many people are under the impression that this is because we have burst out of an age-old strait-jacket. But the fact is that societies swing between prudery and permissiveness; this certainly occurred in Rome, which passed from strictness to license between the time of the Antonines and the Emperors, while the converse change took place in England when Christian missionaries and the Norman invaders between them clamped down on the fertility worship and pagan jollity (largely Celtic in origin) which they found there.

Since such swings have occurred so often in the past, we can be sure that they will occur again, so we must take seriously the possibility that our current permissiveness will again be replaced by severity, perhaps within the lifespan of our own grandchildren. Indeed, there are already some signs of a swing-back. Thus it is a matter of considerable practical relevance to try to uncover and understand the forces and mechanisms which bring about such changes. Furthermore, if we wish to improve our society we must reckon with these vast social processes. It is no good paddling in one direction if the current is sweeping us in another.

But moral attitudes, as will emerge later, are closely bound up with other kinds of attitude. The change from the eighteenth to the nineteenth century involved—and necessarily involved—changes in political outlook, in religious and moral outlook, in social outlook. And very noticeably, it involved a striking depression in the status of women. Thus it is not simply moral change but social change in general on which I hope to shed some light. Are there any generalisations one can usefully make, or is history, as some maintain, merely a random process?

Specifically, the enquiry is designed to test the hypotheses about social and moral attitudes put forward in an earlier work, *Sex in History*, the theory that in history there can be distinguished periods in which the psychological influence of a father-figure is dominant (and these are repressive periods) and periods in which the mother-image predominates (and these are permissive periods). For such periods I proposed the terms 'patrist' and 'matrist'.[1] It is perhaps natural that when mothers are valued above fathers the status of women should be high, and conversely. However, it is not widely appreciated how free eighteenth-century women in most sections of society were. There is a widespread belief that only to-day have women begun to cast off the chains imposed by a man-dominated society. Nothing could be further from the truth. In the next chapter, therefore, I shall take a look at the changing status of women in the period. (In the original edition of this book, this chapter appeared as Chapter Fourteen but I have thought it helpful to place it earlier here, since it gives a good impression of the whole problem and opens up various issues which will be treated more fully later.)

A curious feature of the Victorianising of women was the attempt to depict them as ethereal beings, lacking human desires and appetites. Thus Dr. Gregory, the stern Scottish doctor who left his advice as a legacy to his daughters when he died in 1773, asserts that in women "the luxury of eating is beyond expression indelicate and disgusting".[2] Women must at least pretend to have no appetite. (Harold Nicolson's grandmother recalled women eating in their boudoirs, so that they could display a lack of appetite in the dining-room.)[3] Furthermore,

---

[1] See Appendix for a summary of this theory.
[2] *Legacy*, p. 39.
[3] *Good Behaviour*, p. 246.

women must not look as if they were in good health, as this is also too earthy: they must be 'pale and interesting'. And, of course, they must be ignorant of sexual matters. As one nineteenth-century educator exclaimed: "A woman must become a walking ghost to be styled truly delicate."[4] But a ghost, of course, is an unsuitable image, for a ghost has power to frighten, and this is by no means the role designed for woman. Woman's job is to minister to the needs of husband and children, and so the idea of woman as a 'ministering angel' was born.

This is quite a strange development, theologically. Angels were always held to be another order of beings, devoid of human feeling, whose role was to praise God or to act as his messengers. To the extent that they could be assigned a sex they were masculine, as names like Gabriel and Michael show. Thus the notion that human beings could become angels was novel, and seems to have emerged in the seventeenth century. By the end of this century, the rationalists were characterising the Puritan[5] advocacy of large families (most of whom died in infancy) as 'pure angel-making'. (The French term 'faiseur d'anges' signifies an abortionist, for similar reasons.) By the reign of Victoria, however, a moralist could tell his readers, without any awareness of theological unorthodoxy, "Remember that you are not angels yet, you are only on probation." And Newman as a young man was obsessed by the idea that he actually *was* an angel.

Women, especially, were expected to model themselves on angels, and in the seventeenth century Jeremy Taylor had said that virgins were like angels and must therefore spend much of their time in 'angelical employments'. And Dr. Gregory warned his daughters

[4] *Female Instructor*, p. 216.
[5] The word 'Puritan' is used in this book both in the general sense of a person of severe morality (as in the word 'Puritanical') and in the specific sense of a member of the religious group which flourished in the sixteenth and seventeenth centuries: indeed, it is argued that nineteenth-century severity is derived from the same psychological roots as Puritanism, and that it is historically connected with it. The word has therefore been spelled with an initial capital throughout.
For analogous reasons, the words 'Romantic' and 'Romanticism' have been capitalised regardless of whether the reference is to the specific literary movement or the whole psychological trend of which it was part.

that women would not 'regain their ascendancy' over the male sex 'by the fullest display of their personal charms' because this actually 'reduces the angel to a very ordinary girl'. Such writers were seeking to impose on women a role dictated by their unconscious needs. Angels are mothers who have no sexual interests. In short the change in the status of women is the result of a psychological process, and this is why *The Angel Makers* struck me as an appropriate title.

Those who put forward simplifying theories are invariably accused of selecting the facts which fit their theories and suppressing those which do not. I have therefore tried to present a wide array of facts (rather than a few instances) letting them speak for themselves, before drawing my conclusions. In this way I may, at least, have provided some hard-won data on which a better theory might be erected, even if my own is found wanting. I was the more inclined to do this because of the fascinating and little-known character of much of the material which I found in manuscript and other obscure diaries and pamphlets of the period (whoever heard of 'blood-bombs'?). In particular the diaries of the Methodists have been unduly neglected by modern social historians.

Truth to tell, social history is still in a very primitive state. For instance, I decided to explore the use of cosmetics, as being an objective clue to the change in social attitudes—something visible to every vistor and thus more reliable as evidence than reported opinions about moral attitudes. I imagined, to start with, that histories of cosmetics existed from which it would be easy to draw what I needed. I could find none,[6] and it was some time before I discovered the different significance of 'paint' and 'rouge' (see p. 46). A still more serious lacuna was the lack of any comprehensive account of the changes in methods of bringing up children during the period.[7]

Further to avoid the charge of imposing a preconception on the material, I have noted from time to time the development of my own

[6] A history of this topic was however published in 1972.

[7] The Association for Applied Psychoanalysis in the U.S.A., partly as a result of the publication of *The Angel Makers*, is now preparing such a study and has launched a new publication, *The History of Childhood Quarterly*.

thought, and how what I found sometimes confirmed but sometimes contradicted my hypotheses or called for modifications on them. One of these developments was of major importance. As I dug deeper into the psychology of the key figures in the story, I began to see that the polarisation between patrism and matrism only explained some aspects of the matter. There was a second polarisation, which I have called hard ego vs. soft ego, which seemed able to account for the essential features of the Puritan on the one hand, the Romantic on the other. This dichotomy derives from the tough–tender dichotomy proposed by William James, the great American psychologist, but is defined in more modern, psychoanalytic terms. In Chapters Five to Eight I seek to explore the material which embodies this distinction and to show how it explains aspects of behaviour as diverse as competitive business and garden design. It is customary, in literary and aesthetic studies, to treat Classicism as the counterpart or opposite of Romanticism. We shall see, however, that a sort of pragmatism, in which function is paramount and feeling is non-existent, is the opposite pole from Romanticism, with Classicism as a middle, or compromise, position.

In short, I now see personality, and hence society, as located on two axes: (1) patrism–matrism (2) hard and soft ego. Patrism–matrism is a scale which ranges from authority and self-control to spontaneity and equality. Hard and soft ego represents a scale from tough, isolated competitiveness to tender, group-minded co-operativeness.[8] The Puritan is both tough and authoritarian, the Romantic is tender and equalitarian. The one is for self-discipline, the other for spontaneity. Both factors are needed to explain their psychology adequately. (And to these we may have to add—if we take a psychoanalytic view—other influences such as anal and oral fixations.) When a society becomes dominated by people of a particular personality type, we can speak of a patrist or a hard-ego society (Mary Douglas calls it a success society) just as we can speak of a matrist or a permissive society.

[8] In 1970 the anthropologist Mary Douglas put forward a rather similar theory, on anthropological rather than psychological grounds, under the title *Natural Symbols* (Cresset Press).

The first part of this book presents the sociological facts—when and in what sections of society did the change of ethos originate and of what did it consist? The second section looks at the underlying psychology in the case of the moralists, the third at the psychology of the Romantics who developed the counter-movement. The strange fascination which death had for the moralists, their preoccupation with money and with parsimony, and, in contrast, the pantheistic euphoria of the Romantics, will provide important clues to the psychopathology of the period. The last section seeks to interpret and explain the rather astonishing material thus revealed.

But before plunging into the mass of sociological detail, it may by helpful to take a broader preliminary look, and we can conveniently do this by considering the role of women in the period, which immediately exposes the main psychological forces involved. Women are the key to the whole problem.

1973

PART ONE

HISTORICAL

CHAPTER I

THE BRITISH FAIR

ZETZNER, writing in 1700, while greatly admiring Englishwomen, concedes that "the women of this country are much given to sensuality, to carnal inclinations, to gambling, to drink and to idleness".[1] He wrote just a century and a half before Dr. Acton gave his imprimatur to the view that women were incapable of sexual desire.[2] The change in the conception of British womanhood over the period could hardly be illustrated more emphatically.

The freedom which women—or at least some women—enjoyed at the opening of the eighteenth century is well known. Zetzner was astonished to find that women used the taverns as freely as men, and that they could hire a private room in which to discuss a business matter over a glass of wine, without anyone suspecting anything dishonourable.[3]

Fanny Russell wrote to her brother in 1743, "My mistress [Princess Amelia] and her youngest sister, Princess Louisa, went last night to Bartholomew's Fair: did not come home till one this morning and then went and supped at Lady Ann's and stayed there till two. Lady Harriet and Lady Ann went with them, and the Duke of Grafton, Lord Lydford, Gen. Churchill and Mr. Will Finch."[4]

It has a curiously contemporary ring.

Novels like *Mount Henneth* (1781) or *Barham Downs* (1784) give a vivid impression of the spirited and self-possessed behaviour of young unmarried girls, daughters of the gentry, even if it was also true that a father's word was not lightly to be disobeyed.

---

[1] Zetzner, *Londres et l'Angleterre*, p. 18.
[2] Acton, *Functions and Disorders*.
[3] Zetzner, op. cit., p, 15.
[4] Historical MSS. Commission: Astley MSS, p. 286.

To a very considerable extent the "double standard" was in abeyance: women were accorded the same freedom as men, in this group. Certainly we find women taking the initiative in sexual advance when necessary, writing notes to men they have seen at a place of public resort, or placing advertisements in the newspapers. Le Blanc notes that Englishwomen have "no false modesty". "If a girl fancies a man and can't get to know him, she'll send him a message with her proposal or advertise," and he reproduces one such advertisement.[5] The same writer complains that Englishwomen of condition dress like tarts.[6]

At the same time the foreign observers all agree on the modesty and reserve of the Englishwoman and on her lack of affectation or coquetry. She is not a hoyden or a virago. These types did exist, to be sure, but almost exclusively in the lower classes.

The absence of feelings of jealousy at this date was quite marked. "An Englishman never refuses to let his wife go for a walk with one of his friends; on the contrary, he regards it as a particular honour if anyone wishes to give pleasure to his wife," observes Zetzner in amplification.[7] This is just what we should expect of a matrist age, and contrasts with the patrist's excessive concern for his wife's chastity. Another attitude which springs from the same source is the valuation of virginity, and it is in accordance with the theory which we are reviewing that men of the upper class attached little importance to it.

It was part of this outlook that relatively little disadvantage attached to illegitimacy. For instance, Sir Edward Walpole (Horace Walpole's brother) had four illegitimate children by Mrs. Clements: all married well.

Shebbeare touches upon another point: the willingness of this group to ignore class-barriers. He remarks with surprise, "Men of the highest rank marry women of infamy even, not to say of extreme low birth, and ladies of noble families wed their footmen, players and singers."[8] This is in accord with the theory. Since the patrist is an authoritarian, he sees society as a hierarchical structure in which there are impenetrable

---

[5] Le Blanc, *Letters*, i, 151.

[6] ib., i, 128.

[7] Op. cit., pp. 19–20. Cf. also de La Motraye, *Travels*, i, 146.

[8] Shebbeare, *Letters*, i, 162–3. Zetzner confirms, op. cit., pp. 19–20.

barriers between the various ranks; the matrist, on the other hand, sees society as composed of equals, and so feels that there is no reason why a poor girl and a rich man should not marry.

At first the aristocracy were willing to take girls of low birth as mistresses but not to marry them; but by the end of the century they did not hesitate to do so. Thus when the Earl of Peterborough started the now time-honoured association of the peerage with the chorus by marrying the beautiful Anastasia Robinson, he kept the marriage a secret and gave out that she was only living with him as his mistress. But by the end of the century Elizabeth Farren, the actress, was accepted as Countess of Derby quite readily.

It is not difficult to find evidence of the patrist attempt to limit this freedom becoming effective towards the end of the century. Thus while in *Barham Downs* Annabella and her sister, the daughters of a merchant, wander about freely and pick up a strange young man, there is an evident note of censure when a satirist depicts Caroline, and her relationship with her beau, in the year 1814. She "used to pass whole days in his company, walking and rambling with him; she wore his picture concealed, and everything marked with his hair; wrote to him daily, although they met twice in the day; and rendered herself conspicuous as his *amante*, to the whole town".[9]

Mary Wollstonecraft's *Vindication* is often asserted to be the first major defence of women's rights. It seems clear, in the context of the foregoing facts, that it came when it did only because women's rights were, for the first time in the century, evidently in danger; and that it owed its fame to the scandal it caused in a world already more than half converted to the view that woman's place was the home. When about 1771 the ineffable Thomas Day, in proposing to Honora Sneyd, explained that in his view women should fill a subordinate role, she replied with a spirited defence of women's rights, and Day withdrew, defeated. Even in the relatively provincial environment of Lichfield, opinion seems to have been on Honora's side; and when her sister Elizabeth told Day that he'd better smarten himself up and learn to dance, he tamely went off to attempt to obey her command.[10]

[9] *Hermit in London*, p. 74.
[10] Scott, *Exemplary Mr. Day*, pp. 88 f.

The arguments advanced by the patrists for restricting the freedom of women bear out the predictions of the theory with almost laughable exactitude. According to the theory, women are seen as the source of sexual immorality because they tempt men, and morals are to be reformed by reforming women. Medieval statements of this theme are numerous. It appears unaltered in the eighteenth century—for instance in the *Gentleman's Magazine* for 1772: "It is without reason that we complain of the licentiousness of the present age; the fault is in ourselves. Did we but confine the fair sex within proper bounds and exert that authority which Nature and Reason have given us, everything would return to its proper place." The final phrase even seems to echo the medieval notion of a fixed order of society, albeit Reason is dragged in to make the argument stronger. The writer then continues with a magnificently symbolic coda: he doesn't want, he says, "to beat out their brains . . . for drinking a glass of wine, but to confine them."[11] Since no one has suggested anything so extraordinary, it is legitimate to assume that he is denying his own unconscious wish, and in fact to make women into brainless creatures was precisely what the patrists did propose.[12] In addition, the word 'confine' suggests a *double entendre*—all the more so since to confine women to the house would scarcely prevent them "drinking a glass of wine".

Another curious attack is that of Polwhele, *The Unsex'd Females: A Poem* (1798). Botany, he says, has recently become a favourite study of the ladies, and he declares that their interest in the topic is primarily sexual. He says that they

> For puberty in sighing florets pant
> Or point the prostitution of a plant;
> Dissect its organ of unhallow'd lust
> And fondly gaze the titillating dust.

Quoting *The Botanic Garden* to prove that flowers commit adultery, he ironically recommends to women a course of gymnastics (as recom-

[11] *Gentleman's Magazine*, 1772, p. 370.
[12] Cf. Gregory's demand, ". . . if you happen to have any learning, keep it a profound secret, especially from the men, who generally look with a jealous and malignant eye on a woman of great parts . . ." (*Legacy*, p. 32).

mended by Mary Wollstonecraft) and the study of plant adultery, together with Angelica Kauffmann's "Priapic prints".[13] He is especially shocked by Mary Wollstonecraft's suggestion, "It would be proper to familiarise the sexes to an unreserved discussion of those topics which are generally avoided in conversation from a principle of false delicacy; and that it would be right to speak of the organs of generation as freely as we mention our eyes or our hands."

The steps by which a 'Victorian' conception of women's role was built up, and the nature of that conception, will be examined later. The point which I was attempting to bring into focus at this stage was: by what psychological mechanisms was this change brought about? It is commonly assumed that when women's status is depressed, this is something imposed upon her by men. But I was already inclined to the view that this could not be a complete explanation, for it is most striking, in the period under investigation, how women themselves played a leading part in advocating this change. The majority of the didactic writers are women: Mrs. Chapone, Mrs. Sherwood, Mrs. Opie, Mrs. Trimmer, Hannah More, Mrs. Sandford and many others. All these writers emphasise, with almost sadistic—and quite certainly obsessive—iteration, that women must submit themselves to men, that they must eschew learning, abandon all idea of a career, and so on.

Furthermore, we find even quite worldly women consciously modelling themselves upon the new pattern. Thus the novelist, Sydney Owenson, Lady Morgan, wrote, "The strongest point of my ambition is to be every inch a woman . . . I dropped the study of chemistry lest I should be less the woman. I have studied music as a sentiment rather than as a science, and drawing as an amusement rather than as an art, lest I should become a musical pedant or a masculine artist."[14] This was about 1807, but we can find signs of this new out-

---

[13] "The vegetable passion of Love is agreeably seen in the flower of the Parnassia, in which the males alternately approach and recede from the female. . . . I was this morning surprised to observe . . . the manifest adultery of several females of the plant Collinsonia, who had bent themselves into contact with the males of other flowers . . . neglectful of their own." (*Botanic Garden*, i, 197.)

[14] Cited without source by Preedy, *This Shining Woman*, p. 165.

look emerging in the upper class at a considerably earlier date. For instance, when Meister, visiting England in 1789, criticised English-women for excessive devotion to pleasure, Lady Craven wrote to tell him that this view was out of date, and that English women, in the nobility, spent much of their time walking about the country on foot, as much as eight miles from their dwelling, to give help to the poor without disclosing their identity, founding schools and hospitals, and only rarely making the lavish display called for by their station in life. She adds that they have resumed the practice of breast-feeding their own children, instead of giving them out to nurse as formerly.[15]

The moment at which the upper-class woman first began to change in outlook can, it seems, be dated with some accuracy. Coyer, in 1777, reports that "It is not long since that women of this higher class have turned again to domestic cares; they have changed their tastes".[16]

As a step towards discovering why women should have been changing in this way, it seemed reasonable to start by looking for indications of special psychological attitudes. I was aware of the existence of a number of facts which I felt might throw light on the whole topic. I refer to the very noticeable signs of a desire among women to masculinise themselves, or perhaps I should say to adopt a male role. I first came across this material when studying the development of costume in the period. (Costume is a particularly useful indicator of underlying attitudes, since it is easily observed, and numerous pictures are available, so that there is little likelihood of error about the facts.)

According to the patrist-matrist theory, as put forward in *Sex in History*, in matrist periods clothes will be rich and colourful, in patrist periods, simple and subdued. The drab clothing of Puritans, the brilliant satins and embroideries of the eighteenth century, and the reaction to dark colours and sober stuffs in the nineteenth century illustrate the point and need hardly be supported by instances. But the theory also predicts that in matrist periods the clothing of the two sexes will become similar, while in patrist periods the differences will become

---

[15] In Meister, *Letters*, p. 85.
[16] *Nouvelles Observations*, p. 274.

marked. No one could mistake, even if seen only in silhouette, the trousered and top-hatted Victorian male from his petticoated and bonneted consort. But in Anne's reign, a century earlier, Ward felt, "It seem'd to me as if the World was turn'd Top-side turvy; for the ladies look'd like undaunted Heroes, fit for Government or Battle, and the Gentlemen like a parcel of Fawning, Flattering Fops, that could swear themselves very faithful and humble servants to the Petticoat . . . as if their Education had been amongst Monkeys who (it is said) in all cases give the Pre-eminence to their Females."[17]

According to the *Spectator* (331), women "already appear in Hats and Feathers, Coats and Perriwigs". And Addison warns them that this is hardly likely to impress their male beholders, for "how would they be affected should they meet a Man on Horseback, in his Breeches and Jack Boots, and at the same time dressed up in a Commode and a Night raile?"[18] To complete the picture one should add that women at this time wore no wig, but dressed their hair simply in short curls.

But if women resembled men, the reverse was also thought to be true.

> But *Art* surpasses *Nature*; and we find
> Men may be transform'd into Womankind.[19]

Nor was this a phenomenon confined to the early years of the century. Thus in 1774 we are told, "Whilst the men upon the *ton* take every means to appear effeminate, the women . . . assume the most masculine air in their power. The fashion of riding in the forenoon in Hyde Park will convince any bystander of this observation: the Macaronies in their riding dresses seem but half whelped . . . whilst the truly female Amazonians appear like heroes and . . . wear the breeches literally as well as metaphorically."[20]

[17] Edward Ward, cited by Ashton, *Soc. Life* . . . *Queen Anne*, pp. 87–9
[18] Addison, *Spectator*, 435.
[19] *Almonds for Parrots*, ed. 1705, cited Ashton, *Soc. Life* . . . *Queen Anne*, pp. 87–9.
[20] *Town and Country Magazine* (1774), pp. 245–6.

Now if men choose to dress with matrist freedom, presumably it is because they have identified on their mother: correspondingly, if girls choose to dress like men, it is because they have identified on their father. And if this is so, we should be able to detect in the eighteenth century a masculinity not merely of clothing but of general outlook among at least a section of the female population. Since the extreme cases show the trend most clearly, let us start with them.

An astonishing number of cases of women passing as men, and not infrequently joining the armed services, is recorded. The *Annual Register* notes cases in 1761, 1766, 1769, 1771, 1773, 1777, 1779, 1782, 1793, 1805, 1807, 1810, 1813, 1814 and 1815. In the 1777 case the woman had been three times married, in the guise of a man. In the 1810 case the woman had become an officer in the Spanish Army.

Some of these women became well known, such as Mary Ann Talbot, who served as powder monkey and cabin boy on a man o'war; Hannah Snell, who was wounded at Pondicherry, and who once suffered five hundred lashes without revealing her sex; and Phoebe Hessel, who claimed to have been wounded at Fontenoy, and lived to be one hundred and eight.[21] Charlotte Charke recounts how on various occasions she dressed as a man. In some cases the feminine protest amounted to Lesbianism. The ladies of Llangollen were widely known: "Miss Butler is tall and masculine. She always wears a riding habit. Hangs up her hat with the air of a sportsman in the hall, and appears in all respects as a young man, if we except the petticoat, which she still retains. Miss Ponsonby, on the contrary, is polite and effeminate, fair and beautiful."[22] But Lesbianism was the exception rather than the rule. Mrs. Ann Bousted, alias Heslop, was a wrestler and ploughman of such masculine propensities that, after her husband left her, she kidnapped and carried off a Mr. Sewel and married him.[23] At least one of the female soldiers joined the services in order to find her husband, who had been reft from her by a press gang.

In lower classes this trend persisted until well on in the nineteenth century. In 1835 a woman passing under the name of Bill Chapman,

[21] See Ashton, *Eighteenth Century Waifs*, Chapter 9, for a résumé.
[22] *Brit. Mercury* (ed. Archenholtz), Vol. 15, sub 'Leaders of Llangollen'.
[23] ib., Vol. 16, sub 'An Excentric Female'.

and living as a ballad singer, was brought to court, but the case was dismissed.[24]

Evidence of a corresponding trend among men has already been mentioned in connection with homosexuality, with which it was often confused. Feeling against homosexuality made it necessary to conceal such behaviour more carefully than in the case of women. However, in addition to the well-known case of the Chevalier d'Eon, a number of instances have come to light, such as that of Eliza Edwards, the beautiful actress who, on her death in 1833, proved to be a man.[25]

If in the eighteenth century the idea of passing as a man was seldom realised but by members of the lower classes, yet that the fantasy was common is revealed by a number of popular novels in which it played a role;[26] this fantasy we may call the feminine protest. I have devoted some space to establishing the existence of this attitude in its clinical shape because to many people the idea will seem startling, and the phenomenon is more easily understood in its most extreme form. However, it is with the more diffuse expressions of father-identification that we are primarily concerned.

This fantasy explains the extensive part which women took in what even to-day are regarded as masculine sports. Women not only rode and hunted, but shot, played cricket, rowed, and boxed, though the more active manifestations seem to have been lower-class, as we should expect, since we know that the middle class opposed all spontancity. Nevertheless Hickey mentions a Mrs. Bristowe (née Miss Wrangham)

[24] *Dens of London*, p. 78. Cf. also *The Female Husband named James Allen* (Anon).
[25] See *Annual Register*, 1833, Chron., p. 17. In France, where fear of homosexuality was less pronounced, cases were numerous, e.g. Philippe d'Orléans, the Abbé de Choisy, the Abbé d'Entragnes, de Saralette du Lange, etc. Naturally it is in the German Romantics that we find this trend carried farthest. Bettina von Arnim wrote in 1807 that she had ordered "a skirt? No, a pair of trousers. Hurray, now another era begins to dawn; and a jacket and an overcoat besides." (Cited Kind and Fuchs, *Weiberherrschaft*, ii, 452.) Some of them carried the fantasy to a point of actual sexual interchange. Varnhagen van Ense wrote to Frau Rahel, "You are a great man. I am the first woman who ever lived." Schleiermacher toyed with the idea of becoming a woman, and his wife wrote to him, "You are not a man to me, but a sweet pure virgin." (Cited Kluckhohn, *Die Auffassung der Liebe*, p. 431.)
[26] E.g. Arbuthnot, *Memoirs of the Remarkable Life . . . Miss Jenny Cameron* (1746). Cf. *The History of Miss Katty N—*, by herself (1757).

of St. Helena who rode astride, jumped, was an excellent shot and a pugilist to boot. She had "four blooming children".[27] Roche- foucauld noted that ladies quite often took part in the sport of shooting in England, and that many of them were very good shots.[28] In May 1758, Miss Pond rode 1,000 miles in 1,000 hours, a feat which many others in vain attempted to repeat.[29] The *Gentleman's Magazine* refers to girls engaging in amateur coaching and tandem-driving, and as late as 1805, Silliman was shocked to see a lady driving in her own phaeton in the Park, together with a female friend. It was, he said, "unbecoming but usual".[30]

Women's rowing, apparently lower-class, was still taking place in 1817, when Battersea defeated Chelsea, the prize being carried off by "a strapping woman, the mother of four children". She was "carried in triumph to a public house on the beach . . . her numerous friends crowded after her and drank her health in copious libations".[31] In the same year, Esther Crozier set out to walk 1,000 miles in twenty days, though whether she was successful I have been unable to discover.[32]

In 1811 some "amateur Noblemen" of Hampshire and Surrey arranged a women's cricket match for five hundred guineas a side; Hampshire won.[33] Female cricket was still being played in 1822, when the single women played the married ones on Gandersdown, Alres- ford.[34]

The palm must go however to Elisa Garnerin, niece of the balloonist, who made her first parachute drop in 1815 and who had made a score of drops by 1820, including at least one delayed drop.[35]

---

[27] Hickey, *Memoirs*, iii, 347.
[28] Rochefoucauld, *Frenchman in England*, p. 55.
[29] *Idler*, May 20th 1758.
[30] Silliman, *Journal of Travels*, ii, 43.
[31] Ashton, *Soc. England*, pp. 298-9.
[32] ib., p. 299.
[33] ib, p. 88.
[34] Singles won, and in a return match on Milberry Down repeated their success, Miss Budd scoring forty-one runs. "Much good play was shown by both sides." The village of Marchwood was anxious to take on this redoubtable team, but history is silent as to the outcome. *Annals of Sporting and Fancy* (1822), Vol. 13.
[35] Ashton, *Social England*, p. 89.

In short, in the eighteenth century, in both upper and lower classes, there was not only a normal independence, but a strain of marked father-identification of a clinical character. While the normal upper-class woman did not attempt to be an actual tomboy, the tendency of women to emerge to dominance over men was noted by visitors. Thus Gemelli says that women "do whatsoever they please, and do so generally wear the breeches (as we use to say) that it is now become a proverb that England is the hell of horses and the paradise of women; and if there were a bridge from the island to the continent, all the women in Europe would run thither".[36] In 1765 Grosley asked whether it was the men or the women who ran the house, and was told the latter.[37] In 1833 the position had so changed that when d'Hausset asked the same question he discovered that English ladies "hardly know the names of the guests invited by their husbands. In all that relates to household economy they are not better informed: the husbands order everything."[38]

These facts suggested a conclusion of major importance to my theme; they indicated that the kind of change which was taking place during the period was a change from a phase in which women were identifying on their fathers and men on their mothers, to a phase in which women were identifying on their mothers and men on their fathers.

In studying the relationship between the sexes during the period I was particularly struck by certain signs of the existence of very powerful overt resentments between the sexes. In *Jonathan Wild*, for instance, there is a crackling dialogue between the newly-married couple, in which the woman refuses to concede any affection for Wild, taunts him with sexual inadequacy, declares that she will never admit him to her bed again, and is only shaken from her attitude of independence and superiority when he is stung into calling her a bitch.[39] In *Chrysal*, in

[36] Cited Smith, *Foreign Visitors*, p. 210.

[37] Grosley, *Tour*, i, 252.

[38] D'Hausset, *Gt. Britain in 1833*, i, 87. However, in the lower classes Amazonism continued to manifest itself (vide *Doings in London*, p. 92, which describes how the notorious Lady Barrymore and Kit Bakers threw a man out of a second-floor window).

[39] *Jonathan Wild*. Book III, Chapter 8.

contrast, we are shown a husband who invites his mistress to his wedding, brings her home on his wedding night, and makes love to her in preference to his wife; it seems difficult to imagine any more humiliating way of treating a wife.[40] There is an obvious sadistic desire to humiliate the woman in *Clarissa Harlowe*, and the theme of the deliberate humiliation of one sex by another is developed to its extreme in *Les Liaisons Dangereuses*.

Taine noted this attitude in the English Don Juan, "Unyielding pride, the desire to subjugate others, the provocative love of battle, the need for ascendancy, these are his predominant features. Sensuality is but of secondary importance compared with these."[41] In Don Juanism, the seduction of women becomes merely a method of humiliating them. Correspondingly, women used their sexual attraction to humiliate men: this is often demonstrated in the literature and sometimes we find a quite explicit statement. Thus the *Female Jockey Club* comments on Lady Elizabeth Foster, whose charms were so remarkable that she "thawed the ice of the Duke of Devonshire and inspired the King of Sweden for a time with the desire for *natural* pleasures". It says that her method was to entice lovers, then abandon them "with ridicule and laughter".[42]

The existence of this aggressive element in intersexual relations is not surprising, inasmuch as we have already noted many signs of a high level of aggression in the eighteenth-century personality-structure.

By the nineteenth century such aggressions were generally denied open expression. Indeed, they were deeply repressed, and we can only infer their existence from special cases. For instance, we get a powerful hint of the reality of these feelings when we find Susan Ferrier discussing quite dispassionately with Lady Charlotte Bury "whether a woman of a right way of thinking would not rather be stabbed as kicked by a husband". Miss Ferrier declared, "I am for a stabber, but I daresay you will be for putting up with a kicker . . . I maintain there is but one

---

[40] " 'I have brought my girl,' said he, 'to grace our nuptials. The dear creature insisted on it: and you know I can't refuse her anything.' " *Chrysal*, ix, 162.

[41] Taine, *History Eng. Literature*, ii, pp. 406-7.

[42] *Female Jockey Club*, p. 22.

crime a woman could never forgive in her husband, and that is a *kicking*."[43] Susan Ferrier was a comparatively emancipated individual, and could discuss openly what others could not face up to. The subject came up in connection with Lady Byron's having left her husband: Miss Ferrier thought the only possible explanation could be that he had given her a kicking. The fact that such a conversation could be held suggests that intersexual aggression was something of a commonplace.

Corresponding to this, we find guarded expressions of hostility against men on the part of women. The Rev. William Jones mentions, as if it were quite a natural thing, that he has often heard mothers warn their daughters against the horrors of the married state.[44]

Occasionally we find in the nineteenth century abnormal individuals who ignore the taboos on expressing aggression, and then the resentments emerge clearly. The half-insane Chetwynd, for instance, forced his children to kick their innocent mother and to call her 'whore', while he fornicated with the servants.[45]

In most of these stories I see the pattern of father-rejection. The father-identifier, resenting (at the unconscious level) his mother's betrayal of him with the father, thinks that all women are whores. Hence Chetwynd's cry. And while the father-identifier attempts to secure the chastity of women, the father-rejector deliberately destroys it: Don Juanism is then a deliberate programme of defloration, as if to say, "You pretend to be so chaste, but I'll show how little chaste you really are."

Correspondingly, the woman's resentments of the male are also basically sexual. In the nineteenth century this was deeply repressed, but it sometimes emerges, as in a melodramatic novel which contains the startling passage, "Is he not a cripple in certain abdominal regions?" To which is given the reply, "Hush—a wife's revenge, a woman's awful retaliation."[46] The incident is, of course, a melodramatic

43 Ferrier, *Memoir and Correspondence*, p. 131.
44 W. Jones, *Diary*, p. 179 (June 7th, 1805).
45 Pearl, *Girl . . . Swansdown Seat*, p. 248. Several similar cases are described by Hare, *Years with Mother*, e.g., p. 249.
46 Anon., *Merry Wives of London*, p. 187.

fantasy, but the fact that it could be included shows that readers would feel it to be appropriate. The psychoanalyst will appreciate that castration is precisely the appropriate form for the woman's resentment to take. And, not surprisingly, the 'cripple' is represented as hating women.

Against the background of these facts, it becomes possible to understand the comments of eighteenth-century visitors, such as Shebbeare. "A woman in England is the momentary toy of passion; in France, the companion in the hours of reason and conversation, as well as in those of love. . . . A female of France would blush at the gothic joys which an English lover only thinks of."[47] Dudley Ryder had made the same point forty years before: "Mr. Bowes, I find, as most other young men do now, looks upon women as only fit to be subservient to a man's lust and not to be an agreeable companion."[48]

Before entering on this digression, I had reached the point in the development of the argument at which it was clear that in the eighteenth century a considerable number of men were making mother-identifications, and a considerable number of women father-identifications.

The counterpart of this statement is obviously that in the nineteenth century the position was reversed: men were tending to make father-identifications, women mother-identifications. And just as the first of these patterns produces men in whom the feminine element is exaggerated and women in whom the masculine element is exaggerated, so the second of the patterns produces an exaggerated masculinity in men and exaggerated femininity in women. This is why even people like Lady Morgan felt that they must give up any serious attempt at painting or music lest it make them "less a woman".

I have indicated how in the nineteenth century any aggression towards the opposite sex was inhibited. We can now supplement this by pointing out that the nineteenth-century women were clearly much exercised to retain the approval of men. In many of the moralising books the reason given for submissive behaviour is that this is what men like. But it follows that if a woman has adjusted her whole life to secure male affection, she will feel powerful resentments if rejected—

[47] *Letters on the English Nation*, i, 228.
[48] Ryder, *Diary*, p. 178 (February 6th, 1716).

hence the saying, "Hell hath no fury like a woman scorned". Actually this statement is only true of patrist societies.[49] In a matrist phase women can shrug off rejection philosophically, and "there are plenty of good fish in the sea" becomes a more appropriate tag. (Tishy Snaps makes use of just this argument in the passage from *Jonathan Wild* already mentioned.) Correspondingly, the mother-orientated man feels strong resentments when rejected, and proverbially goes off to shoot big game in Africa, i.e. to assassinate substitutes.

Alternatively, the aggression may be turned against the self: this perhaps explains why in the first half of the eighteenth century many men committed suicide when refused by women, to the point where it was widely commented upon at the time. I therefore assume that the instances of extreme aggression against women, of which I have given some examples earlier in the chapter, represent either the defiance of a father-rejector or the transferred resentments of a man whose mother had rejected him.

But while aggression against the opposite sex was severely inhibited, aggression against the same sex was much less so: hence the 'feminine' mother-identifying woman could rule her daughters with a rod of iron, and deny them pleasures which she had permitted herself. Thus Hannah More condemned playgoing, though she had written plays herself, and Mrs. Sherwood, who had been to balls in her youth and enjoyed them, thanked God that she could say her daughters had never even asked to enter a ballroom in their lives.[50]

Similar factors also affected the nature of the marriage relationship. Cunnington has pointed out that the Victorian marriage resembled a father-daughter relationship.[51] The man took all the decisions and responsibilities, the woman deferred to his superior judgment. It may be added that to make the woman into a daughter is to desexualise her, and this, as I show in the introduction and in Chapter Six, was part of the object of the 'angel-makers'. This observation can be complemented

---

[49] E. Jones argues that the 'separation fear' in women—the fear of being separated from men in general, and the father in particular—is the sign of father-identification, and the converse of the castration complex in men. (*Papers*, p. 445.)

[50] Darton, *Life of Mrs. Sherwood*, p. 15.

[51] *Feminine Attitudes*, p. 110.

by saying that in a matrist society the marriage relationship tends to become a mother-son relationship.[52]

These considerations also account for the tendency of clothing of the two sexes to assimilate in a matrist age, and to contrast during a patrist age. By the same token, the excessive 'masculinity' of the patrist can be seen to be as abnormal as the effeminacy of the matrist; correspondingly, the excessive femininity of the Victorian woman is as abnormal as the masculinity of a Hannah Snell.

It would be pleasant to leave the matter at this point, with everything neatly explained. Honesty, or curiosity, compels me to admit, however, that I uncovered a group of facts which I was unable to fit into the picture, and which seemed to run counter to the theory. This was comforting in a way, for everything had worked out so smoothly, on the whole, that I was beginning to feel that the theory was rather too good to be true.

It has been the tenor of my argument that patrists depress the status of women, matrists elevate it. It was therefore awkward to find in Rousseau a quite definite statement of the desirability of subordinating women: "They will be subject, all their lives, to the most severe and constant constraint, which is that of decorum: it is, therefore, necessary to accustom them early to restraint, that it may not cost them anything; and to the suppression of their whims, that they may the more readily submit to the will of others."[53] Not only the attitude but the very arguments are Puritan. "There results from this habitual restraint a tractableness which women have occasion for during their whole lives, as they constantly remain either under subjection to the men or to the opinions of mankind." The stress on the importance of public opinion is also distinctly recognisable, if a bit strange coming from Rousseau, who so consistently defied it himself. He even remarks that, in order to break women's will, "If, indeed, they be fond of being always at work, they should sometimes be compelled to lay it aside."[54]

Still, Rousseau was perhaps something of a special case, being a Swiss

---

[52] This point suddenly became clear to me when an acquaintance commented that in the United States marriage had the character of a mother-son relationship.

[53] Rousseau, *Emile*, p. 424 (my translation).

[54] ib., p. 424.

living in France. What really concerned me was to discover in Thomson's 'Autumn' the programme he proposes for the "British Fair".[55]

> Far be the pleasures of the chase from them;
> Uncomely courage, unbeseeming skill,
> To spring the fence, to rein the prancing steed,
> The cap, the whip, the masculine attire,
> In which they roughen to the sense, and all
> The winning softness of their sex is lost.
> In them 'tis graceful to dissolve at woe;
> With every motion, every word, to wave
> Quick o'er the kindling cheek the ready blush;
> And from the smallest violence to shrink
> Unequal . . .
>
> To teach the lute to languish; with smooth step,
> Disclosing motion in its every charm,
> To swim along, and swell the mazy dance;
> To train the foliage o'er the snowy lawn;
> To guide the pencil, turn the tuneful page;
> To heighten Nature's dainties; in their race
> To rear their graces into second life;
> To give Society its highest taste;
> Well-ordered Home Man's best delight to make;
> And by submissive wisdom, modest skill,
> With every gentle care-eluding art,
> To raise the virtues, animate the bliss,
> And sweeten all the toils of human life:
> This be the female dignity and praise.

Victoria herself could hardly have disapproved. And this was written in 1730, nearly twenty years before *Emile*, so there can be no question of Rousseau's influence.

On close inspection, it will be seen that though Thomson thinks that

[55] *The Seasons*, 'Autumn', lines 571-608.

women should devote themselves to pleasing men, he does not display any objection to mild pleasure: music and dancing, sketching and embroidery are permitted. Women should occupy themselves with domestic comforts. Religion is not mentioned, and there is no suggestion that women's time should be devoted to visiting the poor. Similarly Rousseau declares, "Do not make of your daughter a good man, as though to give the lie to Nature, but make of her a good woman." And he continues, "Does it follow that she ought to be brought up in complete ignorance, and restricted solely to the duties of the household? Shall man make a servant of his companion? Shall he deprive himself of the greatest charm of society? Shall he make of her a real automaton? Undoubtedly not. Nature will have them think, and judge, and love and know, and cultivate their mind as they do their form."[56] (Though he hastily adds that they should know only what it becomes them to know.)

It seems, then, that Rousseau and Thomson want women to be the ideal mother: feeding them, dispersing their cares, and sweetening their toil. Thomson's objection to their fox-hunting is that it will dispel their "winning softness". No one wants a hearty fox-hunting mother. This is not inconsistent with the treatment of Rousseau and Thomson as matrists, though it is a long way from the "free and daring girls" whom Shelley admired.

A further clue, it struck me, was to be found in the fact that Rousseau in his actions—as opposed to his words—displayed a double attitude towards women. Some, like Mme. Warens, he put on a pedestal, and called 'Mother'. But when he wanted to make a permanent relationship, he chose Thérèse Levasseur, a servant, and she occupied a subordinate position, looking after him in just the way laid down for the eponymous Sophia in *Emile*. As we shall see when we come to consider Wesley, many mother-identifiers find themselves impotent with mother-figures, because of the incest bar, and find they can only establish sexual relationships with those in inferior positions who cannot be regarded as mothers. Rousseau suffered from this type of impotence; we know this from his *Confessions*, which contain a characteristic account of his last-minute panic when attempting to

[56] *Emile*, p. 418.

sleep with the enchanting Zulietta, who has, with shrewd insight, already warned him if he starts not to stop half-way. Soon after, he begins to maintain a mistress, Anzoletta, but says, "I should have dreaded connection with this child . . . as an abominable incest."[57]

I fancy, therefore, that a closer study of Rousseau would reveal considerable ambivalence towards women. It is also significant that when Thérèse Levasseur admitted to him that she was not a virgin, he "uttered a cry of joy".[58]

Despite such individual inconsistencies, the general development of female attitudes during the period under study strongly confirms our main thesis. It is evident that a marked tendency, in the upper (and still more the lower) classes during the eighteenth century, for women to identify with their fathers was gradually replaced by the middle-class pattern of strong mother-identification. This complements the change exhibited by males. We may summarise the two changes by saying that cross-parent identification gave way to like parent identification.

To sum up, then, we find that a dramatic change in the status of women was closely linked with the change in sexual standards. And we find suggestive indications that both these changes were linked to a change in the balance of parental identifications—that is to say, to the individual's relationship to his or her father and mother.

But before looking at the psychological forces which were at work, we need to look more closely at the plain sociological facts. The extent to which a Puritan attitude persisted into the eighteenth century and the changes it underwent have been very inadequately documented. And what were the limits of Victorian rectitude? Not only was there an underworld of sexuality and vice, but an almost pagan attitude persisted in the lower and agricultural sectors of society, with roots in the Elizabethan rather than the Caroline period.

We shall find that the depression in the status of women, like the new moral attitude which was associated with it, was achieved long before Victoria came to the throne in 1838. The term 'Victorian' is a misnomer, for, as we shall see, the swing-back which has led to the present permissive age also started much sooner than is generally realised: the first signs can be detected as early as 1850.

These enquiries will occupy the next four chapters and illuminate some curious and neglected corners of social history.

[57] Rousseau, *Confessions*, ii, 57.
[58] ib., ii, 60.

CHAPTER 2

SERIOUS INCLINATIONS

A TRAVELLER passing through Haworth about 1750 was amazed to see people leaping out of the lower windows of a public-house, springing over a low wall and making off. He thought that the house must be on fire, but, on inquiring the cause of the commotion, was told that they had seen the parson coming. The cleric who had this electrifying effect was William Grimshaw, who became the incumbent about 1742. It was his custom to stand at the door of the church armed with a huge whip, with which he speeded the progress of late-comers. Moreover, during the course of the service, while the psalm before the sermon was being sung, it was his practice to leave the church and scout round the village for truants. If he found any, he drove them before him into church with the aid of his bull-whip[1].

Evidently the eighteenth century, however immoral it may have been, was not without its zealots. Grimshaw is not the only example. In the first decade of the century, for instance, Powell, the mayor of Deal, used to patrol the town in like manner, looking for sabbath-breakers. After he had made an example of some offenders he was able to say, "I could walk through the town on a Sunday, and not see a door open, either in a public house or a shop. If any company is within, it is very privately done, whereas before they used to keep them open." He was even able to scare coach-drivers into abandoning Sunday coach-services from Deal, though in some other parts of the country these were usual.[2]

[1] J. Newton, *Life of the Rev. William Grimshaw*, p. 110. See also E. Middleton, *Biographia Evangelica*, iv, 405.
[2] J. Laker, *History of Deal*, p. 247.

The most significant feature of such stories is that the local population seems to have accepted such behaviour. If Powell had been universally thought unreasonable, he would not have been re-elected to the post of mayor, as he was. If Grimshaw has been thought a fanatic, complaints would no doubt have reached the bishop and he would have been rebuked or even removed. Clearly, then, Puritan feeling was by no means dead in the eighteenth century.

It seemed to me that the first step in the inquiry must be to attempt an assessment of the scope and character of such feeling, for presumably it was from this source that the forces which led to the moral revolution derived. No general study of this topic seems to have been made before.[3] It is not a particularly easy task. While both moralists and scandal-mongers are quick to record and to magnify 'immoral' behaviour, no one troubles to record ordinary virtue. It is therefore necessary to work inferentially.

One cannot read much eighteenth-century material without becoming aware that this reservoir of moral and religious feeling must have been quite extensive. For instance, Pollnitz, visiting England in 1733, speaks of the "zeal for Religion" and the enormous number of books of devotion which was sold.[4] Sterne said that he made more money from his books of sermons than he ever made from *Tristram Shandy*.[5] Two of the most successful religious works of the century appeared at this time: Law's *Serious Call to a Devout and Holy Life* (1728) and Doddridge's *Rise and Progress of Religion in the Soul* (1745). Each ran through many editions, while the religious best-sellers of the previous century (such as Taylor's *Holy Living* in 1650, and *Holy Dying* in 1651, or Baxter's *Christian Directory*) continued to be reprinted. Defoe, though known to-day as a novelist, was primarily a pamphleteer who took a strong moral line less from conviction than because he found it suited the taste of the times. Similarly, Richardson's novels, though unconsciously salacious, were put forward as moralistic, and

[3] Quinlan, *Victorian Prelude*, however contains valuable material. Muriel Jaeger's *Before Victoria* was published while this book was awaiting publication. It covers some of the ground but ignores many important sociological factors.

[4] Pollnitz, *Memoirs de Charles Lewis*, iii, 282, 320, Letter LIV.

[5] Cited Bayne-Powell, *Travellers in Eighteenth Century England*, p. 154.

were introduced as "showing virtue in the strongest light and rendering the practice of it amiable and lovely".[6]

It is easy to pile up details demonstrating the existence of a strong, even severe, morality during the period. For instance, Charlotte Charke speaks (in 1755) of the Puritanical going to public devotions four times a day;[7] in 1731 Mrs. Pendarves writes to Wesley, telling him that there is a religious concert in London on Sunday night— evidently something rare or novel since he has to be informed of the fact—and asking whether it would be proper to attend it;[8] in 1757 there was a public protest when Parliament proposed to permit Sunday drilling.[9]

We can also infer an interest in morality from the moralistic type of play which was beginning to be played in the theatre.[10] Though the Restoration comedies continued to be played, a new type of play was becoming popular. Thus *The London Merchant* (1731) shows an apprentice ruined by a courtesan, while *The Gamester* (1753) teaches that gambling is a sin. One can trace the movement back to Steele's *Lying Lover* (1703), which proves that adultery does not pay, and still further to *Love's Last Shift*, at the close of the preceding century.

The public which supported such plays was the public that bought Hogarth's prints, which contain as much moral as social criticism, and that flocked to buy the novels of Richardson. How strongly people were affected by these last is shown by the parishioners of Slough, who, when Pamela finally reached the port of matrimony without loss of her virtue, rang the bells of the church in celebration.[11] Further

---

[6] Preface to the 1785 edition of *Pamela*, which was "published in order to cultivate the principles of virtue and religion in the mind of youth."

[7] Charke, *Narrative of the Life*, p. 254.

[8] *Letters of J. Wesley* (ed. Telford), i, 78.

[9] Whitaker, *Eighteenth Century English Sunday*, pp. 151–3.

[10] At least as early as 1723 the Middlesex Grand Jury 'presented' the King's Theatre, Haymarket, for a proposal to hold six Opera balls, "conceiving the same to be wicked and illegal practices." Malcolm, *Anecdotes of the Manners and Customs*, p. 335.

[11] Turner, *History of Courting*, p. 106.

confirmation comes in many small ways: for instance, Uffenbach, in 1710, found it difficult to procure a copy of Rochester's poems, while his *Sodom* was not in print at all.[12] The pages of the *Gentleman's Magazine* are occupied with discussions of such moral problems as whether a parson should baptise the children of a suicide. When Hammond's *Elegies* were published in 1742, it emerged that he had bowdlerised these translations from Catullus, in deference to middle-class opinion;[13] and as early as 1718 we find Ancillon promising the readers of his *Eunuchism Displayed* that it will contain no "broad expressions".[14] While many people remember that it was in the eighteenth century that Cleland wrote the celebrated *Memoirs of a Woman of Pleasure*, most of them forget that he was summoned before the Privy Council for doing so, that he agreed never to write another such work, and that Drybutter, the bookseller who published it, was sent to gaol.[15]

I accumulated in my notebooks a great deal of material of this sort. A substantial section of it concerns the way in which the sabbath was observed.[16] Foreign visitors are unanimous that it was phenomenally strict. Misson commented on the extraordinary importance attaching to Sunday just before the century dawned. "I have observed it particularly in the confessions of persons that are hanged," he says. "Sabbath-breaking is the crime the poor wretches always begin with. If they had killed father or mother, they would not mention that article till after having professed how often they had broke the sabbath."[17] The Abbé Le Blanc commented that the English kept the day with Jewish rigour[18] (1747) and Grosley used a very similar

[12] Uffenbach, *London in 1710*, p. 151.
[13] Reed, *Background to Gray's Elegy*, p. 226.
[14] Ancillon, op. cit., preface.
[15] They may also forget that although *The Beggar's Opera* was performed it was over the protests of the Middlesex Grand Jury (Archenholtz, *Picture of England*, p. 298).
[16] On this, in general, see Whitaker, *Eighteenth Century English Sunday*. Whitaker's interpretation of the facts seems to me invalidated by his failure to distinguish sufficiently between the classes.
[17] Misson, *Memoirs*, p. 311.
[18] Le Blanc, *Letters*, ii, 69.

phrase in 1765.[19] La Combe, in 1784, said, "Nothing is sadder or more strange than an English Sunday, whether in London or in the country; the theatres are shut, the public-houses and restaurants are only allowed to open at certain times and under certain limitations; all games, dancing and music are prohibited. The political papers, the staple fare of Englishmen, are suspended, road and bridge tolls are trebled, and people are reduced, when the weather is fine, to walking in the parks."[20] This, it may be noted, is at the period when, according to the Victorian historian Massey, "the depravity of manners reached their extreme point", a depravity, he declared, which operated "throughout the whole order of society".[21]

That strict Sunday observance meant something more than regular church-going is revealed by incidents such as that which the German pastor Moritz records in 1782. He thoughtlessly hummed a lively tune in front of his landlady's twelve-year-old son Jacky. "He stared at me with surprise and then reminded me it was Sunday; and so, that I might not forfeit his good opinion by any appearance of levity, I gave him to understand that, in the hurry of my journey, I had forgotten the day."[22] And we may recall how Dr. Johnson conjured Reynolds on his deathbed not to work on Sunday.[23]

Since some authorities claim that there was a gradual decline in standards during the century I will find space for a citation from the end of the century. Pastor Wendeborn, who was in charge of the German church in London for twenty years, recorded, "The sabbath day is kept in England with more outward decency than I have seen in many countries; and in churches and meeting houses, outward decorum and seeming devotion are very observable, particularly in the country at some distance from the metropolis. About London, the public houses are on Sunday very full indeed; but the ear of passengers is not struck with music and dancing, as is too much the case abroad; nor is there card playing, except that of late some houses of people of quality,

19 Grosley, *Tour*, i, 174.
20 La Combe, *Tableau*, p. 18 (my translation).
21 Massey, *History of England*, iv, 52.
22 Moritz, *Travels*, p. 19.
23 Archenholtz, *Picture of England*, p. 166.

at the west end of town, have, on a Sunday, resounded with musical concerts, and card tables have been in use."[24]

Even the reformers themselves, for all their complaints of the immorality of the times, occasionally let slip a detail which reveals that the standard of observance was actually high. Thus one preacher about 1750 comments:

"In the time of Harvest, when the weather has been unfavourable and the corn or hay is in danger of being spoiled, it would be extremely convenient for the farmers if they might take the opportunity of a fine day to break the Sabbath; but, irreligious as the present age is, the very worst of them do not presume upon such a liberty."[25]

We need not be too impressed by the oft-made claim that the Established Church was corrupt.[26] Bishops, it is true, were often absent from their dioceses; parsons held plural livings, leaving only a curate in charge; and where a cadet of some noble or gentle family had obtained a living, he hunted and drank like the squire. But the picture can be overdrawn. The diary of John Thomlinson of Blencogo reveals something short of licence. If once he spends Sunday in a tavern, he is consumed by remorse for it.[27] He may approvingly recall the reply of the French King to his confessor, but his uncle tells another minister, "Such as you and I should not go to fairs, it gives offence, too secular, etc."[28]

And if the parson was lax, it does not follow that he let his congregation follow his example. Thomlinson was congratulated by his

[24] Wendeborn, *View of England*, ii, 269. As this entry shows, it was only in middle-class circles that such strictures reigned. In lower-class agricultural areas the day was spent "in jollity and junketing" whenever the parson (in consequence of plurality of livings) failed to conduct a service. (*Considerations on Parochial Evils*, p. 22.)

[25] Webster, *Two Sermons*, p. 16.

[26] Sykes says that it is now held that the eighteenth-century Church was not so bad as the nineteenth-century writers depicted it as being. (*Church and State*, pp. 6 ff.)

[27] Hodgson, *Six Diaries*, p. 164, entry of February 3rd, 1721-2.

[28] The King, reproved by his confessor for "med'ling with women", promised to confine himself to his wife if the confessor would confine himself to his favourite dish at every meal. The confessor gave up the attempt after six months (ib., p. 155).

flock for his strong sermons, and in 1718 records, "We churched
G. Storey's wife, and yet uncle does not allow their marriage—
presented for living in fornication."[29] His diary also confirms that
church attendance was not declining. On Good Friday in the same
year, "Uncle said that more have been at prayers this week than any
Easter since he came. . . . Ninety-one communicants, more than ever
on this day since he came, used to think forty considerable."[30]

Claver Morris, in Somerset, was another such. He would allow "of
no Sweet-hart to come to a Maid-servant in his House", and in 1725 he
"turned off my servant Charles Cook . . . because he was too much
in favour with my servant Hannah Beal, & was bolted into his
Chamber with her Sunday Oct: 3 for a considerable time . . ."[31]
Previously, in 1720, he had refused to attend "that vicious Woman
Mrs. Franklin", when she was "dangerously ill of the Small-pox".[32]
On Sunday he reads aloud to his family from The Whole Duty of Man.
Parson Woodforde felt obliged to refuse an invitation to attend a
sheep-shearing on a Saturday evening, as this was "a very improper
time to spend the evening out anywhere".[33] More significant still, he
writes, "As I was going to shave myself this morning as usual on
Sundays, my razor broke in my hand as I was setting it on the strop
without any violence. May it always be a warning to me not to shave
on the Lord's Day or do any other work to profane it pro futuro."[34]
Moralists had long objected to barbers shaving customers on Sunday as
coming under the heading of Sunday work, but it may be surprising to
find the view that one should not shave oneself being put in England as
early as 1765 by the relatively easy-going Woodforde. That considerable genuine religious feeling existed is also shown by the rage to be
confirmed which developed about 1770. So great was this desire that
many had themselves confirmed twice, or more often, and a ticket-

[29] ib., p. 148, (November 21st)
[30] ib., p. 114, (April 11th).
[31] Morris, Diary, p. 126.
[32] ib., p. 82.
[33] Woodforde, Diary, i, 19. (Formerly the sabbath was held to run from sundown on Saturday to sundown on Sunday.)
[34] ib., p. 105.

system had to be instituted to prevent this; some even forged tickets for the purpose.[35] The strain on the bishops was considerable; in 1773 Zachary Pearce taxed himself so severely performing mass confirmations that he died as a result.[36]

As I extended my reading in this material, two distinctions began to clarify themselves in my mind. The first was the need to distinguish between those who led a simple and pious existence, devoting themselves to good works, but without harshness, proselytism or self-mortification, and those of a more obsessive and sado-masochistic type, who were continually censuring the morals of others.

A little casual reading in the diaries and journals of the period reveals many quietly virtuous individuals, entirely free from the licence and debauchery which are supposedly characteristic of the period, but equally free of the Puritanical fear of pleasure and the obsessive drive which mark the reformer. Thus William Stukeley's description of his parents shows two God-fearing, hard-working, charitable, well-liked individuals, the father always engaged in schemes for the betterment of the town, the mother active in helping the needy. These were people with very definite personal standards: the senior Stukeley, who was a lawyer, would never take on a client unless he thought his case just; the young Stukeley went to great trouble, and permanently handicapped his career, in order to pay off the obligations inherited on his father's sudden death, though he could legally have avoided some of them.[37] Or, if we turn to fiction, we can see in a novel like Smollett's *Roderick Random* a family living in a sober or respectable way, occasionally indulging in some harmless fun perhaps, but setting a strict standard of honesty and sexual virtue.

But there is also a great deal of material which reveals a personality of a different type. It emerges, for instance, in a story like the following.

A newspaper report of 1724 describes how respectable tradesmen and their wives used to frequent concerts at the White Lion in Wych Street; a number of prostitutes also attended these concerts, though, since they wore masks, the fact that they were prostitutes was not

---

[35] Rochefoucauld, *A Frenchman in England*, p. 86.
[36] Sykes, *Church and State*, p. 137.
[37] Stukeley, *Family Memoirs*. He was born in 1687 and died 1765.

realised. "Neighbouring moralists," says the report, "waited with impatience for the hour when they should effectually transgress the law", and were delighted when a police raid resulted in the prostitutes being committed to Bridewell.[38] Again, in 1731, a 'threepenny hop' was held over a stable at the upper end of Piccadilly, "attended by footmen, serving maids, butchers, apprentices . . . and common w——s". *Read's Journal*, reporting a raid on it, describes it as "a very sink of hell".[39] The truth behind these descriptions seems to be simply that a perfectly respectable series of concerts, attended by respectable tradesmen's wives, and an equally ordinary dance for young people of the lower class, were closed down because a number of prostitutes gained admittance. Lamentable though it may be that prostitutes should exist, their existence does not automatically render immoral entertainments frequented by respectable members of society; there is a very distinct air of the spoil-sport in the reference to the impatience of the "neighbouring moralists". A similar impression is created when, for instance, a Chester paper reports that a ball has been held, without any of the mishaps anticipated by "the outrageously virtuous"—at a date just fifty years later than the previous incident.[40]

The major conclusion to which I found myself led was that the main repository of moral feeling, and particularly of this reforming zeal, was the middle class; or, since this is a vague term, let me be more specific and say the trading middle class. At the bottom this group extends to the small craftsman who manages to extend his trade enough to employ assistants, and so becomes an entrepreneur. At the top, the tradesman grows into a merchant and begins to speak on equal terms with the class which lies between the middle class and the nobility—the landed proprietor, the university-trained professional man, and the clergy.

We can see these small craftsmen and tradesmen going earnestly about the formation of religious groups in the diaries of William Whiston or Richard Viney.[41] It was from this group that Wesley

---

[38] Cited Malcolm, *Anecdotes*, i, 187–8.
[39] ib., p. 163.
[40] *The Explosion*, p. 32n.
[41] See Whiston, *Memoirs*, p. 202; Viney, MS *Diary*.

recruited most of his preachers. We can study the records of the Middlesex Quarter Sessions, where we find the Grand Jury—composed of substantial tradesmen and merchants—continually attacking both upper- and lower-class gaieties.[42] Powell, the mayor of Deal, was a local tradesman. Grosley, a contemporary observer, says, "The Methodist church consists almost wholly of tradesmen, and people of the lower sort: nothing can be more edifying than their behaviour."[43]

But the most decisive evidence is that provided by the records of the various reform groups which were established from time to time throughout the period. Thus in the time of Queen Anne there were eleven in London alone, with others in Bristol, Canterbury, Nottingham and elsewhere, even as far afield as Ireland.[44] The movement became so extensive and so active that some of the bishops of the Church began to fear that it would get out of hand, and afford a threat to the authority of the Church. Just prior to this had been founded the Society for the Propagation of the Gospel and the Society for Promoting Christian Knowledge, as well as many charitable societies, including one for the augmentation of poor livings. A satirical poem of the period describes how these reformers would march into a tavern and, without authority, arrest people on the smallest excuse.[45]

The first of these groups, the Society for the Reformation of Manners, founded in 1692, employed professional informers to spy upon and report those who broke certain laws, thus enabling the magistrates to inflict fines or imprisonment, and published annual lists of those so convicted. (But, as Archbishop Sharp observed, they made little or no attempt to improve their own behaviour.) According to its own report, by 1725 it had made a total of 91,899 arrests. The Society continued to issue annual reports until 1738, when it presumably lapsed. It was refounded, however, in 1757, and was soon followed by others: de Coetlogon speaks of the foundation of a Sunday Observance

---

[42] Thus in 1723 magistrates banded together as 'The Convention' to suppress gaming. See Dowdell, *Middlesex Quarter Sessions*, for this and similar incidents.
[43] Grosley, *Tour*, i, 357.
[44] Woodward, *An Account . . . of the Religious Societies*, pp. 20 ff.
[45] *The Heaven Drivers.*

Society in 1775;[46] the Proclamation Society was founded in 1789, to give effect to the Royal Proclamation against Vice. The Society for the Suppression of Vice was founded in 1802, and found many imitators. The early nineteenth century yields many such, e.g. the Guardian Society, founded 1815.

A little study shows that these were definitely based in the trading class. Thus, of the groups in London at the opening of the eighteenth century, one consisted of "a body of fifty tradesmen" which claimed to have suppressed "above 500 disorderly houses, and convicted some thousands of lewd persons". Another consisted of "a large body of eminent citizens", while a third was composed of constables, who, from excess of zeal, parcelled out the town for inspection and laid information with the magistrates concerning any breaches of the law which they observed.[47] It was primarily this class, too, which supported the evangelising societies.[48]

I thought it significant that these societies, though their aims were broad, spent the greater part of their time in enforcing the rigorous observance of Sunday, while some were formed solely for this purpose. For evidently moralists would not concern themselves with such lesser offences as Sunday games if gross immorality was common. In such matters it is always difficult to make sufficient allowance for the moralists' desire to paint the picture as black as possible. Thus "A Reformed Rake", in one of the numerous lay tracts on morality which were produced during the period, starts by asserting that his experience, before his reformation, indicates that four women out of every five, of all classes throughout the country, are given to fornication. But later he gives the game away when he happens to mention that prostitutes are recruited from those who have fallen from virtue, in some country town, and have as a result been so completely ostracised

[46] De Coetlogon, *Sermon* . . ., p. 37.

[47] Chamberlayne, *Magnae Britanniae Notitia*, Book iii, Chapter 9.

[48] The Sunday Observance Society which de Coetlogon mentions (in 1775) is described as having been founded "by a number of tradesmen and others". It is also noticeable that the several members who are named in the pamphlet announcing its formation as willing to receive subscriptions on behalf of the society are all merchants or shopkeepers—e.g., a bookseller in Cheapside, a linen-draper in Bond Street, a glass-manufacturer in Fleet Street, etc., (pp. 43 ff.)

that they have had to come to London and take the only course open to them.[49] Clearly, if opinion in country towns was as severe as this, moralists must have been in the majority and lapses from virtue relatively rare. The picture of general debauchery which emerges in a tract like *Hell upon Earth: or the Town in an Uproar* represents the writer's fantasy rather than a picture of reality. There was, one suspects, an actual desire to believe that all the world was a hotbed of vice.

The view that general morals were good is confirmed by the foreign observers, whom we may assume to have been unbiased. In 1756 Shebbeare declares, "Without doubt there are fewer corrupt married women in this nation, than in any in Europe where women have so much liberty; and husbands justly have more reliance on them than in any other country."[50] Twenty years later, the Abbé Coyer comments on the grave deportment of married women, who say to themselves "I am promised, I am bound, I must no longer hear anything", though he adds that this does not apply to women of the upper class, whose marriages (in contrast to those of the middle class) are not intended to last for ever.[51]

The stress upon Sunday observance, also, it seemed to me, reflected another important fact: that the moralists were not concerned simply with the maintenance of morals as expressed in the ten commandments and the law of the land, but were animated by a dislike of pleasure in all its forms.

At a time when men worked long hours, six days a week, Sunday was virtually the only day on which they could dance, drink, play games or sing. Had the moralists welcomed such relaxations on weekdays, the claim that their real object was sabbath-observance might

---

[49] Anon, *A Congratulatory Epistle* . . . (1750).

[50] Shebbeare, *Letters*, p. 229.

[51] Coyer, *Nouvelles Obs.*, p. 273-4. From these letters emerge other revealing details. Even the habit of drunkenness, which so many writers have imputed to eighteenth-century England, is denied by Coyer, who writes, "One rarely sees him [the Englishman] drunk, although he drinks no water. Beer, which constitutes his ordinary drink, does not intoxicate like wine. He is not at all quarrelsome."

have been admissible, but, as we shall see in more detail later, they displayed a general objection to relaxation and especially to music, drink and dancing. Indeed, they did not rest content with forbidding light-hearted entertainment. For instance, Orton, a Presbyterian minister at Shrewsbury, condemned walking about the streets or fields "merely for amusement", as "evidently wrong, and a thing of very bad example", thus reviving a doctrine held by the Puritans a century before. If it was absolutely necessary to health, he added, one must walk alone.[52]

To have located the source of reforming zeal in the trading middle class was an important first step towards the solution of the problem which I had set myself.[53] But before building on this discovery, I felt that I should pay some attention to the lower class, to see whether perhaps reforming zeal were present here also. This was a difficult task, since little data is available. Halévy emphasises that the country towns and villages in the early part of the century were all still high Calvinist.[54]. And the opposition which the crowds offered to the first Methodist preachers seems to confirm this. There is a revealing story of a jolly young woman coming up to Thomas Woolston, the deistical writer, as he walked in St. George's Fields, and saying, "You old Rogue, are you not hanged yet?" Woolston replied, "Good woman, I know you not. Pray what have I done to offend you?" "You have writ against my Saviour; what would become of my poor sinful Soul if it were not for my dear Saviour? My Saviour who dyed for such Sinners as I am."[55] Wesley and his preachers found their converts not in the rural areas or the sleepy country towns, but in the new industrial and urban developments for which the Church had failed to provide adequate care. Wesley's most remarkable achievements were among

[52] Orton, Works, i, 102. Hannah More agreed.

[53] Bebb, Nonconformity and Social . . . Life, p. 57, shows that while at first a few of the aristocracy and many of the gentry belonged to Nonconformist and Dissenting groups, these gradually departed. Then the new Nonconformity, Methodism, arose at the bottom of the social scale, many of its members later becoming wealthy.

[54] Halévy, 'La Naissance du Methodisme en Angleterre'. Revue de Paris, August 15th, 1906.

[55] Woolston, Life, p. 27.

the degraded miners of Kingswood, who lived more like animals than human beings.[56]

But in the remoter country districts moral notions seem to have been tempered by an older tradition, weeks of exhausting manual labour being broken by festival junketings in which sexual opportunities were taken in the pagan manner. An unpublished diary gives a vivid picture of rural life in Northumberland about 1750:

"Whit Monday 14 May. Wm going again to the Cliff end to see what Stirrings at the Sands and Robert Johnson and my self went to Carton Sports—a Saddle, bridle, whip etc. all to be Gallopt for . . . there was very good diversion all the afternoon. Abundance of young men and women diverted themselves with the game or pastime here that they call Losing their Suppers that gave some diversion to the Spectators. And after all they ended their recreation with Carrouzing at the Ale-houses and ye men Kissing and toying away most of the night with their Mistresses. Some with their real Sweethearts and others with their Ladys of Pleasure."

Another entry, for June 2nd, describes Lebberston Sport—"a Copper Pan was play'd for at Qoites . . . there was also a Dove neatly deckt and adorned with Ribbons of divers colours and other fine Trappings which was danced for by the Country Girls . . ." And he adds rather disapprovingly, "After the Diversions out of Doors were all over the Young men and the young women adjourned to the Alehouses and concluded their sport within Doors."[57]

The fact seems clear, that the reputation for immorality which the eighteenth century has gained rests almost entirely on the behaviour of the nobility and their immediate imitators in the upper-middle class.

As the century drew on, these became more numerous. The increase in wealth made it possible for men like Boswell and William Hickey, the sons of a laird and a lawyer respectively, to live on the fringe of the aristocracy and to imitate its vices.

Indeed, as I read further into the material I began to realise that, so far from being immoral, this was a period of intense religious preoccupation. Countless sects, reflecting the differing psychological

[56] For further details see Warner, *Wesleyan Movement*, pp. 166 ff.
[57] MS *Diary* of Beswick.

needs of different personalities, had been thrown up in the previous century and still existed. In addition to the Quakers, there were the Muggletonians, the Traskites, the Familists, with their variants the Anabaptists, the Behmenists, the Fifth Monarchy Men, the Millenaires, the Sabbatarians and many others. The Moravians established successful missions, and in diaries such as those of Richard Viney we get an impression of what these small groups meant to the struggling artisan or craftsman. So great was the religious impulse that laymen felt it necessary to take advertisements in the papers, or to publish tracts, to express their views. Thus in the *Postman* for July 31st, 1716, appears an advertisement asking people whether they have "apprehended their lost condition without a Saviour as revealed in the Gospel"—precisely the question Wesley was to ask more than twenty years later. Another, published in 1732, offers a manual called "Divine Inspiration: or a collection of manifestations to make known the Visitation of the Lord". It is signed by twelve persons, of whom four are women.[58]

It was from this fermenting religious material that Wesley was able to construct his movement. The enormous success which greeted it is well known: by 1751 there were eighty-five travelling preachers at work, and in 1767 the total membership was just under 26,000 members, with many more adherents who were not accepted as members.[59]

I found much further evidence of piety and intense moral preoccupation in diaries of the period. The number of diaries available for the opening of the century is quite small, but a majority of them reveal the tortured self-questioning and feelings of guilt which mark the Puritan personality. Esther Jackson, writing about 1702, fills pages of reminiscence about her temptation to lusts of the flesh and her conversion.[60] Marriott, a Dissenter of the period, leaves 172 pages of painful religious meditations.[61] Narcissus Luttrell spends hours on his knees each night before going to bed.[62]

[58] Malcolm, *Anecdotes*, pp. 229, 241.
[59] Wearmouth, *Methodism and the Common People*, pp. 174-5.
[60] Jackson, MS *Diary*.
[61] Marriott, MS *Diary*.
[62] Luttrell, MS *Diary*.

The diaries of the Methodist preachers also reveal this religious pre-occupation. Most of them note how strictly they were brought up, and record that they had "serious inclinations" or "felt a degree of the fear of God" when they were young.[63] It is difficult to convey in a few words the atmosphere which these diaries breathe. There is an ominous sense of impending punishment or disaster. In Whiston's diaries we see small groups of earnest tradesmen forming religious societies which meet in one another's rooms as if no time could be wasted in erecting barriers against the wrath to come.[64]

In many cases, an internal struggle seems to have been proceeding. Thomas Turner, the East Hoathly tradesman whose diary sheds such a revealing light on village life, oscillates between gaiety and fear of death. At one moment his behaviour is as relaxed as eighteenth-century behaviour is commonly supposed to be. "After supper," he writes in 1757, "our behaviour . . . was downright obstreperous, mixed with a great deal of folly and stupidity. Our diversion was dancing or jumping about, without a violin or any musick, singing of foolish healths, and drinking all the time as fast as it could well be poured down; and the parson of the parish was one amongst the mixed multitude." He reached home at three a.m., "very far from sober"; his wife did not arrive until after five. Soon after, he was knocked up by the parson, his wife and two neighbours. He tried to keep them out, but they threatened to break the door down and his wife admitted them. They poured into his bedroom and proceeded to drag him out of bed "topsy-turvey" and made him dance in his wife's petticoats until they had finished their wine and his beer. It is not until three o'clock the next afternoon that they finally go home, "beginning to be a little serious".[65]

But a few nights before this he has been reading the *New Whole Duty of Man*. And a few pages later he is writing "How careful should I be that I live not in vain—that, as I daily increase in age, so may I also improve in all virtue and godlyness of life!" Often he reads Drelin-

[63] See Jackson (ed.), *Lives of Early Methodist Preachers*, passim.
[64] Whiston, *Memoirs*, p. 202.
[65] Turner, *Diary*, pp. 30-2.

court's *On Death*[66] or a few of Tillotson's sermons aloud to his friend Thomas Davy. As churchwarden, he searches the public-houses while the psalms are being sung, and looks to see whether the barber is illegally practising his trade. On a general fast day he records that the parish has observed it "with a good deal of decorum—the church in the morning being more thronged than I have seen it lately. Oh! may religion once more rear up her head in this wicked and impious nation!"[67]

The earlier and even more naïve diary of the young Dudley Ryder betrays the same combination of high moral aspiration and low performance. One day he is remonstrating with Dr. Lee when he talks "with a very sensible relish" of whoring or noting that "Cousin Joseph has a talent of introducing a kind of bawdy discourse which indeed generally shocks me so much I don't know how to go on with it".[68] The next he is defiantly recording, "Had a mind to fill a whore's commodity, and went about the streets to it."[69] A few pages later he is reading Derham's *Astro-Theology* and entering sententious notes about the importance of children obeying their parents.

Similarly Thomlinson is normally cheerful, and not above flirtation, but he also notes, "Feb. 3—Remorse for sin, spending Sabbath in tavern, etc. This day much dejected and apprehensive of I know not what . . ."[70]

Perhaps one should write all this off as simple hypocrisy. In that case we must recognise that the hypocrisy of which the Victorians are accused existed more than a century earlier, and the problem becomes to explain why it was felt necessary to express elevated thoughts at a time when social pressures to conformity were—so it is alleged—almost non-existent. My own impression was that these incon-

---

[66] Correctly titled *The Christian's Defence against the Fear of Death*, this work was first translated into English in 1675, but did not become widely popular until the following century. There were thirteen editions in English between 1701 and 1751.

[67] Turner, *Diary*, p. 29.

[68] Ryder, *Diary* (1715–16), pp. 313, 371.

[69] ib., pp. 215, 271, 275

[70] Hodgson (ed.), *Six Diaries*, p. 164 (February 3rd 1721–2).

sistencies represent the wavering of those who are balanced on a knife edge between acceptance and rejection of the moral code.

Having said that the focus of reformist feeling was situated in the middle class, it is necessary to add that in the latter half of the century persons of higher rank, chiefly in that class lying just below the nobility, began to lend their support to the middle-class conscience. Since they commanded money and positions of social power, their efforts attracted more attention, whether or not they created more effect, than those of the earnest tradesmen by themselves. Sir John Fielding, the blind magistrate, launched his campaign against crime in the 'fifties. But while his ostensible purpose was to apprehend thieves and similar malefactors, he did not hesitate to suppress the evening entertainments of Mrs. Cornelys, which were widely patronised by the nobility. By 1781 we find Bishop Porteus bringing forward a Bill to prohibit all Sunday amusements, including debating societies; Lord Surrey thought that all Sunday traffic should cease too. In 1783 a reform group was established under the name of the Eclectic Society. In the West Riding, the Rev. H. Zouch, a J.P., started a move to tighten up the local administration, which was cracking under the pressure of the Industrial Revolution; and in 1786 he published *Hints Respecting the Public Police*. ("He displayed," said the *Leeds Intelligencer*, "a most condescending attention to the complaints of the lower classes of society.") Wilberforce, the Yorkshire M.P., set himself to convert this into a national movement, and in 1787 induced the Privy Council to issue a Proclamation which forbade "playing on the Lord's Day at dice, cards, or any other game whatsoever, either in public or in private houses", and enjoined special energy in enforcing the laws against "blasphemy, drunkenness, profane swearing and cursing, lewdness, profanation of the Lord's Day, or other dissolute, immoral or disorderly practices . . . licentious books and prints . . and the supply of refreshments during the times of divine service". A society was immediately formed, under distinguished patronage, to implement it, and a national conference of Justices of the Peace was called.[71]

71 See Webb, *Hist. of Liquor Licensing*, Appendix. In 1792 stipendiary magistrates were set up. For the development of the police force, see Reith, *The Police Idea*.

But two years before this Proclamation, Newte, passing through Manchester, was impressed to find that "the streets are paraded every Sunday during the time of divine service by constables who take all straggling persons into custody. Disorderly houses are searched once in every eight or ten days, about nine or ten o'clock in the evening, care being taken not to let it be known when the search is to be made".[72] Evidently there were local authorities who were ahead of the pressure-group in the capital.

It was at this period that the so-called Evangelical movement first became of importance. Henry Venn had published his *Complete Duty of Man* as early as 1763. His teaching was adopted by a number of active and wealthy middle-class laymen, including a banker and a future Governor-General of India.[73]

Such measures have given some writers the impression that there was an actual raising of moral standards in the latter part of the century. It seemed to me, however, that there was very little real change; only that more sound and fury was created. The middle class had, as I have shown, always held strict views: now these views received public endorsement. But the motives for such endorsement were more often political than moral. Porteus' Bill took the opportunity of suppressing the debating societies in which, it was feared, revolutionary political notions were being discussed. Much of the pressure against Sunday amusements had an economic basis.[74] Thus in 1764 we find the *London Chronicle* deploring "the whole inhabitants of a country village drawn from their harvest work to see a cudgel-playing or a cricket match".[75] As they would probably be "disqualified by intemperance" from work-

---

[72] Newte, *Tour*, p. 39.

[73] Their greater wealth and better education enabled them to press more effectively for religious reforms than could small-time Methodists and Dissenters. They were largely concerned in organising the Proclamation Society and subsequently the Religious Tract Society and the Society for the Suppression of Vice. The Governor-General of India was Lord Teignmouth; but his middle-class status is revealed in Glenbervie's comment on Lady Teignmouth: "a grand, be-velvetted and be-furred, vulgar, Leadenhallish, Bengalish, saint-like, new-fangled lady of quality." *Diaries* (1810), ii, 17.

[74] On this see Webb, *Hist. of Liquor Licensing*, Appendix.

[75] Issue of October 4th–6th, 1764.

ing the next day also, they were wasting one-fourth part of the week. The *Leeds Intelligencer* (1786) said it would be much better to suppress the country feasts entirely, as mischief invariably ensued, and the public "waste their time and money to their own great loss and that of their employers".[76] Here we can detect, no doubt, the Puritan objection to pleasure combined with the tradesman's attention to business. The *Bristol Journal* (1787) declared that it was actually "the business of the magistrate" to lessen "the number of diversions calculated to slacken the industry of the useful hands".[77]

Incidentally, it is noticeable that the reformers, while pressing the prosecution of those who shaved or sold food on a Sunday, turned a blind eye on glass-works, blast furnaces and collieries, where men worked to keep the furnaces going over the week-end.[78] In fact, Sunday labour of many kinds was common—we even read of the work of rebuilding theatres being carried forward on that day—and it was not until well into the nineteenth century that a feeling against Sunday work of an industrial character emerged.[79]

One gets an impression of a quite obsessive determination to bring spontaneous enjoyment under control when one finds Zouch, the Yorkshire magistrate, writing a tract in which he attacks the performance of oratorios in country churches, as bringing together a great number of persons and so creating "drunkenness, disorder and riot". Even the Archbishop of York disapproved of "introducing sacred music in this way".[80]

The theatre provides a further clue to the changing moral picture,

[76] Issue of June 20th, 1786.

[77] Issue of August 18th, 1787. Home Office papers also provide evidence. Thus in 1802 Whitechapel magistrates urged the Home Secretary to refuse a licence to the Royalty Theatre on the grounds that it would affect industrial employees. In the same way Wesley in 1734 protested against the building of a theatre in Bristol on the grounds that "it would be peculiarly hurtful to a trading city, giving a wrong turn to youth especially, gay, trifling and directly opposed to the spirit of industry and a close application to business". *Works*, xii, 189. Archbishop Cornwallis opposed the Manchester Playhouse Bill in 1775 for similar reasons.

[78] Whitaker, *Eighteenth Century English Sunday*, pp. 161–2.

[79] ib.

[80] Zouch, *Hints*, p. 7n.

and in fact it was the evidence from this field which first confirmed me in my suspicion that the nature of the change in morals constituted a genuine historical problem. Thus as early as 1771, Colman, in the prologue to Kelly's *Clementina*, speaks of "these, our moral and religious days".[81] Similarly Murphy, in the epilogue to *Three Weeks after Marriage* (1776), speaks of "this grave, this moral, pious age". If we dismiss this as irony, we must face the fact that plays as innocent as Mrs. Cowley's *A School for Greybeards* (1786) were damned for indecency, while in 1798 Thomson's translation of *Adelaide von Wulfingen* was described as "unnatural and disgusting in the highest degree".[82] Texts were bowdlerised (*The Beggar's Opera* was bowdlerised in 1765; *The School for Scandal* was expurgated in 1777): Sheridan's plays constitute an attempt to adapt the style of Congreve to current taste.[83]

Most significant of all, after 1800 the *Gentleman's Magazine* ceases to print its regular list of current plays, while, almost from the same year, it promotes the Ecclesiastical Preferments from an obscure position in small type at the end of the social announcements to the dignity of a section of its own, and a capitalised entry in the list of contents.

With the capture of the post of censor by a Methodist (Larpent) in 1802, the conquest of the theatre may be said to have been completed.[84] In short, it seems that the theatre was completely 'Victorianised' before ever the eighteenth century terminated. No doubt this was due not merely to a change in public taste, but also to the increasing wealth and numerousness of the new middle class, which forced the playwright to write increasingly for a middle-class and decreasingly for an upper-class audience.

But the change was not confined merely to the theatre. There was evidence that important sections of society had already become 'Victorianised'. For instance, in 1798, Mary Wollstonecraft was

---

[81] In this year the J.P.s of Middlesex urged Garrick not to perform *The Beggar's Opera*.

[82] Cited Nicoll, *Hist. of Late Eighteenth Century Drama*, p. 15.

[83] When Goldsmith wrote *The Good Natur'd Man* (1768) he intended to include a scene in a sponging house. "But in deference to public taste grown, of late, perhaps too delicate," he cut the scene. (Preface.)

[84] See Nicoll, *Hist. of Early Nineteenth Century Drama*, i, 17.

instantly 'dropped' by Mrs. Siddons and Mrs. Inchbald, as soon as it became clear that she had previously been living in sin with Imlay. While it was possible to pretend ignorance, they did so, but the announcement of her marriage to Godwin publicly demonstrated that her relationship with Imlay must have been illicit, and so brought public opinion to bear.[85] Moreover, her sisters wrote to complain that Mary's reputation was making it impossible for them to get employment as companions in respectable households.[86] Indeed, Mary Wollstonecraft herself, for all her brave claims for the rights of women, thought men midwives immoral, and declined to have a doctor present at her lying-in, from reasons of modesty.

Are not these the very accents of Victorianism?

At this point, I took stock of the problem. It already seemed clear that there had been a continuous Puritan tradition throughout the eighteenth century. The most active inheritors of this tradition were often extremely severe, extremely pious: there was no reason to suppose that the tradition was losing force. They were to be found, for the most part, in the trading middle class. Thus it seemed to me that possibly the main problem with which I was faced should not be formulated as, how did the pendulum swing from licence to prudery? but, how did the trading middle class succeed in imposing its views on the rest of society?

In a general way, this was indirectly connected with the fact that the middle class was becoming steadily richer, more numerous and more powerful throughout the period. Its rising status was evidently a part of the story, but only a part. In itself it did not seem enough to account for the still wealthier and much more influential aristocracy abandoning its habits and adopting middle-class values. But before pursuing this question, I felt it would be instructive to study fairly closely the nature and timing of this process. When did the upper class begin to adopt, or conform to, middle-class conceptions of morality and behaviour? And in what did the change consist?

[85] Preedy, *This Shining Woman*, p. 279. (Just after this Lady Jersey was ostracised at a large Assembly at the Duchess of Gordon's, "the ladies made a lane for her and let her pass unspoken to." Farington, *Diary*, i, 199.)
[86] ib., p. 279.

CHAPTER 3

THE REIGN OF THE SAINTS

In 1788, Lady Bridget Talmash observed to the Duchess of Bolton, "Really, I declare 'pon my honour, it's true that a great many People now go to Chapel. I saw a vaste number of carriages at Portman Chapel last Sunday." The Duchess replied, rather crushingly no doubt, that she invariably went to chapel on Sunday, and that when she was in the country she also read prayers in the hall to her family. Lord Robert Seymour thought the passage worth recording in his diary.[1]

This seems to have been a new development, and by 1798 it had grown general enough to engage the attention of Parliament. According to the *Annual Register*, "It was a wonder to the lower orders, throughout all parts of England, to see the avenues of the churches filled with carriages. This novel appearance prompted the simple country people to inquire, what was the matter?"[2]

It seems to have been about this time that the middle class first developed an active and open campaign against the manners of the upper class. In 1795, for instance, the *Morning Post* permitted itself a sarcastic comment on Lady Archer's use of cosmetics; while in 1797 information was laid against Lady Buckinghamshire and four of her guests for playing at faro in her house, and all were convicted and heavily fined.[3] In 1791, Hannah More launched her first broadside in this direction, *An Estimate of the Religion of the Fashionable World*, soon followed by *Thoughts on . . . the Manners of the Great*.

But it was evidently not a complete explanation to suppose that the aristocracy were subdued by these pressures, for an increasing number were reforming themselves from conviction. Thus the Duke of

[1] Cited Russell, *Recollections*, p. 91.
[2] *Annual Register* (1798), Chronicle, p. 229.
[3] Paston, *Social Caricature*, p. 33.

Grafton, after a reprobate youth in which he supported a number of mistresses, including the famed Nancy Parsons, was converted to Unitarianism some time after 1770 and became a correspondent of the pious Arthur Young. Wilberforce underwent a quite definite religious conversion in 1785, while others changed their views more gradually, like William Windham the younger, who became serious towards the end of his life. Cases such as these confirmed my assumption that psychological factors would have to be studied at some point: the explanation could not be simply economic or political. But for the moment I rejected the temptation to pursue this lead and continued the attempt to sketch a picture of the process of change in non-psychological terms.

By quite an early date in the nineteenth century we find upper-class families which have not merely become religious but have adopted the whole pattern of bourgeois behaviour. The lives of the Capels, as described in the *Capel Letters* (1814–17), are completely bourgeois: moral, domesticated, devoid of æsthetic or philosophical interests. Lady Caroline refuses to receive her sister-in-law on the grounds that she is a divorcée, though after Waterloo she "Swallows the Pill" and does so for the thoroughly bourgeois reason that she does not want to offend her brother, who was one of the heroes of that battle.[4]

Lady Holland exclaims at and even approves the domestication of the Earl of Ros, "He is become gardener, carpenter, mechanic, boatman, fisherman, in short always occupied and in consequence always happy. Five children and much love; in short it is a beau ideal of happiness."[5] By 1825 we find Lady Granville speaking admiringly of Mme. de Broglie as "an angel quite as strict and good as the Duchess of Beaufort and Mrs. Money, without one shade of peculiarity, no cant, no humbug, passing her life in acts of charity and thoughts of piety, but living in the world, going to theatres, admired and praised by everybody".[6]

---

[4] *Capel Letters*, pp. 116–17. But people who knew them in Brussels were always asking, "Why is Lady Caroline so *very* Particular? Why don't she let you do as other girls do?" (p. 200).

[5] *Lady Holland to Her Son*, p. 100.

[6] Lady Granville, *Letters*, i, 344.

Such single instances might be exceptional, however, and it would be easy to produce contrary cases. I therefore sought to chart the change by indirect methods. One of the simplest of these seemed to be the use of cosmetics by women, since this is something which can, unless very discreet, be detected by casual observers. (If the use were so discreet as to be unnoticeable, one would presumably be justified in inferring that the person concerned was deferring to public opinion, while not personally convinced that cosmetics were wicked or worldly.)

In 1766 the Princess of Monaco is "the only lady who doesn't wear rouge, for all the rest daub themselves so shockingly it's shocking".[7] But in 1784, rather surprisingly, Rochefoucauld says, "The ladies . . . never use rouge, a practice which has completely disappeared in England; indeed it is as rare a thing for a woman to use rouge in England as for a man to putty his face in France."[8] This is perhaps a bit premature: Rochefoucauld spent most of his time in rather middle-class surroundings in Norfolk, and the statement probably reflects his experience there. However by 1796 Glenbervie comments on the use of make-up by the wife of the Bishop of Winchester, which suggests that the use of rouge was already becoming uncommon.[9] Doubtless it decreased when Queen Sophia and the Princesses gave up the use even of powder in 1793.[10] In 1810 Lady Granville reports that a friend has urged her to use rouge as she looks so pale after her pregnancy, observing that she herself uses it, but "Husbands never see those things;—Lor O. [Lord Ossulton] never finds it out, he would be furious with me."[11] From this it is clear that make-up was now often

[7] Lady Lennox, *Life and Letters*, p. 172.

[8] *Frenchman in England.* A distinction must be made between the use of paint (or enamel), which was used to create a deliberately artificial effect in France, and a mere heightening of the natural colouring with rouge and powder. Thus, even in 1750, Mme. de Bocage observes that Englishwomen use no paint: but in the same year Walpole records how Lady Caroline Peters makes up while inviting him to Vauxhall.

[9] Glenbervie, *Diaries*, i, 89. Archenholtz (1797) says that few, even among women of the town, used paint. (*Picture of England*, p. 330.)

[10] *Book of Elegance*, p. 20.

[11] Lady Granville, *Letters*, i, 17.

used so discreetly as to be invisible. In the same year Glenbervie refers disapprovingly to "Mrs. Panton's pink lip-salve, which looks quite ugly when she is singing".[12]

Apparently, however, a discreet make-up was still used by some for evening occasions, for as late as the 1830s Barbara Charlton refers to the "made-up London girls" who attended country balls; and she recalls how the opening of shutters, at the end of the dance, "was the signal for all those ladies, young or old, who indulged in dyes and paint to scuffle down the staircase and call loudly for their carriages".[13]

At the same time the habit of deep drinking was going out. The middle class had already abandoned it. Johnson could recall when "all the *decent* people of Lichfield got drunk every night, and were not the worse thought of".[14] By 1825, Granby (in Ainsworth's novel of that name) tells his uncle, "Drinking is universally exploded . . . I believe, sir, that you would find that a messtable, now, is quite as temperate as any other."[15] And about the same time Pueckler-Muskau comments, "Much drinking (by men after ladies leave) is now unfashionable."[16] The habit lingered on at places like Cambridge and in country society into the nineteenth century, but by 1827 the Rev. Mr. Knipe, after describing the drinking and pranks of men of "large landed property" in his youth in Cheshire, told Place, "They are all gone now, except one or two of the youngest who still remain stupid, drunken, fox-hunters, and they get drunk alone or in some other company than that of their equals in rank and property."[17]

There were always exceptions, of course, particularly among the established clergy. Samuel Wilberforce records in his diary in 1831, "A good audit dinner: 23 people drank 11 bottles of wine, 28 quarts of

12 Glenbervie, *Diaries*, ii, 48.

13 B. Charlton, *Recollections*, p. 83.

14 Boswell, 'A Tour to the Hebrides,' in *Life of Johnson*, v, 59.

15 Cf. also Farington, *Life of Reynolds*, pp. 66–8.

16 Pueckler-Muskau, *Tour*, ii, 35.

17 B. M. Addl. MSS, 27,827, pp. 108–11. Prof. Pryme said, "When I first went to Cambridge [c. 1800] the habit of hard drinking was almost as prevalent there as it was in country society." *Autobiographical Recollections*, pp. 49–51. Cited Overton, *Church in the 19th Century*, p. 222.

beer, 2½ of spirits, and 12 bowls of punch; and would have drunk twice as much if not restrained. *None, we hope, drunk!*"[18]

The *Annals of Sporting and Fancy Gazette* observed in 1828, "We boast in this age that we have abolished the vice of drinking to excess, but we have substituted in its place that of eating."[19] To judge from the gargantuan menus given by Gronow, and the comments of foreigners, this might seem correct.[20] But Lichtenberg had commented on the vast quantities of food offered in 1774.[21] The main purpose of these banquets was probably ostentation rather than gluttony, as Harriet Granville implies. "We fared sumptuously at the rich man's table", she says, when describing a visit to Trentham. "The dinner for us two was soup, fish, fricassee of chicken, cutlets, venison, veal, hare, vegetables of all kinds, tarr, melon, pineapple, grapes, peaches, nectarines, with wine in proportion. . . . Before this sumptuous repast was well digested, about four hours later, the door opened, and in was pushed a supper in the same proportion, in itself enough to have fed me for a week. I did not know whether to laugh or to cry. Either would have been better than what I did, which was to begin again, with the prospect of a pill to-night, and redoubled abstemiousness for a week to come."[22]

I came to the subject prepared to find that the spread of morality would be accompanied by signs of loss of spontaneity: greater formalism and restraint in social behaviour, and fear of drinking, dancing and other activities which tend to free the unconscious and inhibit the higher centres. The position concerning drink we have seen. No general public condemnation of dancing seems to have developed, although the moralists condemned it severely enough. However, the waltz was strongly condemned, after its introduction in 1812—a handbook of the period refers to "the pollution of the waltz"[23] —and by 1833 all dancing was "forbidden to English wives by the

[18] Russell, *Recollections*, pp. 82–3.
[19] Op. cit., iii, 371.
[20] Gronow, *Reminiscences*, p. 79, etc.
[21] Lichtenberg, *Visits*, p. 49.
[22] Lady Granville, *Letters*, pp. 8–9.
[23] *Ladies Pocket Book*, cited Turner, *History of Courting*, p. 144.

greater part of English husbands".[24] That it sometimes became a matter of conscience even in the upper class is shown by the fact that in 1811 Lady Catherine Graham refused to allow her daughters to learn to dance, and was only with difficulty persuaded to let them learn music.[25]

Dominated as they were by the importance of public appearance, the moralists naturally had more important targets than dancing, which is performed in private, and which, even if it "arouses improper passions", at least has no immediately visible effects. Dancing was not felt to be wicked in itself so much as demoralising: this emerges very vividly in Elizabeth Fry's diary, "The danger of dancing, I find, is throwing me off my centre; at times when dancing I know that I have not reason left but that I do things which in calmer moments I repent for."[26] She also disapproved of singing in company, as leading to vanity and dissipation, and soon after making these entries resolved to give both up.

But I was looking also for a general increase in restraint in manners. Following the French Revolution Moore noted in the higher classes in England "an increased reserve of manner, which had been fatal to conviviality and humour, and not very propitious to wit, subduing both manners and conversation to a sort of polished level, to rise above which is often thought almost as vulgar as to sink below it".[27] This, he said, exerted a proportionate restraint upon all within their circle. Again, the author of *An American in England* (1835) reported that the demeanour of Englishwomen "seemed constrained and formal, as if they were acting each in imitation of some established model".[28]

Lucy Aikin speaks of the long silences which used to take place on social occasions, broken only by an occasional triviality; and this was so even when visitors had come to call.[29] And that this had early infected the upper class is suggested by the Duchess of Dorset's warning

[24] D'Hausset, *Great Britain in 1833*, i, 86.

[25] Reeve, *Journal of a Residence*, p. 231.

[26] Ponsonby, *English Diaries*, p. 323.

[27] Moore, *Life of Sheridan*, p. 217. However, even in the eighteenth century many foreign visitors thought the English middle class restrained, and by 1792 Schuetz (*Briefe ueber London*, i, 155 f) put this view quite strongly.

[28] Op. cit., p. 116.

[29] Cf. More, 'French Opinion of Eng. Society': *Works*, iv, 207.

to Mme. Vigée le Brun, when she came to stay at Knole, "I'm afraid you'll find it very dull; we never speak at meals."[30]

The truly extraordinary character of this inhibition emerges rather vividly in the letters of the Danish pastor, Geijer. He describes a Sunday in Hyde Park in 1810; walking was the only amusement permitted on Sunday. "A stream of people pours at such times over the roads from the town to Kensington Gdns, they rush there and back as on an ant-run. . . . The first sight of this multitude of well-dressed and handsome people is dazzling, and the whole scene would be a vivid pleasure if the entire mass gave any sign of life other than the movement by which they are borne hither and back again. One sees scarcely a smiling lip, one hears no laughter, one hears not a word. Only the sound of thousands of footsteps and a soft murmur of greetings between the human stream which flows forward and that which flows back. It is a running whisper half an English mile in length. And one can swear that ninety-nine out of a hundred of the sounds that they utter are nothing but the words 'How-do-you-do?'"[31]

By 1840 Guizot, the French Ambassador, finds the silence, even on week-days, somewhat oppressive. He notices it immediately on landing at Dover, and again when he gets to London. "Nobody visits or speaks to me, I hear no noise, it is the repose of night without its darkness. I am surrounded by a hive of bees who work without humming."[32]

In fact, it seems clear that the lower class was also substantially affected, at least in the metropolis.

As early as 1805 Malcolm is recording the great improvement in the manners of the populace; there is now no violence and incivility in the streets, no pushing and shoving.[33] By 1825, when Place visited Rotherhithe on Easter Sunday, the transformation has been completed.[34] "There was no noisy turbulence as formerly, no drunken-

[30] Sackville-West, *Knole and the Sackvilles*, p. 197.
[31] Geijer, *Impressions of England*, pp. 165–6.
[32] Guizot, *An Embassy to the Court of St. James*, pp. 2–5.
[33] *Anecdotes of the Manners*, p. 217.
[34] Place MSS.

ness. Two sailors at Rotherhithe had taken liquor enough on board to make them funny, but except these two, no person that I saw in my three hours' walk was in the least disguised by liquor. Formerly hundreds would have been seen drunk at noon on Easter Sunday." He records the general improvement in the housing and the clothes of the people, an improvement produced in the last thirty years, and continues, "Went at five p.m. with my wife up Mill Bank to Chelsea and home through Pimlico and St. James' Park. I expected to see a crowd of people on Mill Bank but was disappointed, there was scarcely any body there . . . We did not see one person who was drunk. Mill Bank the gay, and noisy, Mill Bank, the place for Sunday evening mirth, and vulgarity, and drinking and smoking and obscenity is deserted. There was no company at the two remaining houses near Vauxhall Bridge." His conclusion is, "The class of persons who used to be found at the water side, and at the tea-gardens on Sundays, now amuse themselves at home or walk in the parks, in a much more rational and useful way than they were accustomed to do formerly, and this is the case also with the great body of respectable journeymen, tradesmen, and their families."

In country areas, where Methodism was strong, the lower class was similarly affected. Guest laments that the amusements of the Lancashire weavers have altered. "The Athletic exercises of Quoits, Wrestling, Foot-ball, Prison-bars and Shooting with the Long-bow are become obsolete . . . they are now Pigeon-fanciers, Canary-breeders and Tulip-growers. The field sports, too, have assumed a less hardy and enterprising character."[35]

How different is all this from less than a century earlier, when Pollnitz noted "that aimiable Freedom which reigns in *England*, gives the People an Air of Gaiety that is to be met with nowhere else so universally".[36]

The evidence from the more important field of upper-class manners is less conclusive. La Rochefoucauld was impressed with the amount of informality in 1784, even in his East Anglian milieu: "It would be impossible to be more easy-going in good society than one is in

[35] Guest, *Compendious History*, p. 38.
[36] Pollnitz, *Memoirs*, v, 222.

England. Formality counts for nothing, and for the greater part of the time one pays no attention to it. Thus, judged by French standards, the English, and especially the women, seem lacking in polite behaviour. They never receive any introduction in the subject and all the young people whom I have met in society in Bury give the impression of being what we should call badly-brought-up: they hum under their breath, they whistle, they sit down in a large arm-chair and put their feet on one another, they sit on any table in the room and do a thousand other things which would be ridiculous in France, but are done quite naturally in England."[37]

But Lady Susan O'Brien, commenting on the changes which had taken place between 1760 and 1818, felt that manners had become less formal. In 1760, she says, "great civility was general in all ranks. Form was much abated; none remained that was troublesome, yet there was a sort of respect shewn to elderly people and those of high rank greater than to those on more of equality. Titles were used in common and none but parents or the greatest intimates were ever call'd by their Christian names. Servants always call'd those they served My Lord or My Lady, My Master or My Mistress. They were in general respectful and anxious to please, & continued in the same service.

"Now there is a certain rudeness or carelessness of manner affected by both men and women. Ladies pretty and young may go and seek their own carriages, & meet with no assistance; persons with or without titles are called by their Xtian names, Mary P., Louisa S., etc. Misses likewise give up their titles, Maria H., Emily B.; all follow this laudable humility, & every rank contributes its mite to equality. Every man, tradesman, or farmer is Esqr., & every prentice girl a young lady. Servants speak of their master in the third person, Ld I. or Mr. F."[38]

Age must have gilded Lady Susan's recollection, for the eighteenth century is notable for endless complaints about the effrontery of servants, and the passage has something of the *laudator temporis acti* about it. Often the ill behaviour of a small minority is criticised, as if it were general; as when one observer complains that to a "modern man

[37] Rochefoucauld, *Frenchman in England*, p. 34.
[38] Lady Lennox, *Life and Letters*, Appendix B.

of the world his sisters are good *pieces*, his mother an *old snuffy*, and his father a stingy old *grave-airs* who might as well *kick the bucket*".[39] This was certainly not the most common mode of address.

That some genuine loss of spontaneity occurred is clearly shown by Mrs. Sherwood, never one to paint the picture in very cheerful hues. Recalling social conditions in her childhood (i.e. about 1785-90), she writes that a pastime at county balls was to spread a tablecloth on the stairs, on which all the ladies who were disposed for merriment seated themselves in rows, "and then the gentlemen pulled, and down came the ladies, one over the other, to the utter confusion of all order, and extinction of all decorum. And how many other freaks and gambols of the same refined nature were in the like manner executed, I know not," and adds darkly, "but this I know, that the mothers and grandmothers of persons in high rank, and now living in this country, made parties in these diversions."[40] The implication that manners have changed decisively is clear.

Still, as late as 1826 it was possible in some circles, apparently, to lie full-length on the floor. Pueckler-Muskau was astonished to find, "The practice of half-lying instead of sitting, sometimes of lying at full length on the carpet at the feet of ladies, of crossing one leg over another in such a manner as to hold the foot in the hand, of putting the hand in the armholes of the waistcoat, and so on,—are all things which have obtained admission in the best company, and the most exclusive circles."[41]

The fourth area in which I looked for clues as to the nature and timing of the change was that of language. As everyone knows, the nineteenth century affected a quite peculiar delicacy of speech, much in contrast with the frankness of the early eighteenth century and earlier periods. This is particularly interesting, since verbal prudery does not invariably go with strict morality. In the medieval church, preachers did not hesitate to call a spade a spade, while the church authorities did not object to depicting the sexual act, both in normal and perverted forms, in carvings and elsewhere. Conversely, although to-day we

---

[39] *The Scourge*, vol. 2.
[40] Darton, *Life of Mrs. Sherwood*, p. 32.
[41] Pueckler-Muskau, *Tour*, p. 45.

have returned to a morality nearer that of the eighteenth century than the nineteenth, we have nevertheless retained a considerable part of this verbal prudery, so that it is still dangerous, if not illegal, to use in print many words which Church dignitaries, like Swift, and middle-class moralists, like Defoe, used quite freely. I adopted the assumption, therefore, that verbal prudery is not an index of the same change in personality structure which the data we have so far considered indicate, but of some other change more or less fortuitously associated with it. How this might come about will emerge later; for the moment let us consider language simply as an index of change.

The move towards verbal prudery had proceeded far enough by 1791 for the *Gentleman's Magazine* to comment rather satirically on it, "All our mothers and grandmothers used in due course of time to become *with child*, or as Shakespeare has it, *round-wombed* . . . but it is very well known that no female, above the degree of a chamber maid or a laundress, has been *with child* these ten years past; every decent married woman now became *pregnant*; nor is she ever *brought to bed* or *delivered*, but merely at the end of nine months has an *accouchement*; antecedent to which she informs her friends that at a certain time she will be *confined*."[42] There were a thousand other instances of such changes, the writer continues, "Only the lowest class *sweat*; a person with any degree of refinement 'merely perspires'." It will be noted that he specifically excepts the lower class from these remarks, and as it is easy to show that the upper class did not adopt these refinements until rather later, it is clearly still a middle-class phenomenon with which we are dealing.

The doughtier members of the aristocracy certainly ignored this trend. In 1816, as Susan Ferrier writes, Lady Charlotte Campbell "would dance and sing and go about and *talk blue*, and that is hard work in this town" (Edinburgh).[43] In 1840 Lady Holland speaks of the

---

[42] *Gentleman's Magazine*, LXI (December 1791), p. 1100. Early in the nineteenth century French words were substituted for English ones, as more decent. A writer, attacking this as prudery, adds that to call breeches smallclothes or inexpressibles is "highly ridiculous, and gives rise to improper ideas . . ." *Errors of Pronunciation*, p. 27.

[43] S. Ferrier, *Memoir and Correspondence*, p. 131.

Queen as "showing visibly her *interesting condition*": but as she under-
lines the phrase and uses the word 'pregnancy' shortly after, we may
assume she was parodying popular prudery. Satire was evidently
intended also when she reproved the French Ambassador for remarking "Hell is paved with good intentions". She apologetically
told him, "We never use the word *hell* here, unless in quoting from
Milton; high poetry is the only excuse".[44]

From all these facts, and others which I have no room to cite,
together with developments which have been noted in the previous
chapter—notably the increasing activity of the magistracy and the
emergence of the Evangelical movement—a distinct and rather
startling conclusion emerges. Everything points to the fact that the
period of decisive moral change was not at the time of Victoria's
accession, or even in the nineteenth century at all, but that it took place
during the decade 1790–1800.[45]

This conclusion is confirmed by the fact that many of those living in
the decades following had the impression that some major change in
standards had taken place. Thus the *Christian Observer*, in celebrating
its tenth anniversary in 1811, wrote, "The circumstance with which
we are most forcibly struck is the different aspect which the Christian
world exhibits at the present moment from that which it bore at the
commencement of our course. Nor is its aspect altered only; it is
improved beyond the fondest dreams of a visionary. If one could
suppose some calm, calculating Christian Observer to open his eyes,
after a ten years sleep on the passing scene, would he not find himself in
a new creation?"[46] Coming from a paper with something like a vested
interested in lamenting the existence of immorality, these are emphatic
words.

Many comparable quotations can be found. For instance, Miss Jane
Porter wrote to Hannah More in 1815, recalling that twenty years

[44] *Lady Holland to Her Son*, pp. 187 ff. It is significant that drunkenness also
became unmentionable. See Knight, *Once Upon a Time*, ii, 49. In 1841 Henry
Fox did not even dare to tell Sir Frederick Lamb's Viennese wife that she would
shock the English by using such expressions as "Christ God, you do not say so!"
(*Lady Holland to Her Son*, p. 195.)

[45] Jaeger, *Before Victoria*, arrives at a similar conclusion.

[46] *Christian Observer*, Preface.

previously she had often been horrified when at dinner some people had scoffed at religion without a reprimand from anyone. "Such conduct would not now be tolerated a moment in any company; and the one I speak of was a most respectable circle."[47] The change is well summed up in a remark noted by Harriet Martineau. "Earl Stanhope, the historian, mentions having been told by 'the Lord Lieutenant and for many years the representative of one of the Midland shires' that when he came of age there were only two landed gentlemen in his county who had family prayers, while at present [1850] there are, he believes, scarcely two who had not."[48]

Indeed, England was even becoming known on the Continent for its prudishness, as we can see, for instance, from Schleiermacher's *Letters to Lucinde* (1799), in which he suggests, at one point, that all German prudes should be banished to England, where they will presumably be quite at home.

It is, of course, easy enough to find the usual complaints of the immorality of the period, such as are always made; but, for reasons already given, these contrary declarations seem to me to carry more weight.

I found one authority who was inclined to put the change—or at any rate the inception of the change—as early as 1770. Joseph Farington, writing in 1819 of the year 1770, said, "At this time a change in the manners and habits of the people of this country was beginning to take place. Public taste was improving. The coarse familiarity so common in personal intercourse was laid aside, and respectful attention and civility and address began to gradually give a new and better aspect to society. The profane habit of using oaths in conversation no longer offended the ear, and bacchanalian intemperance at the dinner table was succeeded by rational cheerfulness and sober forbearance."[49] Whenever it was that the change began, this quotation certainly confirms that Farington felt it had achieved itself appreciably prior to 1819.

[47] Cited Roberts, *Memoirs . . . H. More*, iii, 431. A number of similar comments are cited by Quinlan, *Victorian Prelude*.
[48] *Hist. 30 Years' Peace*, ii, 324.
[49] Farington, *Life of Reynolds*, p. 55.

These facts seemed to establish very clearly that the popular conception of the moral tone of the nineteenth century being established by the influence of Queen Victoria was completely incorrect. In point of fact, Victoria in her youth, though earnest and very conscious of her duties, was by no means Puritanical. In the opening years of her reign she came under strong criticism from the middle class for giving too many balls; she preferred whisky to tea, adored gossip and questioned Melbourne closely about other people's behaviour. She ate heartily ("I think I may say she gobbles") and once organised a sweepstake on the Derby at Balmoral. Creevey noted, "She laughs in real earnest, opening her mouth as wide as it can go, showing not very pretty gums."[50]

It was Albert who was the real moralist, as Melbourne makes clear; after his death, Victoria came increasingly to adopt the ideas he had held up to her, so that in the latter part of her reign she came to display many of the genuine characteristics of the moralist. If royalty influenced the process at all, it was rather the pious Adelaide and the bluff William. A bourgeois nation now had a bourgeois Court, and was confirmed in its conception of what was fitting. But it was no more than confirmation of something which already existed.

Not the least interesting feature of this great social change is the smallness of the part which seems to have been played by the Established Church. With a few exceptions, it followed the eighteenth-century pattern of pluralism and non-residence, and even carried it further during the first half of the nineteenth century. Manners-Sutton, an uncle of the Duke of Portland, who was Archbishop of Canterbury from 1805 to 1828, bestowed sixteen livings, to say nothing of numerous cathedral appointments, upon seven of his relations. Richard Watson, Bishop of Llandaff, was chiefly interested in chemistry—he made notable improvements in the manufacture of gunpowder—and paid, in the thirty-four years of his episcopate, only one visit to his see. He held fifteen livings when he retired to the shores of Lake Windermere.[51]

[50] *Creevey Papers*, ii, 326.
[51] See Baring-Gould, *Church Revival*, Chapter 8. Also Emden, *Regency Pageant*, pp. 71-3.

Countless other examples can be given. Porteus, as Bishop of London in the early years of the century, made some gestures of reform—he once obliged the manager of Covent Garden to lower the curtain in the middle of a ballet—but seems to have been actuated more by an opportunist sense of what public opinion wanted than by religious fervour. It is not until the 1840s that we begin to find the Church making a genuine effort to influence the public to piety; and it is not until 1854, I find, that the Convocation of Canterbury recommended clergymen to live in poor districts "preaching, exhorting, visiting the sick and poor in their own homes, and superintending schools". Contrast with this the attitude of Harcourt, as Archbishop of York (1807–47), who, when asked to conduct confirmations in the West Riding, replied that it must be at Wakefield, as that was as far into the West Riding as a gentleman could be expected to go.[52]

It was, in short, not the Court and not the Church which effected the moral revolution: it was the middle class.

It is not difficult to see how it was that the middle class could have come to exert such extensive influence, for it was rapidly growing in numbers and importance. Since the aristocracy could not increase in size, the numerical increase of the middle class—the result of the rapid growth of population—increased its influence proportionately. In addition, it was becoming more urbanised, and in an urban setting the traditional influence of the upper class is at a discount.[53]

Much more important than this, it was becoming richer and better educated. Its buying power influenced the press, to say nothing of the stage and literature, which became increasingly tailored to middle-class preference. But it was also infiltrating the positions of power. The magistracy passed increasingly into its hands from those of the

---

[52] Hammonds, *Bleak Age*, Chapter 13. There were of course individual exceptions, notably the small number of clergymen who belonged to the Evangelical movement. The Methodists and Dissenters were of course a very different matter.

[53] As the Industrial Revolution progressed, an increasing proportion of the population came to live in towns. The aristocracy continued to live in their country seats, and the new urban populations had no aristocratic figures available to fill the role the lord of the manor filled in rural milieux.

country gentry, and from the first the senior officers of the new police were drawn from middle-class ranks. Fielding's ablest assistant had been a grocer, Saunders Welch, who became the High Constable of Holborn, and the tradition continued.[54] Above all, education fell into its hands. This had begun early in the eighteenth century, when middle-class writers like Defoe had started producing books of instruction, while the university-trained class was content to carry on with the inculcation of Latin. It is striking that no public-school master wrote any school text-book during the eighteenth century. When Arnold was selected to be Headmaster of Rugby, there was a major break with the old headmaster tradition; and his pupils helped to spread the new tradition: thus Vaughan became Headmaster of Harrow, where he could influence many members of the upper class.

The middle-class preponderance was aided by the inflations engendered by the American and Napoleonic wars, which impoverished the older landed middle class. As Southey wrote in 1807, "The gentry of small fortune have also disappeared." Thanks to two wars and the ensuing inflation, though they had inherited what their forefathers would have thought an ample income, "they have found themselves step by step curtailed of the luxuries and at last of the comforts of life, without a possibility of helping themselves. . . . Meantime year after year the price of every article of necessary consumption has increased with accelerating rapidity: education has become more costly, and at the same time more indispensable; and taxation falls year after year heavier, while the means of payment become less." In vain does the man of private income get rid of his carriage, and dismiss his footman, there is no escape. "Wine disappears from the sideboard; there is no longer a table ready for his friend . . . ."[55]

While economic forces were slowly driving him out of his accustomed pattern of life, and actually into the trading middle class, his social standing was being actively threatened by the new industrial and financial magnates—such as Arkwright, Abel Smith, the Boultons, and the Wilkinsons. These increasingly took over the social functions he

[54] Reith, *Police Idea*, pp. 30–1.
[55] Southey, *Letters from England*, p. 369.

had formerly discharged, and brought to the exercise of the magistracy, of charity institutions, of local government, the viewpoint of the new trading class.[56]

Its new economic power and status gave the middle class a much greater power of influencing both upper and lower classes. If bankers would only provide capital for sober individuals who went to church and did not squander their substance, then many who might have been a good deal less sober in other circumstances would be obliged to assume sobriety. If employers made it a condition of employment that their employees should be sober, in the literal sense, and that they should attend church, they too would be forced into line. We find evidence of this sort of pressures in von Raumer's observation that domestic servants were obliged to be moral for fear of losing their places.[57]

In addition to exerting moral pressure in this kind of way, middle-class pietists also sought to achieve moral reform indirectly by assisting the spread of religion. To this end they endowed chapels, distributed tracts and supported reform groups. Some went further still, and planned complete campaigns: Mrs. Treffry tells how a Mrs. Walker planned the conversion of the whole of Maidenhead to Methodism and how she used her interest with the mayor to obtain a hall in defiance of the local vicar.[58]

Furthermore, while the upper class was yielding to middle-class pressures, it was also being diluted and infiltrated by middle-class elements. An unprecedented number of new titles was created: between 1812 and 1838 eight new marquesses were created, as many as had been created in the whole of English history up to 1800: only three more were created between 1838 and the end of the century. The manufacture of earls and viscounts proceeded on an even more intensive scale. Forty-four earls and fourteen viscounts were created in the first half of the nineteenth century. Meanwhile the wealthy

[56] See Chambers, *Nottinghamshire in the 18th Century.*
[57] Raumer, *England in 1835*, ii, 34–5. In 1807 Brandy told Stendhal that his sister would have dismissed her maid if she had found him kissing her. (Edwards, 'Stendhal in London' in *London Magazine*, vol. 2, No. 3, 1955).
[58] Treffry, *Heavenward*, pp. 214–15.

members of the middle class were intermarrying with the upper: still more important, they were sending their children to the same schools. The social function of the public school in the nineteenth century was to weld the middle and upper classes together.

Above all, the sober, trading middle class was influencing those other members of the middle class who might not have been so sober. Some perhaps were sinking into poverty because they lacked the money-making qualities, and so out of the middle class. Many more were conforming to the prejudices of those who had jobs to offer or money to lend, in a period which combined both high unemployment and capital shortage.

While the middle class was gradually extending its influence over the upper class (and to some extent the lower) in this way, the code of behaviour standards was itself undergoing change and development, and the development is, I think, of some interest. It did not consist of a heightening of the fundamental moral elements—there was no broad general pressure for a heightened sense of religious conviction or even for a greater degree of restraint in behaviour. It was rather that the secondary and incidental features were developed, and this to a point of exaggeration bordering on imbecility. The standards of delicacy demanded, the extent of verbal prudery, the degree of unreality in the theatre and the novel, grew steadily greater.

Susan Ferrier was censured in 1817 for mentioning the cutting of toe-nails in a letter to a friend.[59] Mrs. Charlton, having occasion to make an entry concerning the lavatory in her private diary, refers to it only by the elliptical phrase "the first place of general interest on entering the house".[60]

The most ordinary activities had to be justified by the drawing of moral lessons. Not merely ladies' magazines but even cook-books were moralised, as the editor of Ackerman's *Repository* testily com-

---

[59] Ferrier, *Memoir and Correspondence*, p. 91.
[60] Charlton, *Recollections*, p. 140. Pillet recorded (1815), "The indelicate who asks at table for a *cuisse* of chicken, who praises a *gigot* of mutton, runs the risk of never being asked again. . . . One must ask for a *jambe* of chicken . . . or mutton." (*L'Angleterre vue à Londres*, Chapter 39.)

plained in 1810, when reviewing a moralised handbook for ladies' maids.[61]

Art criticism became moralised: when Etty exhibited his 'To Arms, to Arms, ye Brave' in the Royal Academy in 1841, *The Times*[62] tut-tutted, "Here is a parcel of half-naked people struggling and tussling, without any motive, and exposing their persons in a way which calls for the interference of the police." Mr. Etty, it said, should know better than to paint such nonsense. It approved, however, his group 'Morning' as "it exhibits none of the indecencies which occasionally disgrace this artist's pictures".

Pamela, which had been offered as a moralistic work in 1740, was now regarded as 'improper'. Sir John Shaw-Lefevre noted how a lady asked to borrow *Pamela* from his library, saying she well remembered the pleasure of it in her youth "but she returned it the next day, saying she was quite ashamed of having asked for anything so improper". *Roderick Random* and *Tom Jones* he dismisses simply as 'unreadable'; though Fielding had also thought himself a moralist.[63] But even Dickens was taboo in some families. Augustus Hare tells how his adoptive grandmother took in *Pickwick* and "read it by her dressing room fire with closed doors, and her old maid, Cowbourne, well on the watch against intruders". Afterwards the copies were destroyed.[64] For the *Edinburgh Quarterly*, even *Jane Eyre* was "of low moral tendency".

The theatre, which is always closely responsive to public taste, reveals what was happening particularly clearly. When the *Double Dealer* was revived in 1802, the *Theatrical Repository* was horrified, "Such a trough-full of villainy and lewdness was surely never before kneaded together. . . . Down, down with it to the lowest pit of hell; and there let devils act the parts, and devils only be the auditors!"[65]

---

[61] *Repository*, ix, 15. Moralised children's games seem to have been introduced about 1792. See Whitehouse, *Table Games*, Chapter 5.

[62] *Times*, May 4th, 1841, p. 5.

[63] Hare, *Years with Mother*, p. 154. *Pamela* had originally been issued as a moralistic work, as noted earlier. Johnson strongly reproved Hannah More for reading *Tom Jones*.

[64] ib., p. 32.

[65] Op. cit. March 1st, 1802 (No. 24).

The censorship became more and more severe. Colman cut such lines as "I love you, and may heaven protect and pardon you" (from *The Rent Day*, 1832). Kemble cut "Oh God, in Thy mercy either restore my mother or destroy the son" from *Jack Sheppard* (1839), and from *Clemence* the remark, "And if one day they tot up all the useless sins, our age will make a bad showing".[66] Von Raumer notes (1835) that the Lord Chamberlain had "made himself ludicrous by striking out the words 'She is an angel' on the grounds of its being impious and shocking".[67]

Reynolds makes a revealing comment when he says, referring to the epilogue of *How to Grow Rich*, acted in 1793, in which Lewis produced from under his coat a lady's pad, "The whole audience receiving this broad discovery with good humour, the effect was electrical. But now [i.e. in 1827] with our present *correct* spectators!—does the actor live who dares risk not only the loss of his profession but of his life, by a similar exhibition?"[68]

In 1844 things had reached such a pitch that the Lord Chancellor, when certain plays had been submitted to him for approval, actually summoned the three managers concerned and rebuked them for their audacity in even asking for a licence for them.[69]

As a result, the theatre began to lose its audiences. The receipts of Covent Garden, which in 1811 had been £98,000, had fallen by 1833 to £43,000. Managers attempted to resolve the difficulty by turning to spectacle and, still worse, by bringing animals on to the stage.[70] A dog named Carlos nightly rescued the heroine from a tank in Reynolds' *The Caravan* (1803) and *Okeania* was advertised in 1804 as involving 8,000 cubic feet of water. By 1835, Fitzball, remarking that he was "determined to have a run of some kind", went to the desperate extreme of introducing a coach and six real horses on to the stage.[71] (It

[66] Nicoll, *History Early Nineteenth Century Drama*, i, 18.
[67] Raumer, *England in 1835*, ii, 217–21.
[68] Reynolds, *Life and Times*, ii, 163–4. The pad is that worn to produce an effect of pregnancy, as was fashionable c. 1793–5.
[69] Nicoll, *History Early Nineteenth Century Drama*, i, 19.
[70] ib., p. 42.
[71] Fitzball, *Thirty-Five Years of a Dramatic Author's Life*, ii, 24.

was in this way that the Drury Lane tradition of spectacle arose.) In the 'sixties, however, a cycle of plays about prostitutes began to be presented; though they were superficially moralised, the tide could be seen to have turned.

The Times, "that cunning old trout the Times, that ranting, canting, trimming old Times, that brazen old slut the stupid Times, and the bloody old Times" (as Cobbett so neatly put it), was quick to see the way the wind was blowing, and began to make gestures towards morality, uninhibited by the fact that its editor, Mr. Barnes, was living in adultery with Mrs. Mondet.[72] In 1815, for instance, it demanded the demolition of a statue of "the vain, obscene, heartless, atheistical Voltaire", a gesture obviously designed to appeal to public opinion, and curiously similar to the demands which sensational papers sometimes make to-day for the banning of certain books or films.[73] Its treatment of art criticism has already been noted.

The reformist groups became bolder in their activities, and more absurd. Thus the Society for the Suppression of Vice wrote a peremptory letter to the owner of Adam House, Piccadilly, ordering him to remove the classical bas-reliefs on the front, and when he failed to comply, wrote again, offensively remarking that an English gentleman would have instantly removed this "gross and filthy exhibition".[74]

The reformers devoted much of their time to making representations to the magistrates for the closure of places of public resort, usually on the excuse that prostitutes were sometimes present. Malcolm records with gratification the closure of the Dog and Duck and the Apollo Gardens, observing, "these places flourished much too long".[75] It was also a sign of the times when a Commission censured the Princess of Wales for "levity of manners" in 1806.

More significant, perhaps, is the series of prosecutions for blasphemy which began about 1811: under this rubric were prosecuted critics of

[72] Hudson, Thos. Barnes of the Times, pp. 42–3.
[73] Times, July 10th, 1815.
[74] Ackerman gives the correspondence in his Repository (1810), iv, 42. The bas-reliefs had been in position for thirty years.
[75] Malcolm, Anecdotes of the Manners, p. 188.

the literal truth of the Bible, such as Robert Taylor, those who criticised the announcements of prelates, the proponents of new creeds, and those, like Richard Carlile, who published works which were judged seditious. As Nokes demonstrates, blasphemy and sedition were equated.[76] The former had been an ecclesiastical crime, not handled by the civil courts; these nevertheless had begun to impose penalties for it in the seventeenth century. In 1819 an Act was passed "for the more effective Prevention and Punishment of Blasphemous Libels"; this led to a fine crop of prosecutions—twenty cases in the years 1820-4 alone. The drive ended in 1842 with the trial of Holyoake, "the last trial for atheism in England". It was under this rubric also that the bookseller Carlile was prosecuted for issuing pamphlets on birth-control.

The literalness with which the moral taboos had to be observed is illustrated by the story of the two ministers who stayed up talking until midnight one Saturday. Suddenly they remembered that they had not yet shaved. It was, of course, impossible to shave once it was the sabbath, equally impossible to appear in their pulpits before their flocks unshaven. With a stroke of inspiration, the host remembered that the kitchen clock was running ten minutes slower than the clock in the sitting-room. Both agreed to regard this as being the more accurate, and they were just able to retrieve the position. While the story is perhaps apocryphal, the fact that it should be told indicates that literalism was a widespread habit.[77]

These excesses seem so ridiculous that it becomes easy to dismiss them with laughter as eccentricities. But when a substantial section of society unites in behaving eccentrically it is clear that we are faced with a psychological phenomenon of some importance, which deserves careful analysis.

Obviously this almost insane trend could not persist indefinitely. The next step therefore seemed to be to look for signs of its changing in

[76] Nokes, *History Crime of Blasphemy*, pp. 80, 103. The passing of the Libel Act in 1792, which made blasphemy officially a concern of the civil courts, marks the change of viewpoint.

[77] It was however told by James Russell as a true story of Dr. Hunter (1788–1866), who was minister at Swinton from 1814-32. (Fyfe, *Scottish Diaries*, p. 561).

character or reversing itself. The phase of moral relaxation was not one which I intended to cover in the investigation, but it seemed desirable to have some idea when it started in order to mark out the limits of the period to be studied.

CHAPTER 4

THE IMPETUS FADES

SIGNS that the moral revolution was beginning to fail can be found far earlier than might be expected—even before Queen Victoria ascended the throne.

The first evidence I came across which seemed relevant was the change of atmosphere in the universities in the 1840s.[1] Thirlwall had been driven from Cambridge in 1834 for condemning compulsory chapel. But by the 1840s, at Oxford, rationalist or free-thinking views were beginning to be expressed; and the works of the Early Fathers had become a drug on the market to the local booksellers, though they still found some demand at Cambridge. By 1851, Lyell says, professors were publishing the most unorthodox views, for which, ten years before, they would have been sent to Coventry.

Lucy Aikin not only confirms this, but puts the date much earlier. Writing to Bishop Channing in 1829, she says, "It is whispered—monstrum horrendum—that Unitarianism is infecting some of the most enlightened clergy of Oxford . . . some of these clergy, and those of Cambridge, also addict themselves to the modern science of geology."[2] (Geology was of peculiar interest, of course, because it suggested a greater age for the earth than the 6,000 years asserted by the Church, and thus threw doubt on the validity of the Bible.)

But according to Lucy Aikin it was not only in the rarefied atmosphere of the universities that orthodoxy was beginning to be rejected. In 1833 she wrote, "It is marvellous to see how much the church is daily losing ground. It has no longer the reverence of the lower classes in general, and by the middling classes it is beginning to be regarded with

---

[1] Lyell, *Life*. Even in 1846, he says, "large parties" were holding forth on rationalistic topics.

[2] Aikin, *Memoirs*, p. 205.

the same feelings here as the lay Tories so generally excite."[3] Lucy Aikin, though pious, was a historian and by no means the sort of person who regularly lamented a decline in moral standards, so that her remarks cannot be written off as yet another example of the tendency to see a decline in manners, such as older people so often display.

Her comments are, in any case, confirmed by actual evidence of the loss of religious faith—a process which may perhaps be called 'deconversion', especially when it follows an early piety. George Eliot, for instance, lost her faith in 1838, after reading Hennell's *Enquiry*, which had been published the same year. But Hennell, before this, had lost his faith when his sister had asked him to explain the discrepancies in the gospels: he set out to do so, but ended up by himself becoming convinced of their unreliability. Miss Hennell, yet earlier, lost her faith on marrying Bray in 1836. Bray, who had started life with "a strong conviction of sin", had been deconverted by a Unitarian, who in trying to wean him from Calvinism wrought more effectively than he intended. Similarly Sterling, who had been an enthusiastic admirer of the unbending and conscientious Thirlwall, was deconverted by Strauss' *Life of Jesus*, which he read in 1839, after which he took up geology.

In fact the middle classes generally were turning to geology. Harriet Martineau says that they were buying five books on geology to one novel in the 1830s.[4] Herschel's *Discourses on the Study of Philosophy* "captivated readers of all classes". George Eliot, while still an Evangelical, revelled in Nichol's *Architecture of the Heavens*.[5] From this sudden interest we may reasonably deduce a stirring of doubt in their minds.

The existence of this reversal of attitude, which some will no doubt be surprised to find dated so early, can be confirmed by reference to secondary social phenomena. It is well displayed in Emily Eden's two novels of upper-class life, one written in 1830, one in 1860.[6] It is

[3] ib., p. 270.
[4] Martineau, *History of the Thirty Years Peace*, ii, 324.
[5] G. Eliot, *Life*, i, 89.
[6] *The Semi-Attached Couple*, though written in 1830, was not published until 1860.

noticeable, as Raymond Mortimer has pointed out, that the requirements of chaperonage are much severer in the first.[7] Other differences are noticeable: for instance, a middle-class wife addresses her husband as 'Mr. Douglas' in the first, the corresponding character in the second calls hers 'John' or 'my dear'. Clothing—always an important telltale of underlying attitudes—also confirms the diagnosis. Women's costume was at its most modest about the time of Victoria's accession. Thereafter it became increasingly provocative: by 1860 evening décolletés are as low as to-day, or lower. For instance, the cleavage between the breasts, barred by Hollywood film-censors until quite recently, is clearly seen in *Punch* illustrations of the 'fifties, and nothing was more bourgeois than *Punch*.[8]

To-day we are apt to think of the crinoline as a device for concealing the lower limbs, but at the time it was very definitely thought of as a device for displaying them. Owing to the way in which the steels were inserted, any pressure on one side caused the other to rise and reveal the legs, and sometimes even the posterior. While prudes complained, William Hardman commented, "The girls of our time like to show their legs. I don't see why they should be interfered with; it pleases them and does no harm to us."[9] Artificial stomachs and breasts, as used in the eighteenth century, seem to have been reintroduced in the 'forties.[10]

Lucy Aikin gives us an explanation for this reaction. The Evangelicals made all the noise; they included "not a few sour and censorious fanatics", and "their moral influence on the whole, and particularly among the lower classes, is in many points unfavourable. They make religion exceedingly repulsive to the young and the cheerful, by setting themselves against all the sports and diversions of common people", and by their "mysterious and terrific doctrines".[11] But to say this is to

[7] *Sunday Times* (December 25, 1955.)

[8] See, for instance, vol. 28, p. 74 (1855), vol. 34, p. 156 (1858), and very marked in vol. 42, p. 31 (1862). In 1799 *The Times* had blushed for the indelicacy of young ladies "who display their snow-white bosoms and panting breasts".

[9] Hardman, *Mid-Victorian Pepys*, pp. 103–4.

[10] In 1847 the *Ladies' Newspaper* was carrying advertisements not merely for 'bust improvers' but for 'lemon bosoms'.

[11] Aikin, *Memoirs*, pp. 197–8.

say that a generation was growing up to whom such doctrines and practices, which had pleased an earlier generation, were unattractive; that is, it argues the occurrence of some psychological change. Moreover, even Lucy Aikin herself felt that this kind of religion was absurd. "I own I am not quite pleased with the prospect of a second reign of the saints, for their rigour and intolerance go beyond the high church themselves."[12]

The fact that some change of outlook was occurring is also demonstrated by the Oxford Movement. Psychologically, the most significant feature of this movement was its insistence on the reintroduction of colour and ritual into church services. These, as we shall see in detail in Chapter Twelve, are indicative of mother-identification. The clashes which occurred in the 'fifties and 'sixties were all over such matters as placing candles and flowers on the altar, or a cross above it, or wearing a surplice. But by 1870 all these ritual features had been adopted in England.[13] The Tractarians simply went too fast for public opinion, with the result that some of them felt that there was no alternative but to enter the Roman Church.

This diagnosis of the Oxford Movement as matrist might seem inconsistent with the fact that the initial impulse was concerned with the location of authority. Newman was anxious to re-establish the Apostolic Succession, that is, the right of the Church to create its own bishops, without interference from the State. Nevertheless, the diagnosis is confirmed beyond all reasonable doubt by Serjeant Bellasis' account of the last sermon which Newman preached before entering the Roman communion. In a voice of great emotion, he cried, "O my Mother, my Mother, how is it that those who would have died for thee fall neglected from thy bosom? How is it thou hast no word of kindness, no sign of encouragement for them?" etc.[14] This settles beyond doubt that for Newman the Roman Church was a

---

[12] ib., p. 226. It was about 1840 that the first complaints that the poor had been deprived of their amusements are heard, and efforts began to be made to provide public parks and to open existing parks on Sundays (Hammonds, *Bleak Age*, Chapter 13).

[13] C. P. S. Clarke, *Oxford Movement and After*, Ch. 8.

[14] Bellasis, *Memorials*, p. 53.

mother- not a father-surrogate. Thus his advocacy of the Apostolic Succession was a plea that the mother be allowed to make her own dispositions as to her children without interference from the father. Further confirmation of this is found in the incident in which he bought a picture of the Virgin Mary and hung it in his brother's rooms at Oxford (much to the latter's horror), and more in the verse which he wrote. Thus it was a movement based on the figure of a mother, even if an authoritarian one.[15]

At this same time the Evangelical insistence upon the importance of conversion was falling into desuetude in the middle classes. After Victoria's accession, it is increasingly obvious that many of those who attend church regularly and who are most careful about appearances are not haunted by any sense of sin or even of deep religious conviction.[16] Indeed, too much religious feeling begins to be suspect: it is 'overdoing it'. D'Hausset noted that there were many Englishmen, "cold, reasoning, positive", who were not religious from conviction, but were so "from a sense of the utility of religion, and from a respect for appearances".[17] Moral feeling begins to undergo a change in character. While appearances remain extremely important, the fear of pleasure drains away, and instead there emerges an increasing preoccupation with welfare matters.

Indeed, so far from the mid-nineteenth century being a period in which moral pressures were increasing, it was actually one in which concessions were being made. By 1857 Parliament found it possible to

[15] Bellasis' own case is also interesting. Brought up a sincere Protestant, he gradually became preoccupied by the question, ". . . what is the authority to which we as Christians are bound to submit ourselves?" And to the reply, "the Church," he returned, "but which Church?" Now, Bellasis' father had died when he was two years old and his mother had remarried. Thus in his own life there were two figures of authority; hence it is perhaps not surprising that, in his religious life, he should have decided that the authority to which he ought to submit himself was the earlier of the two Churches, not the one which had supplanted it, (*Memorials*, p. 69).

[16] Lucy Aikin, pious as she was, told Bishop Channing, "I have never at any period within my memory, viewed death as a subject of dread." (*Memoirs*, p. 253.) The practice of sending an empty coach to the funeral of a respected man also seems significant.

[17] D'Hausset, *Gt. Brit. in 1833*, i, 262.

pass an Act reforming the divorce laws in a liberal sense: making divorce easier and giving the wife right to a legal separation on grounds of cruelty. True, it was not until the 'seventies and 'eighties that Parliament made any comprehensive effort to improve the status of women, but evidently the tide had already turned.[18]

Commentators on the reign of Victoria frequently praise it for having combined a high standard of morality with an attention to social reforms. The fact would seem to be, however, that the phase of increasing reform was a phase of declining moral pressure, at least as far as the leaders of society were concerned. And it was the period of greatest moral pressure which coincided with the worst atrocities of industrialism and individualism. (This, as we shall see later, is a point of some interest for the validity of the theory of matrism and patrism put forward in the introduction.)

The shift in social attitudes is, however, a complex one. While the upper and upper-middle classes were moving towards matrism again, the lower classes—who, as we shall see in the next chapter, had so far been little affected by the moral climate—began to drift towards patrism. Thus, after 1850 we find an increasing degree of restraint and morality in these lower levels, which did not reverse itself until the following century. It is as if the moral attitude of the middle classes were gradually drifting down the social scale. But the whole subject of how a moral revolution reverses itself is so complicated that I felt it necessary to leave it over to a separate study. For this reason, I decided to treat the 1850s as the practical limit of the present inquiry.

While middle-class morality was changing, so also was its whole outlook, and it is a delicate question which should be regarded as cause, and which effect. Whereas in the eighteenth century this class had been struggling to establish its importance, by the time of Victoria's accession it had 'arrived'. It had become much less interested in

[18] The delicate fainting Victorian lady has become a stereotype. But to Lucy Aikin, writing in 1842, it was "forty or fifty years ago" that women had "pale faces, weak nerves, much affectation, a delicate helplessness, and miserable health". But now they have "well developed figures, blooming cheeks, active habits, firm nerves, natural and easy manners, a scorn of affectation and vigorous constitutions". (*Memoirs*, p. 435.)

acquiring modes of behaviour from the upper class, and had begun to establish its own.[19] To close the door to late-arrivals had become more urgent than to make further progress. We can see this clearly enough in the etiquette books. At the turn of the century, these are concerned with teaching the newly rich the usages of aristocratic society: how to manage the table silver, and so on. As time passes, a more definitely middle-class code emerges. Thus it becomes rude to speak French or even to discuss any learned topic, because some of those present may not understand what is being said.[20]

At first it becomes increasingly important to demonstrate one's wealth and standing. Food must be left on the plate, for to eat it all would suggest that one was hungry. One writer refers to the "sneers, nods and derision of the company, when a young lady so far forgot herself as to speak of the flavour of a pineapple, saying she had never before tasted one", and also observes: "It is ungenteel to stare at an opera or ballet as if you had never seen it before," and recommends, "Do not notice a friend in a shabby suit."[21]

But the chief object of these books is to prevent any crossing of class barriers. Thus *Hints on Etiquette* (1834) rules, "Never introduce people to one another without a previous understanding that it will be agreeable to both," and advises that one should always send letters of introduction in advance as this "will prevent your exposure to any slight coldness".[22] Moreover, the reader is told, "Do not strain after great people. Leave it to noblemen to speak to you first," while a special section of Advice to Tradespeople urges them to keep their place, explaining that "Society is divided into various orders, each class having its own views, its peculiar education, habits and tastes; so that the conversation of the one would probably be most uninteresting to the other."[23]

---

[19] Thus, in 1834, *Hints on Etiquette* urges "Do not practise the *filthy* custom of gargling your mouth at table" (i.e. with finger-bowl water) (p. 17). Simond recorded this as an upper-class custom in 1811. (*Journal of a Tour*, p. 47).

[20] This emerges in *The Hermit in London*, v. 3.

[21] *Book of Gentility*, pp. 24–5, 26.

[22] Op cit., pp. 10–11, 7.

[23] ib., p. 25.

Special difficulties arise if a man marries out of his class. "He may be obliged to admit to his table those whom a year ago he would have grudged sitting room in his hall. Strange outré-like apparitions with sandy hair and moleskin smallclothes, call him 'brother' and 'cousin', and plague his existence with petitions for employment; and he almost dreads to take up a newspaper or police report lest he should stumble upon some tidings not of the most flattering nature, connected with his new kith and kin."[24]

Trusler, who also rules that one should not accost superiors, praises a man raised to the baronetcy who asked his old friends to dinner and told them frankly that he should not, in his new station, be able to see them any more.[25] The etiquette of calling is also well designed to prevent attempts to rise in social status.

It is obvious that such rules are designed to maintain a stratified, hierarchical society of authoritarian rather than of democratic type. Pueckler-Muskau was struck by this. "The spirit of *caste*, which . . . descends through all stages of society in greater or less force, has received here a power, consistency and full development wholly un-exampled in any other country. The having visited on an intimate footing in a lower class is sufficient to secure you an extremely cold reception in the next step of the ladder. . . . Every class in society as well as every field in England is separated from each other by a hedge of thorns. Each has its own manners and turns of expression—its cant language as it is called; and above all a supreme and absolute contempt for all below it . . ." And he justly adds, "A society so constituted must necessarily become eminently provincial."[26]

This arrangement had God's sanction. As the vicar of St. Swithin's observed, "It clearly manifests Divine Wisdom in the economy of Providence, that civil society should be composed of subordinate as well as superior classes."

This structure was erected some time after the beginning of the century. Knight, contrasting the 1850s with his youth half a century before, wrote, "The distinction between the trading and the pro-

[24] *How to Woo; How to Win*, p. 20.
[25] Trusler, *System of Etiquette*, pp. 21–3.
[26] *Tour*, iv, 374.

fessional classes was not so nicely preserved as it is now. Respectability was the quality more aimed at by the attorney and doctor than what we call gentility; and respectability did not mean the pretension of keeping a gig and footman—display to the world and meanness for the household."[27]

Early in the century the upper class was still erecting defences against the penetration from below. In a satirical novel of 1811, an old baronet says that he has just "turned off his butcher because he found that he kept his tilbury and mistress" and issues a serious warning to his house-keeper when he finds that her daughter is "learning French, music, dancing and fancy work".[28] The upper class also began to interlard their conversation with French phrases—a trick which was soon copied, for we find it being parodied as a device of the *arriviste* in the 1860s.[29] They also adopted vogue-words and affected accents, or lisps. A satirical novel of 1819 gives the following examples: "My pay (i.e. pa) is sorry he's engeeged, or he would have weeted upon her leedy-ship." "On Tooseday the Dook will be there in his noo carriage." "He'd theen the Printh in the Park, and kithed his hand to a Pruthian printhess, a very thweet woman." Fun is poked at such odd ex-pressions as "to make my adieus" and the ridiculous affectation of pronouncing Guards as if it were spelled Gardes.[30]

We can doubtless see social defences at work in the observation cited by Besant, "Familiarity is the greatest vice of Society. When an acquaintance says 'My dear fellow' cut him immediately."[31] The 'cut', of course, is a social defence pure and simple.[32]

By the middle of the nineteenth century, however, no such defences are necessary. This is very clearly shown in the novels of Emily Eden. In the *Semi-Attached Couple* (written in 1830) the upper class live in a well-preserved remoteness; in the *Semi-Detached House* (1860) they are

[27] Knight, *Passages of a Working Life*, i, 48.

[28] *Hermit in London*, iii, 35.

[29] Of course, many eighteenth-century aristocrats spoke French: but the vogue for mixing the two languages seems to belong to the nineteenth century.

[30] *Hermit in London*, iii, 265 ff.

[31] Besant, *50 Years Ago*, p. 124.

[32] That it had become an established social weapon by 1800 is shown by a satirical poem, *The Cutter*.

shown living in the same building as their bourgeois neighbours, and it is stressed that, because these neighbours make no attempt to presume on the situation, they treat them with friendly familiarity.[33] At the same time, a foreign *arriviste* who seeks to enter upper-class society is shown in unfavourable contrast with this bourgeois family which "knows its station".

While the upper class was still in the stage of erecting defences, the middle class was still feeling the need to demonstrate its importance. In a satire of 1810, we see Mrs. M'Tavish, an uncouth visitor from the Highlands, assuming, as she walks in Kensington Gardens, "an air of dignity which soon *let people know who she was*".[34] The italics are the author's, so no doubt the phrase had recently become popular, and the intention is to satirise behaviour which was already seen as provincial. The lavish meals, the tilbury, and other signs of ostentation evidently had the same function of letting people know "who one was".

The word 'vulgar' in its modern connotation entered the language about this time. Formerly it had meant merely popular or general, without a specific implication of lack of social know-how, as in the phrase "vulgar curiosity". But now it came to mean everything that the middle class was not. Thus was born the dictum, "Nothing is in its own nature so vulgar as vice."[35] In this phrase morals are made a pendant of manners, instead of (as is more normal) the reverse.

Perhaps the most revealing sign of the change which was taking place in the middle-class outlook was the new emphasis on domestic comfort. The idea that the bourgeois class lives in comfort is now so well understood that one readily assumes that this was always the case. During the eighteenth century, however, the trading class was emphatically frugal, and expenditure on anything which was not absolutely necessary was condemned on religious as well as on economic grounds, as I shall show in more detail later. This remained true as late as the 1830s, for d'Hausset particularly notes that "though

[33] However, as early as 1832 the Duke of Devonshire had told Collier, "You are much more worth waiting upon than I am . . . and more fit to be a Duke than I am" (*Old Man's Diary*, i, 36).

[34] *London, or a Month at Steven's*, p. 51.

[35] Utter and Needham, *Pamela's Daughters*, p. 46.

there is great neatness and cleanness, there is nothing that justifies the idea of general comfort" in the average English house.[36] The development of the heavily-upholstered mid-Victorian interior, crammed with unneeded bric-à-brac, signals a fundamental psychological change in the personalities of those concerned.

I explored the question of precisely when the trading middle class succeeded in imposing its morality on the majority of the upper class in some detail just because the answer seemed so contrary to the widespread impression that the Regency was a period of peculiar immorality; and for the same reason I have reproduced the evidence on the timing of the reversal of trend comparatively fully here. The basic explanation of the discrepancy lies in the facts that vice receives more publicity than virtue, and that the Court occupies a position of peculiar prominence. In point of fact, it is at least equally striking that the Prince Regent had to look for companions in debauchery among such fly-by-night characters as Col. George Hanger. The fact that he was surrounded by enthusiastic diarists also helped to propagate the impression of debauchery.

Nevertheless, I could not escape the impression that much of the sexual freedom of the Regency was in fact more desperate, more debauched, than anything which had preceded it. This led to the thought that in a period of repression only those who are particularly strongly in reaction from conventionality will be able to break free of the pressures to conformity. It therefore seemed to me a reasonable hypothesis that the stricter the Puritanical become, the more debauched the libertines will become. Society will thus be split into two sections, ever more sharply sundered. But one of these groups will be increasing in size, while the other will be vanishing away. This seemed to me consistent with the evidence. Early in the eighteenth century freedom of manners had been rather widespread, but not very extreme. By the time of George IV it had become extreme, but confined to a handful of people. By 1840 there was only one example of debauchery on the grand scale left, in the person of Lord Hertford: but what an example! Here the best course is probably to quote Greville without

36 D'Hausset, *Gt. Brit. in* 1933, i, 102.

comment: "There has been, as far as I know, no example of un-disguised debauchery exhibited to the world like that of Lord Hertford, and his age and infirmities rendered it at once the more remarkable and the more shocking. Between sixty and seventy years old, broken with various infirmities, and almost unintelligible from a paralysis of the tongue, he has been in the habit of travelling about with a company of prostitutes who formed his principal society, and by whom he was surrounded up to the moment of his death, generally picking them up from the dregs of that class, and changing them according to his fancy and caprice. Here he was to be seen driving about the town, and lifted by two footmen from his carriage into the brothel, and he never seems to have thought it necessary to throw the slightest veil over the habits he pursued."[37] Among his mistresses had been Lady Strachan, Harriette Wilson, Anne Sissons, Mme. Visconti, Henrietta d'Ambre and Angelique Borel.

The popular notion of the immorality of the Regency is derived in part from Byron and Shelley (though, as I hope to show, they were psychologically quite different from the libertines). But they were regarded with horror by the middle, and even the upper, class. Thus Knight records that in his youth (he was born in 1791) "Wordsworth had not entered the popular mind . . . Southey was voted dangerous . . . Shelley was feared and neglected".[38] Byron had not then arisen; but we can perceive what the upper classes thought of him from Lady Jersey's observation that when he left the room, the ladies drew aside their skirts, lest they be polluted by the floor he had walked on.[39]

The reputation of the Regency thus derives from a small section of society; how limited in extent this area of licence was is indicated by the enormous output of satirical and moralising works pillorying it.

Massey's judgment, that 1770 represents the nadir of immorality, is thus not so much wrong as meaningless, since morality and im-morality must be judged by extent as well as depth. If we leave the lower classes, about which we know so little, out of the calculation, then we may say that immorality was greatest in extent in the early

[37] Greville, *Diary*, i, 105–6.
[38] *Passages*.
[39] Lamington, *Days of the Dandies*, p. 49.

part of the eighteenth century; but if we wish to measure it by its depth, then the early nineteenth century was much worse than 1770. If we take the lower classes into consideration, the middle of the nineteenth century was worst of all: but this is an aspect of the subject with which I wish to deal in the next chapter. A further point of considerable sociological interest which seemed to me to emerge from this material was that the widely-held view that each class imitates the one above it, and hence that social habits drift down through the hierarchy, seems to be false, or at least a serious over-simplification. In the period we have been studying, the middle class sought at first to imitate upper-class manners; but before long it abandoned this, except perhaps in a few exceptional instances, and began to develop its own *mores*. More than this, the upper class began increasingly to imitate and accept middle-class standards and patterns of behaviour. Quite the most striking instance of this is the Court. As has often been pointed out, under William and Victoria the Court became completely bourgeois. And since we have already seen that society adopted bourgeois morals before William, let alone Victoria, came to the throne, it must follow that, if any imitation was occurring, the Court was copying the middle class, and not the reverse. (As a matter of fact, as was pointed out in the previous chapter, the young Victoria came under middle-class criticism for her excessive gaiety.)

At the same time, as we shall see in the next chapter, the lower classes were, at this period, very definitely refusing to imitate the successful tradesmen immediately above them; they were influenced much more by intellectuals from, roughly, the professional classes.[40]

All these considerations confirmed my basic assumption that it was in the eighteenth-century middle, or trading, class that I should have to look for the sources of nineteenth-century morality.

The questions which now arose were, first, what exactly was the moral scheme which the eighteenth-century reformers advocated; and secondly, what made members of the upper and lower classes psychologically ready to accept such teaching?

---

[40] We see this in the popularity of free-thinking tracts like Paine's *Rights of Man*, and novel industrial proposals like Owen's.

But before pursuing the long trails which lead to the answers to these questions, it is desirable, first of all, to consider the question, how far did such teaching really work? How far was the moral revolution really effective?

CHAPTER 5

THE HOLLOW VICTORY

SERJEANT BELLASIS records how a friend set out in quest of a church service in Reading in 1844 "but in this town of 20,000 inhabitants there was no service to be found save in the Catholic chapel".[1] Facts like these indicate that it was not without grounds that the *Christian Visitors' Handbook*, in 1851, asked for the foundation of an English mission to go through the country "to point out the mass of heathenism which so fearfully and extensively prevails in our midst".[2]

Puritan and Evangelical ideals certainly did not appreciably influence the agricultural population, except perhaps near the big cities. Lytton, no moralist, spoke in 1833 of the "shameless abandonment of the female peasantry".[3] The 'Letters on Rural Districts' in the *Morning Chronicle* reveal a startling picture of free-and-easy sexual morality. Thus one clergyman told an investigator that "he never recollected an instance of his having married a woman who was not either pregnant at the time of her marriage, or had had one or more children before her marriage". The rector of a parish in East Anglia said, "The immorality of the young women is literally horrible, and I regret to say it is on the increase in a most extraordinary degree."[4]

What these strictures apparently refer to, however, is not so much a wanton defiance of moral law as the existence of a completely different

[1] Bellasis, *Memorials*, p. 34 n.

[2] Op. cit., p. 46, "In 1714 there were daily prayers in forty-nine churches in London and Westminster, not counting St. Paul's, Westminster Abbey and the three Inns of Court. Today [i.e. 1846] there are only sixteen." (See Bp. of London's *Charge*, p. 184.) *Travels in Town* (1839) estimates that one in six of London's population attend church.

[3] Bulwer, *England and the Eng.*, p. 370. He also mentions the existence of extensive abortion (p. 204).

[4] Cited Kay, *Social Condition*, i, 529–39.

morality, probably derived from earlier conceptions of trial-marriage.[5] The clergy all stress that no guilt was felt. "There appears," one clergyman said, "to be among the lower orders a perfect deadness of all moral feeling on this subject."[6]

An investigator spoke to the wife of a respectable labourer, in the Norwich district, about it; she had seven children, one of whom was then confined with an illegitimate child. She excused her daughter's conduct saying, "What was the poor girl to do? The chaps say they won't marry 'em first, and then the girls give way. I did the same myself with my husband."[7] Mr. Brigstock, the magistrate of Blaeupant, stated that although intercourse between the sexes was very general before marriage, misconduct after marriage was rare.

In the country districts of Wales, and no doubt elsewhere, the ancient custom of bundling persisted, though it is alleged that it was not simply a system of courting but involved actual fornication. "The system of bundling, or at any rate something analogous to it, prevails extensively, the unmarried men servants on the farms range over the country at night; and it is a known and tolerated practice that they are admitted by the women servants at the houses to which they come.[8] I heard the most revolting anecdotes of the gross and almost bestial indelicacy with which sexual intercourse takes place on these occasions."[9]

It would seem that sexual licence at the great annual festivals—long traditional in agricultural areas—also persisted into the nineteenth

[5] Gaskell, *Manufacturing Population*, p. 20, stresses this difference from urban immorality, since there was a tacit understanding that marriage would follow. Bastardy was rare. In the report made by Mr. Lingen on Carmarthen, Glamorgan and Pembroke, a Mr. Trevor observed, "Fornication was not regarded as a vice, scarcely as a frailty, by the common people of Wales. It is considered as a matter of course, as the regular conventional process towards marriage. It is avowed, defended and laughed at without scruple or shame or concealment by both sexes alike."

[6] Kay, *Social Condition*, p. 529.

[7] ib., p. 529.

[8] ib., p. 542.

[9] ib., p. 542. Another witness said, "The farmers connive at young people meeting in their houses after the family has retired to rest." And when clergymen besought the farmers to dismiss maids who behaved thus, they replied that they would soon be without maids at all if they did so.

century, to judge from a *Times* leader of 1858, which complains of the "traditional licence" of Whitsun and Martinmas, and urges that female servants be compelled to return from the festivities before dark, and that employers should refuse to engage those guilty of "unchaste behaviour".

Matters were no different in Scotland apparently. Dr. J. M. Strachan of Stirlingshire, for instance, said that nine out of ten women had had children by the bridegroom on marriage or were pregnant. This, he believed, was the average state among the working classes all over Scotland.

For a view in depth, we can turn to the diary of the Rev. Mr. Skinner, who found his parish at Camerton, near Bath, an extremely discouraging responsibility in the 1820s. In 1823 he records how he persuades one Jacob Balne to marry the woman he has been living with for so long, and at once goes on, "heard this evening some sad accounts of the Somer family, and intend speaking to the Overseer respecting them. The mother presented the Parish with four illegitimate children, and two elder daughters have each had one, and the third is in a fair way to increase the number, and yet we are now maintaining the whole family at the Poor House, when the husband of the woman, Somer, is living with another person at Timsbury, to whom report says he has been married."[10]

At this stage he is still fresh enough to hope that something may be done about such things, but by 1830 he has become resigned, and merely records acidly, "I had to marry a couple at half past eight; the bride was as round as a barrel, and according to custom, I suppose there will be a christening in the course of the honeymoon."[11] The frequency of such events is also indicated by an entry of 1831, "There was a wedding this morning after the Camerton mode, I find, as the woman has already produced.[12]

Mrs. Trew, the schoolmistress, complains to him of the conduct of the schoolchildren; several of those who have left have become prostitutes. Miss Perfett, who keeps the school for young children,

[10] Skinner, *Journal*, p. 50.
[11] ib., p. 248.
[12] ib., pp. 248, 270.

runs off after a man who keeps a disorderly house in Bath, and when her father thrashes her for it, says that if he does so again, she will "go to Bath and get her living there as the others do, upon the town".[13]

The diary also records much petty theft, dishonesty over receipts and the like: even the church is broken into in order to steal the funeral hangings.

Perhaps middle-class notions of morality were influencing the country districts by 1865, however, when we find a Mr. Percival writing to *The Times* after a tour of Westmorland and Cumberland, to complain that "chastity is of little concern" and that one in nine of the children are illegitimate. *The Times* in a leader thought this figure a "delusive minimum" and declared that statistics showed irrefutably that the country was no better than the towns.[14]

If the country people were still largely unaffected by the middle-class morality, so also was the working population of the towns. The works of Mayhew alone would demonstrate this point, but additional objective evidence may also be offered. Not only had the country people taken their permissive outlook with them to the towns, but the Industrial Revolution had given their employers almost unlimited powers of exploitation of female employees, while greatly weakening their possibility of resisting. Thus Gaskell speaks of "the almost entire extinction of sexual decency, which is one of the darkest stains upon the character of the manufacturing population" and traces it to the industrial revolution. The master cotton spinners and weavers took full advantage of the "facilities for lascivious indulgence afforded them by the number of females brought under their immediate control". "Victim after victim was successively taken from the mill . . . an improper intimacy was esteemed creditable rather than otherwise. . . . Houses were established in some localities by parties of young men purposely for the prosecution of their illicit pleasures, and to

[13] ib., pp. 261, 134–5.
[14] Following this letter, the Evangelical Union called a meeting to discuss the matter, and a prize was awarded for an essay on 'The Excessive Immorality of the Two Counties'. The fact that Westmorland and Cumberland seem to have been regarded as abnormally immoral seems to imply that less remote districts were now coming under the influence of stricter notions.

which their victims repaired—nothing loth it is true—to share the disgraceful orgies of their paramours; and in which scenes were enacted that even put to the blush the lascivious Saturnalia of the Romans, the rites of the Pagoda girls of India, and the Harem life of the most voluptuous Ottoman."[15]

The younger relatives of the employers and master-spinners, coming into the mills, were "thrust into a very hotbed of lust . . . the organised system of immorality which was pursued by these younger men and boys was extremely fatal to the best interests of the community. . . . Chastity became a laughing-stock and a by-word". In 1828 Francis Place told D'Eichthal, the Saint-Simonian, that when a friend of his visited a Lancashire mill, the owner had bid him take his choice among the mill girls.[16] Halévy says the streets of mill towns presented a particularly disgusting spectacle, as it was quite common for the mill girls, with their husbands' connivance, to eke out their scant wages by prostitution.[17] The point was reached at which illegitimacy was rationed. "In Manchester . . . an almost promiscuous intercourse prevails in the great mass of the people; insomuch that the magistrates attempt to check the increase of bastard children by inflicting stripes and imprisonment on the women who bear above a certain number."[18]

Conditions were particularly bad in the mining districts, where the miners lived a life quite cut off from the local community. The management of the mine left the payment of the women and children to the miners themselves, "together with full liberty to use them at pleasure for the gratification of their bestial and filthy desires."[19] Ayton records, in his *Voyage Round Britain* (1815), "These gloomy and loathsome caverns [i.e. the mines], are made the scenes of the most bestial debauchery. If a man and woman meet in them and are excited by passion at the moment, they indulge in it."[20]

[15] Gaskell, *The Manufacturing Population.*
[16] 'Condition de la Classe Ouvrière en Angleterre'. In *Revue Historique*, LXXIV, 1902.
[17] Halévy, *Eng. in 1815*, p. 280.
[18] Barber, *Tour throughout S. Wales*, p. 140 *n.*
[19] Halévy, *Eng. in 1815*, pp. 262–3.
[20] Ayton, op. cit., ii, 156, 159.

Chadwick's sanitary reports and Lord Ashley's speeches describe the chaotic conditions ruling even in non-industrial parts of London. "In Mint Street alone there are nineteen lodging houses. The majority of these latter are awful sinks of iniquity, and are used as houses of accommodation. In some of them, both sexes sleep together indiscriminately, and such acts are practised and witnessed that married persons who are in other respects awfully depraved, have been so shocked as to be compelled to get up in the night and leave the house."

Nor was it only in London that such conditions existed. Even in a small country centre not much affected by industrialisation, such as Bath, the City Mission discovered an almost incredible degree of social disorganisation. Thus the report for 1837 speaks of "the overwhelming mass of ignorance, indifference, immorality, irreligion and openly avowed infidelity, which has accumulated around us" and adds, "these are matters of too great notoriety to admit of question." A typical report by one of their agents, upon three streets which he had just visited, reads, "I am of the opinion that all the inhabitants are living in gross sin, and more than half of them upon sin! In many of these places numbers are living in adultery and not ashamed to admit it: prostitution stalks unblushingly abroad in open day," and goes on, "I met with abusive language and cursing from many of the inhabitants."[21] Another typical entry runs, "In the front room, met with two young persons who are living in a state of fornication; they can't read; have not a copy of the Scriptures. Back ditto—in this room, a mother and daughter living in adultery. Front attic, two aged people living in sin. Back ditto, two young people living in a state of fornication."

We can guess that many of these couples were maintaining common-law marriages, and were in no way promiscuous: the facilities and the money for church marriages were simply beyond them.

In these slums of Bath religion was equally neglected. One agent reports, "Visited 109 families, consisting of 436 persons. I conversed with 215 adults, and found that, if their own statements were true, only 20 attended any place of worship: of 118 children I saw, only 17 attended any school, either on the Lord's Day or at any other time." Some of those questioned did not know who Christ was. One woman

[21] *Annual Report*, Bath City Mission, 1838.

had indeed never heard of Him, did not know how He died, and when told that He was the Son of God, replied, "Then God has got a Son, how wonderful!"[22] An eighty-year-old woman, asked what she thought of the future life, replied, "I think it cannot be worse than this, let it be as bad as it may."[23] Many of these, questioned about religion, said that they had actively rejected it, and argued with the agent on rationalist grounds: one was an Owenite. Other agents had similar experiences.

In short the morality for which the early nineteenth century is known was clearly a middle- and not a lower-class phenomenon. But it is also necessary to consider how far, even within the middle class, the moral standards of the Puritans were genuinely accepted. How far was the morality of this period a sham?

In considering this question, the most obvious point at which to start is the subject of prostitution. The extent of prostitution in London in the first half of the nineteenth century greatly exceeded that of the eighteenth century or of to-day, after allowance has been made for changes in the size of the population.

Reformers of the period, acutely aware of the presence of prostitution, give figures which are wildly exaggerated, such as 80,000 or 90,000 prostitutes in London alone.[24] However, we have a number of comparatively accurate counts, which tally well enough with one another and suggest a figure rising to a peak of 9,000 odd in the 1840s, and then declining again.[25] The presence of this peak is interesting, since I have already argued that the 1840s was the period when Puritan feeling was at its height.

These figures are sufficiently remarkable when it is remembered that

[22] Broadsheet attached to *Reports* of Bath City Mission.

[23] First *Annual Report*, p. 18.

[24] Ryan (*Prostitution in London*, p. 59) guesses 100,000. See also Acton, *Prostitution considered*, Chapter 3, for other estimates. Von Raumer shrewdly said in 1835, "When I hear it asserted that there are 50,000 prostitutes . . . I ask myself who has counted them? And who knows whether an o ought not safely to be struck off?" *Eng. in 1835*, ii, 24–5.

[25] The Constabulary returns for 1837 gave 6,371. The Chief Commissioner of the Metropolitan Police gave 9,409 in 1841 and 8,600 in 1857, including 'kept women'. Acton, op. cit., Chapter 3.

the entire male adult population of London in 1851 was well under a million. There was thus approximately one prostitute for every hundred males. (Tait calculated one for eighty-one, and found the proportion in Edinburgh to be similar.)

It appears to be a reasonable assumption that a prostitute may have entertained thirty-five men a week.[26] A simple calculation then suggests that in London some quarter of a million were resorting to prostitutes weekly, out of a total male adult population of 800,000. When we subtract from the figure of 800,000 all those who were maimed, senile, very poor, or on a bed of sickness, it becomes clear that the entire able-bodied population must have been making use of prostitutes at least once every three weeks. Ryan asserts that not one man in a hundred has not had a lewd woman—though no doubt this is an exaggeration.

Whether or not these calculations are thought suggestive, the bare figures show that nineteenth-century prostitution was on an incomparably greater scale than anything known in the eighteenth century.[27] From Misson's account at the beginning of the century we gather that prostitution was confined to one or, at most, two streets.[28] In

[26] Modern inquiries show that London prostitutes receive approximately twenty-five customers a week; and at the low rates of remuneration ruling in the nineteenth century a prostitute would probably have attempted a higher turnover than this whenever possible. Ryan asserts that many girls had six or seven men in a few hours, and mentions one who had twelve men a night at £1 a time. Treating the latter figure as exceptional, and the former as slightly exaggerated, we arrive at a figure perhaps nearer thirty-five than twenty-five. The figures of weekly earnings which Ryan gives, if read in conjunction with the scale of charges, also support a figure in this region (Ryan, op. cit.). Cf. also *London and all its Dangers*, which asserts that "a pretty Cyprian can make £20 to £30 a week regularly" and twice this if really skilled (pp. 33–4).

[27] Police figures put the number of prostitutes operating in C Division territory, including those moving in from other areas for the evening, as 668 in 1838. (C Division covers the Haymarket and West End.) Contemporary accounts indicate that patrons in this area were predominantly members of the upper classes. If a corresponding calculation is made on the basis of these figures, it would seem that a sizeable proportion of the upper-middle-class group were making regular use of prostitutes (Acton, op. cit., Chapter 3).

[28] Quoting Moncony's visit some thirty years previously, *Memoirs*, p. 60.

the mid-eighteenth century the favoured area was round Covent Garden. A moralist complains in 1750 that a search for prostitutes, reported in the *Public Advertiser*, was limited to Drury Lane, Hedge Lane and St. Giles. Why, he asks, did the police not look into the Turk's Head or almost any other house in Bow Street? As this trifling extension of the area is all he can suggest, it seems clear that the 'red light' district was still extremely restricted.[29] While many taverns kept rooms upstairs to which customers could retire with girls if desired, brothels in the strict sense were few. Soon after 1760, however, the trade became organised, and persons with considerable financial resources began to set up houses, furnished in excellent taste, where good food and wine could be obtained, and equipped with selected girls who had been given some training and had been fitted out with good clothes.[30]

Grosley comments on their introduction, "Besides the women of the town, who ply on the streets, London has many wholesale dealers, who keep warehouses, in which are to be found compleat parcels. A warehouse for commodities of this sort goes by the name of a Bagnio: the prices are there fixed, and all passes with as much order and decency as can be expected in a commerce of this nature."[31] But it is clear from Hickey's memoirs that the number was still so small that a man could know every one of the available girls.

By the first years of the nineteenth century, brothels of this character had become numerous, and were patronised even by royalty.[32]

Prostitution grew not only in scale but in complexity, and its rising importance is betrayed by the increasingly elaborate vocabulary which was developed to describe it.

A mid-eighteenth century moralist, attempting to make things look

[29] *Congratulatory Epistle*, p. 13.
[30] *Les Serails de Londres*, Ch. 2.
[31] *Tour to London*, i, 55–56.
[32] By 1841 the police were able to count 933 brothels and 848 houses of resort in London. And by 1857 the number had risen to 2,825. In C Division alone there were fourteen brothels and forty-six places of resort. In short the rate of growth both of brothels and of independent prostitutes was much higher than the rate of growth of the population.

as alarming as possible, distinguished the following 'Gradations of Whores':

> Women of Fashion, who intrigue
> Demi-reps
> Good-natured Girls
> Kept Mistresses
> Ladies of Pleasure
> Whores
> Park Walkers
> Street Walkers
> Bunters
> Bulk-mongers.

The first four groups are, he admits, in a different category, so that there are only six grades of prostitutes properly so called. Ladies of Pleasure are defined as "those in continual waiting (in the House or at the Door) of Genteel Brothels; the others comprise the furniture of (what you call) low infamous Bawdy Houses".[33]

But by the accession of Victoria, the vocabulary is much more elaborate. There are countless synonyms for prostitute, such as Cyprian, Paphian, trooper, academician and horse-breaker. There are specialised terms, such as trulls, who are the followers of soldiers; figurantes, who are those who make a minor role in the theatre the basis of their activities; and stargazers, who frequent hedgerows. There are brilliant metaphors, such as cockchafer, ladybird and bobtail. And there is a whole range of ancillary activities: jockgaggers, who are men who prostitute their own wives; bully rocks, whose job is to keep order in houses of ill fame; crimps, who decoy girls into prostitution; and tallymen, who let out clothes to saloon Cyprians. The cant dictionaries furnish many further terms, such as blowens, mots, and chicksters, for prostitutes, flashmen for their bullies, and covess of a ken for a female brother keeper.[34].

As the Puritan pressures increased, however, a certain change came over the technique of prostitution. Police action against brothels

[33] *A Congratulatory Epistle*, p. 10.
[34] See the Flash Dictionary in *Sinks of London*.

90

increased. The figures show a decline in the number of brothels from 933 to 410 over the years 1841 to 1857, while the number of prostitutes on the street, and the number of places where prostitutes were known to lodge, rose during the period, though not proportionately. To meet this development, two new institutions were elaborated: the introducing-house and the dress-house. The introducing-house, as the name implies, served to bring men together with prostitutes who then took them to their own room, or to a house of accommodation, paying a rake-off to the introducing-house. The dress-house specialised in equipping girls who could not afford good clothes with a suitable rig-out. Such girls ('dress-girls' or 'dress-ladies') were attended on the street by an old woman, to see that they did not run off with the clothes, and to make sure that they brought back the proceeds of business; and if a man picked the girl up and got into a cab with her the watcher got in too. Thus both these institutions served simply to decentralise that part of the process of organised prostitution concerned with the sexual act, in order to avoid the danger of a charge of brothel-keeping. For regular clients, the introducing-house would even send a note of new talent to the customer's club or private address.[35]

An increasingly common practice was for prostitutes to sit at windows, often in a state of extreme déshabillé, or even half naked.[36] For this reason, it became taboo for a respectable woman to sit at her window, or even to look out of it, as an American noted when visiting England in 1835.[37]

Prostitutes continued to go aboard H.M. ships when in port, according to Ryan, often in large numbers.[38]

All witnesses agree that there was a sharp decline in the standard of manners of prostitutes. In the eighteenth century Archenholtz had

[35] From about 1800 until the opening of the Cremorne, the bars of theatres were common meeting grounds, as were the flash houses and dancing rooms. In the nineteenth century the boxes at Covent Garden were provided with retiring rooms to which girls could be taken, and at Drury Lane the doors of the boxes could be locked (*Swell's Night Guide*).

[36] Reported as common in 1807 by Malcolm, *Anecdotes*, p. 183.

[37] *An American in England*, p. 22.

[38] Ryan, *Prostitution in London*, p. 190. Cf. *Statement Respecting . . . Immoral Practices in H.M. Navy*.

been most struck by the good manners and honesty of the better class of prostitute. "Among those of the highest class, a person is secure of not being robbed; he may even give them his purse to keep. They think it dishonest likewise to grant favours to the lovers of their friends." When a friend of Archenholtz's solicits a girl Archenholtz has used, she replies, "Sir, I am a poor girl and forced to live by this trade, and Heaven knows how much need I have of money: but it would be dishonest to consent to this gentleman's proposal!" "At elections for members of Parliament" (Archenholtz continues), "these girls have been known to refuse large sums, and to reserve their favours to those who could procure votes to the patriots whom they esteemed. Such virtues take off from the stigma attached to their professions . . . I have seen well-known persons give them their arm on a public walk. I have even seen more than one Minister plenipotentiary conversing publicly in Vauxhall Gardens with celebrated courtesans.

"It will not be therefore surprising that there should be so many women of the town in London who possess those virtues we admire in the sex, youth, beauty, the graces, gentleness, education, principles, and even that delightful modesty which is the most powerful attraction to pleasure. They give us an idea of those celebrated Greek courtesans, who charmed the Athenian heroes, and who Socrates himself honoured with his visits."[39] Meister confirms this, "And, what is no less remarkable, the priestesses of Venus here have more reserve and timidity, with a degree of decorum and even prudery, beyond anything to be found among bacchants of our country" (1791).[40]

In the first half of the nineteenth century the picture is very different. The American visitor in 1835 records that "the streets swarmed with women, filthy in their dress, openly brutal, and indecent in their advances".[41] Not satisfied with words, they assailed those who passed

[39] Archenholtz, *Picture of England*, pp. 302-9.

[40] Meister, *Letters*, p. 287. Coyer, writing in 1777, had made a similar comment. "In the Bagnios, in most of the Taverns, it is said that one rings for them as one rings for a cup of tea; one thing which is not general, is that whether there or at their own abode, one can complain neither of the slightest injury nor the smallest scandal, thanks to English phlegm and to the Law." *Nouvelles Obs.*, pp. 275-6 (my translation).

[41] *An American in England*, p. 136.

"with gallantries of a more practical kind". He recalls the remark of a Frenchman that there were enjoyments which could be procured in Paris if you desired them; but that in London you must submit to them whether you would or not.[42] *Doings in London* (1840) describes the frequent robbing of customers by prostitutes, either by the crude method of running off with their clothes, or by presenting them with a bill for five guineas for accommodation, and calling in the bully to threaten force if they demur.[43]

By 1854 we read, "Females, dressed in the most costly apparel, parading the wide thoroughfare in groups of six, eight, ten and twelve —ages, various, but mostly young and beautiful—the younger parties attended by their keepers. Gentlemen . . . in numbers nearly equal."[44]

It would seem, therefore, that prostitution reached a nadir of dishonesty and degradation somewhere between 1800 and 1850, i.e. during the period when Puritanical pressures were at their peak.

A general impression of the extensive night life in London at a date only slightly later than that we are concerned with can be gained from a work like *London in the Sixties*: the writer has no hesitation in saying that Edwardian London was 'goody-goody' in comparison. The Haymarket blazed with light till daylight. There were dives where "more blasphemy and filth was to be heard for 1s. than it would appear possible". Gambling for large sums was common.[45] This picture is confirmed by earlier works, like *The Yokel's Preceptor* (c. 1850) and *London and all its Dangers* (1835). The lists of prostitutes with their addresses and peculiarities continued to be circulated covertly, certainly up to 1841.[46]

[42] ib., p. 213.
[43] Op. cit., pp. 94–5.
[44] *London by Moonlight*, 2nd series, No. 1. It is interesting, however, that Acton observed, by 1857, that the "Improved manners of the time do not permit the women to make advances", and adds that "No one will deny the improvement in manners and appearances". He notices too, at the Cremorne, where dancing is now sanctioned, it is the men who approach the girls, few of whom appear to use cosmetics (*Prostitution considered*).
[45] Op. cit., Chapter 4.
[46] Thus *The Swell's Night Guide* contains a list of seventy names—one of those named, a Miss Entwistle, boasting as a special attraction "a large air cushion sofa".

A vivid impression of London's underside is conveyed by some of the cheap novels of the period. The following conversation takes place between an aristocratic rake and his shady valet:

"There's the pic-nic with Towler's and Wilson's girls in R——d Park."

"I hate the whole lot. Sally's as fusty as an old mare, and Polly has grown as common as any Regent Street drab."

"There's the dancing at White-headed Bob's, both men and girls stripped."

"Won't do. Lost my watch and purse last time I was there."

"There's a ball at Mother Carey's, and some new pieces will be there."

"Ah, that might do——"

The valet then reminds him of "the little piece that you picked up, when you were at the Casino the other night", observing, ". . . .s 'elp my tatur, My Lord . . . she's as nice, clean-looking, fresh and virgin a bit of flesh as ever I clapped eyes upon. She's horridly handsome."[47]

From these considerations alone it is clear that, at least as far as male sexual continence was concerned, the moral pressure of the Puritans was ineffective. So far from stamping out illicit sexual relationships, it made them more numerous, and at the same time degraded them to the most sordid physical and commercial level.

The fact is, libido obeys the laws of conservation of energy. It cannot be abolished, it can only be converted into other forms.

This explains the enormous volume of pornography which was produced during the nineteenth century. In a period of censorship, of course, many works which we should to-day regard as innocent—such as texts on birth-control—are prohibited and can only be published *sub rosa*. Such works consequently appear in the bibliographies of erotic works and are technically included under the heading of pornography. But even when we leave aside all such stray entries, we are left with a phenomenal output. A rough check of Reade's *Registrum Librorum Eroticorum* suggests that almost half the entries refer to books either printed or reprinted in the nineteenth century, and if the last two

[47] *Merry Wives of London*, pp. 186 ff.

decades of the eighteenth are included, the proportion would be well over a half. Of course, the development of printing and the growth of the literate population are primary factors in this.[48]

The centre of the trade was in Holywell Street; the principal publishers, Duncombe and Dugdale, were imprisoned repeatedly, Dugdale dying in prison during his ninth term of imprisonment in 1868. While most of the material they turned out was printed as wretchedly as it was written, private subscription societies of wealthy men were formed, for whom de luxe editions were produced. The first of these, as far as I have been able to discover, was the Society of Vice, which was in existence in 1802. Some of the works published were printed in extremely small editions. Of *My Secret Life*, which describes every known perversion in the course of eleven lengthy volumes, only ten copies were printed.

As is well-known, Monckton Milnes, with the aid of Frederick Hankey, who supplied much of the material from Paris—some of it via the diplomatic bag—built up the finest collection of pornography which then existed. Edward Sellon was another who devoted his life to pornography, as did W. S. Potter, who was part-author of *The Romance of Lust*, which has been described by H. S. Ashbee, the great nineteenth-century bibliographer of pornography, as possibly the most lascivious book ever written.[49]

---

[48] What distinguishes nineteenth-century pornography is not so much its volume as its psychopathic character. Eighteenth-century works, such as *The Toast* or *The Memoirs of a Woman of Pleasure*, describe people whose passions are aroused by the sight of a person of the opposite sex, and who in due course perform the normal sexual act in a normal way. Nineteenth-century pornography is increasingly concerned with abnormal sexual acts; it takes off into a realm of fantasy in which sexual activities of a frequency, complexity and elaboration of accompaniments which could be not realised in practice are described. And about these descriptions there is an air of sniggering indecency totally different from the frank bawdiness which characterised most eighteenth-century writing on the topic.

It is evident that these descriptions are not intended as a sauce for actual sexual interests, but as an exclusive substitute. At the same time, while the sexual details are tediously elaborated, all attempt at drawing character or developing plot vanishes. So desperate is the demand for sexual titillation, that the buying public would tolerate the most pitiful literary level of accomplishment.

[49] Fraxi (i.e. Ashbee), *Catena*, pp. 183–9; *Index*, p. 188.

In addition to books, there was a steady output of erotic prints and, later, photographs. When the stereoscope was invented, it was immediately applied to erotic purposes, as the *Saturday Review* notes in 1858, and Victorian clubmen were able to gaze upon scenes of vice in three-dimensional form.[50]

The most striking impression left by an examination of a selection of the material is the prevalence of perversion and particularly flagellation. The output of flagellatory material in the eighteenth century is small up to 1785, but in that year alone three works on the topic appeared, and after that the stream is unceasing. The classics of the subject, such as *The Birchen Bouquet* and *The Rodiad*, were reprinted again and again; classic works, such as those of Meibomius, were translated into English, and new contributions added: even successful journalists like George Augustus Sala were not above trying their hand.

It is not difficult to understand that people who were deeply frustrated, who harboured fierce resentments against frustrating parents, might indulge in fantasies of cruel treatment; and that if in their own experience being flogged was the most painful event known to them, their fantasies would follow a corresponding course. We should also expect that many of them would indulge in actual flagellation, and such is the case. Mrs. Collet's flagellatory brothel at Tavistock Court seems to have been the first house specialising in such matters. It was founded towards the close of the eighteenth century, and such was its fame that it was visited by George IV. Mrs. Collet set up her niece Mrs. Mitchell in the same line at 22, Waterloo Road; Mrs. James in Carlisle Street and Emma Lee in Margaret Street followed suit, as did several others. Theresa Berkley's establishment at 28, Charlotte Place carried the practice to new levels of refinement

[50] A distinct section of this field is constituted by the bawdy song books. These began to appear quite early in the eighteenth century (e.g. *The Frisky Muse*, 1749). No doubt men who were normally careful to conform to public standards would be ready to relax their behaviour after a certain amount of drink and when with trusted companions. Thus there would be a demand for a form of sexual titillation which could be indulged in such circumstances: the bawdy story was no doubt one, but the bawdy song was probably more satisfactory. The output of such books continued steadily during the period. Books of bawdy jokes were also popular (e.g. *The Bagnio Miscellany*, 1792, and numerous reprints).

during the 'twenties, and she funded £10,000 in eight years.[51] Equally significant is the growth of interest in other perversions.

While in my reading of eighteenth-century material the only perverted writing I have actually encountered has been that of Beverland—and that had to be published abroad—by the nineteenth century it becomes much more noticeable. Thus an erotic periodical of 1822 contains a list of twenty-five perversions, sufficiently well-established to have received cant names: of these about twenty can be identified as perversions known to modern psychopathology. The fetichisms seem to have been common by the middle of the century, and the *Englishwomen's Domestic Magazine* was started, in 1858, apparently in order to cater for them.

As it is sometimes supposed that homosexuality is commoner in periods of relaxed morals than in strict ones, it is worth pointing out that in the nineteenth century it was at least as common as in the eighteenth, despite the severer measures taken to repress it. Early eighteenth-century writers, such as Dalton[52] and the anonymous author of *Hell Upon Earth*,[53] give a detailed picture of the homosexual groups in London at the time, and Dudley Ryder comments on its prevalence at Oxford.[54] In the mid-century, the author of *Satan's Harvest Home*[55] thought it was increasing, while Strutwell, in *Roderick Random* (1748), says that homosexuality "gains ground apace and in all

[51] Fraxi, *Index*, p. xli.

[52] *Genuine Narrative of the Street Robberies.* . . .

[53] The anonymous author of *Hell Upon Earth: or the Town in an Uproar* (1729) writes, "They also have their Walks and Appointments, to meet and pick up one another, and their particular Houses of Resort to go to, because they dare not trust themselves in an open Tavern. About twenty of these sort of Houses have been discovered, beside the Nocturnal Assemblies of great numbers of the like vile Persons, what they call the *Markets*, which are the Royal Exchange, Lincoln's Inn Bog-Houses, the south side of St. James's Park, the Piazzas in Covent Garden, St. Clement's Churchyard, &c."

"It would be a pretty scene to behold them in their clubs and cabals," he says longingly, "how they assume the Air and affect the name of Madam or Miss, Betty or Molly, with a chuck under the chin, and 'Oh, you bold pullet, I'll break your eggs,' and then frisk and walk away." (pp. 42-3.)

[54] *Diary*, p. 143.

[55] Op. cit., pp. 45 ff: 'Reasons for the Growth of Sodomy.'

probability will become in a short time a more fashionable device than fornication". If in the last two or three decades of the century we find an increasing number of prosecutions for sodomy reported, it is probably only an indication that middle-class opinion was becoming more effective. We also find an increase in cases of blackmail, which clearly indicates that the climate of opinion had become severer.

With the opening of the new century, homosexual practices were thought to have increased.[56] In 1813 the prosecution of one Cook for keeping a house of resort in Vere Street led to a scandal, as Cook named the people using the place, who included a clergyman and several prominent men. The Home Secretary intervened and Cook was sent to the pillory. "It was not intended that you should have come back alive," the turnkey told him afterwards.[57] A solicitor, who, though condemning homosexuality, was outraged by the injustice of the treatment meted to Cook, made a personal investigation of the whole matter, which had until then been successfully hushed up. He records with naïve astonishment that many of those concerned were not effeminate in appearance. "It is not effeminate men but butchers, blacksmiths, coal-merchants, police runners, who do it and have favourite women." And he adds, "These odious practices are not confined to one, two or three houses, either public or private; for there are many about town: one in the vicinity of the Strand; one in Blackman Street in the Borough; one near the Obelisk, St. George's Fields; one in the neighbourhood of Bishopsgate Street, kept by a fellow known by the title of the Countess of Camomile." And he appeals for some method of "restraining this vice, either by castration or some other cogent preventitive, without waiting for completion of the offence".[58]

By the middle of the nineteenth century things are so bad that "it is not long since that, in the neighbourhood of Charing Cross, they posted bills in the windows of several respectable public houses,

---

[56] Thus *Hints . . . on the Prevalence of Vice* (1811) complains of the great increase in immorality including "the shocking depravity of men's *unnatural passions*, sodomitical" (p. 101).

[57] *The Phoenix of Sodom*, pp. 12–20.

[58] ib., pp. 13, 16.

cautioning the public to 'Beware of Sods'." *The Yokel's Preceptor* says it is necessary to warn its readers to be careful, owing to the "increase of these monsters in the shape of men, commonly designated Margeries, Pooffs, &c., of late years in the great metropolis . . . the Quadrant, Fleet Street, Holborn, the Strand, &c., are actually thronged with them!" There are many in the theatrical profession, it adds, and goes on to describe the signs by which they make themselves known—precisely the same as Parker had described in the previous century![59]

It appears that actual homosexual brothels were established: Ryan, retreating into the decent obscurity of a learned language, and adding two exclamation points, says, "*Sunt lupinaria nunc inter nos, in quibus utuntur pueri vel puellae!!*" And he adds that the cost of obtaining a boy for such purposes was ten pounds.[60]

In my files there is much more data of this sort, but I have perhaps presented enough to dispel the picture, presented in moralised social histories, of a pious era. In actual fact, all that Massey arraigns in the eighteenth century was true of the period in which he himself wrote, and more besides.

For the Victorians, morality meant almost exclusively sexual morality. But before leaving the subject, it is worth while noting that they were almost equally deficient in other kinds of ethically approved behaviour.

Pueckler-Muskau was astonished, in 1828, to find that "Cheating, in every kind of 'sport' is as completely in the common order of things in England, among the highest classes as well as in the lowest, as false play was in the time of the Comte de Grammont. It is no uncommon thing to hear gentlemen boast of it almost openly; and I never found that those who are regarded as 'the most knowing ones' had suffered in their reputation in consequence. . . . Some of the highest members of the aristocracy are quite notorious for their achievements of this description".[61]

Forty years later Ritchie similarly stresses the dishonesty of the supposedly moral upper-middle class; he mentions as typical a case

[59] *Yokel's Preceptor*, pp. 5 f. Parker, *A View of Society*, pp. 85 f.
[60] Ryan, *Prostitution in London*, p. 199.
[61] Pueckler-Muskau, *Tour . . .*, ii, 235.

known to him where the father of a boy who was getting married proposed to the father of the bride that they should join in stocking a cellar for the young couple. He then obtained all the wine at a discount, but billed the other parent for his share at the full rate. To outwit a social acquaintance in this way was considered a source of satisfaction.[62] The diaries of the period contain many other examples: Greville records how, when Creevey died, he left everything to his mistress, Emma, whom he made his executrix, the chief item being his papers, worth some thousands to any publisher. Brougham, and Vizard the solicitor, systematically set out to deceive her as to their value, and Greville is naïvely astonished that Emma "behaved with the utmost delicacy and propriety, has shown no mercenary disposition" while Creevey's upper-class friends unblushingly duped her.[63]

What could happen when the parties were really at loggerheads we can see from Hare's account of the case for libel brought against him by the Catholics, with its suborning of witnesses, perjury, sharp practice, and hushing-up of presumptive murder, to say nothing of the incidental larceny, by the abbess of a nunnery, of candelabra and point lace.[64]

In reading memoirs of the period one cannot fail to be struck by the quite extraordinary rudeness which prevailed. This word rudeness is perhaps inadequate to describe what was really an ill-concealed aggression, a desire to wound and humiliate others by any means which would not actually land one up in court. Robert Lowe probably demonstrates this type at its extreme. Lowe, says Briggs, "liked to be rude," and he describes how, having some time to pass at a railway station, Lowe deliberately picked a quarrel with the carman, saying to the Lord Chancellor, who was with him, "Let's have a row with the carman about the fare."[65]

Or take Lord Brougham, who used to curse his sister-in-law "in the most horrible language before all the guests, and this not for anything she had done but to vent his spite and ill-humour". Hare records how "Col. Jones, the day before his marriage, stamped all his bride's things

---

[62] cf. also *London in the Sixties*, Ch. 11.
[63] Greville, *Diary*, i, 11.
[64] *Years with Mother*, Chapter 14.
[65] Briggs, *Victorian People*, p. 245.

down into one box, ruining the dresses" and proceeded to drag her all round Scotland in a pony trap. When Mary Browning's maid, in the goodness of her heart, cooked a dinner for the lonely Bulwer Lytton, he threw it out of the window.[66]

That such aggression was often generated by nineteenth-century upbringing is not surprising. I mention it simply because it is important to remember that the Victorians were not, as we now tend to think them, calm, beautifully-mannered people moving gracefully through an orderly social dance: this is the romanticisation we retrospectively make. Such restraint as they achieved, they achieved at the cost of severe tensions, and they performed the dance often with considerable anxiety.

It would not be difficult to demonstrate the underside of nineteenth-century morality in every other sphere. The eighteenth century is known as a period of gambling, and remembered for the South Sea Bubble. But the nineteenth century saw the deliberate manipulation of the funds by Cochrane Johnstone, later Lord Admiral Cochrane, and the speculation mania of the Railway Age.[67] The number of gambling dens in London increased from six before the French Revolution to fifty by 1820.[68] The eighteenth century is known as a period of frankness amounting to indecency. But in the nineteenth periodicals such as *The Town* were notorious for their grossness and indecency, while *Paul Pry* (founded 1856) carried on the tradition. Stead's *Pall Mall Gazette* found a way of serving up the prurient thinly disguised as moralising, which, though still common to-day, has no parallel in the eighteenth century, and seems much more repellent than the unvarnished statements of that period.

Let us now discuss the broader implications of all this material. It is clear, in the light of such facts, that the popular conception of the nineteenth century as a period of undeviating morality must be drastically modified. In point of fact, prior to 1850 'morality', as the Victorians understood the word, was confined almost entirely to the

[66] *Years with Mother*, p. 200.
[67] Smith Hughes, *Six Ventures*, Ch. 1.
[68] According to an estimate by *The Gaming Calendar*, cited Rosa, *Silver Fork School*, p. 26.

middle, and to a less extent the upper, class, and even in these sections its grip was partial. Moreover, appearances mattered more than reality: and people were prepared to subscribe publicly to a strict code while privately observing a much lower standard.[69] In this sense at least the Victorian reputation for hypocrisy seems to have been justified.

But while the nineteenth century does not live up to its reputation for morality, as I have shown, the eighteenth century also does not live up to its reputation for immorality. The question therefore arises, in what did the change between the periods really consist? Was there, indeed, a moral change at all? Did the moralists achieve anything more than the placing of a decorous screen in front of immoral behaviour? I think it must be concluded that, in any quantitative sense, the moral change is too slight to assess: it may even be that the sum total of immorality was higher in the nineteenth century than in the eighteenth.[70]

The only realistic question which can be asked in this context is, why do historians regard the eighteenth century as immoral, the nineteenth not? How, in fact, does an age acquire its ethos, or at any rate its reputation?

One is tempted to reply that in the eighteenth century the upper class was literate and had the leisure to write diaries, while the trading middle class did not: whereas in the following century the middle class had become so numerous and so wealthy that it produced diaries in greater numbers than did the upper class. Add to this the fact that vice was pushed out of sight, so that few nineteenth-century diaries refer to it, and we have a plausible explanation of the situation.

Still, this does not mean that no change occurred, nor that there is

[69] This was Mrs. Sherwood's view: "If (in the eighteenth century) the great were more coarse, they were then more hospitable; if they were then profligate, they are now, I fear, equally so, although in a more refined and guarded manner." (Darton, *Life of Mrs. Sherwood*, p. 32.)

[70] By making normal sexual activity more difficult, they increased the amount of auto-erotic, perverted and fantasied sexual behaviour; but since these kinds of behaviour are obsessive in character, individuals who exhibit them have recourse to it more frequently than normal individuals have recourse to normal sexual behaviour.

nothing to explain. Whether or not the Puritan group achieved any actual gross balance of moral reform, there is no doubt, first, that it attempted to do so, and, second, that it forced vice out of sight. And it would be absurd to deny that in the process it influenced a great many people, some to greater piety, others to sense of guilt, while yet others were negatively influenced, in that they reacted from piety towards the other extreme.

In short, the problem which I set out to analyse has changed very greatly in character. A social process remains to be examined, though not the kind of process it had seemed to be at first sight. Moreover, the fact that the middle-class victory was so incomplete itself constitutes a problem requiring explanation. Why did genuine religious conviction remain so largely a peculiarity of the middle class? And why was the lower class almost entirely unaffected by the pressures which the middle class exerted, despite the occurrence of numerous religious conversions among it?

The crucial factor, it seemed to me, was the fact that in the same individuals religious feeling was associated with the 'commercial virtues' of conscientiousness, industriousness, parsimony and so on. The consistency of the association is most striking. Clearly, this psychological conjunction is sufficient to account for the concentration of moral feeling in the middle class. For if any lower-class individual displayed such a combination of traits, he would tend to rise into the trading class. And, in fact, we can see this happening in many of the Methodist and Quaker diaries.[71]

The Methodists, indeed, sought to achieve this for their converts and lent them capital for the purpose. As early as 1763, Wesley declared that "Methodists in business have increased in substance sevenfold, some of them twenty, yea, an hundred fold".[72] The practice, which

[71] See, for instance, Emden, *Quakers in Commerce*.

[72] *Journal*, v. 30–1. Janion notes how one man borrowed five guineas to start in the potato trade and a few years later was worth 500 guineas. (*Some Account*, p. 72–3.) Lackington, the bookseller, is another well-known example. By 1786 Wesley was becoming shocked at the mania for making money, and in 1789 the Methodist Conference felt it necessary to condemn it. See Warner, *Wesleyan Movement*, for further details.

Methodists made a quite explicit policy, of boycotting tradesmen whom they regarded as immoral and of giving their custom to those they approved, would also tend to bring this about, both by accelerating the economic rise of the latter and driving into bankruptcy the former.

The possession of the 'commercial virtues' also assisted the promotion of those who were not in business on their own. Masters of iron works and collieries went out of their way to appoint Methodists as foremen and managers, finding them especially hard-working and reliable. Thus it came about that the group which held moral convictions was also the group which held extensive economic power.[73]

But the fact that the 'commercial virtues' were associated with moral and specifically religious feeling requires explanation. Many writers have assumed this to be a natural if not an inevitable conjunction. But once we take a longer historical perspective, we can see this is not so. The Early Fathers of the Christian Church, so far from being impelled to cautious, industrious, accumulative behaviour, neglected all commercial activity, eschewed property and lived in the desert. The followers of St. Bernard and other medieval groups embraced poverty and preferred the voluntary service of their fellow men to paid activity. At the other extreme, we can see around us to-day many who are industrious and who accumulate wealth, while having no religious convictions at all. Thus it is not only a question why moral feeling should be associated with commercialism, but it is by no means inevitable that society should contain a pietistic group at all. In a large society there may indeed be a small minority of zealots, but—as we see in our own society to-day—their teachings may be ignored as ridiculous and exaggerated. The real problems behind the change which I am attempting to examine are, therefore, why did society contain an appreciable number of people prepared to be influenced by pietistic arguments, and why was such readiness also commonly associated with the commercial virtues? Troeltsch, Tawney and others have, to be sure, pointed out the significance of the association of

[73] Habershon, *Chapeltown Researches*, pp. 129–42. Everett describes how the owners of a lead-mine, exasperated by dishonest agents, sought out a Methodist for the job (*Wesleyan Methodism*, pp. 221 f.)

Protestantism with capitalism.[74] But they have not made it clear why such an association occurred. Sometimes it has been argued that the bourgeois adopted Protestantism because it sanctioned his commercial ambitions, sometimes Protestantism has been made the cause and capitalism the result.

In my view, both these groups of attitudes were acceptable to the bourgeois because of certain underlying elements in his personality, and the problem is to identify these elements. Thus, while at a crude level of analysis the social and historical change can be interpreted in economic terms, on closer analysis it calls for psychological analysis. Let us now turn, therefore, to the psychological aspect. Let us, however, consider the evidence dispassionately, before attempting to offer any explanation of it. We may start by considering the nature of Puritan moral theories more precisely.

[74] Tawney, *Religion and the Rise of Capitalism*: Troeltsch, *Protestantism and Progress*. See also Robertson, *Aspects of the Rise of Economic Individualism*.

PART TWO

THE MORALISTS

CHAPTER 6

ON THE SIDE OF THE ANGELS

THE PURITAN MORAL CODE is embodied in a great mass of literature, produced by writers of varying religious affiliations—Calvinist, Methodist, Dissenting, including Quaker—and also by laymen.[1] It spreads over two centuries, for the works of the seventeenth-century writers like Baxter and Taylor continued to be reprinted throughout the eighteenth century. But, on examination, it proves to speak with a consistent voice on all topics relevant to our present purpose. There is a coherent moral conception running through this whole corpus of writing.

Nevertheless, it is quite a strange conception, differing in many ways from that of an earlier period. While some aspects of it reflect precisely

---

[1] There is, first, the main stream of the Puritan tradition, represented by such books as Law's *Serious Call* (1728), and the *New Whole Duty of Man* (1744) which pick up the themes laid down by such seventeenth-century writers as Baxter, Jeremy Taylor and the author (probably Allestree) of the *Whole Duty of Man*. This line of thinking runs on without a perceptible break into the Evangelical movement, of which the source book is Venn's *Complete Duty of Man* (1763). Also part of this tradition, despite differences of view on dogmatic points, are Nonconformist works such as those of Philip Doddridge, whose *Rise and Progress of Religion in the Soul* appeared in 1745. As I shall show, Wesley's teaching was in a similar psychological tradition. Secondly there is the group of moralising, but less specifically religious, writers, such as Steele and Addison at the beginning of the century, Samuel Richardson in the middle, and the group of writers, chiefly female, on child upbringing and the role of women who emerged towards the end of the century; it includes such names as Mrs. Pennington, Mrs. Chapone, Mrs. Sherwood, Miss Edgeworth, Mrs. Trimmer and many others. The mere existence of this mass of material gives some indication of how strong moral preoccupations continued to be throughout the period, especially when it is remembered that almost all these books ran through numerous editions, while the works of seventeenth-century divines also continued to be reprinted.

the attitudes which, as I have argued in *Sex in History*, are associated with father-identification, other aspects remain mysterious, and clearly call for some further psychological explanation.

With this theory in mind, I expected to find in the teaching the basic ideas of submission to authority, low status for women, and the sinfulness of pleasure, especially sexual pleasure. And indeed, these ideas permeate this literature through and through. It is only necessary to give a few of the numerous instances, for one can open almost any one of these books at random and find these themes apparent. Baxter speaks of the importance of "subjection to God" in 1673[2] in words hardly different from those used by Wilberforce in 1797 when he actually *defines* sin as "rebellion against the authority of God".[3] This is simply an inverted way of saying that nothing is worse than disobedience. Venn, the father of the Evangelical movement, enjoined "absolute submission" to God's will and "obedience without exception" to parents.[4] Wesley took a similar view.

The women moralists all made obedience the foundation stone of their teaching. Mrs. Cockle (1809), for instance, declares the obedience of children of all ages to their parents is "one of the most sacred of the divine commandments"[5]—though how one can discriminate between the sacredness of the commandments is not clear.

That parents should expect obedience is natural, but the emphasis is excessive. And such emphasis was not universal. Thus in some country districts fathers used to encourage their sons to attack them, and when a son had succeeded in knocking his father down, he was considered to have reached manhood, and to be ready to stand on his own feet. It is inconceivable that the moralists of whom we have been speaking could ever have admitted such a practice.

If submission is good, it follows that independence is bad. Hannah More exclaims, in 1799, "Who can forbear observing and regretting in a variety of instances, that not only sons, but daughters, have adopted something of that spirit of independence and disdain of control, which

---

[2] Baxter, *Christian Directory*, p. 85.
[3] Wilberforce, *Practical View*, p. 291.
[4] Venn, *Complete Duty*, pp. 32, 188, 271.
[5] Cockle, *Important Studies*, p. 54.

characterises the times? The rights of man have been discussed, till we are somewhat wearied with the discussion. To these have been opposed . . . the rights of women. It follows that the world will next have—grave descants on the rights of youth—the rights of children—the rights of babies!"[6]

So strong was this fear of independence that *Robinson Crusoe* was condemned on the grounds that it might, as Maria Edgeworth said, have the dangerous effect of inspiring young readers with a taste for adventure.[7]

Obviously persons who constitutionally favour submission to authority cannot be expected to favour liberty. During the eighteenth century liberty had been so popular a catchword that no doubt it took some time before anyone could come right out with a condemnation of liberty. However, in 1811 a clergyman, the Rev. Mr. Cecil, roundly asserted, "The love of liberty is one of the most dangerous passions of the heart of man. . . ."[8] Others continued to use the word liberty, but in a different sense, as Halévy[9] explains: in the first fifteen years of the nineteenth century, "the word liberty no longer bore for them the sense it had borne for their fathers. They now understood by liberty restraint self-imposed and freely accepted as opposed to restraint forcibly imposed by the Government."

The second strand in the web is the taboo on pleasure: this is perhaps not quite so explicit. Pleasure appears more as a temptation which may distract one from attention to business or from religious devotion. The earlier writers indicate that sexual pleasure is especially suspect: Taylor, for instance, gives a list of "Rules for suppressing Voluptuousness".[10] The later writers avoid anything so indelicate as an open reference to sexual pleasure, but that it is in their minds is clear enough. Thus for Burder (1805) the "dancing of both sexes together" is a practice which "more or less must, I conceive, be liable to awaken improper passions".[11]

[6] More, *Strictures*, p. 109.

[7] The revision of *Robinson Crusoe* was the final achievement of Plumptre, the great expurgator who went so much further than his better-known contemporary.

[8] In *The Female Instructor*, p. 348.

[9] *England in 1815,*

[10] *Holy Living*, p. 72.

[11] Burder, *Lawful Amusements*, p. 17.

(Unfortunately, almost every other form of amusement is equally undesirable, and when he has finished his catalogue, hardly anything is left permitted except homosexual dancing.)[12] He, too, feels that the true Christian will, in any case, have no time left from his duties for pleasure, however innocent.

Such views merely echo the franker statement of Law, three-quarters of a century earlier, that "the vigour of the blood, the gaiety of our spirits, and the enjoyment of sensible pleasures" (i.e. the pleasures of the senses) are "the undeniable proofs of dead Christians".[13]

The Puritan condemnation of the theatre, the novel and other social pleasures was also repeated. The author of *Fashionable Amusements* (1827), while condemning the writers of bad novels as "moral assassins", would permit "select novel reading to be cautiously allowed".[14] But Mrs. Chapone felt that "novels mislead your heart and understanding",[15] Mrs. Cartwright thought that they only tend to vitiate children's morals and corrupt their hearts.[16] In 1793 the *Evangelical Magazine* roundly declared that, "All novels, generally speaking, are instruments of abomination and ruin."[17] Fairy tales were especially condemned. According to a correspondent in *The Guardian of Education*, Cinderella is "one of the most exceptionable books ever written for children. It paints the worst passions that can enter into the human heart, and of which little children should, if possible be totally ignorant; such as envy, jealousy, a dislike to mothers-in-law and half-sisters, vanity, a love of dress, etc., etc".[18] Mrs. Trimmer, the editress,

---

[12] The Puritans in general were opposed to 'gynecandrical dancing', i.e. the dancing of the two sexes together. Men might however dance together in one room, women in another. Cf. Increase Mather, *An Arrow against Profane and Promiscuous Dancings*; Wesley, *Works*, vii, 34.

[13] Law, *Christian Perfection*, p. 27. Chapters 4, 5 and 6 comprise a sustained attack on enjoyment. "Christianity calleth all men to a state of Self Denial and Mortification". "We ought to refuse Pleasures and Satisfactions". "Suffering is the proper state of this life", pp. 148, 153.

[14] Op cit., p. 111.

[15] *Letters*, p. 181.

[16] *Female Education*, p. 17.

[17] *Evangelical Magazine* (August 1793), pp. 78-9.

[18] *Guardian of Education* (August 1803), ii, 448.

agreed, and the Society for the Suppression of Vice expressly denounced it.[19]

The Methodists and Dissenters continued to attack the stage with a Puritan severity: Gisborne[20] and Burder[21] condemn it; John Styles' *Essay on the Character, Immorality and Anti-Christian Tendency of the Stage* (1806) bears comparison with the earlier diatribes of Law (1720) (for whom it was "absolutely unlawful") and Jeremy Collier, and he declares that it was a "luckless hour" when Shakespeare took to writing for it.[22]

These are all attitudes which reflect the presence of father-identification. But in the Puritan code are other attitudes of a less expected sort. Chief of these is a profound belief in the need to suppress all spontaneous impulses. This belief is often expressed in the form of injunctions to 'self-restraint' or 'self-control'.[23] Thus Hannah More says that the great secret of religious education consists in training young men to "an habitual interior restraint, an early government of their affections, and a course of self-control".[24] Here the central idea is not that of submission to an authority deserving of respect, but that of inhibition of impulse. It is not simply that we should restrain ourselves from wicked impulses; it is an inhibition of all impulse, even the most innocent, which is desired. Wesley, for instance, reproved Adam Clarke for displaying grief at the death of his daughter.[25] Some sixteenth-century Puritans went still further: one of them would not even permit himself to pat his dog—surely one of the most extraordinary instances of inhibition that one could ever find![26] Laughter was forbidden. Baxter quotes *Ecclesiastes* ii, 2, against laughter;[27] similarly Venn condemns all jesting and urges not only modesty of

---

[19] Darton, in *Camb. History Eng. Lit.*, xi, 380.
[20] Gisborne, *Enquiry . . . Duties of Female Sex*, pp. 164 ff.
[21] Burder, *Lawful Amusements*, pp. 5 ff.
[22] Op cit., p. 55 *n*.
[23] See Schuecking, *Familie*, Ch. I., for a survey.
[24] More, *Estimate*, p. 91.
[25] Cited Bowen, *Wrestling Jacob*, p. 378.
[26] Cited Schuecking, *Familie*, p. 14.
[27] Baxter, *Christian Directory*, p. 335.

manners but "tranquillity of countenance".[28] Gouge urges control of the gestures, in terms no different from those of a Victorian governess.[29] This notion re-appears unchanged in the secular writers. Mrs. Cartwright, though one of the milder authorities, prohibits all practical jokes;[30] Louisa Hoare (1819) declares that children must show no undue eagerness nor indulge in loud laughter.[31] By 1841 Mrs. Gore (writing about the first decade of the century) depicts Lady Vandeleur teaching her son Cecil to keep "in the background of the picture". "You talk too much, you laugh too much," she tells him.[32]

One of the impulses which we must resist is that of talking. The Puritan Allestree devoted a whole book to *The Government of the Tongue*. Watts only condemns "a talkative or tattling humour"[33], but Mrs. Chapone states that "many are of the opinion that a young woman cannot be too silent in company".[34] As I have already recorded, inhibition did in fact become so considerable that long silences ensued even on social occasions. Brandy told Stendhal that none of the passengers spoke in the whole course of a coach journey which he made from Bath to London.[35]

Often these themes are combined, as when the moralists insist that children should never interrupt their parents, a rule which Mrs. Cartwright mentions as common in 1777, though she dismisses it as stupid.[36]

As one might imagine, restraint is particularly important for women, who are expected to put up even with unreasonable treatment "with

[28] Venn, *Complete Duty*, pp. 193, 265.

[29] Gouge, *Domesticall Duties*, p. 163. Cf. Aikin (*Memoirs*, p. 435): "All Europe declares that we have *no* gestures . . . All governesses proscribe it."

[30] Cartwright, *Female Education*, p. 25.

[31] Hoare, *Hints*, pp. 129 ff.

[32] Laughing had, however, been condemned in the eighteenth century even in aristocratic circles, e.g. by Lord Chesterfield, *Letters*. See Allen, *Tides in Eng. Taste*, Chapter 2, for a discussion.

[33] Watts, *Preservative from the Sins*, p. 49.

[34] Chapone, *Letters*. p. 160.

[35] Edwards, 'Stendhal in London' in *London Magazine* (1955), vol. 2, No. 3.

[36] Cartwright, *Female Education*, pp. 54-5. Mrs. Sherwood's mother was among those who "never suffered her children to interrupt conversation". (Darton, *Life*, p. 33.)

uncomplaining meekness". Restraint is to be physical and verbal as well as moral. As Mrs. Sandford puts it, she must not "play the romp, leap a five-barred gate, or affect the Di Vernon."[37]

All this constitutes what has been called the Puritan ideal of sobriety: the choice of word is significant, for actual intoxication produces just that freedom from inhibition which they thought sinful.[38] Naturally, intoxication itself was feared and condemned. It is logical, therefore, that in the nineteenth century, when the middle-class view had triumphed and was beginning to infiltrate the lower class, we find, for the first time, a general temperance movement developing.[39]

Allied with this is the fear of 'caprice' or, as we should probably say, impulse. Isaac Watts objects to all caprice or 'humoursome behaviour', as well as to rashness, heedlessness, impatience, fickleness and even profuseness (by which he means prodigality).[40] Mrs. Cockle, nearly a century later, advises, "Avoid, above all things, indulging a capricious disposition."[41]

Between the ideas of restraint and submission there is .a certain natural kinship, but the Puritan code also expounds a set of values of a more unusual sort.

Thus in many of the seventeenth- and eighteenth-century moralists there is a strange preoccupation with the use of time. Baxter had devoted a whole section of the *Christian Directory* to the subject.[42] Law made eighteen rules for himself when entering Cambridge: four of them express the identical thought, that one must not waste time.[43] Often this preoccupation takes the more definite form of urging

---

[37] Sandford, *Woman in Soc. and Dom. Character*, p. 17.

[38] That it was not merely sinful impulses which had to be restrained is shown, for instance, by the objection to whistling, and even to such innocent actions as eating apples in the street. Dissenting ministers lost their congregations if they displayed such 'levit'. (See *Metrop. Pulpit*, p. 13.)

[39] Webbs, *Hist. of Liquor Licensing*, stress the relative lateness of this development. Wesley, though strongly against spirits, permitted himself two or three glasses of wine with his meals (Hampson, *Memoirs*, p. 84).

[40] Watts, *Preservative from the Sins*, Ch. 4.

[41] Cockle, *Important Studies*, p. 59.

[42] Op cit., Part 1, Chapter 5.

[43] Overton, *William Law*, pp. 6–7.

activity, and not merely activity in religious exercise, but assiduity in one's trade or profession. Thus Taylor not only urges "diligence in the pursuit of employment" but declares that one must never do anything merely "to pass the time away".[44] The festivals of the Church must in no sense be days of idleness "for it is better to plough upon holydays than to do nothing".[45] In view of the strong feelings about avoiding work on the sabbath, this is a strong statement. In just the same way, Venn insists that it is the duty of parents to inspire their children with an abhorrence of idleness.[46] Isaac Watts continued this doctrine:[47] it was he who wrote the hymn "How doth the little busy bee" which maintains that Satan will find work for idle hands to do.

Not only was work a good thing, but the possession of wealth was approved: indeed, it was a mark of God's esteem. Thus Venn, "But if, while your heart is whole with Him, He is pleased to make prosper whatever you do, your wealth is plainly His gift, as much as if it came to you by legacy, or inheritance . . ."[48] For such Bible fundamentalists as were the Puritan moralists, this was a surprising departure from the teaching of Christ that a rich man would find it more difficult to get into Heaven than a camel to pass through the eye of a needle. By the same token, thrift emerged as a virtue; a due proportion is to be given to charity, but there is to be "no prodigality".[49] The words "Give *all* thou hast to the poor" are forgotten. Law, however, perceived the difficulty, and argued that "the words *sell all* are only used as a Form of Speech", and mean only that one should part with the enjoyment of wealth, i.e. that one should not spend it.[50]

These, of course, are the so-called 'commercial virtues'. It is obvious that they are not derived from the Bible, but in spite of it, and we are justified in inferring the existence of unconscious motivations. In due course, I shall try to show what they were. The commercial character

[44] *Holy Living*, Ch. 2: 'Rules for the Use of Time' (Rules 2 and 6).
[45] ib., Rule 4.
[46] Venn, *Complete Duty*, p. 267.
[47] Watts, *Preservative from the Sins*, pp. 34-5.
[48] Venn, *Complete Duty*, p. 296.
[49] See, for instance, Kettlewell's diatribe against prodigality in 1705.
[50] *Christian Perfection*, p. 105. Law is ready enough to take a text literally when it suits his purpose, however, and even to go further.

of Puritan thinking is revealed by Watts, when he asks rhetorically, "What is injustice?" and then replies, "Taking what is not due to me."[51] Mrs. Cartwright suggests that children should be given money as soon as they can count, so that they can "practise Œconomy". They should be made to keep accounts and render them every month.[52]

Religion itself was invaded by these commercial notions: the Judgment Day became a sort of general audit, at which one would have to "give an account of oneself" to one's heavenly Father, much as Mrs. Cartwright's pupils were accustomed to account to their earthly one. And, as a celebrated hymn later expressed it, God became a kind of "good risk", to whom moral capital could be lent with the certainty of a handsome reward.[53]

Now the vital point which emerged was that these notions had not invaded a previously pure religion from an adjacent commercial morality external to it. They had grown up within the very heart of the Puritan tradition advocated by persons themselves quite uncommercial; and it was clearly going to be of interest at a later stage to study more closely how these notions had developed.

In this system, special attention was devoted to the status of women. All authorities agreed that the woman must be completely subordinate to her husband; she must submit herself completely, even when she knows him to be wrong. But the late eighteenth-century writers modified the picture of women's dependent role in a manner quite foreign to the seventeenth-century Puritans. Women must not only avoid any show of independence: they must try and increase their dependency: "There is something unfeminine in independence. It is contrary to Nature, and therefore it offends. A really sensible woman feels her dependence, she does what she can, but she is conscious of inferiority and therefore grateful for support. . . . In everything that women attempt they should show their consciousness of dependence."[54]

[51] Watts, *Preservative from the Sins*, p. 25. Cf. also his advice to avoid fickleness because there is "no profit in it".

[52] Cartwright, *Female Education*, p. 17.

[53] "Whatever, Lord, we lend to thee
  Repaid a thousand fold shall be.
  Then gladly will we lend to Thee . . ."

[54] Sandford, *Woman in Soc. and Dom. Character*, p. 13.

It is to be noted that they must not only be dependent, but must draw attention to the fact as much as possible, instead, as one might have thought, of trying to conceal it. The reason for this is frankly stated: it will ingratiate them with men. "They should remember that by them influence is to be obtained not by assumption, but by a delicate appeal to affection or principle. Women in this respect are something like children—the more they show their need of support, the more engaging they are."[55]

Thus the problem with which this leaves us is, why the men of the period should have preferred women to be childlike and dependent rather than mature and independent; and why should women—for this passage was written by a woman—have endorsed the view?

Women must also lack self-confidence. Shyness is "a thousand times preferable to boldness," exclaims Gausenna Minor in 1762.[56] The influential Dr. Gregory goes rather further in a passage of considerable psychological interest: "One of the chief beauties in a female character is that modest reserve, that retiring delicacy, which avoids the public eye and is disconcerted at the gaze of admiration. When a girl ceases to blush, she has lost the most powerful charm of beauty. That extreme sensibility which it indicates may be taken as a weakness and an encumbrance by the other sex, but in females it is peculiarly engaging. Pedants, who think themselves philosophers, may ask, why should a woman blush when she is conscious of no crime? It is a sufficient answer that nature has made them to blush when they are guilty of no fault and has forced men to love them because they do so."[57]

Thus it appears that Dr. Gregory wants women to behave as if they had committed a crime; and we, who know more about the unconscious than Dr. Gregory did, will realise that women will in fact only behave in this way when, at the unconscious level, they feel they have committed the crime in question.

It was part of this conception that women were not to display any social ease—to do so was 'effrontery'. They must never aspire to write

[55] ib. Girls should be led to mistrust their own judgment. (More, *Strictures*, i, 116.)
[56] *Gentleman's Magazine*, xxxii, 70.
[57] *A Father's Legacy*, pp. 36 ff.

a 'good' letter. If they happen to have any learning they must keep it "a profound secret".[58] It is unbecoming even to offer an opinion on political matters.[59]

The woman was also conceived as being particularly the guardian of the moral virtues, and having a special role in influencing men. Gisborne makes this point,[60] and the author of *Female Tuition* (1786) says, "All virtues, all vices, and all characters, are intimately connected with the manners, principles and dispositions of our women."[61]

But by 1831 the view has developed further: "The fair sex . . . are the chief sources of all graces and charms of life and have even been the main supports of human civilisation. Without them men would have been warlike hordes and ever contending barbarians. . . . Their milder character is ever operating insensibly to soften his asperities and infuse a softer spirit into his mind."[62]

Women became peculiarly responsible for religion. As Gregory frankly said, "Women must not be indifferent to religion, as even men who are themselves unbelievers dislike infidelity in you."[63] Moreover, "Men consider absence of religious feelings as proof of that hard and masculine spirit which of all your faults we dislike most." And with his usual astonishing naïvety he adds, "Besides, men consider your religion as one of their principle securities for that female virtue in which they are most interested."[64]

Mrs. Sandford, as a woman, provides a different reason. There is nothing so adapted as religion to her wants. Women have many trials, and therefore peculiarly need support, and religion is their asylum. Religion is just what woman needs, without it she is ever restless or unhappy. But she adds, "And it is the domesticating tendency of religion that especially prepossesses men in its favour, and makes them, even if indifferent to it themselves, desire it at least in their nearest

[58] Gregory, op cit., p. 31.
[59] Anon, *Females of the Present Day*, p. 1.
[60] Gisborne, *Duties of the Female Sex*, pp. 12 ff.
[61] Op cit., p. 30. Cf. also *Sacred Meditations*, p. 242.
[62] Anon, *Females of the Present Day*.
[63] Gregory, *Father's Legacy*, p. 22.
[64] ib., pp. 9 ff.

female connections."[65] The preoccupation with female chastity could hardly be more clearly stated.

As the way in which women were to behave became more and more clearly defined, there gradually emerged an important new concept: that of delicacy. There were circumstances in which a man was expected to display delicacy, but it was the whole of women's existence. Since the term still has some currency to-day, it is easy to take this development for granted, but it is in fact a strange one, and of considerable psychological interest.

I collected a considerable number of references to this notion: it seemed to be used in a bewildering variety of senses. But on consideration, I felt that I could detect in it the following fundamental ideas.

Firstly, there is physical delicacy. Women are expected to be physically weak, easily startled, and even devoid of the most normal appetites. I have already quoted Dr. Gregory's remark that "the luxury of eating" is in women "beyond expression indelicate and disgusting". This idea is confirmed by the nineteenth-century etiquette books, "It is not genteel to eat much."[66] There is one appetite which they are especially not to feel: that of sexual desire. As Dr. Acton said, it is a "vile aspersion" to suggest that woman is even capable of such a feeling.[67] Here, as I have indicated in the introduction, is the nexus of ideas which gave rise to the conception of women as being like angels.

More extraordinary still, women have even to feel ashamed of being able to love. Although there is no reason why she should feel ashamed of an attachment to a man of merit, "nature has annexed a sense of shame to it. She feels a violence done to her pride and to her modesty when she has to recognise it."[68] It is a maxim that the woman must never fall in love with a man first, but only after he has fallen in love with her. Gregory then adds, with apparent inconsequence, that it is extremely unlikely that the man the woman loves will be the man who loves her, so that she must resign herself to marrying without love. That is, she must resign herself to a marriage in which passion will be

[65] Sandford, *Woman in Soc. and Dom. Character*, p. 45.
[66] *The Book of Gentility*, p. 24.
[67] Acton, *Functions and Disorders*.
[68] Gregory, *Father's Legacy*, pp. 80 ff.

difficult or impossible. And he adds the astonishing command, "If you do love your husband, do not ever say so."[69]

By the same token, her appearance must not seem to provoke desire. As Mrs. Jameson said of Amelia, "Her neck is likewise too protuberant for the genteel size, especially as she laces herself, for no woman, in my opinion, can be genteel who is not entirely flat before."[70] (In this sentence, 'neck' is of course a delicate periphrasis for the word 'breast'.)

This physical delicacy was to be supported by a virgin innocence—or, more brutally, ignorance—of all wrong-doing, of the mere fact that many people act from wrong motives, and above all the existence of physical functions, and especially sexual ones. Not merely the sexual act, but the process of child-bearing came to be thought indelicate. As early as the middle of the century Richardson's Pamela is shocked by her husband's oblique hint that she may be going to have a baby.

Here again we have the attempt to display woman as sexually immature. Even "the duties of a mother are by some thought to be indelicate", as the *Female Instructor* remarked. "A woman must become a walking ghost to be styled truly delicate."[71] In *The Monk* (1795) Lewis satirically depicts a girl so genteel that she does not know the difference between a man and a woman,[72] while in *Burrcliff* (1853) we even find a girl who does not know what love is—criteria which suggest that lack of sexual knowledge is the core of delicacy. But this is precisely what Jeremy Taylor had advocated: "Virgins must contend for a singular modesty; whose first part must be an ignorance in the distinction of sexes or their proper instruments."[73]

The idea of knowledge had long been equated with sexual know-

---

[69] To anticipate the psychological discussion which follows in later chapters, it may be observed that these statements mirror the Œdipal situation; the child must not desire the parent of opposite sex.

[70] In *Pamela*. Cf. also *Joseph Andrews*, Book 1, Chapter 5, by the much more outspoken Fielding. By 1790 the flat bosom was general: Meister comments that even the prostitutes have no bosoms, and that women use artificial means to conceal them (p. 223).

[71] *Female Instructor*, p. 216.

[72] Op cit., p. 216.

[73] Taylor, *Holy Living*, p. 100.

ledge (cf. Adam knew Eve) and this perhaps explains why women were to be deprived of all knowledge. In Sarah Fielding's *David Simple* (1744), for instance, a mother snatched away a book from her daughter with the remark, "Miss must not inquire too far into things, it would turn her brain: she had better mind to her Needlework." Jane Austen caustically observed, "Imbecility in females is a great enhancement of their charms," while the *Female Instructor* declares that a female must not even be able to converse, though it concedes that she should know how to read and write.[74]

Finally a woman must be very careful of her reputation for delicacy, and it becomes a form of indelicacy to perform any action, however innocent in itself, which might jeopardise that reputation, however unjustifiably. Thus the heroine of *The Wanderer*[75] (1814) cannot collect some money which is due to her, and which she desperately needs, because women are supposed to be above such material matters; and she has to cancel a cross-Channel passage when she finds the man she admires is crossing on the same boat (although no one knows her feelings) in case it should ever, at some future date, be said that she had been pursuing him.

A truly delicate girl, furthermore, will not marry any man who has been a rake, for fear of seeming to countenance immorality; in Mrs. Brunton's *Self-Control* (1814), the heroine, who is obliged to make such a marriage, redeems herself by refusing herself physically to her husband until the grave. But if the delicate girl is wise, she will also not disclose that this is her reason for rejecting him. In Edgeworth's *Patronage* (1814) Caroline is in this position. "It is a subject ladies cannot well discuss; a subject on which the manners and customs of the world are so much at variance with religion and morality, that entering upon the discussion would lead to greater difficulties than you are aware of."[76]

The opposite of delicacy, incidentally, is 'coarseness'; in 1811

---

[74] Op cit., p. 28.
[75] By Fanny Burney.
[76] See Utter and Needham, *Pamela's Daughters*, for a valuable survey—but, I think, a very faulty analysis of this topic.

Mary Shelley writes, "Coarseness is completely out of fashion."[77]

This multiple concept of delicacy is almost synonymous with that of genteelness (not quite the same as gentility), to which the appropriate antonym is vulgarity. In these terms, the concept is given a class basis. The masses behave with coarse vulgarity, the middle classes with genteel delicacy.

Finally, the concept of delicacy applies with special force to language, which, as we have already seen, was a special preoccupation of the period—to a point which seemed ridiculous to the upper classes. A sturdy writer of 1817 exclaims that "to call Breeches smallclothes or inexpressibles is highly ridiculous, and gives rise to improper ideas, which would not otherwise exist". And of the word 'chemise' he says, "Prudery and affectation first gave rise to the idea that it was improper for a lady to say *Shift*: why should it be less decent than to talk of a *Shirt*? It is ridiculous to suppose that, by putting it in a foreign language, the word is rendered more chaste."[78] (Yet the same writer condemns as "very low" the word 'mulligrubs'.)

During the eighteenth century the word 'prude', which originally indicated probity and moral feeling, gradually came to be used of persons who paid lip-service to a standard of morality higher than they really felt to be necessary.[79] This hypocrisy is satirised by Sheridan, who shows Lydia Languish hiding her worldly novels, such as *Tanzai* and *Bijoux Indiscrets*, and putting out *Human Duties* in their place.

From such incidents we can infer, I think, not only that the worldly sometimes accused the genuinely moral of pretence, because they found it hard to believe that such delicacy could be genuine, but also that a good many people, predominantly women, felt it necessary to conform to a strict standard, even when personal conviction did not impel them to.

The word prudish is often used of the verbal periphrases to which I have referred earlier. I think that this does not mean simply that such phrases were used by strict persons, but usually implies that there was an

[77] Cited Acland, *Caroline Norton*, p. 50.
[78] Anon, *Errors of Pronunciation*, p. 27.
[79] Cf. *Gentleman's Magazine* (1762), xxxii, 70, in which a writer uses the terms of Prudes and Coquettes in simple contrast.

element of pretence or hypocrisy in thus refusing to call a spade a spade. But in many cases, I make no doubt, the people who used such phrases found the original words truly shocking, and did not simply assume a polite language for use in public, while privately using a franker one. To this extent, we cannot regard their prudery as hypocritical.

But this raises the interesting question of what is meant by the term 'shocking'. The point is of central importance, for the way in which a morality is commonly built up is by the moralist condemning what actually shocks him (or her). So much so that the word 'shocking' became the habitual equivalent for immoral or wicked and on the Continent is still thought characteristically English.

The answer may be given in a simple apophthegm: people are shocked by events which arouse their unconscious anxieties. In the course of this book I hope to show in more detail the truth of this assertion. However, the word shock may also be used whenever a state of affairs, or a continuous motion, is suddenly interrupted. The moralist tends to be shocked by any event to which he is unaccustomed, which is one reason why he is frequently critical of new fashions; later, when they have ceased to be new, he often defends them against yet newer fashions. The two analyses are quite compatible, for, as I have argued, the patrist prefers his father's way of doing things, and those who flout this code, flout authority—flout, in fact, the father, and this for them is the most anxiety-creating situation.

To sum up, it should not be thought that the examples I have given are isolated ones, dimly foreshadowing a development which has not yet occurred. They are simply representative extracts from an extensive literature giving a comprehensive and broadly consistent picture. Nor are the works cited the obscure productions of cranks or eccentrics. All of them enjoyed extensive and prolonged sales throughout the period: relative to the population, they achieved sales exceeding those of many modern best-sellers, and continued to sell for a century and upwards. Often two or three were bound up together: thus we get Mrs. Pennington's advice bound up with Dr. Gregory's *Legacy* and Mrs. Chapone's *Letters for Her Niece*, and published in 1847.

From this survey certain facts, I believe, emerge. First, one is struck by the virtual unanimity of these writers on the main features of the moral scheme. Though separated by many points of dogma, they agree on all those propositions which, according to the theory we are investigating, reflect the father-identification, and we are entitled to infer the existence of a common patrist element in their personality structures.

The second striking feature is the almost unanimous stress on the "commercial virtues". These are by no means an integral part of the patrist conception of morality. Medieval moralists would have disagreed profoundly about the importance of industriousness and the possession of wealth; the stress upon not wasting time is also novel. Significance also attaches to the tremendous stress put upon *self-control*, a concept psychologically different from submission to authority. It was clear to me that any psychological analysis I might, in due course, make would have to account for the presence of these unusual features in the moral scheme, and for the personal preoccupations which gave rise to them.

A further unusual feature was the treatment of women: while the normal patrist aim of restricting women's freedom, as a means of ensuring their chastity, was present together with the demand that women be subordinated to men, there was nothing of the usual patrist view that women are sexual temptresses and morally vile. Instead, women were provided with a new role: they were to behave *as if* sexually immature; and it soon came to be held that they were devoid of sexual feeling, in actual fact. This too required further analysis.

In short, it was clear that while the theory of parental identification could explain some of the main features of the moral scheme, it could not explain all of them, and evidently other forces were simultaneously at work. The scope of the analysis would, evidently, have to be broadened.

But while it thus exposed certain problems of interpretation, the survey strongly confirmed the impression already received, that the sources of the social change which we are studying lay not in the reign of Victoria, but very much earlier. Nineteenth-century morality, far from being a creation of the Victorian reign, was the outcome of a continuous moral tradition. Quite to the contrary, it is about the 1830s, as we have seen, that we find a decline in this tradition. At this time there seems to be a definite fading away of the extreme guilt-laden religious element.

No more religious books on the theme of how to live one's daily life are written commanding the sales which works like the *Christian Directory*, *Holy Living* and *The Whole Duty of Man* commanded; and the reprints of these works begin to become fewer and further between, despite the increasing numbers, wealth and literacy of the population. Keble's *Christian Year* (1827) is perhaps the last flaring-up of this inspiration.

The harshness, the ideal of self-control, the interest in money and the dislike of idleness, these continue until almost the end of the nineteenth century. But long before this the status of women has begun to rise, and other changes have taken place in the ideal. These are changes which belong to another study, the study of how moral standards gradually relax themselves. Thus when we speak of Victorian morality, we refer to a period of let-down, of relaxing controls. The subject of the present study is how the spring was wound up. It appears it was substantially Puritan morality which wound up the spring.

I have used the word 'moral' without prejudice, but there is a distinction to be made between 'moral' feeling and religious conviction. When, in 1797, Wilberforce published his influential work, *A Practical View of the Prevailing Religious System*, he stressed that he was not complaining about unsatisfactory behaviour; his complaint was that those whose behaviour was satisfactory were insufficiently religious. These people, he said, believe that it is what one does that matters. But this is quite false; Christianity does not merely call upon us to live moral lives, it requires us to believe certain propositions.[80] It is not enough to submit to "the horrors" of Sunday observance, as people call them: one must *enjoy* them.[81] We find exactly the same attitude in the writings of Lackington, the Methodist bookseller. He says that his wife "is in her moral conduct one of the most perfect beings I ever saw" and that she "always thought she ought to be as good as she could", but he complains that "she had not the least knowledge of religion beyond that of being as good as she could. . . . As to going to church or private

[80] Wilberforce, *Practical View*, p. 248.
[81] ib., p. 193.

devotion, she could not see of what use it could be to her. As she wanted for nothing, she did not know what she should pray for; she had never done any person any harm; she had never slandered, back-bited, or ridiculed any person, nor did she know that she had com-mitted any other sin, and so she had no need of praying for pardon".[82]

This was a dreadful state of affairs, of course; so Lackington sends off for a staggering array of literature—Watson's *Apology*, Porteus' *Compendium*, Butler's *Analogy*, Paley's *Evidences*, Pilgrim's *Good Intent*, Pascal's *Thoughts*, Addison's *Evidences*, and many more, to say nothing of volumes of sermons, of biblical exposition, of rules for the Christian life, and the entire works of Hannah More. "For some time, one sermon was read on Sunday, but soon Mrs. Lackington began to like them, and then two or three were read in the course of the week; at last one at least was read every day, and very often part of some other book of divinity . . . and now Mrs. Lackington sees very important reasons for going to church, sacrament, &c."[83]

This suggests the striking conclusion that it was not in fact religion, as people like Wilberforce and Lackington understood that term, which brought about the moralisation of behaviour; the religion had to be injected afterwards. Alternatively, we must believe that these men were wrong in regarding dogma and (what Wilberforce insisted on) the sense of sin as actually the constitutive element in religion. Be that as it may (and only the theologians can decide such a point), it seems clear that some psychological influence must have been at work on the 'religious' individuals, to create their overpowering sense of sin. What this factor could be, I had, at this stage, no idea, nor had I any data which seemed relevant. But the fact that these feelings of religious necessity became more pronounced towards the end of the century and reached a peak at the beginning of the century following, suggested that this factor must have been becoming more powerful and more widespread.

I also noted that the religious demand had a perfectionist—that is, an

---

82 Lackington, *Confessions*, pp. 51–3. But the same point had been made as early as 1726 by Law, *Christian Perfection*, pp. 30, 59. "Christianity is not a school of virtue . . ."
83 Lackington, ib.

obsessive—character.[84] Although human nature was inherently wicked, nevertheless the demand was made that one should achieve absolute perfection. The Scripture says, "Be ye perfect"—so one cannot be too strict. So it was argued. It also says, "Thy will be done in earth, *as it is in Heaven.*" This means that we must behave no whit less well than the angels do.[85] Religion, declares Wilberforce, requires *all* one's time. "There are no little sins."[86] "Remember," he says, "that we are all fallen creatures, born in sin, and naturally depraved. Christianity recognises no *innocence* or *goodness of heart.*"[87]

Finally, I was struck by the extreme fatuity and inconsistency of the arguments advanced to support these doctrines. The best argument that Watts can produce for avoiding 'lewdness' is that "Modesty is a natural Virtue to a child" so that "Lewdness makes him appear like a Monster".[88] Mrs. Chapone advocates that children should only be allowed to make friends with children six to eight years older than themselves, and that they should always invite their friends to their own house, never themselves to go to their friends' houses—rules which are clearly self-defeating and incapable of general application.[89] Practical jokes are prohibited because once one caused a girl to die of surprise. One wonders whether such anecdotes were not invented for the purpose.

It is clear that all these writers are providing reasons, *post hoc*, for views that they already hold. They are rationalising. When people of high intellectual calibre engage in this exercise, they often find very convincing reasons: when lesser men attempt it, the results are more obviously ridiculous. Thus Burder's *Sermon*, Gisborne's *Duties*, are so vapid and weakly argued, it is obvious that they could have convinced no one. They were, in fact, preaching to the converted; and it is

---

[84] All the classic religious works worry each point *ad nauseam*, coming back again and again to the same phrases and ideas, in just the same way as certain pornographic works do, and the air of obsession is most noticeable. See, for instance, Law's *Christian Perfection.*

[85] Wilberforce, *Practical View*, p. 147.

[86] ib., p. 153.

[87] ib., p. 437.

[88] Watts, *Preservatives*, p. 33.

[89] Chapone, *Letters on the Improvement*, p. 76.

because people enjoy seeing their convictions asserted and supported more impressively than they could themselves manage that such works sold.

This supports my view that, by and large, books do not bring about changes, though they may hasten and clarify a change which is already in progress. They are only bought because they express something which people, however obscurely, feel. When a book is written which advocates views which are not part of the trend of the times, it causes a scandal or is ignored; to take but one example of this in the period, Madan's *Thelyphthora* (1781) argued that polygamy was part of the Mosaic Law, and hence that England should revert to it—a suggestion the impeccable logic of which caused a frenzy of exasperation.

The pattern of behaviour which emerges in these quotations is quite familiar: its familiarity may blind us to its peculiarity. Against the perspective of history it emerges as a very extraordinary perversion of the human spirit. For me, at least, it raised in an acute form the questions: why did the reformers of the period conceive of morality in precisely this one form? And how did they manage to impose such a restrictive code on such an important section of the population, in face of all those in the eighteenth century who favoured robustness, spontaneity and a permissive morality?

To answer such questions, it is necessary (as I think) to dive beneath the surface into unconscious processes. But it was not my wish to force the material into the mould of a preconceived theory. My policy was to examine the historical material for signs of psychological tension; and then, having gathered together what seemed to be significant, to see what explanation naturally arose from it. I had not read far into the subject before I began to realise that the people of the eighteenth century, or at any rate very considerable numbers of them, exhibited one overwhelming obsession: an obsession with the idea of death. This, therefore, seemed a good starting-point.

CHAPTER 7

AH, LOVELY APPEARANCE
OF DEATH!

IT WAS WIDELY RECOGNISED in the early eighteenth century that the English were extraordinarily subject to melancholia and, as we should now say, to depressive states. Indeed, gloom was known all over the Continent as "the English malady".[1]

Foreign visitors repeatedly comment on it. Le Sage, who visited England in 1715, calls the English the most unhappy people on earth; thirty-five years later Grosley felt it necessary to devote a whole section of his account of England to the English melancholy, noting the gloom of children, the rarity of laughter, and "the natural bent" of the English to suicide, despite the heavy penalties.[2] It is for this reason, he suggests, that all bridges are equipped with high walls, and barriers close off the roads which run down to the river. Addison speaks of melancholy as a kind of demon that haunts the island;[3] Stukeley (like Sydenham before him) says it constitutes fully one half the chronic disease in England.[4]

The existence of an elaborate vocabulary on a topic is generally an index of interest in it. By 1732 the *Gentleman's Magazine* could print a letter from a doctor stating, "When I first dabbled in this art, the old distemper called Melancholy was exchang'd for *Vapours*, and afterwards for the *Hypp*, and at last took up the now current appellation of the *Spleen*, which it still retains, tho' a learned doctor of the west, in a little tract he hath written, divided the *Spleen* and *Vapours*, not only

[1] Cheyne made this phrase the title of his work on the subject in 1733. For the whole topic discussed in this chapter (but not the interpretations offered), see Moore, *Backgrounds of English Literature*, Chapter 5, which I have found invaluable.

[2] *Tour to London*, pp. 165–85. Cf. also Le Sage, Muralt, Prevost, etc.

[3] He wrote several essays on the topic; cf. *Spectator*, 419.

[4] Stukeley, *Of the Spleen*, p. 73.

into the *Hypp*, the *Hyppos*, and the *Hyppocons*; but subdivided these divisions into the *Markambles*, the *Moonpalls*, the *Strong-fives*, and the *Hockogrokles*."[5]

Caring for the victims of this depression became a full-time task for many members of the medical profession. Mandeville settled in England on the grounds that it was the ideal place for a nerve specialist; Cheyne specialised in melancholia, and was consulted by such eminent figures as Gay, Swift, Pope, Young, Arbuthnot, Hume, Hervey and Richardson. Numerous medical treatises were written on it, the most famous being Cheyne's *The English Malady* (1733).

These facts struck me as extremely significant, for the cause of any kind of grief is the loss of a loved object, and the usual cause of neurotic (that is, exaggerated and irrational) melancholy is now generally recognised to be the loss of a mother-figure. This does not mean that the individual has necessarily lost his mother in reality: a sense of rejection or abandonment by the mother is sufficient to produce it. Melancholia of this obsessive kind derives in fact, like almost everything else in psychoanalysis, from the Œdipal situation. The child's first love is its mother, its first rival the father. If the stresses developed in this situation are unduly severe, some permanent disturbance results. Evidently something of the kind was occurring on a widespread scale during the eighteenth century. The explanation which suggested itself, provisionally, was that actual severity on the part of the mother was reinforcing the primitive sense of loss. The relationship of this malady to the mother-figure seems to have been suspected at the time, for Purcell mentions that it was popularly known as "fits of the mother".[6] He observes that a majority of people are afflicted with it, which confirms the idea that this was an element in the general personality structure and not just the peculiarity of a few.

Now depressive states are well known to practising psychiatrists to-day. It has been noticed that, in very many cases, states of depression alternate with states of euphoria, and just as, in the former, activity is reduced, in the latter it is usually increased. These euphoric states are technically known as manias (a word which has a rather different

[5] *Gentleman's Magazine*, November 1732, p. 1062.
[6] *A Treatise of . . . Hysteric Fits*, p. 1.

connotation in popular use, where it is often applied to obsessions) and the condition is generally known as manic-depression. The alternation however is not in any way a regular one; it is possible to go through a number of depressive phases without any intervening manic phase, and so on. The depressive state is often accompanied by headaches, blurring of vision, temporary black-outs and other symptoms.

Many cases of insanity in the eighteenth century can be identified as manic-depressions. Christopher Smart, the poet, who was confined in Bedlam, and whose best work, *Song to David*, was written while in the manic state, also suffered bouts of depression.[7]

The insanity of George III seems to have been manic-depression, as might be inferred simply from the fact that he had to be physically restrained. His case serves to show how closely the loss of super-ego control is associated with a freeing of sexual impulses. In normal periods he was somewhat severe in morality, as we know from many incidents: for instance, he deprived Meadows of the Rangership of Richmond Park because he kept a mistress, no unusual thing at the time. But during the onset of one of the manic phases (he was attacked by insanity on at least five, possibly seven, occasions)[8] he slapped the bottom of a respectable middle-aged lady at Brighton, exclaiming, "What a pretty little arse!"[9] On another, while out hunting, and seeing an Evangelical director of the Bank of England riding by, he exclaimed, "I hate such canting Methodists," and began singing aloud, "Youth's a season fit for joy, love is then our duty."[10]

In his periods of actual insanity, he had to be restrained from exposing his person, and he often roared for the Queen to come and satisfy his desires "in a voice like thunder and in a situation as to dress extremely distressing to behold".[11] Other excesses which he practised hardly bear repeating.

[7] McKenzie, *Christopher Smart.*

[8] See Guttmacher, *America's Last King,* for a full discussion.

[9] Stuart, *Regency Roundabout,* p. 1.

[10] Whitwell, *Analecta,* pp. 142–5. On another occasion, according to Withers, he declared, "As to religion, damme if I care one farthing about it. I am determined to eat, drink and whore as long as I can—and no longer" (*Hist. Royal Malady,* p. 44).

[11] Withers, *History of the Royal Malady,* p. 34.

Apart from those who actually had to be confined, there were many who simply underwent alternations of feeling. The case of Cowper, the poet, is worth studying in some detail, partly as helping us to understand the nature of this malady, and also as illustrating its connection with religious feeling. In it can be seen also the elements of fear of death, personal inadequacy, sense of guilt, and fear of the all-powerful father, in the form of a stern deity.

"I was struck, not long after my settlement in the Temple [1753] with such a dejection of spirits, as none but they who have felt the same, can have the least conception of," he writes.[12] "Day and night I was upon the rack, lying down in horror and rising up in despair. In this state of mind I continued near a twelvemonth." A little later, having been recommended a change of residence, he went to Freemantle, near Southampton, in beautiful country. Taking a walk one splen'id day, and sitting down on an eminence, "it was as if another sun had been kindled that instant in the heavens, on purpose to dispel sorrow and vexation of spirit. I felt the weight of all my misery taken off; my heart became light and joyful in a moment; I could have wept with transport had I been alone. I must needs believe that nothing less than the Almighty fiat could have filled me with such inexpressible delight."[13]

Returning to London he abandons his religious exercises, which he perceives were simply the reaction to his depression. But after a while his anxieties return when he finds himself about to become a clerk in the House of Commons, and feels himself inadequate for the post. He toys with the idea of suicide; tries to say the Creed, but has mysteriously forgotten the words. "I laid myself down, howling with horror, while my knees smote against each other. In this condition my brother found me, and the first words I spoke to him were, 'Oh, Brother, I am damned!'" His brother, according to the pious custom, sent for Martin Madan, who attempted to impress upon Cowper his utter sinfulness. Not surprisingly, he awoke next morning with a sense of terror and depression ten times stronger than before. He remained in this state of mind from December 7th, 1763, until the middle of the

12 *Memoir of the Early Life* . . . *by himself,* p. 9.
13 ib., p. 11.

following July. Writing this account in later life, he sees the irrational character of this sense of guilt, for he describes how "the accuser of the brethren was very busy with me night and day, bringing to my recollection in dreams the commission of long-forgotten sins, and charging upon my conscience things of an indifferent nature as atrocious crimes".[14] Fortunately, at this stage he consults a doctor, not a divine, and when the doctor assures him it is all a delusion, he feels better and begins to sleep well. In the course of his autobiography he describes several more such phases of elation and depression.

Psychiatrists tend to take the view that both melancholia and mania are regressions to a more primitive phase of psychic development: melancholia represents regression to the anal phase, mania to the oral. The manic returns to the primitive state in which the mother's breast was the source of all satisfaction and he was filled with bliss in his intimate contact with her. The manic, we may say, retreats to his infancy, and denies the reality of all painful later experiences. Since this involves a more drastic regression than melancholia, this would help to explain why it is a rarer phenomenon.

Regression is a process which occurs under stress (which is why we scream, as a baby does, when severely hurt) and so the existence of manic-depression in the eighteenth century certainly establishes the fact that people were finding adjustment difficult. Since manic-depression is much less general in the nineteenth century, some change of circumstances must have occurred: I saw that it must be part of my inquiry to discover, if possible, what that change was.

Another writer on this topic, Lewin, notes that in some kinds of mania the object of the operation seems to be to deny the demands of the super-ego. The mania has the character of a "flight into reality" in which painful thoughts are kept at bay by filling the mind with other ideas.[15] This seems to fit such cases as that of Cowper very well, and is not inconsistent with the previous explanation. Bearing in mind that the super-ego is formed by the introjection of a parental, principally a

14 ib., p. 60.
15 *Psychoanalysis of Elation*, Ch. 3. By the same token, the depressive phase represents an extreme consciousness of the demands of the super-ego; i.e. it reflects a sense of guilt, the real origins of which are unconscious.

paternal, image, it occurred to me that regression to the manic state could therefore be regarded as an escape from the father. The case of George III, with its obvious flouting of the rules of behaviour and freeing of impulses, is (it at once struck me) a clear instance of some kind of denial of the super-ego.

But Lewin makes the additional point that this explanation does not apply to all cases; and this seems to be confirmed by the fact that Cowper did not manifest such anti-social behaviour during his manic phases, but was simply filled with euphoria. I was puzzled by this, as I did not have any alternative explanation available—though I had some hunches about where to look for one. For the time being, however, I put the problem aside, and continued to study the negative aspect—the ideas of inhibition, depression, melancholia, and so on.

The period also shows a phenomenal incidence of suicide. This development, as far as I have been able to determine, became evident about the beginning of the century, and reached a peak about 1755, in which year, according to Gray, suicide was 'epidemical'. It remained a feature for which England was noted until the nineteenth century.[16]

In 1720 *Mercurius Politicus* says that more people commit suicide in Britain than in the rest of the world combined. By 1754 the *Gentleman's Magazine* writes, "Suicide begins to prevail so generally, that it is the most gallant exploit by which modern heroes chuse to signalise themselves. . . . Almost every day informs us that the coroners inquest has sat on the body of some miserable suicide and brought in the verdict *lunacy*."[17] The poets of death refer to it: Blair called it "Our island's shame, That makes her the reproach of neighbouring states", and Young, in his *Night Thoughts*, apostrophises the nation "O Britain! infamous for suicide". Foreign visitors such as Muralt and Pollnitz also note it: one of them (doubtless Le Blanc), writing anonymously in *Fog's Journal* in 1737, says that he heard almost daily, for several weeks after his arrival, of suicides, and could not restrain his astonishment. The point was reached at which insurance companies began to offer to

---

[16] However, Coyer said in 1777 that it was rarer than he had been led to expect—though he confirms the gloom of the English (*Nouvelles Observations*, pp. 259–60).

[17] *Gentleman's Magazine*, 1754, p. 95.

insure people against the possibility of their committing suicide, limiting the premiums to £300. Grosley adds that a special form of prayer against its temptations was introduced by the Church.[18]

In 1755 *The Gentleman's Magazine* carried a satirical advertisement, describing methods of committing suicide without inconveniencing others. The pistol shot, it points out, is not to be recommended, as it is liable to blow the brains about the room, "spoiling the paintings and other furniture, and leaving the body bloody and mangled, the countenance distorted and the features defaced; and at the same time alarming not only the family but the neighbourhood, so that all attempts to conceal it by pretending apoplexy or sudden death are ineffectual." It recommends instead the *Stygian spirit*, "a small vial of which may be held by a person in the midst of a large circle of gentlemen and ladies" and which is so potent "as instantly to kill him without affecting any other of the company". It is available at the Two Blue Posts in Frith Street at a guinea a phial, or gratis to any person who has been certified as a proper object of charity.[19]

Humour is frequently employed as a method of deflating a threat which is too alarming to accept at its real value, and I think it is in this sense that we must read the foregoing passage.

A school of writing defending suicide as a reasonable course emerged. However, this movement did not develop as far in England as it did on the Continent, probably because Englishmen were too alarmed by the topic. A storm of protest greeted *Biathanatos*, while Hume was ruined by Warburton for his essay on the topic, even though it was not actually published.

The existence of depressive states is not the only pathognomonic sign in the first half of the eighteenth century, however. Equally striking is the extraordinary preoccupation with the subject of death.[20] Funerals attracted immense attention and were staged with elaborate trappings of woe: invitation cards were sent out decorated with skulls, tomb-

[18] Grosley, *A Tour to London*, I, 229–34.

[19] *Gentleman's Magazine*, 1755, p. 43.

[20] Moore dates this from 1688, when William III came to the throne, and the traditional attitudes which had been in abeyance under the Stuarts again became fashionable, (*Backgrounds of English Literature*, pp. 152–3).

stones and other emblems of mortality, and the tombs themselves were often similarly garnished. Many a Puritan wore a ring garnished with a death's head to act as *memento mori*.[21] The author of *The Pilgrim's Guide, from his Cradle to his Deathbed*, a work which contains rules for funeral processions and hints on funeral etiquette, regrets living in a small village, since it means he so seldom has a chance to attend a good funeral. Major funerals evoked not only suitable sermons, often reprinted and circulated among the connoisseurs, but also poems, like that which celebrated the interment of the Duke of Grafton:

> "They divided his bowels, and laid at his feet
> Whilst they imbalmed his body with spices so sweet;
> Six weeks together they kept him from the clay
> Whilst the Nobles appointed his funeral day."[22]

Misson in his *Memoirs* (1698) comments on the unhealthy eagerness of the English to study dissolution at close range,[23] and the phenomenon became so striking that Steele was driven to criticise it in 1702 in *The Funeral, or Grief à la Mode*.

Naturally, this preoccupation evoked a considerable literature;[24] John Dunton, who recalls that he had been haunted by the fear of death from childhood,[25] made a considerable reputation as a religious bookseller, issuing an immense stream of necrophilous works. Drelincourt's *Defence Against the Fear of Death*, first translated in 1765, suddenly became popular about the end of the century, and had reached a seventeenth edition by 1751. Other popular works included *A Mourning Ring* (with blank space on the title-page for name of deceased).

It became the thing to spend a part of every day contemplating one's own funeral. The religious reformers, like Law, advised it; and lay writers repeated the invitation in language more mellifluous but no less

---

[21] See, for variants on this theme, Weber, *Aspects of Death in Art*, pp. 134 f.

[22] *The Noble Funeral of that Renowned Champion the Duke of Grafton*.

[23] Op. cit., pp. 88 ff. See also Le Blanc (1747), p. 67. Meister (*Letters*, p. 291) says, "The dead are kept longer above ground here than in any country in Europe."

[24] See Moore, *Backgrounds of English Literature*, Chapter 4.

[25] Dunton, *Life and Errors*, i, 26.

compelling. "Let us therefore now, kind Reader, every day make Funeral processions, or at least visit in meditation every hour our Tomb, as the place where our bodies must make so long abode. Celebrate we our selves our own Funerals, and invite to our Exequies Ambition, Pride, Choler, Luxury, Gluttony and all the other Passions."[26]

In the 'forties a fresh wave of death literature (though of a more romantic type) swept over the reading public. Young's *Night Thoughts*, a 10,000-line poem which Boswell called "a mass of the richest, grandest poetry that human genius has ever produced", appeared from 1742-5. Blair's *The Grave* was published in 1743 and had reached as many as forty-seven editions by 1798. Hervey's *Meditations among the Tombs* went through twenty-five editions between its appearance in 1745 and 1791. Parnell's *Night Piece on Death* (1721), Warton's *Pleasures of Melancholy* (1745), and the Wesleys' *Funeral Hymns* (1753) may also be mentioned.

In all these works there emerges an extraordinary *Schadenfreude*, but sometimes the person whose death is wished is another, sometimes it is oneself; that is, sometimes the feeling is sadistic, at others it is masochistic. Thus Dunton is struck by the thought that, since all must die, the whole world is but a kind of graveyard, and in this notion he finds something pleasant. "The entire world is but as it were a Cœmitary or Churchyard," he writes; "a walk into Church-yards and Charnels, though it be sad and melancholy, hath nevertheless something agreeable in it." Then comes the explanation: the thought of one's own mortality is more bearable if one can be sure that everyone else, and especially those one dislikes, will also be involved. Like Samson pulling down the temple, the depressive is prepared to write off his own future if he can at the same time ensure the destruction of everybody else. Dunton makes this clear enough when he continues, "How often have I taken pleasure to consider a great number of Dead men's Sculls arranged in one pile upon another with this conceit of the vanity, and arrogance, wherewith otherwise they have been filled."[27] Thomas Warton took pleasure in attending executions (as did many in the

[26] Dunton, *Pilgrim's Guide*, p. 195.
[27] ib., p. 196.

eighteenth century) and wrote sadistically gory ballads. Hervey observes with relish, "The poor voluptuary is himself a feast for fattened insects; the reptile riots in his flesh."[28]

Schadenfreude in its purest form is exhibited by Dunton's most successful publishing venture, *The Second Spira*, which describes in detail the agonies of mind of an avowed atheist when at the point of death. It sold 30,000 copies in six weeks; significantly enough, the sales slumped when it leaked out that it was only fiction.[29]

But in contrast with these, we find another and more specifically religious group, in which the idea of death is coupled with the self alone, and welcomed.

> "Ah, lovely Appearance of Death!
>   No Sight upon Earth is so fair.
> Not all the gay Pageants that *breathe*
>   Can with a dead Body compare.
> With solemn Delight I survey
>   The Corpse when the Spirit is fled,
> In love with the beautiful Clay
>   And long to lie in its stead,"

So Charles Wesley exclaims rhapsodically, in a hymn entitled 'On the Sight of a Corpse'[30]. The masochism becomes even more pronounced in another hymn:

> "Pain, my old Companion, Pain
>   Seldom parted from my Side,
> Welcome to thy Seat again,
>   Here, if GOD permits, abide:
> Pledge of sure-approaching Ease,
>   Haste to stop my wretched Breath,
> Rugged Messenger of Peace,
>   Joyful Harbinger of Death."[31]

[28] Hervey, *Meditations among the Tombs*, p. 76.

[29] Dunton, *Life and Errors*, i, 157.

[30] J. and C. Wesley, *Funeral Hymns*.

[31] J. and C. Wesley, *Hymns and Sacred Poems* (1749). Cited Ingram and Newton, *Hymns as Poetry*, pp. 134-5.

This seems to be the plea of one who not only finds life intolerable but has also given up all hope of conditions improving. Thus it unites the mood of depression with the death-wish.

But while the writer expects 'sure-approaching Ease' for himself, the religious individual almost invariably insisted that the after-life was going to be even more painful than this one for most people. One of the ghastliest books of piety of the period is a forgery entitled *The Visions of John Bunyan, Being his Last Remains, Giving an Account of the Glories of Heaven, and the Terrors of Hell, and of the World to Come* (1725). Attempts to describe the torments of the after-life, too painful to quote here, were common in the period.[32] John Wesley rejected Swedenborg's account of hell on the grounds that it asserted that hell was not filled with everlasting fire, but merely with red-hot ashes.

How closely the whole idea of death came to be associated with the idea of piety is well expressed in Law's remark, to which reference has already been made, "The vigour of the blood, the gaiety of our spirits, and the enjoyment of sensible pleasures, though the allowed signs of living men, are often the undeniable proofs of dead Christians."[33]

Law carries the masochistic element further too when he argues that "Suffering is to be sought", to "pay some part of that Debt which is due to Sin".[34] Not merely "self-denial", but "self-persecution" is necessary, indeed "even more necessary than they were in the first days of Christianity". However, "Christianity has no other Interest in this World than as it takes its members out of it."[35] The body, he adds, "is a mere sepulchre of the soul."

Wesley, not content with masochism, must needs impute sadism to God. God, he explains in a careful gloss on the scriptures, was *pleased* that Christ should be bruised for our iniquities.

Curiously enough, however, this elementary sado-masochistic element never gained a strong foothold: sadism was expressed only in sublimated forms, and justified on grounds of morality.

[32] Cf. Bunyan's *Grace Abounding*.
[33] Law, *Christian Perfection*, p. 27.
[34] ib., p. 148.
[35] ib., p. 41.

After working through a certain amount of this material, I formed a strong impression of the existence of a sort of mass neurosis. To analyse it was evidently an imperative necessity if one hoped to understand the period.

This did not present great difficulty. It was clear that the key to the subject was aggression. Suicide, it is now generally recognised, is caused primarily by the turning of aggressive impulses, which had formerly been directed outward, against the self. The sense of impending death is also derived from aggressive wishes, and specifically those rooted in the Œdipal situation. The infant's mind works in a primitive way: when frustrated it wishes blind destruction on the frustrating object, and, like the primitive savage, it believes that its wishes are magically powerful and effective. Accordingly, when, in the Œdipal situation, it sees the father as the interloper, it directs towards him annihilating wishes. Believing these wishes to be potent, it fears the results of its own action, for if it annihilates the father, it will be left without support. At the same time, it fears the father's retaliation. The more powerful its own annihilating wish, the more powerful the father's retaliation is expected to be. Thus the father-image grows in stature in proportion to the infant's frustration: this, incidentally, is why the father (when introjected to form the super-ego) is more severe and terrifying than the human father could ever be, and may even be terrifying when the real father is mild and permissive.

In short, the sense of impending doom, the fear of death, is the product of the infant's frustration. If parents are in fact severe, this frustration will be increased, and the aggression strengthened. Thus the whole picture can be related to a struggle between the infant and the father-image. Such, at any rate, is the account which psychoanalysis would offer, in its most simplified form. It suggested that my next step should be to look more closely for signs of some such struggle in this depressive religious group.

But it also suggested that the whole subject of aggression, and how it is handled, is of central importance in the eighteenth century, and the next logical steps in the investigation seemed to be to examine the whole question of aggression as impartially as possible, in its various manifestations.

The most obvious form which aggression took was that of an interest in violent and bloodthirsty sports. Bull-running and bear-baiting, the interest in boxing, the readiness of the crowd to hurl stones and filth at those in the pillory, betray another kind of violence. It is sometimes said that these interests were based on a pleasure in cruelty, i.e. on sadism. This does not seem to me to be the case.

Such contests were often cruel, but the cruelty was not the *raison d'être* of the proceedings. People were not interested in cruelty, they were simply impervious to it. The owners of bulls and other animals kept for baiting treated them with great kindness between bouts, in just the same spirit as the owner of a whippet might to-day. (Archenholtz emphasised that the English are remarkably kind to animals, and explains that cock-fighting is not considered cruel, as each bird has a chance.)[36] The only sport which might seem an exception to this assertion was "throwing at cocks"—a contest in which men threw wooden billets at a tethered cock, or duck, until it was dead. The man who delivered the *coup de grâce* was awarded the corpse (there was also a variant, 'threshing the hen', in which the bird was carried by a man on horseback). Here the main interest was a display of skill, coupled with the element of prize-winning. In any case, this was a medieval activity, proper only to Shrovetide, which was rapidly going out and which disappeared about the middle of the century.

What the onlooker seems to have been interested in was a situation of a very special type: a situation in which two creatures were locked in a conflict not of their own choosing, from which there was no escape except by death or complete defeat. Great ingenuity was displayed in finding variants on this theme: it was not simply that dogs were set on bears—an ape would be tied to a donkey, fireworks would be tied to a bull, and so on. The reaction of eighteenth-century man to a conflict situation is beautifully shown by an incident that took place in America, in which a settler came upon a man locked in the embrace of a grizzly bear. Though armed himself, his immediate reaction was to drop his gun and cheer on the contestants.[37]

The placing of a person in the pillory may also be seen as the placing

[36] Archenholtz, *Picture of England*, p. 262.
[37] Communicated by Mary Settle.

of a person in an intolerable situation, and the pelting of such people (curiously resembling the throwing at cocks) drew large crowds whose interest was to see how the victim would stand up to it.

In some parts of England contests were held in which men attempted to kick one another to death. Here again is a situation of no escape; the demand is made that one should show determination and courage in face of pain. And the period is full of stories of detachment in appalling circumstances, like the man who, on seeing his leg shot off by a cannon-ball, exclaimed, "Dead Chelsea, by God!"[38] Perhaps one can link with this kind of attitude the stoicism of the dandies, or of Hervey when Lord Cobham spat into his hat. ("Has your Lordship any further occasion for my hat?" he said, before challenging him to a duel.) Here, it may be said, is the ideal of self-control in a very different context from that of the Puritans.

But it was not my purpose to pursue the question of stoicism and self-control at this point. I was looking for instances of aggression. The next most obvious instance was that of the Mohocks and their kin. Lecky says, "The impunity with which outrages were committed in the ill-lit and ill-guarded streets of the eighteenth century can now hardly be realised. In 1712 a club of young men of the higher classes, who assumed the name of Mohocks, were accustomed nightly to sally out drunk into the streets to hunt the passers-by and to subject them in mere wantonness to the most atrocious outrages. One of their favourite amusements, called 'tipping the lion', was to squeeze the nose of their victim flat upon his face and to bore out his eyes with their fingers. Among these were the 'sweaters', who formed a circle round their prisoner and pricked him with their swords till he sank exhausted to the ground, the 'dancing masters' so-called from their skill in making men caper by thrusting swords into their legs, the 'tumblers', whose favourite amusement was to set women on their heads and commit various indecencies and barbarities on the limbs that were exposed. Maid servants, as they opened their masters' doors, were waylaid, beaten, and their faces cut. Matrons inclosed in barrels were rolled down the steep and stony incline of Snow Hill. Watchmen were

[38] That is to say, a candidate for the Chelsea Hospital for wounded soldiers

beaten unmercifully and their noses slit. Country gentlemen went to the theatre as if in time of war, accompanied by their armed retainers."[39]

This trend had begun to emerge a century before: the Mohocks were the logical descendants of the Roaring Boys and Roysters of 1604, and the Tityre-tues and Bugles twenty years later. This kind of behaviour continued, on and off, right into the Victorian period.[40] It seems to be marked by a desire to humiliate, and to represent a fairly straightforward type of resentment. The young men involved went about in gangs, and, in one or two accounts, they flee when offered determined resistance by a much smaller party. So no question of proving personal courage was involved, it would seem.

As usual, we must turn to the most extreme instances of aggressive resentment if we wish to discover what processes were at work. Perhaps the epitome of aggressive resentment is found in the second Lord Camelford, who was apparently so uncertain of his own courage, or so resentful of dominance, that he must always resent any slight, even imaginary ones. When only twenty-two and an officer in the Navy, he challenged the captain of his ship to a duel. The following year he killed his first man, and a series of such events followed. In 1799 he was fined £500 for knocking a man downstairs. In 1801 he fought a mob single-handed. A contemporary plate shows his aggressive stance and jutting chin.[41] Captain Macnamara was a rather similar case, Squire Mytton another, who liked to hunt cross-country at night, and deliberately overturned his carriage when a guest said he'd never been in a carriage accident, just to show him what it was like.

In cases such as these, aggression is no doubt coupled with the need to prove one's potency, and the duel, with its obvious sexual symbolism, embodies this principle. The duel is fought to protect honour, and what worse imputation upon one's honour than impotence?

"Mad Fitzgerald" is perhaps a more complex case. In addition to numerous duels, in some of which he did not scruple to fire at his opponent while on the ground, he was involved in many extraordinary

---

[39] Lecky, *History of England in the Eighteenth Century*, i, 142.
[40] For a full account, see Jones, *Clubs of the Georgian Rakes*, p. 14.
[41] See White, *Scandalmonger*, Ch. 2, for an account and a reproduction of the plate.

incidents. He shot up the house of a man who failed to invite him there; called at Lord Altamont's and asked to see his wolfhound, which he promptly shot; and fired at Denis Browne, Altamont's brother, in broad daylight in Sackville Street, Dublin. On another occasion he hunted Browne, who was a relative, through the bogs on horseback. Among other exploits, he kidnapped his own father for failing to pay his allowance.[42] (Such incidents indicate the presence of father-rejection, in addition to the need to prove his own valour.)

To sum up, then, we find many aggressive individuals in the eighteenth century—some force must have been at work to produce such a high level of aggression. But these aggressive individuals may be divided into two broad groups: those that directed their aggression outward, on to others, and those who turned it inward on themselves, as we have seen that the Puritans and moralists did.

Having reached this conclusion, I began to feel that the whole inquiry was resolving itself into two questions. First, why was there such a high level of aggression? Second, why was this aggression increasingly turned against the self? For it was this trend which seemed to be behind the increasing force of reform. Actually, the issue is not as simple as that, but the questions are good ones; and to the second the theory we have been engaged in discussing provides a plausible answer: aggression is turned back on the self when the father becomes too dangerous a figure to threaten. In the next chapter I shall attempt to show that this is precisely what was occurring.

It promptly occurred to me that the preoccupation with situations of conflict to which I have just been referring, in which the opponents were equally matched, reproduced very closely the severe struggle which was occurring between the individual and his father-image, at the unconscious level. For in this case, too, the conflict could only be solved by the defeat or death of the weaker. (In the next chapter I shall bring forward evidence encountered in another field which strongly supports this conclusion.)

Moreover, it is a conflict which depends on strength of will rather than physical equipment. The cock which loses its nerve and runs

[42] Ashton, *Eighteenth Century Waifs*, pp. 135–76. See also Sir Jonah Barrington's *Personal Sketches*.

away, like the man who refuses a duel, spoils the sport. The ideal is not an overwhelming victory but to get two equally matched opponents and see which can hold out longer. To these elements in personality we shall return from time to time for further comment.

To resume the argument so far, the eighteenth-century personality is marked by two factors working hand-in-hand—to say nothing of others, discussed elsewhere—these being a tendency to depressive states, and a preoccupation with death. It may be the case that the introjection of aggression itself contributes to a sense of depression—a sense of impending doom is obviously not very encouraging.

And there, for some time, I left it. It was not until many months later, when reading through biographical material of the Victorian period, that the last link in the chain fell into my hands. I read how Sterling, a year after the death of his loved wife, himself died of no specific cause. And a year later still, his sister died equally inexplicably. At the same time I read how the elder sisters of F. D. Maurice turned to a more Calvinist, and thus death-centred, form of religion after the death of two loved cousins. I then realised that to experience the death of a loved person is the thing which most powerfully activates the melancholic's death-wish. Thus the two themes of death and depression are finally linked.

So the point reached in the argument is this. The problem which the average individual faced in the eighteenth century was to escape from the pressure of his death-wishes, a pressure which was created by the terrifying nature of the father-image. One solution, as we have seen, was regression, first to the depressive, then, if necessary, to the manic state.

Mania, however, is not the only way in which the psyche can cope with the depression caused by too severe a super-ego. There is a more radical kind of adjustment possible, to which the name 'conversion' is given—though conversion is a word which seems to be applied to two or three different psychic processes which are clinically distinct. Conversion was, of course, an important feature of Methodism, though Methodism had no monopoly of it, and played an important role in the period under review. Let us therefore examine it in detail.

CHAPTER 8

THE RAPTUR'D SOUL

RELIGIOUS CONVERSION, in the eighteenth century, is principally associated with the name of Wesley. Actually, it was widely practised before him by the Moravians, by Hwel Harris and others in Wales, as well as by Whitefield; while it remained a central feature of Evangelical belief until the middle of the nineteenth century and also figured in the Tractarian movement. A well-known mid-century example is the conversion of Brownlow North in 1854. Diaries recounting the writer's conversion are even commoner in the early nineteenth century than the eighteenth. The psychological state which gave rise to it must, therefore, have continued to exist throughout the period, and the psychological consequences of conversion must have continued to be active in society.

As evoked by Wesley it was a pretty strenuous experience. "Some said they felt just as if a sword was running through them; others, that they thought a great weight lay on them, as if it would squeeze them in to the earth. Some said they were quite choked, so that they could not breathe; others that their hearts swelled ready to burst; and others that it was as if their hearts, as if their inside, as if their whole body was tearing all to pieces."[1] Elizabeth Booth screamed, "He is tearing off my breasts, he is pouring melted lead down my throat," and tried to throw herself out of the window when Wesley approached.[2]

So powerful was Wesley's technique that in the years 1739–43 he drove twenty-three persons mad (nine of them permanently), struck two blind, caused eighty-five to drop as dead, and induced in un-counted numbers convulsive tearings, groans and trembling.[3] The

[1] Wesley, *Journal*, iii, 69–70. Cf. also vii, 153.
[2] *Journal*, iv, 70–71.
[3] Dimond, *Psychol. of the Meth. Revival*, p. 127.

numbers may indeed be greater—these are only the recorded cases—and they certainly would have been greater if Wesley, alarmed at what was happening, had not gone out of his way to discourage such responses.[4]

Clearly this is a phenomenon of importance to the present study. In order to discover something about its origins and significance, I turned first to the diaries of the earliest Methodist ministers, which are fortunately numerous since Wesley specifically instructed the earliest converts to record their experiences. All agree that conversion produced a lightening of the spirits, even a positive ecstasy. Conversion provided (as Christopher Hopper said) "a glorious and undeniable change".[5] Peter Jaco said, "In that moment, it seemed to me as though a new creation had taken place. I felt no guilt, no distress of any kind. My soul was filled with light and love."[6] Joseph Cownley said that suddenly the darkness vanished away from his soul and the Sun of righteousness arose with healing in his wings. "He was filled with Divine joy, pleasure smiled in his eyes, and heaven reigned in his heart."[7] These are words which recall Fox's famous account of his conversion, "All things were new; and all the creation gave another smell unto me than before, beyond what words can utter. I knew nothing but pureness and innocency and righteousness, being renewed up into the image of God to the state of Adam, which he was in before the fall."[8]

Jaco felt "no guilt"; Fox "innocency and righteousness". Pleasure smiled in Cownley's eyes. The change was clearly one which relieved a sense of guilt.

It is quite noticeable in the lives of those who have undergone conversion that, though fundamentally serious, they are cheerful in their manner, and seem free from those fits of depression which formerly afflicted them. We can see this not only in Wesley himself,

---

[4] Dimond, *Psychol. of the Meth. Revival*, pp. 127 ff, based on an analysis of 234 recorded cases.

[5] Jackson (ed.), *Lives of the Methodist Preachers*, i, 189.

[6] ib., i, 262.

[7] ib., ii, 4.

[8] *Jnl. Bicent.*, i, 28–9. See also Brayshaw, *Personality of George Fox*, p. 79.

but in such figures as William Wilberforce at the end of the eighteenth century, or Hurrell Froude in the nineteenth. It seems reasonable, then, to regard conversion as a psychological adjustment whose actual purpose is to relieve guilt and free the individual from his sense of depression. It may well be that other forms of conversion exist, and I would not put this forward as universally true, but it seems to have been true of conversion as it was known in the eighteenth century. I therefore looked for material which might throw light on how this very desirable adjustment was achieved.

The second feature of such conversions, as Dimond points out, is that the behaviour described may in many cases be interpreted as a struggle with the converter. Elizabeth Booth clearly felt that some frightful aggression was taking place; and the 'rage' and 'fury' of the victims are explicitly stated in a remarkable passage of a letter written by John Cennick to John Wesley in 1739:

"On Monday night, I was preaching at the school, on the forgiveness of sins, when numbers cried out with a loud and bitter cry. Indeed it seemed that the devil and the powers of darkness were come among us. My mouth was stopped. The cries were terrifying. It was pitch dark; it rained much; and the wind blew vehemently. Large flashes of lightning and loud claps of thunder mingled with the screams and exclamations of the people. The hurry and confusion cannot be expressed. The whole place seemed to resemble the habitation of apostate spirits; many raving up and down, and crying 'The devil will have me; . . . I am gone, gone for ever!'

". . . Some cried out with a hollow voice, 'Mr. Cennick! Bring Mr. Cennick!' I came to all that desired me. Then they spurned me with all their strength, grinding their teeth and expressing all the fury that heart can conceive. Their eyes were staring and their faces swollen, and several have since told me, that when I drew near, they felt fresh rage, and longed to tear me in pieces. I never saw the like, not even the shadow of it before."[9]

According to the best authorities, conversion generally occurs after the loss, and especially the death, of a loved person, usually of the

[9] Cited Tyerman, Life . . . of John Wesley, i, 263, from the Methodist Mag. (1778), p. 179.

opposite sex. Thus St. Augustine's conversion followed the loss of his beloved mistress. With this in mind, I was inclined to look for some evidence of this sort in the diaries of the Methodist preachers. However, I found nothing of the sort: what I did find was, first, that in many cases conversion followed the death of the father, or sometimes of a father-figure, and secondly that this father was not loved but hated.

Thus John Haime says that as a boy he was "very undutiful to his parents, given to cursing, lying and sabbath breaking". Then he describes a vivid and striking incident. One day he went into a lonely field, and after a passionate bout of weeping, he "threw a stick at God, with the utmost enmity". As he stood there he was filled with the urge to curse God. He tried to do so, but could not bring himself to take the risk. Suddenly he abandoned the overwhelming struggle, and at once he experienced a revulsion of feeling and his heart was filled with love for God.[10] It seems pretty clear that he is struggling against a severe father-figure, whom he hates, but the dangers of so doing are too great, and he finally submits. He represses all the hatred, leaving only the love at the conscious level.

As I have already noted, the regular psychological mechanism is for the child's fear of the father to be proportionate to the strength of his own annihilating wishes towards the father. He feels, so to speak, that the more powerfully he hates the father, the more powerfully will the father hate him. Moreover, owing to the infantile belief that such wishes are magically effective, he tends to interpret any misfortune to the father as a result of such death-dealing wishes, and this produces guilt. These processes, familiar to the clinical psychologist to-day, can be seen at work in the Methodist diaries very vividly. For instance, John Nelson writes, "When I was turned a little of sixteen, my father was taken ill, which I thought was for my wickedness"; and he adds that he earnestly prayed to God that he might be allowed to die in his stead—an almost explicit statement of the way in which the death-wish is turned against the self.[11]

In the diary of Christopher Hopper we find an even more explicit

[10] *Lives of the Methodist Preachers*, i, 272.
[11] ib., i, 7.

statement. Before his conversion he "took a diabolical pleasure in hanging dogs, worrying cats, and killing birds and insects, mangling and cutting them to pieces". He particularly recalls smashing up a large number of frogs with stones. The same night he had a terrifying nightmare. "I dreamed I fell into a deep place full of frogs and they seized on me from head to foot, and begun to eat the flesh off my bones. I was in great terror and found exquisite pain until I awoke, sweating and trembling and half dead with fear."[12] The frogs which he had sought to destroy end by destroying him.

Hopper also demonstrates the influence of the father-figure, for after the death of his father, and despite the fact that the farm had to be sold up, he became happy, recovered his health, and began to see the world in a different light. "I saw transitory objects in another point of view than I had done during the time of my illness," he says, revealing that he realises his depression *was* an illness.

His fears returned, however, after he had had a narrow escape from death, and it was the preaching of a Mr. Reeves, in 1742, which effected his final conversion.[13]

Thus while, on the face of it, the death of the hated father should seem to be a relief, and a removal of the threat, at the unconscious level, this event is liable to activate the guilt feelings. At the same time, though the father is hated, his love is always deeply desired, and to some extent it is true to say that he is hated for not being loving enough. Thus his death removes all hope of ever establishing a love-relationship with him, while it also leaves the son obliged to stand on his own legs, without support. Acceptance of the heavenly Father thus represents a desperate solution: one which restores the wanted love-relationship, and it is also significant that the heavenly Father is also seen as offering support, "Eternal Father, strong to save. . . ."

Another noticeable feature of the Methodist diaries is that, in almost

[12] ib., i. 181.

[13] These patterns are repeated with extraordinary uniformity. Thus Pawson, -when fifteen, was tempted to curse his parents, but after reading *Grace Abounding* trembled exceedingly when he heard of anyone coming to an untimely end, fearing that that would one day be his fate. Pawson, *A Short Account*, pp. 97–8. Cf. also Longden, *Life*, pp. 6–7, 35.

every case, it is stated that the sense of guilt, depression, and fear of the father-figure date from infancy. Thus Jaco states, "From my infancy, I had very serious impressions, and awful thoughts of God."[14] Joseph Cownley "reflected on eternity and the awful concerns thereof", from "his first conscious perceptions".[15] William Hunter "felt a degree of the fear of God when very young, and sweet drawings of love. Sometimes the thoughts of death were very dreadful to me, so that I felt very unhappy".[16] This supports the idea that the psychic situation which provides the conditions for conversion are laid down at a very early age.

Hunter also adds, revealingly enough, "My father was very severe with me and I dreaded him much: and yet I was often guilty of much disobedience against him."[17] The fear of death is also a constant factor, and so is the idea of judgment. Thus John Nelson writes, "When I was between nine and ten years old I was horribly terrified with the thoughts of death and judgment, whenever I was alone."[18] He was particularly terrified when his father read to him aloud from *Revelation* xx (which describes the Last Judgment) and had a vision in which he saw that only a minority would be saved. His statement also betrays the fear of punishment for sin, as when he says, "Whenever I had committed any known sin, either against God or man, I used to be so terrified that I shed many tears in private." And again, "When I was about sixteen, I heard a sermon in our own church, which deprived me of rest in the night; nor durst I sin as I had done before for many days." That the sins to which he was tempted soon became pre-eminently sexual is suggested by the fact that he prayed repeatedly that "God would preserve me, and give me a wife, that I might live with her" in order to prevent him from falling into "scandalous sins".[19]

Jaco's experience was very similar. He had "many a restless night"

[14] *Lives . . . Methodist Preachers*, i, 261. The same is true of later conversions; (Pawson, Bourne (ed. Walford)), etc. It is also true of women. (See, for instance, *Life of Selina, Countess of Huntingdon*.)

[15] *Lives . . . Methodist Preachers*, ii, 2.

[16] ib., ii, 240.

[17] ib., ii, 241.

[18] ib., i, 6.

[19] ib., i, 6, 7, 8.

and suffered from bad dreams. He adds that his father was "a very serious man".[20]

The picture which emerges from these and similar testimonies is distinctly that of a threatening father-figure, whose punishment for sin is greatly to be feared. So powerful are the aggressions that the unhappy wretches are often tempted to suicide, as Thomas Mitchell records.

At the same time, there are signs that what these unhappy men really desired was to be loved by this father whom they felt to be so severe. This is well brought out by Haime, who, after he had become filled with the love of God, was told by one of Whitefield's preachers that this was simply an illusion, "the work of the devil". The sense of despair which ensued was so great that he nearly caved in entirely. But one day, crying to the Lord for mercy, he was answered by an impression of the words, "I have loved thee with an everlasting love", whereupon "my soul melted within me and I was filled with joy unspeakable".[21]

The way in which the guilt-ridden individual struggles with the father-figure is demonstrated with great clarity in the case of John Newton, the slave-trading skipper who afterwards became the prophet of the Evangelical movement and the friend of Cowper.[22] His father, a sea-captain who had been educated by the Jesuits, was haughty in manner and severe with his son. During his absences at sea the child was left much to his mother, a pious Dissenter, who had taught him, by the age of six, to repeat from memory the whole of Dr. Watts' *A Preservative from the Sins and Follies of Youth*. He was particularly struck by the Biblical passage in which children who mock the prophet Elisha are eaten by bears. His mother died when he was six, and after a few years at school, where he was severely treated, he was taken off on voyages with his father, and was left alone for long periods, for the crew did not dare speak to the severe captain's son. During this period he continued piously reading the scriptures, fasting and practising penances.

[20] ib., i, 261.
[21] ib., i, 276.
[22] See Martin, *John Newton*.

At the age of seventeen he was seized by a press gang and sent to sea. He seems to have felt resentment against his father, who could have obtained his release but did not. Soon after, he left the ship without permission, probably to visit his father, whose own vessel happened to be nearby, and was flogged before the Fleet for desertion. This experience, which he resented as most unjust, developed in him a terrific rage; he toyed with the idea of murdering the captain of his ship, who had ordered the flogging. He became a militant atheist.[23] Obtaining a transfer to a slaver, he became "exceedingly vile", preaching atheism and libertinism to his companions, and writing a song mocking the captain. Here we see, clearly enough, rejection of the father-figure and of his morality, under the stimulus of intolerable injustice and pain.

His reconversion to acceptance of the father shows the characteristic signs of death-fears. Despite a strong constitution the slightest indisposition filled him with the feeling that he might be going to die. If letters from his betrothed in England failed to reach him at the ports at which his vessel called, he at once speculated that she must be dead. On his return from Africa at the age of twenty-three, the ship encountered a tremendous storm and seemed, after some days, to be in danger of foundering. Faced with a genuine threat of death, he began to pray. Soon afterwards the storm abated: the rescue seemed to him miraculous. Not long after this, he read Doddridge's work *Some Remarkable Passages in the Life of the Hon. Col. Jas. Gardiner*, a story similar to his own: Gardiner, the son of a religious mother, renounced Christianity, but was reconverted by a devotional book. Newton now became so pious that his fiancée refused for a while to marry him, as being too good for her. It is, I believe, significant that his conversion took place in the same year as the death of his father (and presumably soon after that event).

We may suppose that it was his growing fear of death which made him reluctant to return to the dangers of a seafaring life; for after postponing this event on various pretexts, when he could do so no longer he suddenly fell down and remained insensible for an hour.[24] Although

23 Later he toyed with moon-worship: the moon is a mother-symbol.
24 Though described as a stroke, the facts suggest a sub-arachnoid hæmorrhage. William Grimshaw also fell down without warning and was unconscious for some time. See *Grimshaw of Haworth*, p. 63.

there were no after-effects other than some temporary headache and dizziness, he never went to sea again.

This account makes it clear, I think, that libertinism must be regarded as a rejection of the father-figure. Whereas matrism consists of having a permissive morality, libertinism consists of an active defiance of patrist morality. The matrist may have illicit relationships, but they are usually of some duration and have a profound emotional basis while they last. The patrist engages in a career of seduction, as if to prove to the world how little he thinks of chastity, and the trouble he often takes to advertise the fact supports the interpretation. Similarly, while the matrist worships something in the nature of a mother deity (I am speaking of matrists of all periods, not just those of the eighteenth century) the patrist feels a need to tear down and humiliate a father deity: this provides an explanation for the activities of the Hell-Fire clubs, which were reputed to engage in parodies of religious worship. (Whether they really did so seems to be a matter of some doubt: but the mere fact that this was thought the sort of thing they were likely to do is itself indicative.)[25] We can also see the element of father-rejection in a libertine like the fourth Duke of Wharton, whose first act on reaching his nonage was to ally himself with the Young Pretender, that is, the leader of the rebellion against the monarch. The fact that later, after his father's death, he settled down to a life of sober statesmanship is also suggestive. (That he was able to do so without a religious conversion I take to indicate that, although he rejected the father, he carried a relatively small load of guilt.)

If this analysis is correct, it follows that a libertine is not a different species of animal from a Puritan: he is only a Puritan in reverse. A Puritan is one who accepts the father-figure, a libertine is one who rejects it. Excessive severity may provoke libertinism—as, for example, it did in the case of the Quaker John Howard's son[26]—and Puritanism finds its most powerful recruits in libertines who come to abandon their defiance of the father-figure.

It is therefore erroneous to speak of Puritanism as a reaction to libertinism, or vice versa; or to argue, as moralists often do, that

[25] Jones, *Clubs of Georgian Rakes*, Ch. 3.
[26] Field, *Life of John Howard*, pp. 48-9.

Puritans had to be strict in order to cope with the licentious behaviour with which they were surrounded. The only conclusion which such facts justify is that the methods of child-upbringing were such that, instead of finding a reasonable compromise between acceptance and rejection, many people were driven into extreme positions. Puritanism and libertinism are both pathological states, and the results of the same causes. The defect of eighteenth-century upbringing was that it produced very many people whose psychological tensions were so acute that they could not maintain equipoise, and tended to swing to one or other extreme.

To sum up, then, conversion represents an escape from an intolerable situation.

The next step seemed to be to study how it was that conversion was induced. In many cases, the person concerned seems to have felt a vague sense of dissatisfaction, and to have gone about looking for some solution to his problems. Thus Mitchell, together with a friend, "were both . . . under deep convictions, but knew not what to do to be saved." Nelson went to London, looking for he knew not what. He tries in turn Catholics, Dissenters, Quakers and other sects. The Quakers nearly "suited the state of my soul" but "showed no remedy".[27]

Before conversion occurs, the sense of guilt and depression reaches an intolerable pitch. Jaco's conviction of guilt increased till he was "driven to the brink of despair", and continued in this state for four months.[28] Hanby was seized with such horror as made him run home and shut the door with all speed.[29] Wright's eyes were "a fountain of tears". Cownley says he frequently threw himself upon the ground, "crying out to God with inconceivable anguish of mind, 'No misery is equal to this: a wounded spirit who can bear?' "[30] Many of them denied themselves necessary food, and "thought by abstinence and mortification to appease the Divine displeasure".

When one has read a score or more of these frightening descriptions of such extremes of mental agony, it becomes patent that we are look-

[27] *Lives* . . . *Methodist Preachers*, ii, 240–2.
[28] ib., i, 262.
[29] ib., ii, 118.
[30] ib., ii, 2–3.

ing at men who are absolutely at the end of their tether. There is no alternative for them but to make some drastic psychological readjustment, or go mad. Some did go mad, and it is, relatively, an indication of strength that others made a readjustment, even if it was a pathological one, in the sense that it represented a partial retreat from reality. The thought which brings release is, of course, the thought that Christ died to save *them* personally. They all stress this: that Christ died to save others, they have heard: but they never applied it to their own case. As Charles Wesley cried—and the italics are his:

> I felt my LORD'S atoning Blood
> Close to *my* Soul applied:
> *Me, me* He lov'd—the Son of GOD
> For *me*, for *me* he died!

Then came the deep, ineffable peace, and it inspires these rather unimaginative, ill-educated men, whose writings are normally pedestrian in the extreme, to a sudden burst of poetry, "I felt such a sudden and delightful change as I never before conceived possible. My joy was indeed unspeakable; my hope full of immortality; and my peace flowed like a river."[31]

The conversion, it should be added, is often followed by a relapse; doubt creeps in again, and it is often after a narrow escape from death, or some other situation of stress, that faith is restored. No doubt there were many who never recovered it. It is also noticeable that many achieved the moment of conversion by reading devotional books; by studying these books we can uncover the process involved.

The Dissenters developed a systematic technique for activating the death-fears. The first stage is to intensify the conviction of sin and the fear of death; then, when a suitable tension has been induced, the hope of salvation is suddenly held out. Thus Law says that the proper subject for evening meditation is death, "Let your prayers contain everything that can affect and awaken your mind into just apprehensions of it." He recommends the following exercise, after retiring to bed

---

[31] Duncan Wright in *Lives* . . . *Methodist Preachers*, ii, 118.

each night: "Represent to your imagination, that your bed is your grave; that all things are ready for your interment; that you are to have no more to do with this world; and that it will be owing to God's great mercy, if you ever see the light of the sun again, or have another day to add to your works of piety. . . . All this in the silence and darkness of the night is a practice that will soon have excellent effects upon your spirit."[32] Doddridge is even more explicit. He announces at the start that he "will labour to fix a deep and awful *Conviction of Guilt*" upon the conscience of the reader. He will strip him of his excuses, show him God's condemnation, and how helpless he is—to each of these aims a chapter will be devoted. Then he will explain the doctrine of salvation through Christ. Then, assuming that the thoughtless reader has been suitably affected, he will turn and address himself "as compassionately as I can, to . . . *a Soul overwhelmed* with a sense of the greatness of its sins, and trembling under the Burthen, as if there were *no more Hope* for him in GOD". Nor is the death-wish forgotten, for after some excursions on the subject of Languor in Religion, he says, "We shall then labour to illustrate and assist the *Delight* with which he may *look forward* to the awful Solemnities of *Death* and *Judgment*."[33] This was the book which converted William Wilberforce.

Wesley's technique was similar; we are told that the crowds he addressed tended to pass through curiosity, astonishment, and fear, to awe. While to upper-class gatherings Wesley usually adopted a stern tone, to lower-class audiences he spoke tenderly, emphasising the peace of mind to be attained: "By this faith we are saved from all uneasiness of mind, from the anguish of a wounded spirit, from discontent, from fear and sorrow of heart, and from that inexpressible listlessness and weariness, both of the world and ourselves, which we had so helplessly laboured under for many years. . . . In this we find that love of God and all mankind which we had elsewhere sought in vain."[34] The appeal to desire for paternal love could hardly be stated more clearly.

Dimond says that Wesley sought to produce a suspension of critical

---

[32] Law, *Serious Call*, p. 339.
[33] Doddridge, *Rise and Progress*, Chapter I, Design.
[34] *Earnest Appeal*, p. 5.

faculties: the listeners were to feel, not to think. So effective was his appeal that crowds of several thousand gathered to hear him.[35]

Religiously-inclined parents also took, as we shall see further later, great trouble to exacerbate these death-fears as much as possible.[36] James Clegg records how he was boarded out, at the age of eight, on a certain Mrs. Bury. Mr. Bury was "a ffudling man" but his wife was a serious Christian. One evening she told him how "the wicked must be tormented in fire, and that to eternity". "I shall never forget," he writes, "how that word struck me." Mrs. Bury, with a sharp psychological insight, then went out, leaving the eight-year-old child in the house alone. "I fell to thinking of that eternity, and the more I thought at it, the more I was amazed, frightened and troubled. I wept bitterly, fearing it would be my lott to be so tormented. Then I began to pray as well as I could, but continued full of trouble all that night, and for some time after, and I cannot say that the impression ever quite went off." Later, these impressions were powerfully reinforced by hearing a funeral sermon, and he subsequently became a Nonconformist minister.[37]

These considerations may enable us to understand better the difference between Calvinism and Methodism. In Calvinism the proposition put forward is that there is absolutely *nothing* which men can do to ensure that God receives them into his love. God has decided in advance whom he will receive (the "doctrine of election") and if you are not on the list there is nothing to be done. Psychologically, therefore, we must regard it as an attitude of total despair about the possibility of winning the father's affection. The only possible solution is the masochistic one of enjoying the position. Thus Jonathan Edwards, the New England Calvinist, writes referring to the doctrine of predestination, "From my childhood up, my mind had been full of objections to the doctrine of God's sovereignty, in choosing whom he would to eternal life, and rejecting whom he pleased; leaving them

---

[35] Dimond, *Psychol. of the Meth. Revival*, pp. 115 ff. Whitefield attracted crowds of up to 20,000 (see *Gentleman's Magazine* 1739).

[36] In Chapter 16, where the whole question of the upbringing of children will be discussed.

[37] *Diary of James Clegg*, p. 19.

eternally to perish, and be everlastingly tormented in hell. It used to appear like a horrible doctrine to me. But I remember the time very well, when I seemed to be convinced, and fully satisfied, as to this sovereignty of God, and his justice in thus eternally disposing of men . . . I have often since had not only a conviction, but a *delightful* conviction. The doctrine has very often appeared exceedingly pleasant, bright, and sweet. Absolute sovereignty is what I love to ascribe to God . . ." etc.[38]

Since it is natural to regard the doctrine of predestination as 'horrible' it is clear that the adjustment achieved is an unnatural one; that is to say, to convince oneself that eternal torment, from which one has not even an outside chance of escaping, is delightful represents a retreat from reality. Some peace of mind is obtained at the cost of refusing to recognise objective facts; this is the course followed by the psychotic.[39] It is a doctrine which is apt to lead to the awkward conclusion that, if one is certainly damned, one may as well enjoy oneself as far as possible in this life (a doctrine known as Antinomianism): Calvinists had to go to some lengths to find a way round such an unpalatable conclusion.

Methodism, on the other hand, says: One can attain to God's love, provided one has faith, i.e. performs an act of psychological adjustment in which the guilt-feelings arising from aggression are dispersed by an act of faith, while, at the same time and by the same formula, the converted person secures for himself a father's love. Here again the result is achieved by a retreat from reality. Unable to find himself an earthly love-object, the converted person settles for a supernal one. In fact, if we take the view that the Deity is not in fact either a father or a mother, since these are human roles, and that to see the Deity as either represents the projection of such roles on to Him to meet a need in the projector, then we can say, without necessarily implying any disbelief in the existence of the Deity, that the converted person substitutes for a

38 Edwards, *Some Account*, i, 60–2.

39 The same is true of Jansenism, which may be regarded as a Catholicised Puritanism. Groethuysen writes, "The Jansenist experience of life is tragic without mitigation. Therefore, unlike St. Augustine, they emphasise the prospect of salvation, when they meditate on the secrets of predestination". *Origines de l'Esprit Bourgeois*, Pt. I, Sec. 4.

real love-object an imaginary one. Imaginary parents may be more satisfactory, in some respects, than real ones, since we can mould them nearer our heart's desire, but in others they are bound to be less satisfactory. Thus the solution represents a retreat into fantasy, based on inability to accept an actual situation in its full unpleasantness. (This tends to lead to the equally awkward conclusion that having once performed the adjustment there is nothing more to worry about, and Methodists in turn had to go to some lengths to get round this unpalatable conclusion.)

Methodism is thus a less despairing doctrine than Calvinism, a doctrine for those whose fathers have rejected them, but not so decisively as to exclude all hope. This enabled me to understand, for instance, why the elder Maurice sisters were driven by the death of their loved cousins to abandon Unitarianism for Calvinism: this final blow convinced them that it was useless to attempt to build relationships of love.

It is noticeable that Wesley had little success ·in strongly Calvinist districts: he returned from Scotland having made hardly a single convert. His successes were in the new industrial areas, among the miners of Cornwall and Kingswood, and in the capital, where presumably upbringing was less severe.

The Methodist technique was superior to that of the Moravians, from whom Wesley learned, and it is interesting to study the circumstances of Wesley's own conversion.[40] Prior to his meeting with the Moravians, he was engaged in a constant struggle to dominate himself. He drew up codes of rules for himself, engaged in ascetic practices, and seemed to be dominated by the idea of obedience to God's *law*. In other words, he was dominated by the need to submit to authority, as well he might, having been taught from childhood that salvation depends on "universal obedience". This was a period of constant struggle and depression at the hopelessness of the task.

But in 1737 Spangenberg introduced him to a quite different notion: that the struggle was unnecessary and useless, for Christ had

---

[40] See Halévy, 'Naissance du Methodisme . . .' in *Revue de Paris*, 1906, pp. 846–7; Rattenbury, *Conversion of the Wesleys*, passim; Dimond, *Psychol. of the Meth. Revival*, pp. 75 ff.

saved mankind. All that was necessary was to believe this completely. Wesley was attracted by this idea, but found himself unable to believe that it was true. An agonised period followed, in which he was under the guidance of Bohler, a Moravian, whose method was a constant repetition of the importance of belief. In a letter to Wesley, still extant, he manages to repeat this idea seven times in nine sentences. Wesley, now extremely depressed, resorts to prayer. Bohler urges Wesley to preach this doctrine to others until he finally comes to believe it himself; this he does, in several London churches, to the point at which he is banned from further preaching. But he still doubts that salvation is 'instantaneous'. Bohler plies him with references from the Bible and also with modern instances. Finally, one day at Blendon, Wesley announces that he has come to see the necessity of conversion by faith, and that such conversion is instantaneous. His brother Charles, appalled, cries, "Revolting!" and walks out of the room.

But almost immediately Charles himself discovers a case of instantaneous conversion: a tremendous internal struggle ensues in which he is physically ill; on May 3rd he feebly announces that he is convinced, and receives the Sacraments. But though he now "thirsts for Christ", still nothing happens. Then, on the even of Pentecost, he is awoken in the middle of the night by a voice crying, "In the name of Jesus arise and believe, and thou shalt be cured of all thine ills." Believing it to be the authentic voice of God, Charles undergoes actual conversion and finds himself "at peace with the Lord". Actually, it is only the voice of a Mrs. Musgrave, piously trying to assist the workings of divine providence: the deception is effective.[41]

John Wesley, apparently chagrined at being outstripped by his brother, makes renewed efforts and, at nine-fifteen in the morning three days later, feels a "warmth in his heart" and is convinced that he is personally saved too. However, his faith is so fragile that the same evening he has renewed doubts, and hurries to consult the Moravians. "Do not struggle," they tell him, "just seek a refuge in the wounds of Christ."[42]

[41] Halévy, op. cit., p. 846.
[42] Contrast the conversion of Simeon. On reading the words "The Jews knew what they did when they transferred their sin to the head of their offering," he

A study of his later remarks makes it very doubtful indeed whether in fact he achieved a conversion, in the sense in which the term has been used in this chapter. For example, he wrote to a brother in October of the same year, "Some measure of this faith which bringeth salvation or victory over sin . . . I now enjoy . . . though in very deed it is in me as a grain of mustard seed. For the seal of the spirit, the love of God shed abroad in my heart, and producing joy in the Holy Ghost, joy which no man taketh away, joy unspeakable and full of glory—this witness of the Spirit I have not; but I particularly wait for it." Literally scores of his hymns, some written much later in life, express this sense of disappointment; thus:

> That sudden flash of heavenly light
> Which once broke in upon my sight
> Has made my darkness visible
> And left me to a deeper hell.
> Ah, what availed the short-lived power,
> The triumph of the lucid hour!
> Again enthralled and doubly cursed
> I am, and viler than at first.

Rattenbury has made a detailed study of the subject.[43] He points out that Wesley never used the word 'conversion' of his own experience, though he used it of other people's. And he quotes the extraordinary passage in cipher in Wesley's diary (which was, in any case, in an obscure shorthand), "I do not love God. I never did. I never believed, in the Christian sense of the word. Therefore I am only an honest heathen. . . . And yet I dare not preach otherwise than I do . . . I have no more fear than love. Or if I have any fear it is not of falling into hell, but of falling into nothing."

---

was struck by the thought, "What! May I transfer all my guilt to another?" Accordingly, he sought to do so. By Wednesday, "began to have a hope of mercy," and by Sunday, "had the sweetest access to God . . ." Carus, *Memoirs of Simeon*, p. 14.

[43] Rattenbury, *Conversion of the Wesleys.*

All this seems to me extraordinarily confirmatory of the theory here advanced. Wesley was dominated by his mother; she was the disciplinarian who made him learn the whole alphabet in a single day at the age of five, who prayed with him, and who determined that he should be a great figure in the Church. His father was a weak nonentity. Evidently, if Wesley was disturbed by any conflict with the parental image, it was with the mother, not the father. His insistence on a subordinate role for women betrays his barely repressed fears of female domination.[44] For Wesley, therefore, reconciliation to a father-figure was not a process of symbolic importance, and it could not arouse a major response.

That some psychological shift did occur is, I think, certain: for he definitely lost his oppressive sense of guilt. But his ability to believe himself loved had been permanently impaired. And so he was left with nothing but "the fear of falling into nothing".

As the reader will have noticed, all the cases of conversion of which I have given an account are those of men. It is worth observing, however, that women were converted in greater numbers than men. Many of these conversions seem to have followed the same course as those of men: a phase of struggle—such as that in which Elizabeth Booth felt that Wesley was assaulting her—followed by a supernal peace. Sometimes the result was a trance-like state of ecstasy. Wesley studied one of these female ecstatics closely, remaining near her for the best part of a day and speaking to her at times, and questioning her after she returned to normality. Ann Thorn said that she was at times "visited with such overpowering love and joy that she often lay in a trance for many hours". Patty Jenkins had enough strength to utter "ejaculations of joy and praise; but no words coming up to what she felt, she frequently laughed while she saw His glory". But when it was time for Wesley to leave for Cockaigne-Hatley, "her strength was restored in a moment."[45]

That women should be converted in greater numbers than men is, I think, not surprising, for a woman can submit to a father-figure more

[44] For details of this, see pp. 226–8, where the psychology of Wesley is discussed further.
[45] Wesley, *Journal*, iv, 334.

easily than a man. The Œdipus situation does not place her in rivalry with the father for the mother, as it does a man: her basic conflicts are more likely to be with her mother. (Presumably we should find such evidence of conflict if a woman living in a society which worshipped a mother-deity underwent conversion.) Moreover, women at this period were taught from childhood that it was their duty to submit to a man. Hence it would only be women who happened to be father-rejectors who would be driven to behave as Ann Thorn did.

In this attempt to analyse the process of conversion, I have confined myself almost entirely to conversions of the Methodist type. It would be a considerable research—and a very interesting one, though difficult —to study how far these factors are reproduced in later instances. From rather sporadic evidence, I am inclined to think that they are, and I certainly came across none inconsistent with this analysis.

For instance, Mrs. Sherwood, the moralistic writer, who later became an active Calvinist, reveals an early preoccupation with death, which started, she says, with her mother's canary, which she carefully encoffined. But since other children have also had pets which died, it is reasonable to suppose that this incident merely aroused an existing susceptibility. She tells how she begged from her father a funeral invitation which, in the fashion of the day, showed "representations of every horrible circumstance belonging to natural death—graves, and skeletons, and coffins, and shrouds, skull and cross-bones, and so on. I cannot comprehend where the temptation lies of poring over such dismal matters . . . I sought them so diligently that I contrived to be taken to see the vault in Stanford Church, and when the funeral arrived, with all the paraphernalia of nodding plumes, flowing scarves and cloaks, coal-black steeds and mourning coaches, I stood at my play-room window, which commanded the church, and gave myself up thoroughly to the contemplation of the scene".[46] This was about her eighth or ninth year.

Again, Miss Cullern, later Mrs. Treffry, at the age of six, was "power-fully convinced of sin" by hearing repeated the following lines of Dr. Watts:

[46] Darton, *Life . . . of Mrs. Sherwood*, p. 47.

> There is a dreadful hell
> And everlasting pains,
> Where sinners must with devils dwell
> In darkness, fire and chains.

In due course she joined the Methodists, but not until the age of thirty-eight did she "receive knowledge of pardon of sin".[47] Mueller (1805–98), himself later to effect so many conversions, displays almost the identical picture of libertinism followed by repentance which we have seen in the case of Newton. He was converted in 1825. In 1833 alone, he converted at least sixty persons, and influenced many more.[48]

But, whatever modifications further research might suggest, I have, I think, established the fact that many in the eighteenth century were preoccupied with the father-figure in a very special kind of way; and since it was precisely those who were involved in this struggle who were the moralising force, I had provided support of a rather detailed and elaborate kind for the general proposition that behaviour is influenced by parental images, and also for the more specific proposition that moralistic attitudes are the product of a father-introjection. For myself, I felt I would now add the introjection of a *severe* father-figure, while recognising that the severity derived in the first instance from the frustrations of the introjector, though no doubt fortified when the father was in actual fact severe.

By way of coda to the discussion, let me report a pendant observation.

The Christian doctrine of the period displays two themes of some interest: the first is a preoccupation with the idea of abandonment, of casting into outer darkness, and of God turning away His face.[49] This is easily understandable, in the light of what has been said. The second is a preoccupation with the idea of annihilation and its complement, "everlasting life". This interest in immortality is so common in Christian feeling that it will not strike any Christian reader as odd; but

[47] Treffry, *Heavenward*, pp. 3, 31.
[48] Mueller, *Autobiography*.
[49] Thus Jonathan Edwards was preoccupied with the idea of abandonment, Wesley with that of "falling into nothing". See p. 163.

against the historical scale it can be seen to be quite arbitrary. Many peoples have displayed only a minimum of interest in the question of *post mortem* existence, and have assumed that, such as it is, it will be the lot of all. The Christian, however, speaks of everlasting life as a blessed hope to which he may attain through Christ's help. It becomes possible to understand this when we recall the depressive's death-wishes towards the father, and his fear of annihilatory retaliation. Only if the father forgives him can he cease to fear annihilation.

By pursuing such lines of argument as these I was led into a psychological interpretation; and, interestingly enough, it was an interpretation which depended more on the concept of aggression than on the balance of parental images. Nevertheless, it did give an important role to the father-figure, and I felt that progress in dissecting the personality structure of the period had been made. The next would evidently be to investigate the mother-image in a similar manner. But before doing this, perhaps it would be as well to round up all my material concerning the Puritan or guilt-ridden character. If I were on the right trail there should be a certain coherence between the parts; and having a clear picture in my mind would make it easier both to detect Puritan elements at work in areas of social life which are not normally considered to be influenced by them, and also to spot any items which did not fit into this picture.

I propose for this purpose to take most of my examples from the actual Puritans of the seventeenth century, in whom the pattern is seen in its clearest form. Later I shall consider how far these elements persisted during the period with which we are concerned.

CHAPTER 9

THE PURITAN PERSONALITY

THERE ARE four areas of behaviour which seem to me fundamental to the whole conception of Puritanism.

The first is the all-important factor of guilt-feelings. I have already probably given enough examples to show how intense these feelings were. The unfortunate victims wept, prayed, banged their heads on the floor, went without food, tried to do away with themselves.[1] Often whole congregations would "roar for disquietness".[2] The sense of impending punishment was all but intolerable; and the elaborate descriptions of hell merely represent a way of saying how guilty the writer felt, that such horrors should be necessary to provide an adequate punishment.

It became evident to me that this burden of guilt was much too great to be accounted for solely by the Œdipal situation. There are many individuals who must certainly be put down as father-identifiers, who do not display guilt in anything like this quantity, if at all. Thus the typical country squire of the period, and many bishops, were undoubted patrists: they believed in a hierarchical structure of society and an authoritarian approach to political problems; they were much more preoccupied with the chastity of their womenfolk than with problems of welfare and the evils of poverty and starvation; they accepted a father-religion, and regarded the rather more matrist Roman Catholic religion with horror. Yet they indulged themselves, drank, swore, and in general showed no signs of guilt. To some extent, the Puritan's guilt might be due to the greater severity of his parents, but this is not a

---

[1] *Lives of the Methodist Preachers*, passim.
[2] ib., ii, 74-5. A similar phrase is used by John Murlin and others.

sufficient explanation. If one had been severely punished by parents for offences, one might expect that the punishment which God would mete out for offences would also be severe, but this would not account for the persistent feeling that some dreadful unspecified offence had been committed. It is a curious thing that although all these Methodists, Calvinists and Evangelicals declare that they are the most depraved of sinners, they rarely produce any evidence to justify the claim. (Bunyan, for example, felt that God's wrath was going to descend on him because he had joined in bell-ringing at the church. When only nine or ten he felt crushed under the weight of sin when playing games.)³ Hence I felt that I should have to locate some special mechanism capable of accounting for this terrible guilt-feeling before I could regard the analysis as complete.

The father-figure with whom the Puritan is preoccupied is essentially a severe one: he is a father who is depicted not only as punishing but sometimes even as *hating* the human race, and the punishment which he metes out is not reluctantly given, nor adjusted to the severity of the crime; man is a disgusting object whom he consigns to the flames with as little compunction as one would crush an insect. This view reaches its most extreme expression in the writings of Jonathan Edwards.

In a sermon entitled 'Sinners in the Hands of an Angry God', he tells his listeners: "You would have gone to hell last night had he not held you like a loathsome spider over the flames by a thread. Every moment of delay accumulates wrath."⁴

This image of being suspended by a thread seems to fascinate him; and God appears to him not only to hate man, but to be angry with him. In another sermon he draws this picture: "If we should suppose that a person saw himself hanging over a great pit, full of fierce and glowing flames, by a thread that he knew to be very weak and not sufficient to bear his weight, and knew that multitudes had been in such circumstances before and most of them had fallen and perished, and saw nothing within reach he could take hold of to save him, what distress he would be in!

³ Talon, *John Bunyan*, pp. 41 ff.
⁴ Edwards, op. cit.

"How ready to think, that now the thread was breaking, that now *this minute* he should be swallowed up in those dreadful flames—would he not be ready to cry out in such circumstances?

"How much more those that see themselves in this manner hanging over an infinitely more dreadful pit, held over it in the hand of God, who at the same time they see to be exceedingly provoked! No wonder they are ready to expect every moment when this angry God will let them drop, and no wonder they cry out at their misery, and no wonder that the wrath of God, when manifested but a little to the soul, overbears human strength."[5]

Since Christianity is nominally a religion based on love, one might have thought it impossible for anyone who supposed himself a Christian to have been able to corrupt its intentions so completely, and to depict a religion of fear and hate so explicitly: but history and anthropology show that men can twist and adapt any myth to suit their unconscious needs.

Naturally the Puritan fears this angry father-figure rather than loves him. And he seeks to propitiate him by self-abnegation and prayer. Prayer can be conceived in several forms, for instance it may be a form of meditation or a spiritual exercise. The prayers of Puritans are almost entirely appeals for mercy. And these prayers must be offered almost continuously. Taylor makes it a rule that one should pray every hour on the hour, as well as in other intervals in one's work. Besides this, one should set aside a period every year for "prayer, fasting and confessing to God". Jonathan Edwards says, "I was almost constantly in ejaculatory prayer, wherever I was. Prayer seemed to be natural to me."[6]

Finally, the father is not only punishing but rejecting—this is implied in Jonathan Edwards' sermons, quoted above—and in general the Puritan continually expressed his sense of isolation, of having been cast out, of having no refuge. He beseeches the father to bestow on him the gift of love once again, to accept him into his love, to cherish and protect him.

[5] Edwards, *The Distinguishing Marks*, pp. 11–12.
[6] Edwards, *Some Account*, p. 6.

But the Puritan does not only seem isolated from God, he seems isolated from his fellow men, and, in a personal sense, uninterested in them. It has been said that the Puritan seems incapable of maintaining a relationship of love and interest with his fellow men, and in this role he is enabled to display great interest in the life of the other party, and even concern for his welfare, without any risk of jeopardising his own emotional position. Another such relationship is that of social investigation (John Howard's work on prison reform, for example) or other charitable or reformist activities. To condemn his fellow men, and to urge them to desist from their folly, represents an outgoing relationship, but at a very low level. It is the best he can do, for all more spontaneous manifestations have been inhibited. Miller and Johnson comment on the strange insensitivity of the Puritan to any great bereavement. Sewall, for instance, briefly records in his diary, for May 26th, 1720, "About midnight my dear wife expired to our great astonishment, especially mine."[7]

The Puritan's diminished interest in others is complemented by his excessive preoccupation with himself. He spends a large part of his time brooding over the state of his soul and his prospects for the future. This has led Schuecking to speak, in an apt phrase, of the Puritan's "moral hypochondria".[8] So concerned is he about his own salvation that he often neglects the needs and wishes of others. He also neglects the larger issues of social progress and society's needs. As has been said, the Puritan's God is concerned only with individuals, not with mankind: and what is true of his God is true of the Puritan, who, like all men, makes his God in his own image.

It is significant that the Puritans make use of many word phrases beginning with 'self': self-indulgence, self-will, self-control. The very word 'selfish' is a Puritan introduction of about 1660.[9] Terms such as 'self-indulgent' suggest some kind of splitting of the personality, as if there were an indulger and an indulged within the ego; and this impression is strengthened by the term 'self-will', for it is difficult, short of hypnotism, to think of any other kind of will. For the Puritan, of

[7] Cited Miller and Johnson, *The Puritans*, p. 391.
[8] Schuecking, *Die Familie im Puritanismus*, p. 13.
[9] Aikin, *Memoirs*, p. 201.

course, self-will was set in opposition to God's will: or, in psycho-analytic terms, ego was in opposition to super-ego. And since the super-ego is an introjected father-figure, ego is in opposition to the father.

This preoccupation with the self betrays a fear of loss of self, and it is interesting to find it said that Wesley feared not the pangs of hell but loss of self.[10] This is significant for, as we shall see, loss of the sense of individuality is often displayed by mother-identifiers, who welcome the experience.[11]

It struck me as an interesting point to note that the Puritan introduced a rather unexpected virtue in the form of 'self-knowledge'. There was nothing in my theoretical analysis which had predicted this, and no very satisfactory explanation occured to me. However, I added the point to the list of unsolved problems, in the hope that it might prove relevant at a later stage.

The Puritan finds a curious way of stressing his personal importance when he declares himself to be the most extreme of sinners with, as we have seen, so little justification. Jonathan Edwards admits, "When I ask for humility, I cannot bear the thoughts of being no more humble than other Christians. It seems to me that, though their degrees of humility may be suitable for them, yet it would be a *vile* exaltation in *me*, not to be the *lowest* in humility of all mankind."[12]

This desire for the lowest possible place represents a kind of inverted pride, for to be the most frightful of sinners is a kind of distinction, and to the most humble of men is a kind of virtue. The real motivation is betrayed by the "theory of reversal" embodied in so much Puritan literature: the thesis that on the day of reckoning the last shall be first, and the first last. Thus he who is the worst of sinners may expect to sit on the right hand of God. The ambivalence of Edwards' wish for humility is revealed by the fact that immediately after wishing to lie "infinitely low before God" he adds, "And yet, I am greatly afflicted with a proud and self-righteous spirit, much more sensible than I used to be formerly."[13]

[10] See p. 163. But Jonathan Edwards sometimes wished to be 'annihilated' *Some Account*, p. 16.
[11] See p. 209.
[12] *Some Account*, p. 16.
[13] ib.

The reversal theory derives, I suspect, from a train of argument in the unconscious which goes, "Since trying to attain my goal in this way has failed me completely, I shall now try doing exactly the opposite." A similar mechanism perhaps lies behind the "blessing in disguise" theory, according to which God's severest blows are really blessings because they make ultimate salvation more certain.

The Puritan's concealed preoccupation with status is revealed by his association of the word dignity with gravity. The word 'dignified' has come to mean a grave, restrained and perhaps rather pompous attitude, and has quite lost its original meaning of "one to whom honour has been paid". It is also interesting that he makes it his ambition to be placed on God's right hand, a position of evident status. Jonathan Edwards was particularly anxious that, when the day of reckoning came, God should start His reform in the New World rather than the Old, so that he might be first in the queue for supernatural dignities.[14]

When this underlying sense of self-satisfaction emerges visibly, we get the type of Puritan for whom the word 'prig' was borrowed.

Certainly the Puritan personality displays signs of sadism, which may be defined for present purposes as pleasure in the sufferings of others, as distinct from blind rage or mere callousness. Furthermore, sadism is invariably associated with masochism, or pleasure in one's own suffering; one passes into the other so smoothly that it is usual to refer to the two attitudes jointly, as sado-masochism. Ranulf made a study of the Thomason collection with a view to determining how far the Puritans were sadistic; he concludes: that they had "a fundamental unreasoned desire to see suffering inflicted upon human beings. This desire, which may conveniently be termed sadism, was . . . partly disguised as a wish to see that sinners were severely punished for their sins."[15] He also notes the Puritans' censoriousness. The Puritan's sadism is usually justified on the grounds that punishment is good for one. As Arthur Young exclaimed of Lord Carrington, "The Lord show mercy to him, and by interrupting his prosperity or lowering his

[14] 'Thoughts on the Present Revival' (*Works*, iv, 128-9, 131-2).
[15] Ranulf, *Moral Indignation*, p. 76.

health, bring him to repentance!"[16] Conversely, if a man undergoes misfortune, it is evidence that he must have sinned; while one's own misfortunes thus reinforce one's existing sense of guilt.

It is this sadism which lies behind the Puritan's misanthropy and harshness. It was a regular feature of the theology of the period that the blessed in heaven would be able to see, all the time, the tortures of the damned. To-day most people feel that the spectacle would detract somewhat from the satisfaction of being in heaven; it is significant that such a thought did not occur to the Puritans, and only to a few of their critics. Some, like Bunyan, thought it would be one of the positive attractions of the place. Jonathan Edwards comments that the inhabitants of heaven will look on this spectacle and praise God's justice; but, we may add, hardly His mercy. And note that to be more interested in justice than mercy is a regular feature of the Puritan personality.

The Calvinist, with his conviction that he is irretrievably damned, seems to be turning his aggression against himself; sadism has passed into masochism.

The Puritan ideal of self-control would be understandable enough if it referred only to the control of those impulses which he regards as sinful. But, as we have seen in Chapter Six, it is noticeable that self-control becomes an end in itself, and that impulses of every kind are to be inhibited, even praiseworthy ones. Joanna Baillie's father, though an excellent parent, never kissed or caressed her in her whole life, and her mother was equally inhibited. "Joanna spoke to me once of her yearning to be caressed when she was a child. She would sometimes venture, she said, to clasp her little hands about her mother's knees, who would seem to chide her—'but I know she liked it.'"[17]

Schuecking suggests that the Puritan's main desire is "not to give himself away". This curiously commercial phrase seems to describe the reaction of one who had made emotional advances and has been repulsed. It is when others have refused us their love and approval that we are anxious not to make fools of ourselves by opening ourselves to a

---

[16] Young, *Autobiography*, p. 361.
[17] Aikin, *Memoirs*, pp. 7f.

fresh rebuff. Here in fact is the origin of the emotional freezing-up which makes the Puritan unable to maintain a normal relationship with his fellow men, or even to respond adequately to bereavement. Schuecking makes the further suggestion that one reason for the popularity of animal pets in the period is that one cannot "give oneself away" to an animal: it is, of course, just those animals which respond to affection of which pets were chiefly made.

In psychoanalytic work, the concept of self-control is often found to be the nucleus of a group of attitudes, all of which have a common origin—and in fact the whole of this constellation of attitudes is found in the typical Puritan. We have gained some impression of them in Chapter Six, where they were seen reflected in Puritan teaching concerning ideals of behaviour. They are, first, the display of rigid self-control and self-discipline, coupled with a strict attention to duty and a fear of wasting time. The word 'strict', with its connotations of constricted or held in, admirably epitomises the notion of severity towards the self ('self-discipline') and towards others; the Puritans were, as we shall see later, extremely strict with their children. Secondly, the display of interest in the accumulation of wealth or property, all the more surprising in conscientious Christians in view of Biblical injunctions to dispose of wealth and embrace poverty. It is not just a blind acceptance of inherited wealth, nor a liking for comfortable living: on the contrary, Puritans regard the making of money as a positive virtue, and the spending of it as something like sin.[18] Though they give some to charity, they spend the minimum on themselves, and go to some trouble to buy at the keenest price. Retentiveness seems to be part of the character: many of them, for instance, boast of their retentive memory. Of others it is said: "no detail escapes them."

Thirdly, we may often note considerable preoccupation with the idea of cleanliness, either physical or moral, or both—an association so well

---

[18] The moralists, such as Watts, all oppose 'prodigality'; attention to business is mandatory because as one's business is run so will one's life be. And then if God "is pleased to make prosper whatever you do, your wealth is plainly his gift, as much as if it came to you by legacy or inheritance" (Venn, *Complete Duty*, Chapter xlii).

recognised that it has given rise to the phrase "Cleanliness is next to godliness". The Puritan is also strangely interested in words, both written and spoken: they seem to him to have immense significance, and an almost magical power of affecting the behaviour of others. In religion, he is much addicted to the sermon: the early Puritans believed that in the sermon they had found the answer to all ecclesiastical problems, and to some of them two sermons on Sunday were "a necessity of salvation". The sermon remained an important feature of worship throughout the eighteenth and nineteenth centuries, and not only of worship, for they were printed in large numbers for reading in the home. The Puritan is equally concerned with prayer, as we have already seen, and these prayers are by preference spoken aloud. Family readings, as well as family prayers, were also regarded as of crucial importance. At the other extreme, the Puritan is immensely scandalised by statements denying what he approves, even when unsupported by action. During the seventeenth and eighteenth centuries many kinds of statement were brought under the laws of blasphemy, including those which had no relation to the Deity: prosecutions were even brought for proposing the disestablishment of the Church.[19] In Chapter Three we have already noted the pressure towards a constant refining of the language, all words with even remotely sexual physical connotations being gradually replaced by substitutes. The Puritan's objection to novels and plays also seems to display this element.

It struck me that this preoccupation with words might also account for the Puritan's stress on the importance of precept. This is beautifully demonstrated by Lucy Aikin, a strict but by no means unreasonable writer, when she debates whether example is more effective than precept in teaching a child. She decides, of course, in favour of "noble precepts supported by just reasoning".[20] Since it is now a widely accepted fact that the reverse is true, this seems a splendid example of the triumph of wish over reality.

To this list other details might be added. For instance, a resentment of thwarting or interference, an extreme persistence and attention to

[19] Cf. R. v. Jordan, 1799. See Nokes, *History of Crime of Blasphemy*, pp. 108 f.
[20] Aikin, *Memoirs*, p. 46.

detail, a preoccupation with enumerative or classifying activities—all these are often found in conjunction with the characteristics previously mentioned. The consistency with which these traits are found together is quite remarkable, as most people can verify from their own knowledge. Some common cause must evidently exist to account for them. And in fact this group of characteristics is well known to psychiatrists and has been shown to be associated with the way in which a child is 'house-trained' or taught anal control.[21] The subject is one which many people seem to find repellent, and the explanation is much resisted. Yet the matter is so fundamental to an understanding of the Puritan character that I cannot avoid treating it.

The general proposition that powerful emotions felt by the child tend to become generalised and to become embedded in its personality is well established, as we can see in the case of the Œdipus situation. The infant's first sensory experiences are concerned with its mouth, and the first deprivation it suffers may be an abrupt weaning. A second important group of sensations and experiences is concerned with the other end of the alimentary canal. It is not difficult to see the symbolic relationship between the retentiveness and accumulation on the one hand and the training which a child receives in anal self-control; and this also demonstrates the origin of the belief in self-control. The symbolic equivalence of money with faeces, which one would expect to follow, emerges clearly in dream analysis, but it is also betrayed by the tendency to describe money as filthy—filthy lucre, stinking with money and, so on.

At this point it will begin to be clear why anal fixation is also associated with the idea of cleanliness.

The association of these ideas with that of duty is sufficiently demonstrated by the fact that defaecation is often called "doing one's duty" and this reminds us that anal training is not only concerned with the idea of retention, but also with the idea of production, and especially production at a given time. If the productive act is rewarded by the parent (or failure to produce punished) we may expect to find a sense of

21 For a discussion of the anal-erotic group of character traits, see E. Jones, *Papers on Psychoanalysis*, Chapter 24.

the importance of productivity in the adult, whether it be literary production or commercial, or any other form. The reasons advanced for the preoccupation with words are somewhat recondite and perhaps not entirely convincing. I shall omit them, merely observing that (a) it is usually important, in the Puritan view, for words to be held in or inhibited; a free, uncontrolled flow of words, sometimes called logorrhea, is regarded as reprehensible; and (b) words can be used to smear and damage.

Psychoanalysts also point out that the anal type frequently betrays signs of sadism: sadism can of course be associated with oral activities (as in biting) and with genital ones (as in rape), but it seems especially closely associated with the anal, so that the term anal-sadistic is used to indicate the combination.

In Freudian theory, the infant concentrates its disposal of psychic energy, or libido, first at the oral level, later at the anal, and finally at the genital. When the move is made some part of the energy remains 'fixated' at the earlier level. Whether or not we choose to employ this particular terminology is not important here: but it is an observable fact that some persons display a kind of dependency which can be shown to have a detailed relationship to the ideas of sucking and biting, and to the whole process of suckling, together with an unusual interest in oral stimulation. Correspondingly, the result of anal fixation is to cause an interest in such ideas as retention, in the way I have described. Finally fixation at the genital level can be shown to be related to sexual activities. Moreover, in conditions of stress, an individual may regress, or retreat down this ladder. Similarly, as libido fails, old people tend to regress to the anal and later the oral. I mention this part of the theory, because from it derives the proposition that if a person has the bulk of his libido concentrated at any one level, he will have little left for the others. Thus it is predictable that the anal character will, on the one hand, display little sign of dependency or of interest in food and drink, or in consumption; and on the other that he will have little energy available for sexual enjoyment.

When stress has been laid on the dirty nature of the excreta, we get the passion for cleanliness, and this may lead to a feeling that everything within the body is filthy. (Cf. the Puritan complaint that people are whited sepulchres, fair without, a mass of dirt and corruption within.) This in turn may lead to hypochondria. Again, since the untaught child values what it has produced and proudly shows its excreta to an approving parent, removal of the excreta would explain the strong interest in injustice, and the resentment of being interfered with which many anally fixated people of this type display. In a more sublimated form, it may appear as a morbid passion for 'purity'.

Psychoanalysts have traced the connection between anal fixation and certain other related concepts, such as the passion for definition or classification, for "making one's mark", for fresh air, and so on, but there is no need to pursue the analyses further here. Finally, the anal type objects to being thwarted, an attitude which may lead to marked individualism, self-willedness, obstinacy, irritation and bad temper.

Anal traits, it must be borne in mind, are often valuable; they include "determination and persistence, the love of order and power of organisation, competency, reliability and thoroughness, generosity, the bent towards art and good taste, the capacity for unusual tenderness, and the general ability to deal with concrete objects of the material world". On the other side of the penny, however, we find "the incapacity for happiness, the irritability and bad temper, the hypochondria, the miserliness, meanness and pettiness, the slow-mindedness and proneness to bore, the bent for dictating and tyrannising, and the obstinacy which, with other qualities, may make the person exceedingly unfit for social relations". [22]

Whether or not one is prepared to accept the explanation advanced by the psychiatrists, it remains true that these characteristics are often found in association, and that they are repeatedly so found among Puritans such as we have been discussing.

To sum up, in the Puritan personality, as displayed in its pristine form in the seventeenth century, there are four main elements: extreme guilt, preoccupation with a severe parental figure, preoccupation with the self, and the whole constellation of anal elements. Having made this analysis, the question which arises is: how far do we find these characteristics displayed during the period actually under examination?

[22] E. Jones, *Papers on Psychoanalysis*, pp. 436-7.

Since it is so often said that we are still influenced by Puritanism to-day, it is curious that no one (as far as I have been able to discover) has made a comprehensive effort to trace the persistence of Puritanism. To do so exhaustively would require a whole book: but an answer which will serve our present purpose can be sketched fairly rapidly.

The fact is, all the anal elements can be found, precisely as predicted, in the moralistic groups right throughout the period; and sometimes the similarity of behaviour is quite astonishing. Thus Sewall's entry about the death of his wife in 1720 is almost paralleled by the entry which Philip Gosse made about the birth of his son in 1849, "E. delivered of a son. Received green swallow from Jamaica."[23] (As Edmund Gosse later commented, the fact that his birth was put first does not indicate that it was more important, only that it happened earlier in the day than the arrival of the bird.) The "taboo on tenderness" has continued down to this day in some sections of society. The case of Joanna Baillie, noted earlier, derives from the early nineteenth century. The preoccupation with words, which continued until late in the nineteenth century, has already been noted, as have the prosecutions for blasphemy. The sermon remained popular.[24] Schuecking has shown the importance attached to family reading of sacred works, and has shown how the practice persisted during the eighteenth century.[25] The continuance of the accumulative and productive spirit, which is the basis of early capitalism, has been analysed by every economic historian. We have already seen how the Puritans urged industriousness. Strictures on idleness—especially the idleness of employees—are still a commonplace to-day. We have seen, too, how the Puritans advocated cleanliness; it is significant that foreign visitors

[23] Gosse, Father and Son, p. 6.

[24] The mania for sermons was one of the commonest complaints of Church writers at the end of the seventeenth century. See Overton, Life in the Eng. Church, 1660–1714, Chapter 6; and cf. Macaulay's story of the congregation clamouring for Burnet to reverse the hour-glass and preach another hour. (History of England, i, 413.)

[25] Die Familie im Puritanismus, especially Chapter 3 and Chapter 8. Also the importance attached to family prayers, as distinct from individual prayer, as argued in such tracts as The Necessary Duty of Family Prayer, by W. J. The point is taken up further in Chapter 16.

repeatedly comment on the English passion for cleanliness, and this despite the blackening effect of the many coal fires.[26]

A full treatment of the subject would have to trace how these ideas gradually influenced secular ideals and aristocratic manners. For instance, one can trace the gradual incursion of the idea of self-control into the concept of the gentleman. The Restoration rake had thought himself a gentleman, but self-control was no part of his code. However, the hero of Steele's *Conscious Lovers* (1722) bitterly reproaches himself with his loss of self-control when insulted; likewise, the hero of Richardson's *Grandison* (1754) reproaches himself for losing his temper with two ruffians.

Similarly a comprehensive study would note the parallel between Mason's *Self Knowledge* (1824) and Baxter's *Mischief of Self-Ignorance* a century and a half before, while the same notion can be traced in a secular sphere in Tennyson's praise of "Self-reverence, self-knowledge, self-control".

It is of course the presence of these anal elements which accounts for the presence of the "commercial virtues" in the moralistic individual, and hence for the association of morality with economic advancement to which I drew attention in the previous chapters. To have identified them so satisfactorily marks a major step towards completing the present investigation. For instance, it enables us to see why it was that morality was associated with economic success. And it enables us to see why the lower class remained, to a very considerable extent, anti-Puritan in character: for there would be a tendency for any members of the lower class equipped with the anal morality to rise out of the lower class into the lower-middle or trading class. On the other hand, members of the upper class would less generally be inclined to drift into the trading class, even if anal in outlook, both because they would

---

[26] Rochefoucauld was much struck by the cleanliness of the English, at least as regards outer appearances. He noted that the floors of houses were washed weekly, that there was no dust anywhere, and the people were clean in their persons—but the kitchens were filthy. (*A Frenchman in England*, pp. 25 and 42.) Grosley also noted that "the churches are conspicuously clean" (*Tour to London*, i, 304), and added that "This taste for cleanliness has banished from London those little dogs, which are kept at Paris by persons of all ranks . . ." i, 73.

have less economic incentive and because they would tend to retain their upper-class classification even if they did engage in industrial activity—as in the case of the Duke of Bridgewater, who sank his fortune in canal-building.

Once this proposition has been accepted, we can use it to document more closely the gradual conquest of upper-class *mores* by middle-class ones. Thus the upper class felt no shame about matters of excretion: women of the upper class would step down from their coach to relieve themselves,[27] and even George III would do the same.[28] St. Fond noted an English upper-class custom: "Wines are the great luxury of the table in England, where they drink the best and dearest that grow in France or Portugal. If the lively champagne should make its diuretic influence felt, the case is foreseen, and in the pretty corners of the room the necessary convenience is to be found. This is applied with so little ceremony, that the person who has occasion to use it, does not even interrupt his talk during the operation. I suppose this is one of the reasons why the English ladies, who are exceedingly modest and reserved always leave the company before the toasts begin."[29] This was in 1784 and the practice was still in use in 1819, as we know from Simond.[30] He was much shocked, and noted that the operation was "performed very deliberately and undisguisedly". But as early as 1765 the country parson, William Cole, had been shocked both by Mme. du Deffand's frank references to the Dauphin's malaise, and also when a Frenchwoman on the Channel packet had asked for a "*Pot pour faire lâcher l' eau*" and had made use of it, "with as little Shame as Decency and Ceremony."[31] By the early days of the nineteenth century, it would seem, the upper class was beginning to

[27] Alexander, *History of Women*, p. 3.

[28] Withers, *A History of the Royal Malady*, Chapter 2.

[29] St. Fond, *Journey Through England*, i, 253. Frequently the sideboard contained a lead-lined compartment in which the pot was kept, as the Duc de Liancourt's son noted with astonishment.

[30] Simond, *Journal of a Tour*, i, 49. Stendhal, during his visit to London in 1817, noted that after the ladies retired, "we drank for half an hour, after which we went up in procession to piss on the roof." Edwards, 'Stendhal in London' *London Magazine*, Vol. 2, No. 3, 1955).

[31] Cole, *Journey to Paris*, pp. 271, 362.

accept the middle-class taboos, for when Lord Sheffield's daughter tells a scatological joke about "little houses", Glenbervie comments, "There must be squeamish critics who are not amused."[32]

Consideration of the persistence of these anal characteristics enabled me to understand a point which I had previously found quite puzzling. The eighteenth century had praised 'liberty' and this could be regarded as symptomatic of its rejection of authority: but in the nineteenth century, when society was considerably more authoritarian in pattern, and subordination to authority was held out as an ideal, we still find individuals who resent interference with their activities and who practise in the economic sphere an extreme individualism. I now realised that this apparent contradiction could be explained, at least in part, by the persistence of anal elements: for both obstinacy and dislike of interference are part of this constellation.

Frequently, of course, we find several of the items combining in a single behaviour pattern: for instance, the introduction of the cold bath combines the ideas of cleanliness and asceticism, and the fact that it should be taken on rising, and that one should rise early, introduce the idea of saving time.[33] The enumerative element is amusingly combined with guilt in Toplady's curious calculation, "Our careful account stands as follows. At ten years old each of us is chargeable with 315 millions and 360,000 sins. At twenty with 630 millions and 72,000 At thirty, with 946 millions and 80,000. . . . At eighty, with 2,522 millions and 880,000."[34]

A full account would also have to consider how far different individuals and movements displayed anal characteristics.[35] Thus we find many in Wesley. He declared, "Cleanliness is next to godliness" and, "Money is unspeakably precious."[36] He also said, "Idleness

[32] Glenbervie, *Diaries of Sylvester Douglas*, ii, 4.

[33] It has been argued that the habit of the cold bath was brought back from China by travellers, a typical example of the attempt to explain historical developments in terms of influences. It is not explained why the habit of wearing pigtails was not adopted at the same time.

[34] *Gospel Magazine*, March 1776.

[35] The anal-expulsive attitude is also found in Sterne and others. See de Froe, *Laurence Sterne*.

[36] *Works*, v, 139. See Warner, *Wesleyan Movement*, for further instances.

slays," and provided himself with an elaborate code of rules for the disposal of his time.[37] He accepted the idea of self-control, when he made one of his rules, "Avoid all manner of passions," and another, "Labour for a grave and modest carriage." His belief in the sermon is too well-known to need proof, and he advocated "frequent and fervent prayer". His persistence and dislike of interference are well-known.[38] We must therefore put him down as having considerable anal elements in his character, though naturally a much fuller analysis would be necessary to account adequately for all the elements in his personality.

But while we find these anal elements present on an extensive scale, it would seem that the other factors were of decreasing importance. The father-figure remains of importance, but ceases to be so severe. The morbid preoccupation with death vanishes, suggesting that aggressions have become much reduced. The quantity of guilt declines, though not to vanishing point by any means. The fear of pleasure is Œdipal in origin, and this too fades away. The typical Victorian figure believes in hard work, self-control, cleanliness, the importance of words, and suppression of tenderness, but he does not believe in asceticism, he does not "howl with disquietude".[39]

This illuminated a problem which had been bothering me. I had not been at all happy about the morality of the Victorians: it seemed to me to display considerable harshness, but the purely patrist elements evidently faded out quite early in the century. I now realised that this could be readily accounted for on the assumption that the anal elements continued to be present in character after the patrist ones had faded out. This seemed to receive confirmation from the continued interest in production, in cleanliness, in duty and other typical anal items.

This suggested that a closer examination of the eighteenth century ought also to reveal at least a few individuals who displayed anal

---

[37] See also *Works*, vii, 39, for importance of application to business. It does not matter if one has intercourse with drunkards and fornicators, provided it is in the way of business. *Works*, vi, 466–7.

[38] Cf. also the rules which he drew up for helpers, at the 1744 conference. They included "Be serious" and "Avoid laughing as you would cursing and swearing ".

[39] It is significant that the classic Puritan works of piety, such as Baxter's *Christian Directory*, ceased to be reprinted with any frequency after about 1830.

without displaying Œdipal elements. I at once realised that the rather numerous misers of the eighteenth (and indeed the nineteenth) century supplied the gap. Of these the best known is Simon Elwes: as expected, he shows none of the usual signs of guilt-feelings: he was a bold horseman, a gambler (this is reaction from the retentive to the expulsive aspect) and not an ungenerous host. His uncle, Sir Harvey Elwes, whose fortune exceeded £100,000 and who spent only £110 per annum, living exclusively upon partridges shot on his estate, was an even more extreme example.[40] If this interpretation is correct, it should also be possible to demonstrate the existence of female misers, since presumably severe anal training would be given to both sexes alike. A brief inquiry revealed that these were equally common—for instance, Elizabeth Bolaine (1723–1805) and Mrs. Tomlinson (who died c. 1827).[41]

The converse cases, individuals who display guilt without anal characteristics, are, of course, too numerous to mention.

In this way there was forced on my attention the fact that 'morality' has two distinct psychological roots, anal and Œdipal. And in fact Ferenczi spoke long ago of a "sphincter morality". The same thought is startlingly expressed in one of the Moravian hymns, when the worshipper, apostrophising the Deity, repeats, "Templum Pacis, thou mak'st Churches ex Cloacis."[42]

But, as I have explained, the child progresses from the oral through

---

[40] Redding, *Remarkable Misers*, pp. 41 ff.

[41] ib.

[42] *Hymns Composed for the Use of the Brethren*. If the Puritan, because of his own constricted and retentive attitude, conceives God as disinclined to give out love, it would seem to follow that he would also find an analogy between the loving aspect of God and freedom of anal movement. This is such an extraordinary proposition (as many readers may think) that it must be regarded as strongly confirmatory of the theory that such hymns can be found, e.g., Isaac Watts:　　　　　　　　"His heart is made of tenderness,
　　　　　　　　　　　　　　His bowels melt with love."
(see Methodist Hymn Book, 1904, No. 193. Wesley included this hymn in his Charlestown Hymn Book).
Cf. also,　　　　　　　　　"Let's feel thy Love, our Bowels move
　　　　　　　　　　　　　　To open thee thy Door."
(Hymn VII in *The Works of Mr. David Culy*, p. 162).

an anal to a genital stage. The adoption of an anal morality suggests that regression has occurred: and no doubt this is due, at least in part, to the blocking of genital outlets. It is this blocking which provides the energy for the anal persistence and obstinacy.

But this suggests the further thought, that occasionally a regression must occur to the oral phase and that there must also be such a thing as an oral morality. The last stage of regression is to the womb, and I already knew that the Moravians had exhibited signs of such regression, for a short period. The point is of some interest, for it demonstrates how ruthlessly myth is adapted to the needs of personality. The Protestant dogma, based on a male figure, Christ, hardly seems adapted to a womb-regression, but in fact several solutions were found. One hymn declares:

> Holy Ghost, a mother thou
> Most suitably are named.[43]

But the commonest solution was that expressed in the following verse:

> O precious Side-hole's cavity
> I want to spend my life in thee . . .
> There in one Side-hole's joy divine,
> I'll spend all future Days of mine.
> Yes, yes, I will for ever sit
> There, where thy Side was split.[44]

Another hymn actually compares the worshipper to "th' Infant leaping".[45] Even without adducing further evidence, it will be

[43] Hymn 24 in *Hymns Composed for the Use of the Brethren* by C. Z.

[44] Cited from a *Collection of Hymns Consisting Chiefly of Translations from the German Hymn Book of the Moravian Brethren* (1749) by Ingram and Newton, *Hymns as Poetry*, pp. 115–16. Cf also Hymns 42, 57, etc. Note also that, in *Hymns Composed for the Use of the Brethren* by C. Z., the Devil "has no side's incision."

[45] Toplady's well-known lines "Rock of Ages, cleft for me, Let me hide myself in Thee" may perhaps be explicable in these terms. In Christian thought a rock is usually regarded as a foundation on which to build rather than as a place to hide. Caves, of course, are womb symbols.

appreciated that these hymns strongly support the theory of a womb-regression.

It therefore seemed an interesting way of checking the general analysis to inquire whether any of the hymns of these minor sects displayed signs of adapting the Christian myth to oral purposes. Without much trouble, I found a hymn by Culy in which the oral elements implicit in the ideas of the Eucharist and the Lamb of God are clearly brought out by introducing the concept of cooking:

> "Now we afresh has eat Christ's flesh
> Not raw, but throughly boil'd,
> Not sod [i.e. stewed], nor unapprov'd to God,
> In whom he's reconciled.
> God tasted first of that Lamb roast
> The Priest has offered,
> He likes the Smell and Savour well,
> This is our Father's Bread."[46]

There remained, however, a group of important cases which, I felt, could not be adequately accounted for in terms of either of the foregoing factors, Œdipal guilt and anal trauma. Of these the best-known example is the Quakers. The Quakers clearly show strong anal elements. They were always canny in business, honest, carefully enumerative, persistent in face of opposition.[47] (George Fox himself had investments in the shipping industry.)[48] They were conspicuously

---

[46] Hymn v in *The Works of Mr. David Culy* (pp. 159–60). Oral images accur in many of Culy's forty-two hymns; Christ is almost invariably referred to as "the Flesh" without further identification. There are also some remarkably frank anal and genital references. (See Hymn VII and XXIX.)

[47] See Emden, *Quakers in Commerce.*

[48] By 1715, it was said of the Bristol Quakers that they are "large traders and very rich. Their number may be supposed about 2,000 and upwards; and their wealth not less than £500,000." Cited Evans MS at Dr. Williams' Library, by Bebb, *Nonconformity and Social . . . Life*, p. 52. Cf. Brayshaw, *Personality of George Fox.* Fox was not only insistent on cleanliness, but repeatedly commented on smell. His phrase for his conversion experience was that creation had a new smell. Foul smells seem to have had for him an evil connotation, for he attributed the

clean and decent in their clothing. They were preoccupied with words, as their refusal to force oaths demonstrates. They also betray marked signs of guilt. Fox had a powerful sense of sin, which his conversion alleviated, but in a rather unreliable way, since he had several subsequent spells of intense depression. But, unlike the Puritans, the Quakers did not feel rejected by God, they did not invariably conceive Him as a punishing figure. On the contrary, during his exalted phases Fox felt an almost mystical sense of union with God. This ecstatic element was to fade away as the century progressed, but it was common in the early days of the movement, and can be paralleled in some of the lesser-known sects. The difficulties become still more marked when we ask whether they can be regarded as father-identifiers. The Quaker's refusal to doff his cap to authority, even to his own father, suggests a defiance of the father-figure, and the Quakers defied authority often enough in their early days. At the same time, they put women in a subordinate position, and their fear of pleasure indicates that their guilt clearly has an Œdipal origin.

I felt that if the patrist-matrist theory had been wholly wrong, many other such exceptional cases would have been found; the fact that there was only one exception suggested that some special modifying factor would be found to account for it. Without feeling unduly discouraged, therefore, I put the problem aside for attention later on, when I should have completed my psychological analysis.

At this stage, in fact, I put aside, for the time being, the whole subject of the father-figure and the restrictive morality, and turn to the other side of the penny, the mother-figure and the outgoing morality.

---

foul smell he noted in Ireland in 1669 to the massacres. On another occasion he ordered an ill child to be washed and re-washed, as if somehow the disease could be washed away. The cleanliness of Quakers in general is well-known; and, conversely, many early Quakers, in accesses of mania, smeared themselves with excrement and ran through the streets, as if to say "Look how filthy (i.e. wicked) I am."

PART THREE

THE IMMORALISTS

CHAPTER 10

WEIRDEST OF THE WEIRDEST

WHILE I WAS WORKING THROUGH the foregoing material, I was keeping at the back of my mind the thought that in due course, when I came to investigate the mother-identifying pattern, it should present, in many respects, just the opposite picture. If the patrist was subject to fits of depression, then the matrist might display fits of elation; if the patrist thought man fundamentally wicked, the matrist ought to think him fundamentally good; if the patrist thought God to be severe and remote, the matrist ought to think him beneficent and near at hand; if the patrist was inhibited, the matrist might be expected to be noticeably uninhibited and spontaneous.

I knew, of course, from my previous work, that, generally speaking, the matrist was the opposite of the patrist in many respects—his sexual permissiveness, his democratic attitude, his view of women, and so on —but my study of the Puritan character had greatly extended my original conception of patrism, and what I was now looking for was a corresponding extension of the concept in matrism.

In *Sex in History* I had identified the Romantics of the late eighteenth and early nineteenth century as exemplifying matrism.[1] Their general spontaneity, their tendency to idealise women, and their interest in movements of an anti-authoritarian character are well known, and are clear indicators. Such general impressions can be confirmed in detail. For instance, as I have argued that the patrist distrusts scientific inquiry and popular education, as likely to unsettle the order of society, so the matrist should tend to support popular education. Thus where patrists from Mandeville to Gardiner[2] condemned popular education, Words-

[1] Op. cit., Chapter 10.
[2] Gardiner attributed the Nore Mutiny to the spread of popular education. Cf. also Davies Giddy's speech in the Commons, 1807, against the Bill to establish parish schools supported from the rates.

worth looked forward to the day when the State should recognise its obligation to provide universal education.

> Oh for the coming of that glorious time
> When, prizing knowledge as his noblest wealth
> And best protection, this imperial Realm
> While she exacts allegiance, shall admit
> An obligation on her part to *teach*
> Those who are born to serve her and obey.[3]

Matrists also display what is perhaps less well known, very clear signs of incest preoccupations: incest is the theme of Shelley's *Laon and Cythna* and *The Cenci*, and appears also in earlier works, like Walpole's *The Mysterious Mother*. Byron not only introduced incest in his *Manfred*, and possibly his *Parisina*, but, as is now generally accepted, seems to have had an incestuous relationship with his half-sister Augusta. (Even if, as Mario Praz claims, he merely sought to give this impression in order to torture his wife, it still betrays his preoccupation with the subject that he should have chosen this method.)[4] This is quite decisive evidence that they must be classed as matrists.[5]

Nevertheless, to identify the Romantics as matrists, though satisfactory as providing an instance, was not satisfactory from the viewpoint of historical interpretation generally. The Romantics were a very small group in themselves, even if they had links with similar groups in France and Germany. To detect the presence of ideas derived from the mother-image it is clearly necessary to show that Romantic ideas had permeated the thinking of a wider public during the period. And it looked as if I should have to investigate the question of how this group came into being, for, if the assumptions made in the present book are correct, no widely influential group could have emerged overnight, but must have grown out of some pre-existing trend in personality formation.

---

[3] 'The Excursion', *Poems*, ix, 293–8.

[4] Praz, *Romantic Agony*, p. 73.

[5] Incest themes also appear in the works of Continental Romantics. Cf. Chateaubriand's *René*.

The first step was therefore to analyse the attitudes of the Romantics, first with the idea of seeing whether they displayed those further characteristics which I now associated with matrism, but for which I had not looked in the earlier study; and secondly, in order to distinguish that part of their thinking which derived from the mother-image from other elements which might be present.

It did not take much study to answer the first of these questions. For instance, in contrast with the Puritans, the Romantics held that man is fundamentally good. Thus Wordsworth speaks of

> . . . his noble nature, as it is
> The gift which God has placed within his power.[6]

This conception is usually regarded as being derived from Rousseau, whose *Emile, or a Treatise on Education*, starts with the words, "God makes all things good."[7] It argues that "the original goodness of human nature is still intact, though the minds of men are corrupted by the prejudices derived from their deplorable education and social environment". It is worth noting that there is here a further point of contrast: the Romantic places the source of evil outside man, in his environment, whereas the patrist places it within him. These alternative attitudes are frequently displayed in our own day.

Coupled with this belief in the essential goodness of man is, on the one hand, an optimistic outlook—a belief not necessarily in the inevitability, but certainly in the possibility, of social progress. Things can be made better: a more harmonious society can be evolved. Tennyson's vision of the future, with precedent slowly broadening down to precedent, was an example which came at once to mind. But we can see a degree of optimism in the many plans for social reform which the Romantics concerned themselves with. Southey and Coleridge were prime movers in a scheme to found a new community on the banks of the Susquehanna, and Coleridge looked forward to the day when

[6] *Poems*, ix, 355–60.
[7] But in fact this view was held by Fr. Bernard Lamy, by whom Rousseau was much influenced.

> each heart
> Self-governed, the vast family of love
> Raised from the common earth by common toil
> Enjoy the equal produce.[8]

words very similar to those of Wordsworth, quoted above. This sense of optimism and of the possibility of progress contrasts with the Puritan's sense of depression and his feeling that everything is getting worse—a feeling so commonly expressed as to give rise to the expression *laudator temporis acti*.[9]

If the patrist is authoritarian, the matrist is democratic. The Romantics felt that social co-operation could readily be attained without any authoritarian organisation. Goodwill would hold the community together and ensure co-operation. In Southey's words, the ideal society would be

> One Brotherhood,
> ONE UNIVERSAL FAMILY OF LOVE.[10]

This is going even further than espousing a democratic attitude: it seems to state a sense of kinship with others. And in fact the Romantics were strongly imbued with a sense of the brotherhood of man, and it was because they assumed that other men could also feel this sense of kinship that they believed society could be run on a simple basis of voluntary co-operation. This sense of kinship was so marked that it also extended to animals. Thus Coleridge exclaimed, "Innocent foal, I

[8] *Poetical Works*, 53–60.

[9] Cf. "We are decidedly of opinion that the present age surpasses in degree and variety of wickedness all that have preceded it . . . the influence of rational religion on the 'minds of men is gradually declining . . . etc." ('On the Deterioration of Natural Morals': *The Scourge*, 1811.) This at the time of greatest moral pressure and strictest behaviour! The indictment is indistinguishable from that of sixty years before: "The almost universal Contempt of Religion, the total Perversion of Morals, especially of the lower class of People . . . are become the subject of every man's complaint . . . etc." *Vices of the Cities*, p. 1.

[10] *Joan of Arc*, Book ix, LI, 743–4.

hail thee brother!"[11] on seeing a young ass, thus providing an opportunity for mockery which patrists did not fail to take.

This sense of kinship contrasts perfectly with the Puritan's sense of personal isolation.

But while the Romantics were undoubtedly matrists, equally undoubtedly there were other factors at work in their personalities which are not present in matrism as we find it at other periods in history—for instance the tough, aggressive matrism of the early Celts.[12] The most noticeable of these, perhaps, is the element of nostalgia and longing, the sense of something lost. Since what the matrist loves is the mother-figure, the clue to follow here seemed to be to ask whether, in some sense or other, the Romantics had lost their mother. A little biographical reading disclosed that some of them, at least, had lost their mothers in a quite literal sense. Southey, for instance, was brought up by an aunt; Rousseau's mother died at birth and he too was placed in the care of another woman. Rousseau makes it clear in his *Confessions* that what he was looking for all his life was a mother-substitute: he called his mistress, Mme. de Warens, "*Maman*" and also speaks of his later mistress, Thérèse Levasseur, as "a successor to *Maman*".[13]

Similarly, when Shelley tells us that in the clear prime of his first youth's dawn there was a Being whom his spirit often met, we are not surprised to find that it was a female one.[14]

I do not suggest that this is a complete explanation of the problem, but at least it suggests that the nostalgic element can be explained in terms of a traumatic childhood experience.

A related feature of the eighteenth-century Romantic is Arcadianism —the belief that long ago man lived in a state of primitive simplicity and happiness, untroubled by material problems of winning an existence and equally untroubled by moral doubts and conflicts. This, of course, is a myth of great age and probably of universal distribution. We all of us can dimly remember that in our own distant past we lived

[11] *Poetical Works*, 'To a Young Ass', p. 86.
[12] See Briffault, *The Mothers*, Chapter 28.
[13] Op. cit., ii, 60.
[14] 'Epipsychidion.'

in a state of bliss, untroubled by doubts, all our wants supplied by our mother. In the view of some authorities such memories stretch back actually to a pre-natal state, but it is sufficient for our purpose to regard them as derived from infancy. It is a myth which carries meaning for patrists as well as for matrists. But the patrist has resigned himself to the loss of the primitive bliss; he has rejected the mother who betrayed him. So in his version of the myth, Adam, having been thrown out of Paradise by the father, faces up to the necessity of earning his own living and satisfying his own needs. The matrist, on the other hand, has not accepted the father's right to do this, and he still hopes to regain the mother. So he can continue to hope that he will also regain the primitive simplicity and satisfaction which she once afforded him.

Evidently the two ideas are closely connected. Nostalgia for the lost mother is at the same time nostalgia for the lost bliss and innocence. The bliss which is lost is the primitive state of guilt-free calm and security before the development of the Œdipus conflict: thus it is that both Arcadianism and nostalgia appear in close association with the idea of innocence.

It is therefore quite in harmony with this interpretation to find that, for the nostalgic type of matrist, childhood carries a quite special sort of importance. The child is conceived to be innocent, and this har-monises with the general desire to see human beings as good rather than wicked. "All children are by nature evil," said Mrs. Sherwood, but the matrist dwelt on the idea of "innocent little children".[15] "Heaven lies about us in our infancy," said Wordsworth.[16] Further-more, the child is spontaneous, it follows its impulses, and sometimes at least these impulses are friendly and co-operative. Thus the child also symbolises effectively two more of the attitudes which the matrist exhibits.

Failure to appreciate this has led many critics into quite untenable judgments. Thus one writer speaks of Shelley's Classicism on the grounds that he had a strong feeling for Greece.[17] But Shelley was a

[15] Cf. Hannah More, "Is it not a fundamental error to consider children as innocent beings . . ." *Strictures*, p. 44.
[16] Intimations of Immortality, *Poems* iii, p. 5, and passim.
[17] Beers, *History Eng. Romanticism*, p. 5.

quite undoubted Romantic, as his rejection of his father, his pre-occupation with incest, his sexual morality, and much else shows. The Greece which he idealised was not the historic Greece, in all its complexity: a society which included grinding poverty, bloody warfare, magical practices and the dark gods of earth. It was an idealised landscape of shepherds and their nymphs: a world of sun and sea and the smell of thyme. Contemporary Greece appealed to him not for itself but because it was in revolt against a tyrant. Thus Shelley's love of Greece was simple Arcadianism: the very word shows how fully Greece had come to represent the Golden Age of the past. Hence Shelley's love of Greece proves his Romanticism, not his Classicism.

It is always necessary to ask, as the anthropologists have demonstrated, what a particular practice or belief *means* to the person who adheres to it, for the same item can mean opposing things to different people.

Thus, for instance, the idea of Nature meant, for the Romantic, wildness, irregularity, lack of order. But to seventeenth-century man, Nature implied harmony, balance and the expression of God's great design.[18] He stressed the mathematical balance of planetary movements, and the functional purpose of mechanisms which might at first sight seem arbitrary or wasteful. Hence it is not enough to know that a man praised Nature, to be able to label him a Romantic; and the same goes for many other attitudes.

In much the same way, to the German Romantics the Middle Ages came to have an Arcadian quality, a quality which had almost nothing in common with the disease, superstitution, persecution, neurosis and poverty which characterised the Middle Ages in historic fact. For this reason, some writers have come to regard an interest in the Middle Ages as synonymous with Romanticism. Thus some critics have been led into the absurd error of regarding Walter Scott as a Romantic.

Scott was always a Tory—that is, a conservative, and so a father-identifier. He opposed both political reform and prison reform, and thought Lancaster, who wished to put schools on a less authoritarian basis, a mountebank. In his only political pamphlet, *The Visionary*

18 Lovejoy, *Essays*, Chapter 5: 'Nature as Æsthetic Norm'.

(1819), the authoritarianism emerges nakedly. Democracy, he says, can only end in social disorder, and that disorder must be quelled by dictatorial methods. Ruskin said that he learnt Toryism from Scott's novels.

His novels express none of the characteristic Romantic attitudes. They glorify obedience to the King, conformity to custom, submission to external authority. "Even an admitted nuisance of ancient standing should not be abated without some caution," says a character in *Guy Mannering*. Scott himself said that his object was to reintroduce realism into the novel, which had been drifting in the direction of romantic fantasy. Really, it is difficult to see how any writer of perspicuity could classify him as a Romantic. As Benn rightly says, "Scott may best be described as one who worked up romantic materials into classic forms, and who used romantic motives for classic ends."[19]

Similarly, some writers have confused Arcadianism with Conservatism, since both display an interest in the past. It will be clear enough from the foregoing discussion how erroneous this is.

A second factor in Romanticism, though it is not present in every Romantic, is the tendency it shows to become associated with ideas of gloom and death. Many critics regard the 'Gothic' novels of the late eighteenth century as a Romantic phenomenon, while Mario Praz has tried to make such ideas the main criterion of Romanticism.[20] The present analysis, however, suggests that such an interpretation must be regarded as incorrect. As we have seen, such ideas were common in the period, and were held by many patrists. Naturally they influenced many matrists too.

More interesting than either of these factors, because far more mysterious, was the special attitude which the Romantic poets exhibited towards Nature: its importance is indicated by the fact that it is the thing for which they are most widely renowned.

This attitude is much more than a mere admiration of the beauties of nature; many writers have described it as 'pantheistic'—but since that is a term which can be used in a number of ways, it may be as well to examine in detail what is meant. For this purpose I shall consider the

[19] Benn, *History Eng. Rationalism*, pp. 311–12.
[20] Praz, *The Romantic Agony*.

works of Wordsworth, who displays this attitude in its clearest form.
In the first place, Nature is for Wordsworth a moralising influence:

> One impulse from a vernal wood
> May teach you more of man,
> Of moral evil and of good,
> Than all the sages can.[21]

This is not an idea to be found in orthodox Christian teaching, though
some of the Christian mystics (e.g. St. Bernard) felt thus: those that did
so usually came under the criticism of their Church.

But Wordsworth goes much further: sometimes he speaks explicitly of going into a kind of trance, in which he has a special insight
into the nature of things, or rather, the 'life' of things. It is a pleasant,
indeed a joyful, experience.

> "We are laid asleep
> In body and become a living soul:
> While with an eye made quiet by the power
> Of harmony, and the deep power of joy,
> We see into the life of things."

This insight seems to consist of an awareness of the *living* character of
all natural objects, and this discovery possesses a profound air of
significance:

> To every natural form, rock, fruit and flower,
> Even the loose stones that cover the highway,
> I gave a moral life; I saw them feel,
> Or linked them to some feeling: the great mass
> Lay bedded in a quickening soul, and all
> That I beheld transpired with inward meaning.[22]

---

[21] *Poetical Works.*
[22] 'Prelude'. Cf. Byron: I live not in myself, but I become
Portion of that around me; and to me
High mountains are a feeling . . .
Childe Harold, Canto 3, lxxii.

In the above quotations, the experience is not explicitly linked with the divine, but we also find the following odd passage, in which the divine is asserted in remarkably pagan terms:

> O'er the wide earth, on mountain and on plain
> Dwells in the affections and the soul of man
> A Godhead, like the universal PAN;
> But more exalted. [23]

Thus it seems that Wordsworth had, specifically, a sense of a divine presence: this presence seems to dwell both in Nature, both animate and inanimate, and also in the soul of man; it is 'good' rather than 'evil', or at any rate it teaches one the nature of good.

It is in the "Lines Written above Tintern Abbey" that Wordsworth gives us the fullest account of this experience, and here he introduces still more specifically the idea of an actual living presence, or spirit: it is not so much that this spirit is present in Nature—for it is everywhere, in man too—as that in surroundings of natural beauty one most easily becomes aware of it. The passage is worth quoting fully.

In his youth, he says, he had a passion for Nature, but he experienced no special mystical insight.

> The sounding cataract
> Haunted me like a passion: the tall rock
> The mountain, and the dark and gloomy wood,
> Their colours and their forms, were then to me
> An appetite; a feeling and a love
> That had no need of a remoter charm
> By thought supplied, nor any interest
> Unborrowed from the eye.

But later the meaning of nature for him grew more subtle.

> For I have learned
> To look on nature, not as in the hour
> Of thoughtless youth; but hearing oftentimes

[23] *Poetical Works*, 'Prelude.'

The still, sad music of humanity,
Nor harsh nor grating, though of ample power
To chasten and subdue. And I have felt
A presence that disturbs me with the joy
Of elevated thoughts; a sense sublime
Of something far more deeply interfused,
Whose dwelling is the light of setting suns,
And the round ocean and the living air,
And the blue sky, and in the mind of man:
A motion and a spirit that impels
All thinking things, all objects of all thought,
And rolls through all things. Therefore am I still
A lover of the meadows and the woods
And mountains; and of all that we behold
From this green earth; of all the mighty world
Of eye, and ear—both what they half create,
And what perceive; well pleased to recognise
In nature and the language of the sense
The anchor of my purest thoughts, the nurse,
The guide, the guardian of my heart and soul,
Of all my moral being.[24]

Thus Nature is a sustaining force; a nurse, and a powerful influence for good: and it is appreciated as a living 'presence'. 'Presence' is a word which occurs often in Wordsworth's works.[25] These ideas are repeated several times in 'The Prelude' and elsewhere.

Wordsworth ended with the conviction that this 'presence' was not just a figment of the imagination, but had objective existence:

> Nor less I deem that there are Powers
> Which of themselves our minds impress.[26]

and he expressly disclaimed having "given way" to animism (the practice of attributing personalities to trees, streams, and other natural

---

[24] 'Tintern Abbey.'
[25] For a survey see Havens, *Mind of a Poet.*
[26] 'Expostulation and Reply,' 21–2.

objects) though he does so in language which implies that he was tempted to it.[27]

That the Romantics should look favourably upon Nature is not in itself surprising, for Nature is traditionally a mother-figure, but Wordsworth's attitude clearly goes much further than that. There seem to be two main elements present: first, a sense of the divine character of all objects, which are seen as emanations of a single divine matrix ("bedded in a quickening soul"). This is, of course, a very ancient idea, found at many periods, as Huxley has demonstrated in *The Perennial Philosophy*. It is the staple of mysticism, and is also termed pantheism. (In theology, various dogmatic distinctions in the use of these terms are made, which need not concern us here.) This leads to the second idea, which is that, since all creatures are emanations of one deity, all are kin—sons, as it were, of the same mother. This accounts, then, for the insistence on the idea of brotherhood in the political thought of the Romantics.

Curiously enough, while the Romantic strongly feels his kinship with other creatures, and even with what are normally regarded as inanimate objects, he also feels the divine presence as something other: the Godhead which is present is not himself.

Here, then, was a special state of mind which must be coupled with the group of attitudes derived from mother-identification to provide an adequate account of the Romantics. Before offering any psychological interpretations on this phenomenon, it seemed best to inquire whether signs of it could be found at some earlier point in the story. For if so, it must be regarded as the product of forces in society affecting the formation of personality, and not as the rare peculiarity of a few individuals.

By good fortune, I came almost at once upon a most striking example, located at the very start of the eighteenth century, in the works of Shaftesbury. These sound the almost animistic note which we have seen in Wordsworth with a quite astonishing fidelity. Take, for instance, the following passage:

[27] "I assure you, I have never given way to my own feelings in personifying natural objects or investing them with sensation without bringing all that I have said to a vigorous after-test of good sense . . ." Letter to W. R. Hamilton, December 23rd, 1829, cited Havens, pp. 68–9.

"But here mid-way the *Mountain*, a spacious Border of thick Wood harbours our weary'd Travellers: who now are come among the ever-green and lofty Pines, the Firs, and noble Cedars, whose tow'r'ing Heads seem endless in the Sky; the rest of the Trees appearing only as Shrubs beside them. And here a different Horror seizes our shelter'd Travellers, when they see the Day diminish'd by the deep Shades of the vast Wood; which closing thick above spreads Darkness and eternal Night below. The faint and gloomy Light looks horrid as the Shade it-self: and the profound Stillness of these Places imposes Silence upon Men, struck with the hoarse Echoings of every Sound within the spacious Caverns of the Wood. Here *Space* astonishes. *Silence* it-self seems pregnant; whilst an unknown Force works on the Mind, and dubious Objects move the wakeful Sense. Mysterious Voices are either heard or fancy'd; and various Forms of *Deity* seem to present them-selves, and appear more manifest in these sacred Sylvan Scenes; such as of old gave rise to Temples, and favour'd the Religion of the antient World."[28]

This is an extraordinary passage to find written in 1698, in a period when the untamed landscape was normally regarded with dislike. The parallels with the Romantic poets of a century later are extraordinarily exact: the emphasis on gloom and mysterious silence, and the pervading sense of the supernatural.

At this point it occurred to me that if the Romantic considers Nature to be not merely beautiful but good, comforting, and in some sense divine, the Puritan should regard Nature not simply as ugly but as harsh, and in some sense bad and bereft of the divine. I knew of nothing to support this, at the time, and I felt it would show the theory to have some predictive value if the point could be proved. Sub-sequently, investigation showed that this attitude was general in the seventeenth century. The secular Defoe thought Westmoreland a county "eminent only for being the wildest, most barren and frightful of any that I have passed over in *England*",[29] while Miège admired southern England because it was "generally a flat and open country,

---

[28] Shaftesbury, *Characteristicks*, p. 390.
[29] Defoe, *Tour*, iii, 231.

not overgrown with wild and unwholsom Forests, nor dreadful high Mountains'.[30]

Theologians, feeling the difficulty of condemning as ugly what God had created, put forward the view that the earth had originally been created flat and smooth, and had only become mountainous and irregular at the time of, and as a result of, the Fall of Man. As Dr. Burnet said in *The Theory of the Earth*, originally there was "not a Wrinkle, Scar or Fracture in all its Body; no Rocks nor Mountains, no hollow caves, nor gaping channels, but even and uniform all over".[31] At the Day of Judgment this state of smoothness is to be restored: this is why the Isaiah says, "Every valley shall be exalted, every mountain and hill laid low."

This opus was immensely popular, going into six editions and being widely discussed. Addison was among those who praised and quoted from it.

From the psychological viewpoint, in which the Fall corresponds to that point in infancy at which the child feels it has been ousted from its mother's affection by the father, the image is wonderfully exact. For, on the one hand, Paradise itself is conceived as Nature in its original perfection, a sort of Kew Gardens replete with splendid specimens of every kind of plant, while on the other, the (earth) mother is naturally thought of as having been fair and perfect before the rejection, but foul and repellent after.

As the century advanced, and the elements in personality shifted back towards a balance, we should expect to find the actively repellent character of Nature fading out. Sir R. Blackmore exclaims:

> But can the objector no convenience find,
> In mountains, hills and rocks, which gird and bind
> The mighty frame, that else would be disjoined?[32]

And Edmund Law, translating William King's *De Origine Mali* (1702) in 1729, goes further: "Mountains . . . which many Moderns have

---

[30] Miège, *New State of England*, i, 13.
[31] Op. cit., Book I, Chapter 6.
[32] 'The Creation', iii, 412 ff, in Chalmers, *Works of Eng. Poets*, x.

misrepresented as deformities of Nature . . . afford to other Animals the most commodious Harbour and Maintenance. . . . To them we owe the curious Vegetables, the richest and most useful Metals, Minerals and other Fossils; and, what is more than all, a wholesome Air, and the conveniences of navigable Rivers and Fountains."[33]

And, of course, the truth does lie between the two extremes. Nature at times seems to obstruct man's endeavours and to bring him into discomfort and danger; at others she aids him in his struggle for existence and adds to his comfort and convenience. It is precisely in moments of pessimism that we see the picture in black hues, in moments of optimism that we see it in rosy ones. Thus the dichotomy which we are developing may be seen also to reflect the distinction between optimism and pessimism, between excitement and depression, to which reference has already been made.

The parallel between Shaftesbury and the Romantic poets goes, however, a good deal further than this. In his *Enquiry Concerning Virtue* he explicitly states his belief in the inherent goodness of man: he maintains that men, so far from being born to evil, have an innate moral sense.[34] This was, for the period, a completely new and challenging proposition. Hobbes had argued that man was motivated only by pleasure and pain. Only on the assumption that *post mortem* rewards and punishments are exactly matched to behaviour would such a system of motivation produce right action. The Church had held that men knew what was right to do only because God had laid such matters down. But Shaftesbury held that men instinctively knew what was right and were motivated to do such things.

Furthermore, Shaftesbury feels that Nature is not merely haunted by the divine, but actually beneficent. His dialogue *The Moralists: a Rhapsody* argues that even those aspects of Nature which seem to be bad work for a good end, and that everything is, as he himself says, for the best. But a still more striking statement is made later in the argument. In a passage in which the persons of the dialogue first retire to a

[33] As we shall see in Chapter Twelve, the view of Nature as a convenience is still a basically patrist attitude in contrast with the matrist tendency to see Nature as a source of aesthetic feeling.

[34] *Characteristicks*, Vol. i, Treatise IV.

beautiful spot, they start by appealing to the *genius loci* to "make us feel *Divinity* present in these solemn Places of Retreat!" Apparently the genius obeys their behest, for there follows this remarkable apostrophe:

"O Glorious *Nature*! supremely *Fair* and sovereignly Good! All-loving and All-lovely, All-divine! Whose Looks are so becoming, and of such infinite Grace; whose study brings such Wisdom, and whose contemplation such Delight . . . O Thou impowering DEITY, Supreme Creator! Thee I invoke, and Thee alone adore. To thee, this Solitude, this Place, these Rural Meditations are sacred; whilst thus inspired with Harmony of Thought, tho' unconfin'd by Words, and in loose Numbers, I sing of Nature's Order in created Beings, and celebrate the Beautys which resolve in Thee, the Source and Principle of all Beauty and Perfection."[35]

While Shaftesbury thinks of Nature as good, as a moralising influence, and as imbued with a divine presence, he does not express so clearly the idea of a kinship based on the fact that all things are emanations of the divine. Nevertheless such ideas were common at the time at which he wrote, and the word 'pantheism' was coined to describe them. Toland was the first to introduce the term. In his *Pantheisticon* (1705) he explains, "Our age has produced not a few who, desirous to dispute freely . . . instituted Entertainments, not unlike those of the *Socratics* . . . They are called for the most part Pantheists . . . They maintain 'All Things are from the Whole, and the Whole is from all Things' . . . From that Motion and Intellect that constitute the Force and Harmony of the infinite Whole, innumerable species of Things arise, every Individual of which is both a Matter and a Form to itself."[36]

The pantheist element can perhaps be traced as dimly present in Shaftesbury, when he writes, "Is there any difficulty in fancying the Universe to be *one Intire thing*? Can one otherwise think of it, by what is visible, than that All hangs together, as *of a Piece*?" This seems to express the conviction of the unity of all life which is the hallmark of pantheism.[37]

---

[35] ib., ii, 345.

[36] Op. cit., pp. 13 ff.

[37] *Characteristicks*, ii, 347. The pantheists tended to be Euhemerists: that is, to regard all religions as being variants of the worship of the one and only divine

But pantheism comes to a much more explicit statement in the work of the Deist poets of the first half of the eighteenth century: particularly in such authors as Thomson, *The Seasons* (1726–30), Baker, *The Universe* (1727), Brooke, *Universal Beauty* (1735), Akenside, *The Pleasures of Imagination* (1744). These poets are commonly referred to as Nature poets, but this is to classify them by a single aspect of their work. In point of fact they put forward a homogeneous conception of the world on precisely the lines I have described: in it, not only is Nature beneficent, but is seen as an aspect or emanation of the Deity; while to man is held out the hope of perfecting himself and of a final reunion with that Deity on lines which are more pantheist than Christian. Thomson indeed added to *The Seasons* a 'Hymn' so frankly pantheist that his first editor thought it best to exclude it from his collected works for the sake of his reputation. This hymn claims that the seasons "are but the varied God".

> "To HIM, ye vocal gales
> Breathe soft; whose SPIRIT in your freshness breathes.
> SOFT ROLL your incense, herbs, and fruits and flowers,
> In mingled clouds to HIM; whose sun exalts,
> Whose breath perfumes you and whose pencil paints . . .

> "God is ever present, ever felt,
> In the void waste and in the city full;
> And where He vital breathes there must be joy."

Finally he apostrophises "UNIVERSAL LOVE . . . from seeming evil still educing good," and he ends by foreseeing that one day he will "lose self in HIM, in LIGHT INEFFABLE!"

It would be instructive to pursue the history of such ideas further, but for the purposes of the present inquiry it is enough to know that this special state of mind was by no means unique to the Romantic

---

spirit. This contrasts with the view of most orthodox Christian dogmatists that their own religion is the only true religion, all others being not merely erroneous but actively devoted to the service of the Prince of Darkness.

poets, but was at least a sporadic feature of the entire period from 1700 to 1850. And that there were many in the population who also had sympathy for such ideas, so vastly different from traditional teaching, is shown by the considerable readership which the works of Shaftesbury, Thomson and others attained.

I next began to look for an explanation of this type of experience. The most instructive description seems to be Tennyson's:

"I have never had any revelations through anæsthetics, but a kind of waking trance—this for lack of a better word—I have frequently had, quite up from boyhood, when I have been alone. This has come upon me through repeating my own name two or three times to myself silently, till all at once, as it were out of the intensity of consciousness of individuality, individuality itself seemed to dissolve and fade away into boundless being, and this is not a confused state, but the clearest of the clearest, and the surest of the surest, the weirdest of the weirdest, utterly beyond words, where death was an almost laughable impossibility, the loss of personality (if so it were) seeming no extinction, but the only true life. I am ashamed of my feeble description. Have I not said that the state is utterly beyond words?"[38]

Thus Tennyson describes it as "loss of consciousness of individuality", or, in psychiatric terms, some kind of disruption of the ego. A similar idea is implied by Coleridge, when he says that by an effort of love we can make

> "The whole one Self. Self that no alien knows,
> Self far-diffused as Fancy's wing can travel!
> Self spreading still. Oblivious of its own,
> Yet of all possessing!"[39]

Tennyson's experience is not without modern parallels. Thus Dr. Bucke had such an experience one evening when driving home after an evening with friends, and it impressed him so much that he spent the rest of his life collecting further examples. He speaks of it as "a

[38] Letter to B. P. Blood in *Memoirs of Alfred Lord Tennyson*, ii, 473, cited James, *Varieties of Relig. Exp.*, p. 285 *n*.
[39] 'Religious Musings,' *Poetical Works*, pp. 53–60.

sense of exultation, of immense joyousness accompanied or immediately followed by an intellectual illumination impossible to describe. Among other things, I did not merely come to believe, but I saw that the universe is not composed of dead matter, but is, on the contrary, a living Presence; and I became conscious in myself of eternal life. I saw that all men are immortal. . . . The vision lasted a few seconds and was gone; but the memory of it and the sense of the reality of what it taught me has remained during the quarter of a century which has since elapsed."[40]

Freud also noted this experience, which he christened the 'oceanic feeling'.[41]

The conclusion to which all this tends is that the Romantic poets suffered from a disturbance of the ego, i.e. that part of us which we consider to be 'I myself'. It is easier to see how such a thing might be possible when we recall that the infant is unable to distinguish the subjective and the objective. As developmental psychologists have shown, it is only by repeated and often painful experience that it learns which sensations come from inside it, and which from outside. At the psychoanalytic level, therefore, we might regard the 'oceanic feeling' as a regression to infancy—to the period when the child is blissfully warm and comforted in the arms of its mother, whom it cannot distinguish from itself. Such an interpretation receives some support from the fact that the Romantic often sees Nature as 'mother Nature' and, as Wordsworth indicates, as a source of support. Such regression results from severe frustation of the child's emotional needs.

It is not necessary to insist on the point, however. It is enough if we stick to the observed facts and say that the Romantic distinguishes only weakly between 'I' and 'not I'. Perhaps it is not too fanciful to say that the walls which contain his ego are thin and sometimes dissolve altogether. Evidently the Romantic's tendency to see all mankind as his brother is related to this, and it is confirmatory that he sees not only mankind but animals and even stones as somehow included in this relationship. Moreover, if, in pantheist terms, all these creatures and objects are seen as emanations of the divine spirit, then 'brothers' is the

[40] Bucke, *Cosmic Consciousness*, pp. 8 ff.
[41] Freud, *Civilisation and its Discontents*, pp. 20 ff.

appropriate simile, for all are the offspring of the same mother spirit.

At this point, I turned back to consider the Puritan personality: for if the Romantic ego was to be called 'thin-walled', then presumably the Puritan could be called 'thick-walled'. And at once this threw light on the Puritan's striking sense of isolation from his fellow men. Again, whereas the Romantic mystic feels himself identified with the Deity, the Puritan feels himself infinitely remote from the Deity, and cast out. And where the mystic feels embraced by His love, the Puritan feels that God's love has turned to hate. These two patterns seemed to complement each other perfectly. Hence if one is to regard the Romantic mystic as having some defect in his ego structure, the Puritan must be regarded as having a defect equally serious but of opposite type.

The idea that the coherence of the ego might be involved in the story was rather alarming, for it opened up a new dimension. Thus far, I had conceived the problem largely in terms of super-ego and id: the patrist was the man with the severe super-ego, caused by introjection of a severe father-figure, the matrist by contrast had a more permissive super-ego, due to introjection of the milder mother-figure. As a result his spontaneous impulses were less repressed, and he appeared as spontaneous where the patrist was inhibited.

This discovery immediately raised in my mind the question of whether disruption of the ego occurred exclusively in conjunction with matrism, or whether patrists of this type could also be discovered.

But while it raised new problems, it also gave promise of illuminating much that had previously been mysterious, and it seemed wise to pursue the clue further. Instead therefore of following up the whole question of Romanticism at this point, I shall attempt in the next chapter to explore the question of ego further, and to show its relation to the various other factors in personality which we have noticed.

CHAPTER II

THE GREAT AMPHIBIUM[1]

THE NEXT STEP seemed to me to be to check my diagnosis that the Romantics suffered from some defect of the ego by reference to a different Romantic school, and for this purpose I took the Romantic movement in Germany.

The earlier German Romantics of the Storm-and-Stress period, such as Hamann[2] and Herder,[3] show the characteristic feeling for a pantheistic conception of the universe—they favoured the views of Spinoza—and they provide, in addition, the usual signs of matrism: for instance, they accorded a high status to women and observed a permissive morality.[4] But it was among the later German Romantics of the nineteenth century that I expected to find the process most

---

[1] "Man is that great and true amphibium whose nature is disposed to live, not only like other creatures in diverse elements, but in divided and distinguished worlds." Sir Thomas Browne, *Hydriotaphia*.

[2] Hamann (1730–88) devoted his whole life to recommending spontaneity. Of him, Goethe said, "The principle behind all Hamann's utterances is this, 'Everything that man undertakes, whether it be produced in action or word, or anything else, must spring from his whole united powers.' " (*Werke*, x, 563). Hamann liked to be called Pan.

[3] Herder (1744–1803), an admirer of Shaftesbury, stressed a loving personal relationship with God, and believed in the divinity of Man's intuitions. He was a Spinozist. On these and other early German Romantics see Pascal, *The German Sturm und Drang*.

[4] See *Sex in History*, Chapter 10, on this; also R. Huch's contribution to Keyserling's *Book of Marriage*. The German Romantics also stressed feeling against intellect. Their pantheism was converted into Roman Catholicism of a mystical sort, and in this the matrist element emerges, as when Novalis saw a vision of his beloved Sophy transfigured as the Virgin Mary. Others, however, became authoritarian in outlook, and the nature of this change needs investigation. See Willoughby, *German Romantics*; Pascal, *German Sturm und Drang*.

vividly displayed, since it was they who carried the Romantic movement, in its literary sense, to the furthest extreme. This expectation was rewarded even more generously than I had imagined possible. E. T. A. Hoffmann, in particular, displays a degree of ego-disruption which can have few parallels outside the casebooks of psychiatry. He sums the whole matter up in so many words when, in *Die Elixire des Teufels*, he makes Brother Medardus say, "My own Ego, the sport of a cruel accident, was dissolved into strange forms and floated helplessly away upon the sea of circumstances. I could not find myself again." And, to make it quite clear, he adds, "I am that which I appear to be and I do not appear to be that which I am. At strife with my own ego, I am an unanswerable riddle to myself." Later, he hears his own voice calling, "Little brother, lit-tle brother Medardus . . . I am here, I am here . . . le-let me in . . . we will g-g-go into the woo-woo-woods, to the woo-woo-woods," and he sees his own face pushing up through the floor.

In the *Golden Jar*, the very notion of ego ceases to have any meaning. The ugly old Dresden apple-woman is also the beautiful bronze knocker on Registrar Lindhorst's door, and is at the same time the odious fortune-teller, Frau Rahesia, and the heroine's kindly nurse, Lise. The archive-keeper is a registrar by day and a salamander by night: the stolid registrar at one point steps backward into a bowl of blazing arrack and allows himself to be drunk up. In *Klein Zaches*, one of the characters continually finds himself absorbing items from the personalities of those he meets. Elsewhere Hoffmann says, "I imagine myself to be looking at my ego through a kaleidoscope—all the forms moving round me are Egos, and annoy me by what they do and leave undone."

This is ego-disruption with a vengeance. Hoffmann's fellow Romantics were little different. As Brandes sums it up, in a work by no means concerned with psychiatry, "They proceeded to decompose the human personality."[5]

An idea which had a peculiar fascination for these writers was that of the *Doppelgänger* or *alter ego*—we find it in Kleist's *Amphitryon*, von

[5] *Main Currents in Nineteenth Cent. Lit.*, Vol. 2, p. 160.

Arnim's *Die Beiden Waldemar*, and several other works. This school also represents characters as living before their birth, after their death, and so forth; in their plays the characters speak "out of character", or argue with the stage hands. Sometimes there are plays within plays, and even plays within plays within plays, in an endless sequence, so that the characters of one are the spectators of another and speak in each of these roles. Brandes comments, "They split the ego into strips, they resolve it into its elements. They scatter it abroad through space, as they stretch it out through time."[6]

It is hardly necessary to quote further instances to prove the point that the German Romantics suffered from some very severe disturbance of the ego. It seems however to have been a disturbance of a somewhat different type from that of the Romantic mystic, for the ego was not dissolved so much as split into parts.

Reflection suggested that the Puritan also suffers a split, but of a different sort. When he speaks of self-indulgence or self-control, he conceives of a controlling part of the ego and of a part which is controlled: thus he splits the ego, so to say, horizontally, where E. T. A. Hoffmann split it vertically. The split which the Puritan makes is, in fact, between ego and super-ego, and it can be expressed by saying that ego and super-ego are not fully integrated, a notion not uncommon in psychoanalytic work.

As I pursued the subject, other instances came to light. Fichte, for instance, argues the identity of the ego and the non-ego. Rousseau speaks longingly of the "short moments in my life when I became *another* and ceased to be *me*".[7] Edmund Gosse, in his youth, felt himself to be two, and thought that one self could watch the other from somewhere near the cornice of the room.[8]

Bertrand Russell, with sharp insight, says that the Romantic seeks to prevent others from impinging on his ego.[9] This seems reasonable

[6] ib., p. 161.

[7] Cited Seillière, *Les Etapes*, p. 4. Rousseau's treatment of the ego sometimes resembles that of the German Romantics. Thus in *La Nouvelle Héloïse* 'St. Preux' is a pseudonym under which several accomplices conceal themselves and we never learn his true identity.

[8] *Father and Son*, pp. 41-2.

[9] *Hist. West. Philosophy*, p. 708.

when one thinks of the fantastic pressures which Gosse's parents exerted on him. Russell further says that the Romantic cannot sustain a love affair for long, since the demands of the other begin to be felt as trammels. "Hence love comes to be conceived as a battle in which each is attempting to destroy the other by breaking through the protecting walls of his or her ego"—an observation which strangely reproduces the concept of ego-walls adumbrated above.[10]

I could see that the whole question of ego-structure needed exploration in the light of this insight. The egos of the German Romantics were evidently diseased, but in a rather different way from those of the English Romantics: instead of the boundaries dissolving, their egos merely split into a number of miniature egos, each still sharply defined. And again, it would be interesting to see how narcissism, or self-love, fitted into the picture: the fact that Rousseau's first play was called *Narcissus* seemed to provide a clue here. But this was a task for another book; it was enough for the moment that I had confirmed my impression that some disturbance of the ego was at work in the English Romantics.

All this time, I had been uneasily conscious of neglecting a small but important group in England, who were alleged to have influenced the thinking of the pantheist group at the beginning of the eighteenth century. These were the Cambridge Platonists, the school of religious philosophers who emerged at Cambridge in the middle of the previous century.

Though the movement was born in the stern Puritan atmosphere of Emmanuel College, the members seemed to betray the general earmarks of loss of ego-definition. They read deeply in the mystical works of Plotinus. Powicke, the best authority on this school, speaks, for instance, of Sterry as being virtually pantheist and stresses his affinity to the German mystic, Boehme.[11] Henry More (1614–87) may stand

---

[10] ib. These observations suggest that the Romantic is reacting from a very dominating kind of supervision in childhood: while this was certainly the case with Edward Gosse, it is not clear that it was so with all Romantics, and other factors are probably at work. Certainly, not all those who are thus supervised become Romantics.

[11] Powicke, *Cambridge Platonists*, p. 185 n.

as a type of this group for our purposes. From childhood he had "an inward sense of the divine presence". His favourite text was, "He that dwelleth in love, dwelleth in God and God in him." Like the Romantics, he loved solitude, but said that he never felt less solitary than when alone. "Many passages in his writings illustrate his delight in Nature, and scarcely less was his delight in music." He lived in perfect health and was "happy all day long". Sometimes he was quite "mad with pleasure"—especially under the influence of Nature or of music. As he gave up the practice of fasting on Fridays and saints' days and lived in simple luxury, one may conclude that he was free of guilt feelings, and of aggressions turned against the self—indeed, he seems to have been free of all aggression. This finds confirmation in the fact that he rejected the Church doctrine of predestination.[12]

His affinity with Catholic saints is emphasised by the fact that his body possessed the property known as "the odour of sanctity".[13]

But while in many respects he resembled the Romantics, he also wrote strongly in defence of the father. We may also see signs of subordination to the father in the fact that he criticised the Quakers and the Familists[14] (with whom he had so much in common) just because they had thrown off the authority of the Church. He himself reverted to the Church of England liturgy at a time when to do so was a crime. In general, too, the Cambridge Platonists stressed that the basis of religion was moral obedience.

Facts such as these compelled me to conclude that these men were, in

[12] ib., Chapter 6.
[13] His body possessed strange properties. Certain products "had naturally the odour of violets". "His breast and body, especially when very young, would of themselves, in like manner, send forth flowery and aromatic odours from them, and such as he daily almost was sensible of, when he came to put off his clothes and go to bed." His contemporary, Valentine Greatrakes (the medical empiric) had a similar property (R. Ward, Life of More, pp. 123–5). It seems possible that the guilt-free man's consciousness of a pleasant odour may be the counterpart of the guilt-ridden man's consciousness of a bad odour, to which reference was made in Chapter Nine; this receives some confirmation from those who, like Fox, felt after their 'conversion' that creation 'had a new smell'. On the odour of sanctity among Catholic saints see Thurston, Physical Phenomena of Mysticism, Ch. 9.
[12] The Familists, or Family of Love.

general, father-identifiers, and this established the important point that ego-defect is not a phenomenon only associated with mother-identification.[15]

Ego-defect must have been common during the seventeenth century, for there was, as Rufus Jones has said, a huge outburst of mysticism: not only were there numerous "Nature poets" of a mystical character such as Crashaw, Traherne, Herbert, and Vaughan, and other writers such as Quarles, Southwell, Penington, Hales and Fr. Baker, but there were also numerous sects based on doctrines of this type.[16] Of these the Quakers are now the best known, because they have persisted. At the time, they were very different in character from to-day, and very similar to such other sects as the Family of Love. All stressed that God was love, and religion a matter of experience of that love, rather than of belief in dogma.

Fox, the founder of the Quakers, is another character whose personality would repay a full investigation in the kind of terms here developed. He seems to have been a manic-depressive, oscillating between a rapturous sense of God's goodness and love, and a black awareness of an "ocean of darkness and death".[17] Thus at times he betrayed a gentle, tolerant attitude similar to Henry More's; at others he assailed whoredoms, lewdness, swearing and playhouses in the veritable accents of Puritanism. His dreams were largely occupied with escape from a danger usually appearing as a grim black man who was fettering his legs with a cord, but once as a bull which wishes to devour him.[18] The bull is the commonest of symbols of male sexuality and, significantly enough, he turns on it with another such symbol, a wooden stake, and "chopped it down his throat and to his heart and laid him still". This, like the Quaker refusal to uncover in the presence of one's father or superior authority, suggests the presence of father-rejection. That the Quakers also show clear signs of anal disturbance

---

[15] This raises the interesting questions why, in the eighteenth century, ego-defect is found exclusively in conjunction with mother-identification, and whether in the seventeenth it was ever found in conjunction with mother-identification.

[16] Jones, *Mysticism and Democracy*, pp. 8-12.

[17] Contrast *Jnl. Bicent.*, i, 10, with i, 19-20.

[18] *Journal* (Friends' House), iv, 124.

has already been demonstrated. In short, it seemed that one could account for the main features of early Quakerism by saying that they were father-rejectors, with marked anal features, and perhaps—certainly in Fox's case—some tendency for the ego-walls to dissolve.

As I considered these various behaviour patterns, I felt that my comprehension of the forces at work in personality was being expanded, while the main lines of the conception were being confirmed. I was able to put yet one more piece of the pattern in position when I came to consider the attitudes displayed by the influential theological writer, William Law (1686–1761).[19]

In the first part of his life he betrays the usual Puritan characteristics. He writes against the stage, against books and idle conversation, which he especially hated. He betrays extreme guilt and masochism. "Suffering is to be sought, to pay some of the debt due to sin," he says. His preoccupation with death has already been mentioned: "Christianity . . . has no other interest in this world than as it takes its members out of it." The body is a mere "sepulchre of the soul".[20]

Actually, his morality was more anal than patrist. The strict rules he made as to behaviour, his horror of waste of time, and his intense inhibition support this conclusion. His inhibition was so extreme that when Byrom came to make his acquaintance the two men walked up and down in silence, after the initial greeting, before Law could bring himself to utter a word; finally Law broke the silence with "Well, what do you say?"[21]

But as his life progressed he gradually became interested in the works of Jacob Boehme, and slowly turned into a near-mystic of the father-identifying type.

This case forced to my attention the fact that in many individuals the structure of personality is not even approximately fixed, but undergoes progressive change. Here the change seemed to be in the one factor of ego-definition, and this raised the questions (a) whether other factors in personality can also exhibit progressive change, and (b) whether any other striking instances of change fall within the period.

---

[19] See Overton, *William Law*, for the facts here given.
[20] W. Law, *Christian Perfection*, pp. 148, 41.
[21] Byrom, *Journal and Remains*, i, 616.

I had already become aware of the fact that decisive changes occurred in the personality of most of the later English Romantics. Thus Wordsworth, whose plea for universal education has already been quoted, had by the time of the Reform Bill come to doubt the value of education. "Mechanics' institutes make discontented spirits and insubordinate and presumptuous workmen,"[22] he complained; and later he asked in even more general terms, "Can it, in a *general* view, be good that an infant can learn much which its parents do not know?"[23]

Coleridge is an even more striking example. In youth his natural leaning towards a pantheistic outlook was marked; and as late as 1810 he praised Schiller's pantheistic *Uber die Sendung Moses*. But from the time he failed to finish 'Christabel' some change seems to have set in. Not only did he lose the capacity to write poetry, but he abandoned his Unitarian views for orthodox Christian ones; he held the Bible to be not only inspired, but the only revelation needed. His death fears grew so acute that he used to wake the house with his screams, and it was this fear of dying, as he told Sarah Hutchinson, which caused his addiction to laudanum.[24] He himself spoke of the 'disease' of his mind, and said, "I have been so forsaken by all the *forms* and *colourings* of existence, as if the *organs* of life had been dried up."[25] As I shall show in more detail in Chapter Thirteen, an awareness of form and colour is characteristic of the uninhibited Romantic personality. Fausset, summing up the change, says that "all that was prosaic and self-centred in his nature was in the ascendant".[26] As we have seen how the preoccupation with self is characteristic of the thick-walled ego, this judgment neatly confirms the diagnosis, implied by the facts noted above, that some progressive thickening of the ego-walls was occurring.

When I first noted the existence of this sort of change, I assumed it to be some kind of switch from matrism to patrism; but the diagnosis did not seem quite satisfactory: I was puzzled, for instance, by the case of

---

[22] *Prose Works*, i, 347.
[23] ib., i, 345. Samuel Palmer, the painter, is an example of such a change in another field of activity.
[24] Fausset, *Coleridge*, p. 226.
[25] ib., p. 191.
[26] ib., p. 266.

Southey, in whom the change smacks of disillusionment and cynicism. After the failure of his plan to start an ideal co-operative community on the banks of the Susquehanna, he exclaimed, "Man is a beast, and an ugly beast, and Monboddo libels the orang outang by suspecting them to be of the same family."[27] A cynic is a disappointed optimist, and if he satirises the folly of man's behaviour it is because he believes or at least wishes that it might be different. In this, I rather think, he differs from the patrist, whose preferred weapon is not satire but invective, and who seems almost pleased by the wickedness of men, which serves to emphasise his own virtue. The discovery that the prime factor in the change was concerned with the ego rather than the parental image went some way towards clearing up the problem, although leaving much unresolved.

The recognition that personality can show progressive variation is of course a commonplace of psychiatry, but it was an aspect which I had hitherto quite neglected. In *Sex in History* I had been concerned only with the broad issues over a long period of time, and, as I now realised, I had been led into speaking of personality as if, once it had been determined in a patrist or a matrist sense, it remained fixed. While this was of no consequence in a study taking such a general view, in the present inquiry I had continued to make this assumption. The realisation that people could at first reject and later accept the father-image had dealt the first blow to this assumption. My reaction to this was to read again the views of Freud, Ferenczi and others on parental identification: they suggested that father-identifications are laid down, as it were, on top of mother-identifications, so that the rejection of the father represents a regression to an earlier phase of development.[28] If in later life patrist ideas are adopted, presumably there has been some re-absorption of the father-image. The discovery of the role of ego-boundaries served to clear up the aspects of this sort of change which had not been covered by such an analysis.

But if individual personality can change in this way, this must be an important factor in the general process of social change which we are

27 *Life and Correspondence*, iii, 5.
28 This statement is drawn from the basic analysis of the difference between patrism and matrism. See Appendix.

studying. Until this point it had been my assumption that social change, on the historic scale, took place primarily because children felt differently from their parents—whether by carrying their views to a new extreme or by reacting from them. But if definitive changes can take place in individuals—as distinct from a mere adaptation to prevailing opinion—then this whole assumption becomes subject to doubt. However, these wider issues I did not wish to consider until all the evidence had been collected.

As the reader will have realised, the development of the inquiry had gradually led me to a much more detailed analysis of personality than the simple matrist-patrist picture with which I had started. At this point therefore it may be as well to summarise what I felt I had learned, as a preliminary to applying the findings to the interpretation of social change on the broadest scale.

In point of fact six factors have proved to be relevant to our purpose. Let us recapitulate what we have learned.

1: *Parental image.* The original scheme of matrist and patrist was modified a little in Chapter Eight where I pointed out that a distinction could be drawn between identification with the mother and rejection of the father. I analysed the libertine (such as the Duke of Wharton) as one who was primarily concerned to deny the father and what he stood for; the distinction was most obvious in the field of religion, where the libertine does not substitute a mother- for a father-religion as a matrist would, but seems chiefly concerned to deny the father-religion, and to ridicule its ceremonies. Similarly in the field of morals, he does not simply maintain a mistress, he flaunts her to the world, or seduces a whole string of women and boasts of having done so. Again, where the mother-identifier rejects the use of force in favour of persuasion (and believes in the fundamental willingness of men to co-operate) the father-rejector simply opposes force by force: politically this seems to correspond to the anarchist, who wishes to destroy the existing system not in order to substitute some other, but in order to maintain a state of 'an-archy', or no government. And where the matrist values welfare above chastity, the father-rejector is simply concerned to depreciate chastity or to destroy it. If the motive behind the patrist's stress on chastity is the Œdipal one of preserving his mother for himself against the incursion of the father, then the father-rejector seems to say, "I have been, as it were, cuckolded by an intruder", and so he may find a source of pleasure in seducing other men's wives, and so reducing them to his own state.

If father-rejection was to be distinguished from mother-fixation it followed that mother-rejection must be distinguished from father-fixation. I could not think, off-hand, of any male person in the period who corresponded to this pattern, but I attempted to infer the features of this personality pattern from the three cases already studied. Presumably the mother-rejector would also reject religion, but, since he would be tied to persuasive methods rather than force, he would be some kind of rationalist rather than a militant atheist or conoclast. He would reject tenderness and love, without substituting force; this seemed to be the pattern of behaviour which Suttie has called the "taboo on tenderness": it is a rejection of tenderness which conceals a basic desire for it.[29] In this description we can recognise the man who is hard to others, and to himself. Arguing further, if the professional soldier represents the pure father-identifier, with his acceptance of an authoritarian system, we can suppose that the ascetic element, so often displayed, derives in part from an accompanying mother-rejection. Finally, since the patrist attaches importance to physical welfare, we should expect the mother-rejector to destroy and undermine welfare, while remaining unconcerned about chastity.[30]

While the period under study does not, I believe, display this type in its pure form, no doubt mother-rejection plays a major part in the severity and emotional inhibition displayed by many moralists. A logical development from this point would be to examine a considerable number of cases of parental acceptance and rejection with a view to discovering what causes these processes. Such an investigation could only be done adequately with contemporary case material, in which the attitudes to both parents had been fairly fully explored. Casual inspection of biographical material in the period 1700–1850 suggests

[29] Suttie, *Origins of Love and Hate*, Ch. 6.

[30] An extreme instance of the type may perhaps be Genghis Khan and other Khans of that same dynasty, but I know of no obvious instance in the period covered by the present study.

that, as one might expect, a severe or unloving parent is often rejected. The second Duke of Wharton rejected the severe upbringing given him by the first Duke, but the third Duke repeated the pattern of the second. Newton rejected his father, as we have seen, after extremely cruel and unjust treatment by a father-figure, coupled with rejection by his own father. We can at least conclude that in this period a good many people were deeply disturbed in personality by unsatisfactory relations with their parents.

2: Guilt. In considering parental images I was led to make a distinction concerning the presence or absence of guilt. It is obvious that the conservative fox-hunting squire, with his vast meals and heavy drinking, is radically different from the ascetic and guilt-ridden Puritan. Yet he shows such decisive signs of patrism as authoritarianism, conservatism, belief in a father deity, and a tendency to restrict the freedom of women, whose chastity seems to him important; at the same time he is not deeply exercised on questions of welfare. This seems to me to represent father-identification without the presence of guilt. If so, it becomes clear that the Œdipus situation does not in itself automatically provide a supply of guilt-feelings, and some other source or some special circumstance must be sought to account for them.[31]

If we can distinguish guilty and non-guilty father-identifiers, should we also distinguish between guilty and non-guilty mother-identifiers? Before attempting to answer this question let me proceed to the third element.

3: Aggression. Having drawn attention to the existence of strong aggressions turned outward in individuals such as Lord Camelford and 'Mad' Fitzgerald, I interpreted the preoccupation with death as due to similar aggressions turned inward, and suggested that the process of reform might be, to some extent, a story of the introjection of aggression—though to this one should add that it would be necessary to explain why such powerful aggressions were generated in the first place.

But I also explained ascetic and masochistic practices as due to

[31] At a later stage in the investigation I found the probable source of this additional guilt, as will appear in Chapter 16.

aggression against the self; here there seems to be a slight discrepancy, for it appears that it is possible to have a preoccupation with death without exhibiting asceticism. We may find a clue in the fact that Wesley practised austerities before his conversion but not afterwards, yet he retained his interest in death, as we have seen. Moreover, aggression was clearly present, as shown by the severity of his regimen for the children at Kingswood, of which I shall say more in a later chapter.

Evidently 'conversion' (if conversion it was) removed the need for *self*-punishment and made possible the projection of aggression. It is guilt which necessitates self-punishment. Guilt and aggression are, of course, closely associated. If guilt is the trepidation inspired by a punishing father, aggression directed towards that father makes him seem still more severe. But in Wesley's post-conversion existence the father has ceased to be conceived as punishing, and hence the thought of death has ceased to be alarming and has become actually pleasant, since it means reunion with him.[32]

This enables us to understand the mother-identifier's death-wish, which is also pleasurable. Since the mother is not normally a severe and authoritarian figure, the matrist death-wish is not normally guilty. It would be, however, if the mother happened to be unusually severe.

4: Spontaneity. In describing the Puritan character I stressed both the actual inhibition of the Puritan (as in Law) and his belief that impulse *ought* to be controlled. In the next chapter I shall show how fully the Romantic believed that impulse *ought* to be indulged; that he actually indulged it is well known.

This dichotomy is closely connected with the parental figure, for it is by introjection of the father-image that the super-ego is normally established and self-control achieved. Introjection of the much milder mother-image creates a mild super-ego, though here again the possibility of introjecting a severe image of the mother exists, so that an inhibited matrist type is not impossible.

---

[32] This analysis, however, fails to distinguish between the harsh self-denial of the Puritan and the actual masochism of a man like Hurrell Froude, or Wesley in his pre-conversion period. This may be only a difference of degree, but the point needs further investigation.

5: *Level of Fixation.* In describing the Puritan character I explained how libido can be fixed at the anal level, and explored the implications of this. As I mentioned, it can also be fixed at the oral level, producing a dependent type of personality, not very common in the period in question (unless perhaps among the female sex), for which reason the point need not be pursued. In contrast with the personality elements we have just been discussing, it would seem that the level of fixation does not depend directly on the parental image; however, since it may be the case that severe taboos on sexual gratification force regression to the anal level, there may be an indirect connection.

6: *Ego-boundaries.* This point has just been explored in detail and I need not recapitulate.

These six factors are found combined in various patterns, as I have already indicated. Thus the Cambridge Platonists can be regarded as father-identifiers with little guilt and weak ego-boundaries. The Quakers are guilty father-rejectors with marked anal characteristics, and in the early years of the movement they possessed thin-walled egos. Jonathan Edwards is a guilty father-identifier with a strong ego, but no anal features, whereas the young Law presents the same pattern but with anal features. Thomas Day is an inhibited mother-identifier with strong ego and marked anal features, and so on.

Now there is no theoretical reason why every conceivable combination of these elements should not occur in actual life, and we might therefore expect the various types to appear in approximately equal numbers. However, while instances of almost every combination can be found in real life, the striking thing is that, in practice, most of the combinations are rare: sometimes only a single instance can be found. In contrast, one, or perhaps two, combinations appear quite widely. Moreover, the proportions gradually alter. Father-identification is commoner than mother-identification throughout the period, and as the century progresses guilty and inhibited father-identification becomes still more widespread. Similarly, anal characteristics appear with increasing frequency. It follows that major cultural influences—probably in the field of child environment—must have been at work to produce this result.

In making this broad statement it is important to emphasise that extreme instances of even the common combinations are almost always rare in the population as a whole. The majority of the population will display mild degrees of mother- or father-influence, mild degrees of ego-hardening or weakening, and so on. As with such other variables as intelligence, the cases are distributed about a mean point; the more extreme the case, the fewer the instances of it. But the extreme individual is influential because his bias enables him to express the corresponding attitude especially vividly. The young Romantic admires Shelley or Byron because they express for him, in a pure form, an aspect of his own personality. The moral statements of a Dr. Gregory or a Hannah More were bought by hundreds of thousands because they expressed succinctly views which the purchasers held but could not phrase so well, and supported them by arguments which the purchasers lacked the wit or application to devise.

The fact that extreme cases tend to be rare makes it all the more remarkable that throughout the period such comparatively large numbers of persons approximated closely to the anal-Puritan type.

It may be useful to discuss what light all this throws on the definition of Romanticism. This is a subject on which much ink has been spilt. Bernhaum lists twenty-six distinct definitions in his *Guide Through Romanticism*, while Lovejoy finds the subject so confusing that he suggests that we should speak of Romanticisms rather than of Romanticism.[33] Words, of course, can mean whatever men agree to make them mean: thus the Germans choose to confine the term Romanticism to the very last phases of the story, from 1795 onward, and thus exclude Goethe, whom many consider a major Romantic, but who was out of sympathy with the later Romantics, such as Schlegel and Herder. But while there is no 'true' meaning of the word, there is certainly a quite well-defined social and cultural phenomenon to which it may be applied. This phenomenon consists in the association of the mother-identification with ego-breakdown. In some cases this grouping was also associated with guilt-feelings and death-wishes. Most of the definitions listed by Bernhaum vary simply in laying more stress on one of these items than on the others; and the problem of

[33] *Essays in the Hist. of Ideas*, Chapter 12.

deciding whether a particular individual can be classed as Romantic is frequently a matter of deciding whether a man who betrays only one or two of these personality items should be included with those who display more.

This concludes the summary of personality factors with which we shall be concerned. As I evolved it, I felt a sense of excitement as I found it providing good working explanations of the various personality types I had noted. Before I hit on the notion of ego-defect, there were many cases (such as Law) which I could not fit in, but in the end every important case had been accounted for.

I say every case; but there is one which I have not yet discussed, and it happens to be especially important to our period. This is the case of John Wesley. At first sight Wesley appears to be a clearly-defined authoritarian. This was so generally recognised that he was known as Pope John. Hampson said, "He was the most absolute of monarchs—his will was the law. He never thought his authority secure but when exerted to the full."[34] The last phrase may give us pause, for the authoritarian does not normally doubt his authority; nevertheless, the general picture is clear. He always supported the authority of the established Church and of the monarchy: he wrote an emphatic letter to *Lloyd's Evening Post* condemning the American colonies for rebelling against the King.[35] He declared that a "wife must be beneath her husband in every respect."[36] As did Law, he drew up a set of rules by which he hoped to be saved. He feared impulse, and even when he was a child his mother observed, "Jacky will do nothing until he gives a reason for it."[37] He certainly believed in a father-deity (and this deity was until his conversion remote and rejecting), and he certainly valued chastity.

Nevertheless, a closer examination of his life reveals undeniable signs of mother-fixation, and especially that most diagnostic of all signs, incest-fears in his relations with women. He constantly toyed sentimentally with women, usually those in a dependent position, and he

---

[34] Hampson, *Memoirs of Wesley*, iii, 202–8.
[35] *Journal*, iv, 60–1.
[36] ib.
[37] Cited Bowen, *Wrestling Jacob*, p. 17.

always precipitated a crisis when marriage came in view. At Oxford it was Betty Kirkham; at Staunton Mrs. Pendarves;[38] on board ship going to America, Mrs. Beata Hawkins: she abandoned him for another man when she saw she was getting nowhere. In Georgia he tantalised the unfortunate Sophey Hopkey, half proposing to her, bringing her back to England, and keeping her on tenterhooks until she finally lost patience and went to another man. Wesley then made a terrible row, and she offered to return; at once he nervously recoiled.

It is a psychoanalytic commonplace that individuals who suffer from incest-fears can often overcome them only with women of inferior class, whom they can dominate and feel no compulsion to regard as their mother. It is therefore significant that when Wesley finally brought himself to propose it was to Grace Murray, an ex-domestic, who had nursed him when he was ill (note the maternal element).[39] Extraordinary to relate, he could not bring himself to go through any marriage service with her, but made a contract *de praesenti* in the medieval manner, though this was not legally binding.[40] She travelled about with him "like a sister". (Meanwhile Wesley displayed interest in other women, notably Molly Francis.) Finally unable to bear this intolerable position, she told him that one Bennett wanted to marry her. Again Wesley created a brouhaha, as he had with poor Sophey.

When, in 1751, Wesley finally brought himself to undergo the marriage ceremony, it was again to an ex-domestic, Molly Vazeille, who had nursed him. Again he flirted with other women. Her constant jealousy sufficiently indicates her own frustration, and the situation finally drove her into imbecility. Soon after, Wesley became enamoured of Sarah Ryan, yet another ex-domestic, whom he met

---

[38] He said that she "summoned up for him the image of God". Cited Bowen, *Wrestling Jacob*, p. 90.

[39] Bowen gives a good account of these events in *Wrestling Jacob*.

[40] In medieval times a valid marriage was effected by a mutual declaration of intention. Failure to have the marriage blessed by the Church was a contravention of canon law, and called for penalties but did not invalidate the marriage. Such a contract could be immediately binding (*de praesenti*) or effective at some future date (*de futuro*).

while visiting one of his female friends. She had the disadvantage, from Wesley's point of view, of being trigamously married, but Wesley said that God had shown him it was all right to trust her, and placed her above his wife at table and in conference. His wife, "foaming with fury", dragged him round the room by the hair of his head, accusing him of adultery.

And, to complete the picture, after Molly's death he undertook to edit the letters of Jane Cooper, also a domestic, who had died aged twenty. It is consonant with this preoccupation with women that he allowed women to preach—the first occasion was in 1761—although this was prohibited by the Church to which he claimed to belong.[41]

Such an extraordinary array of evidence (here given only in summary form) cannot be explained away, and we are bound to conclude that Wesley was fixated on a mother- rather than a father-figure. His sympathy with the poor, his genuine charities and his efforts to ameliorate the lot of the unfortunate also indicate a matrist interest in welfare.

I have little doubt that the explanation is that Wesley was fixated on a mother who had herself been fixated on a severe father.[42] In this way he acquired many of the patrist characteristics at second hand. Susanna Wesley was the daughter of that notable Puritan, the austere Samuel Annesley, who believed in the divine right of kings and personally taught his daughter the "performance of duties". She was the strictest of disciplinarians—for instance, she gave her children one day in which to learn the alphabet. "Rigid rules, a precise spacing of time, a stern insistence on method that brought everyone in Epworth parsonage to an almost mechanical state of regularity" was her system.[43] She was much preoccupied by the danger of eternal damnation, and emphasised to the children "the lost and miserable state" in which they were by nature. Overton observes that she had "a strong and masculine

[41] The wife who is described as like a sister (i.e. barred by the incest laws from consummating the relationship) appears in analogous situations in other periods, e.g. St. Paul. On this, see *Sex in History*, pp. 278-9.

[42] See p. 164, where it was argued that Wesley's conversion was impaired by the fact that he was preoccupied with a mother- rather than a father-image.

[43] Bowen, op. cit., p. 4. See Kirk, *Mother of the Wesleys*, Ch. 7.

mind. She showed, too, a masculine spirit in her brave struggles with poverty".[44]

Against this, Wesley's father was weak and ineffectual, as well as revengeful and vindictive. Brought up a Dissenter, he became a High Churchman for reasons of self-advancement. The mother was the dominant figure in the family, and when her husband was away, she did not hesitate to preach, without his authority, in his church. Thus it was evidently from his mother (or rather his grandfather, via his mother) that Wesley derived his patrist characteristics.

This resulting curious mixture of matrism and patrism I shall call 'patromatrism': we shall find its influence at work throughout the years which followed, and not simply among the Methodists. It is this that accounts, in some measure, for the way in which moralists began to concern themselves with the evils of this world, such as cruelty and slavery, which earlier Puritans had regarded as inevitable. The patromatrist is also distinguishable by his ambivalent attitude to women, whom he both courts and denigrates.

Obviously, girls can also fixate on a severe mother, and this should tend to produce a moralistic and reforming type of woman—such as we in fact find in Mrs. Sherwood, Mrs. Opie and others.

By analogy with these patterns we should expect to find instances of fixation on a mild father which should give rise to a permissive moral outlook, nevertheless marked by homosexual preoccupations; in this case it is the girls who will display the puzzling mixture, combining a preference for the society of men with an inability to come to terms with them, despite a permissive morality. And they will be inclined both to put men on a pedestal and to prefer men of lower status.[45]

To sum up: though the influence of parental introjections is closely intertwined with that of other elements, the evidence presented justifies the conclusion that it plays a primary part in the determination

[44] *Life in Eng. Church*, p. 156. Overton adds a vague tribute to her "feminine delicacy". But, as we have seen, this was primarily a masculine attitude, to which women were expected to conform.

[45] My knowledge of the women of the eighteenth century is insufficient for me to give examples of this type, but I know of clear instances in the contemporary world.

of behaviour, and it certainly plays a major part in determining those attitudes which we regard as moral.

Furthermore the evidence we have examined shows beyond doubt that during the eighteenth century severe disturbance of parental relationships was occurring, causing both wholesale rejection of parent figures and, to an increasing extent as the century wore on, intro-jection of rejecting mother-figures. The task of accounting for the social and moral changes we have observed becomes a matter of tracing the preponderance of such images, and of accounting for them. Why, in short, did not only fathers, as previously, but also mothers, come to be seen by many children as rejecting them?

Were there any changes in the upbringing of children which might account for this?

But before pursuing this question, I felt I should round out the picture of the period by analysing it more broadly in the light of the understanding of personality which I felt I had now gained.

CHAPTER 12

DELICIOUS DECLINE

O U R   T A S K is now to look at the culture—meaning the whole network of social beliefs, attitudes and practices—for indications of two contrary attitudes which can be referred to the two broad trends in personality which we have been tracing.

For reasons which will presently become clear, I shall start by considering the field of æsthetic judgments and the idea of beauty.

If we examine the development of taste during the eighteenth century, we at once become aware that a battle was in progress: this battle is usually described as being between the Classical conception of art and the newer, Romantic conception. The thought immediately presents itself: could these two conceptions reflect patrist and matrist elements in the personality? As I shall now attempt to show, this is on the right track, but the answer is slightly less straightforward.

Let us forget the labels 'Classical' and 'Romantic' for a minute, and simply ask ourselves what was the chief respect in which æsthetic positions differed. We find at one extreme a group which feels that art consists in the imitation of approved models, and the obeying of immutable rules of taste. Thus, in 1718, Gildon declared that even the greatest genius was never justified in breaking any of the rules.[1] At the other extreme we find those who feel that the artist should be free to follow his own imaginative impulse, however extraordinary. Hurd, in 1762, says that the poet has no need to observe the "cautious rules of credibility" and denies that he need "follow Nature", for he has a world of imagination to range in.[2] Between these two extremes lies a compromise position, in which 'reason' is to keep imagination in

---

[1] Gildon, *Complete Art of Poetry*, p. 96.
[2] *Letters on Chivalry and Romance*, Letter x.

check; the artist should not imitate Nature exactly, but rather, after studying Nature, seek to form generalised images which shall be more perfect than any individual instance in Nature.[3]

Even stated in these formal terms, this difference of view seems consistent with the patrist-matrist dichotomy. For the first group is one which appeals to the authority of rules established by our forebears, and stresses the importance of Classical models, while the contrary group wishes to free fantasy (i.e. the unconscious) from the control of 'reason'. The parallel becomes still more evident when we consider a different formulation. Young, writing in the middle of the battle, in 1759, saw the issue thus: "Modern writers have a choice to make. . . . They may soar in the regions of liberty, or move in the soft fetters of easy imitation."[4] Thus he equates the one view with liberty, the other with restraint—a dichotomy which closely reflects the proposition that the matrist welcomes spontaneity and lack of inhibition, while the patrist prefers discipline and restraint.

Many of the best-known writers on taste in the eighteenth century took up positions between these extremes; in their writings they were frequently concerned to modify the severity of the older (patrist) view. It is sometimes forgotten with what strictness this was often held. Shakespeare, for instance, was condemned because he failed to observe the Classic unities.[5] Vanbrugh was held to be the worst major architect in England.[6] Reynolds, defending him in 1786, said that he was "defrauded of the due reward of his merit" and claimed that he "showed a greater display of imagination" than any other architect.[7] But, for the patrist group, imagination was not a merit: it was felt to be morbid or actually immoral. Johnson, though taking a position between these extremes—he praised Shakespeare, despite his breaking

---

[3] See, for instance, Sir J. Reynolds' *Discourses*, iii (December 1770). Cf. also Johnson, "He [the poet] is to exhibit in his portraits of Nature such prominent and striking features, as recall the original to every mind; and must neglect the minuter discriminations . . . etc." *Rasselas*, Chapter X.

[4] Young, *Conjectures*, p. 19.

[5] Blair, like Hume, thought him "deficient in just taste, and altogether unassisted by knowledge of art".

[6] Steegman, *Rule of Taste*, p. 27.

[7] *Discourses*, xiii, 1786.

the rules—nevertheless regarded imagination as "a licentious and vagrant faculty"[8] and thought its current prevalence dangerous.

Now insistence on the primacy of the imagination is characteristic of the Romantics, and we can describe one of the two extremes from now on as 'Romantic'—although, as I have already sought to show, Romanticism also embodies elements drawn from aspects of personality other than the mother-identification.

But it is evident that the term 'Classical' does not suitably describe the other extreme. With its insistence on a balance between 'reason' and imagination, and the compromise it finds between art-as-imitation and art-as-creation, it seems rather to represent the position of balance between matrism and patrism. Let us assume for a moment that this is the case—I shall attempt to demonstrate the point more fully in a moment—and ask ourselves, what æsthetic character must be assigned to the third position, corresponding to undiluted patrism, in which imagination is totally inhibited? Works produced by this group, it would seem, must be quite devoid of æsthetic content. In the field of literature, for instance, the patrist position would be represented by a straightforward factual statement, in making which no consideration has been given to euphony or prose rhythm, as also none to emotional connotations. In architecture, it might be represented by a building erected solely for utilitarian reasons.

I have proceeded to consider what meaning should be assigned to the terms 'Classical' and 'Romantic' at this early stage in the argument partly in order to be free to use them myself, partly in order to obviate any confusion which might be caused by readers hastily assuming that Classicism was to be equated to the patrist position. Let us now return to the task of comparing differences in æsthetic viewpoint with differences on the patrist-matrist scale.

Differences of this kind can also be detected in the field of æsthetic theory. Two contrasting views are found: that beauty is objective, and that it is subjective. Burke, for instance, accepted the Renaissance view that beauty was absolute and resided in the object. Like Renaissance theorists, he held that certain proportions, such as the Golden Section, were absolutely beautiful, and there could be no two opinions about

[8] *Rambler*, No. 125, May 28th 1751.

them. But if beauty derives from certain predetermined elements, it becomes theoretically possible to lay down objective canons of taste which all must accept; and since all beautiful objects must be made according to a set of universal rules, it follows that if an object is beautiful it must necessarily resemble the approved models. If any individual fails to find the approved models beautiful, it argues only his lack of taste. This is evidently a patrist view.

The Romantics, on the other hand, believed that beauty was subjective—that it resided not in the object but "in the eye of the beholder". An object might legitimately seem beautiful to one person, ugly to another: hence the individual must be free to pursue whatever appeared to him to be beautiful, however novel, however little others might agree.

From the Classical view it followed that no one could appreciate beauty, let alone create it, without a knowledge of Classical models: it was for this reason that the Grand Tour was considered necessary to form one's taste. But from the Romantic viewpoint it followed that to appreciate beauty one must develop one's sensitivity (or, as the eighteenth century called it, sensibility) rather than one's art-historical knowledge. In short, both these views are necessary concomitants of the basic psychological biases of the two groups.

We can verify this interpretation by showing that each of these two attitudes to æsthetics was held by persons of the appropriate psychological type. Thus, as we know that Burke was a conservative, we are not surprised to find that he supported a Classical conception of beauty.[9] Knowing that Hogarth supported a much more Romantic conception of beauty we can predict that he must have been preponderantly matrist—as it seems indeed that he was.[10]

The patrist conception of reason as controlling the dangerous forces of imagination resembles his moral conception in which reason controls impulse, impulse being usually sinful. That this is something more than an analogy is suggested by the readiness with which, even to-day, moral and æsthetic judgments are assimilated, the terms appropriate to

9 See his *Essay on the Sublime.*
10 This can be inferred from his *Frolic,* as well as from the preoccupation with physical welfare in his subjects.

each being interchanged: a curious fact, which we too lightly take for granted. Thus we still speak of 'ugly' behaviour, or of a 'purity' of line. The eighteenth-century critic often praised a 'chaste' design, but the moralists saw a more specific correspondence. Thus one writer condemns the 'caprice' of Romantic designs—we have already noted that moralists (e.g. Isaac Watts) regarded caprice as a defect. Similarly, they criticised designs for their 'profusion'.

Furthermore, a man who preferred a capricious or fantastic design was not merely æsthetically mistaken, but morally defective. It is therefore interesting to find that Romantic critics made a similar assumption, although their æsthetic standards were just the opposite of the Puritans'. Thus Tilson depicts in Micio a man whose libertinism does not merely reflect but actually accounts for the bad (that is, Classical) taste with which his garden is laid out;[11] while Shenstone declares that "an obvious connection may be traced between moral and physical beauty, the love of symmetry and the love of virtue".[12]

It will be evident to the reader that the subject we have opened up in this chapter—the influence of parental identifications on æsthetic attitudes—is one which extends far beyond the bounds of the period with which this book is concerned. If one is correct in inferring such a relationship, then it must be valid for the whole of art history; conversely, one must examine a broad range of art history before one can legitimately make generalisations about the influence of parental identification on æsthetic attitudes. Now I had in fact made such an analysis before starting on the present inquiry, and had published part of it elsewhere.[13] In approaching the question of eighteenth-century taste, I naturally fell back on this wider treatment, the main points of which I shall now indicate as briefly as possible.

I approached the subject empirically. For instance, it is noticeable that the Puritan fears and dislikes brilliant colours: the 'sober costumes' on which the Puritans insisted are well known, while in churches they

---

[11] In a paper (No. 67) in *The World*, cited Allen, *Tides in Taste*, ii, 191. Cf. also Jackson, *Essay* (1754): a person who chooses bad wallpaper is obviously immoral.

[12] Shenstone, *Works*, ii, 273, 'On Taste.'

[13] 'Psychology, Architecture and the Patron', in *The Architect's Yearbook*, No. 7 (1956).

removed all gilding and decorative colouring.[14] Similarly the Puritan fears fantasy—we have already noted how the reformers attacked even such innocent fantasies as fairy tales—and insisted on an extreme literalism. On the other hand the Romantic lets his imagination flower elaborately—how elaborately, the fantasies of Hoffmann show. These differences stem from the basic dichotomy of impulse versus control.

In the sphere of painting I thought to put the matrist preference for fantastic and symbolic forms, such as we find in Blake, in contrast with realism or the exact depiction of life. But on closer study I realised that the extreme patrist is not necessarily interested in realism: what we see if we examine certain types of early medieval religious art, for instance, is utilitarianism.[15] Pictures are used to convey a message: the figures are flat and formalised: often they show different phases of the action like a strip cartoon: thus a single picture shows Christ both lying in the tomb and also rising from it. The Bayeux Tapestry is a well-known example of this pictographic treatment. The patrist does demand photographic accuracy in a portrait or a view, because in such cases the purpose, as he sees it, is to depict the original. I have already noted his utilitarianism in the sphere of architecture: when the patrist designs a house he attends solely to convenience of design or functional efficiency. If he adds decorative features it is to demonstrate his wealth and prestige, or for some other non-æsthetic purpose. The individual who is at a point of balance between matrism and patrism finds a compromise by seeking to show an idealised reality: thus some Renaissance painters held that painting was superior to Nature because it could depict, for instance, a chariot drawn by four identical horses, whereas in life the horses could never be identical.

Consideration of the shape of buildings led to another conclusion. It is a striking feature of the Classical designer that he insists on symmetry. This can be seen in Renaissance architecture, and also in paintings such as Raphael's *Disputa*. (In many paintings the garden of Eden appears symmetrically laid out: in Andreini's *L'Adamo* even the

[14] Cf. Stukeley's anger at the introduction of light and colour into Peterborough Cathedral in 1747. (*Family Memoirs*, iii, 70.)
[15] See Hauser, *Social History of Art*, for fuller treatment of this point.

animals in Paradise are symmetrically disposed.) The Romantic, on the other hand, prefers the more complex kind of balance which can be produced in asymmetrical designs. In architecture, this corresponds to the rococo. The patrist counterpart seems to be a geometrical lay-out produced with ruler and compasses; this provides a transition to the subtler symmetries of the Classical style. The same development may be noted in the lay-out of towns: first an *ad hoc* treatment, then a geometrical lay-out, finally a calculated asymmetry. The symmetrical composition is one in which the masses and voids are balanced: it therefore has a static quality. The planned asymmetry of a Romantic composition is, in contrast, full of movement. It is striking that it is the balanced composition which is preferred by the man with the personality which, at least as far as parental introjections are concerned, is in balance.

Nevertheless, some readers will probably feel that the Classical feeling for symmetry was rather a matter of style—of borrowing from a Classical tradition which, as it happened, was symmetrical—and will scout the idea that it represented some deep-seated need of the personality. It therefore offers some verification to find this sense of symmetry expressed in a field remote from architecture, where the probability of any such idea being borrowed or adapted for merely stylistic reasons is almost non-existent. Thus Dr. Burnet complained about God's failure to make the heavens symmetrical.[16] The stars, he said, "lie carelessly scattered, as if they had been sown in Heaven like seed in handfuls, and not by a skilful hand neither." The effect would have been far more impressive "if they had been placed in rank and order, if they had all been disposed into regular figures, and the little ones set with due regard to the greater; then all finished and made up into one fair piece of great composition according to the rules of art and symmetry." He also criticised the lay-out of the oceans on similar grounds, acidly observing, "If the seas had been drawn round the earth in regular figures and borders, it might have been a great beauty to our globe."

Finally, the patrist prefers to work within a system of rules, which must be strictly observed; the matrist, who admires originality, defies

[16] *Sacred Theory of the Earth,* cf. Book 1, Chapters 6 and 9.

rules and conventions. Between these lies an imaginative use of rules and conventions. These findings may be tabulated thus:

PATRIST	INTERMEDIATE	MATRIST
1. Inhibited	Disciplined	Spontaneous
2. Fears colour	Controlled use of colour	Revels in colour or strong chiaroscuro
3. Dislikes fantasy	Some fantasy	Elaborate fantasy
4. Utilitarian (or geometrical) design	Symmetrical, static compositions	Asymmetrical, dynamic compositions
5. Pictographic (or geometrical) images	Natural forms and images	Fantastic, symbolic forms and images
6. Works within strict framework of rules	Imaginative use of rules and conventions	Exalts originality, defies rules

When writing the present chapter I realised that a seventh point could be added. The Romantic prefers curves, as more sensuous, where the Classicist prefers formal patterns based on straight lines. Hogarth's *Analysis of Beauty* is chiefly concerned to justify the use of the curve. The patrist, constructing his design for utilitarian purposes, uses lines straight, curved, or erratic as he needs them; and if he uses a curve he does not seek to endow it with any internal harmony. (Here again the moral criterion creeps in. John Trusler, the doctor who so industriously adapted aristocratic notions to the understanding of the middle class, explained in 1768, "It was long the opinion of his [Hogarth's] professor that the standard of beauty was a right line; in consequence of this *In recto decus* became an established maxim. Indeed of late again it has, rather, been considered in a moral view; yet still, it is plain, it took its rise from imagery . . . Mr. Hogarth was the first person who contradicted this erroneous notion; he published a treatise in order to shew that the line of beauty is serpentine."[17]

---

[17] Trusler, *Hogarth Moralised*, p. xix. But in fact Queen Caroline had ordered the construction of the Serpentine River in Hyde Park. Pope's friend, Lord Bathhurst, however, is said to have constructed the first winding stream at Ryskins, near Colebrook. (Allen, *Tides in Taste*, p. 135.)

Surveying this table, the reader will realise that the centre column corresponds broadly to Classicism, the right-hand column to Romanticism. The discovery that Classicism is really a position of compromise is highly significant: it means that Classicism cannot with complete accuracy be placed in opposition to Romantic, as is so frequently done. Classicism actually contains, it is legitimate to say, certain Romantic elements: it makes *some* use of colour, *some* use of imagination. It is, so to say, a controlled Romanticism.

Of course, in making broad generalisations about Classical and Romantic styles, such as are made in the table just given, we must remember that such terms are used in varying senses by different people. One writer will stress the elements of discipline in Classicism, another the imaginative elements. This is particularly true when moral judgments intrude. The moralist, attacking Romantic spontaneity and impulse, sees Classicism as nearer to his own ideal, and tends to assimilate it to his own position: for him, Classicism comes to stand for the virtues. Conversely, the Romantic, attacking the narrow-mindedness of the Puritan, tends to feel that the Classicist, who is also interested in æsthetics, is on his side. These tendencies seem worth mentioning, because they have often led to inconceivable confusion on the part of pedants masquerading as literary or artistic critics.[18]

It may be added that Romanticism and Puritanism suffer from the tendency to define them by their most extreme developments, but can at least thereby be presented in clear-cut form; whereas the concept of Classicism, consisting as it does of compromises, cannot be made so precise.

Let us now try to apply these distinctions to the period we are examining. It is not difficult to see the application of these criteria in the art of the eighteenth century. The reader will no doubt perceive at once how in poetry the measured tones and analytic purpose of a Pope give way to the remote or supernatural scenes and evocative language of a Coleridge or a Wordsworth. He will see how in painting the flat realism of a Kneller contrasts with the dreamlike images of Blake or Fuseli; and how in architecture the calm symmetry of the Classical designer, such as Gibbs, contrasts with the fervid imagination of

[18] Instances are given later on pp. 251–3 and 344–5.

Vanbrugh, in whose buildings all thought of practical convenience is sacrificed to æsthetic effect. And he will remember how, in this field too, fanciful designs derived from remote countries (e.g. China) and remote periods (e.g. the medieval) gradually supersede the soberer Classical taste.

To have discovered that æsthetic attitudes reflect parental identifications was, I felt, a major achievement, since it integrated a whole field of human experience into the general pattern I was trying to build.

But it is not necessary for the purposes of this book to undertake a complete analysis of the art of the period in psychological terms. It is enough to demonstrate the bare fact that psychological factors of the sort we have been considering can be seen at work in æsthetic attitudes.

To this end I propose to consider a field with which the reader may be less familiar, the treatment of gardens and gardening, where the psychological factors can be seen at work with particular clearness. (At first glance this might seem a somewhat trivial field of application; actually it is of the highest relevance because it expresses an attitude to Nature, and this, as I have shown, is a matter which persons with ego-defects regard as specially significant.)

Up to the end of the seventeenth century, gardens were customarily laid out, as at Versailles, on a symmetrical plan, the pattern being rectangular, without free curves, and the various sections neatly marked off with hedges of box or yew. The flowers were planted in formal parterres: the whole pattern was completely subordinated to a conception of order, and no resemblance to Nature was attempted. If water was used, it was in stone-edged basins, not in informal ponds or streams.[19]

But already by 1712 Addison was arguing for the "beautiful wildness of Nature" as against "the nicer Elegancies of Art". He liked "trees and shrubs growing freely" and a stream that runs "as it would do in an open field".

[19] See Gothein, *History of Garden Art*, Chs. 10, 12, 13. As Allen points out (*Tides in Taste*, i, 138), seventeenth-century gardening books were wholly utilitarian. The garden itself was utilitarian, being designed for the production of fruit and vegetables or for use as an outside room.

When Joseph Warton wrote *The Enthusiast* in 1740, he lauded the superiority of Nature over Art, and denigrated Versailles, while Lord Kames, introducing the moral note, said it was an example of "vicious" and "depraved taste".[20] It was in the same spirit that Bishop Berkeley said, when he saw the natural gardens at Muckross, "Another Louis Quatorze may make another Versailles, but the hand of the Deity only can make another Mucruss."[21] Lord Bathurst, at Ryskins, was the first to make a winding stream through a garden. "So unusual was the effect that his friend, Lord Stafford, could not believe it had been done on purpose, and supposing it had been for economy asked him to own fairly how little more it would have cost to have made the course of the brook in a straight direction."[22]

The preference for a curving course can be explained on the grounds that it resembles Nature, but it is nearer the mark to say that the Romantic prefers the sensuous elasticity of the curve to the rigidity of the line, and prefers nature partly for this reason. The preference for curves also affected paths, which ceased to be straight and were made serpentine. Some called this "nonsensical zigzaggery", but Dr. Johnson, characteristically substituting a moral for an æsthetic judgment, declared that a walk made to appear longer than it is, is more than a deception, "a lie, Sir, is a lie, whether it be a lie to the eye or a lie to the ear." It has been said that the Classicist feels awe where the Romantic feels wonder. This distinction is well exemplified in the ways in which the two schools thought it proper for a house to be approached. The Romantic recommended the placing of plantations of trees; this, with the serpentine drive, would ensure that one came upon the house suddenly, thus increasing the dramatic effect. In many of the consciously-landscaped gardens, such as the Leasowes or Stourhead, there was a prescribed order of viewing the features of the garden, for the same reason.[23] The Classicist, in contrast, prefers to approach a house

[20] Kames, *Elements of Criticism*, ii, 394, 396.

[21] Derrick, *Letters*, Vol. ii, No. xxxix.

[22] Mr. Barrington in 'On the Progress of Gardening' 1728, *Archæologia*, Vol. v. Cited Reynolds, *Nature in Eng. Poetry*, p. 252.

[23] Batty Langley conceived that it was the purpose of a garden to surprise by continually presenting new objects. *New Principles*, preface.

by a long straight avenue: this produces an impression of grandeur but eliminates shock.

Or again, waterfalls were favoured by Romantics as providing a sense of movement; fountains, such as appear in Classical gardens, were disapproved as too formal.

But for the purposes of the present study the most striking feature among these preferences is the Romantic dislike of boundary walls. Allen says, "Addison contended, moreover, that the contemporary garden failed to yield one of the keenest imaginable pleasures: the astonishment and thrilling sense of liberty derivable from greatness or vastness of extent when the eye is conscious of no boundary to its vision short of the horizon itself. So Addison hazards the suggestion that the whole estate be turned into a 'kind of garden' embracing even the meadows and 'fields of corn'." The idea was revolutionary; the garden was no longer to be regarded, as it always had been from the earliest times, as a walled-in, self-contained enclosure, but as a visual creation including in its effect, if not in actuality, the whole landscape in its compass. The conception led in practice to the tearing down of all walls and fences, and to the concealment of every boundary.[24]

In the seventeenth century, not only had the garden been separated from the countryside by walls, but the garden itself had been chopped up by clipped walls of yew.[25] Huet said, "Polite society . . . requires palisades erected with the line and at the point of the shears."[26] For these palisades the Romantic substituted that most characteristic invention, the sunken ditch, or ha-ha. Walpole stresses its importance. "But the capital stroke, the leading step to all that has followed, was (I believe the first thought was Bridgeman's) the destruction of walls for boundaries, and the invention of fossés—an attempt then deemed so astonishing that the common people called them Ha! Ha's! to express their surprize."[27]

24 Allen, *Tides*, ii, 124, referring to *Tatler*, 161, 218; *Spectator*, 414, 477.

25 Allen calls the Elizabethan garden "an outside room". The high walls and hedges enclosed it for privacy. Thus while the patrist unites the garden to the house, the matrist detaches it from the house to unite it with the landscape.

26 *Huetiana*, LI, p. 120.

27 Walpole, *Essay on Modern Gardening*, p. 53.

Actually, as Allen shows, the credit must go not to Bridgeman (who died in 1738) but to Stephen Switzer. London and Wise, the leading gardeners at the turn of the century, had insisted that boundary walls were necessary to give dignity to gardens (a characteristically Classical requirement) and to unite them architecturally to the house;[28] but Switzer said that he would "throw the Garden open to all view".[29]

This seemed to me a quite astonishing discovery, uniting as it does the ideas of Nature, boundlessness, and liberty in a single feature. Just as the walls of the Romantic ego vanish, until it becomes indistinguishable from its environment, so the walls round the garden vanish, till it likewise becomes continuous with its environment. The purely subjective quality of the Romantic's desire for boundlessness is well shown by Shenstone. "I conceived some idea of the sensation . . . from walking but a few minutes, immured, between Lord D——'s high shorn yew hedges." It was "like being condemned to labour at the gallies".[30]

Actually, though Bridgeman abandoned symmetry, and planted loose groves of oak, he still marked the main lines with clipped yew; and it was Kent, his successor at Stowe, who brought the Romantic garden to fruition. "Study Nature and follow her laws" was his motto.[31] His most important gardens were planned between 1730 and his death in 1748. Shenstone's the Leasowes (described as "new-formed" in 1754), Wooburn Farm and Pain's Hill (described as "but lately laid out" in 1761) are key examples.[32]

Just as the Romantic feeling for Nature and for boundlessness is coloured by the death-wish, so we find similar notions introduced into the concept of the beautiful; and this is often combined with the sense of nostalgia for a lost past. Such feelings are well expressed by ruins, which demonstrate by their presence the existence of change and

[28] *The Compleat Gard'ner,* 1699: *The Retir'd Gard'ner,* 1706.
[29] Switzer, *Ichnographia Rustica,* Preface.
[30] Shenstone, *Works,* ii, 116: 'Unconnected Thoughts on Gardening'.
[31] Cited Reynolds, *Nature in Eng. Poetry,* p. 260.
[32] ib., pp. 261–2.

decay, and recall a vanished grandeur and perfection.[33] Moreover, if a building collapses, it ceases to be symmetrical, even if it was so before, while the idea of unbalance and impending movement is presented. Romantic paintings frequently show a shattered arch, the remaining segment of which seems about to crash upon the ground: sometimes they show buildings on fire and in the act of falling.[34]

To the extreme patrist, whose approach is purely utilitarian, ruins seem a pointless addition to the landscape. If genuine, they deserve a certain respect as being the work of our forefathers, and they may have some educational value; but the Romantic practice of deliberately constructing ruins for the æsthetic effect seems to him perverse. (Chippendale even designed a ruined chimney-piece.)[35]

At first the natural garden approximated to Nature in its most peaceful and attractive forms: it represented an idealised Nature, shorn of its more savage features. But gradually, as Romanticism itself developed, the conception of the garden became wilder and more savage. Payne Knight attacks the gardens of 'Capability' Brown as too smooth. He says that Brown

> "Levels each broken bank and shaggy mound
> And fashions all to one unvaried round;
> One even round, that ever gently flows,
> Nor forms abrupt, nor broken colours knows;
> But, wrapt all o'er in everlasting green,
> Makes one dull, vapid, smooth and tranquil scene."[36]

It is at this point that one must introduce the conception of the picturesque.[37]

[33] Ruins please "both by the greatness of the object, and also by giving us a melancholy idea of their past grandeur and magnificence". *Spiritual Quixote*, 1773.

[34] To this feeling, no doubt, we owe the fact that Salix babylonica, when it was introduced from China, was named 'weeping willow'.

[35] Allen, op. cit., ii, 172.

[36] Knight, *The Landscape*.

[37] This term meant having the quality of a picture, and was applicable to landscapes. To speak of a painting as picturesque is a meiosis.

For the later Romantics it was not enough that there should be natural water, it should be in movement, and preferably lashed by storms. It was not a peaceful meadow which they wanted, but a beetling cliff topped by a blasted pine.

Uvedale Price is the recognised exponent of this concept. He starts by making the usual distinctions: a winding road, he says, creates tension and surprise—what will be round the next bend?—whereas a straight, broad road reduces tension and generates boredom. Price also clearly indicates the significance of symmetry, when he says, "Beauty goes with symmetry, asymmetry with the picturesque."[38] But then he goes further: he contrasts the "animation" of windblown trees with the "tameness of poor, pinioned trees" in gentlemen's plantations. He prefers dead and decaying trees to live ones, for they exhibit "a variety of tints, of brilliant and mellow lights, with deep and peculiar shades", which fine timber trees cannot exhibit. (Here is the predicted preference for colour and chiaroscuro explicitly stated.)

For Uvedale Price, the picturesque and the beautiful are quite distinct. A smooth, placid lake is beautiful, but a lake lashed with waves, or a waterfall, is picturesque.[39] Time, he says, converts a beautiful building into a picturesque one. A little reflection will show why this should be so. Lichen and weathering break up the uniform colour and texture of the surfaces, and the plain tints of classic stone or marble are converted to rusts and yellows, or blackened by dirt. (This was also one of the reasons for admiring ruins.)

Another feature of the picturesque landscape was the grotto, which Uvedale Price regards as a specific feature of the picturesque, simply on the grounds that caves are a feature of natural scenery. Reading Barbara Jones' *Follies and Grottoes* suggested to me, however, a thought almost too ridiculously obvious to be true, and I record it without being wholly convinced of its correctness. Since many 'follies' consist of tall towers and other vertical objects, such as are now widely re-

---

[38] Price, *On the Picturesque*, Chapter 2. Price chooses to confine the use of the term beauty to Classical forms where we, to-day, use it to embrace both Classical and Romantic conceptions.

[39] Op. cit., Chapter 3. Contrast Burke, for whom smoothness was an essential ingredient of beauty.

cognised as phallic symbols, it would be logical to regard caves and grottoes as womb-symbols. They were not provided merely for their visual effect in the landscape, since many of them can hardly be seen from the outside. Compared with the other features of the landscape which Price mentions, such as trees and waterfalls, caves are rare, and it seems hardly necessary to go to the expense of constructing them. In any case, the appeal to Nature cannot account for the construction of vertical follies, such as the towers and columns which were so common on eighteenth-century estates.

While my first thought was that Classicists might feel drawn to towers, Romantics to grottoes, it later struck me that caves indicate rather the wish to regress, while follies perhaps reflect the impotence which seems to have been a distinctive feature of the period, and which often springs from the incest-preoccupation: hence both indicate matrism, in slightly different forms. In point of fact, both seem to have been matrist productions.

Uvedale Price did not make his analysis of the picturesque until the very end of the century. If I am right, however, in linking Romanticism with the decay of ego-boundaries, it ought to be possible to find similar views expressed by Shaftesbury. It is therefore a confirmation of the thesis to find such passages as this:

"Even the rude *Rocks*, the mossy *Caverns*, the irregular unwrought *Grotto's*, and broken *Falls* of *Waters*, with all the horrid Graces of the Wilderness itself, as representing NATURE more, will be the more engaging, and appear with a Magnificence beyond the formal Mockery of princely Gardens."[40]

My argument could hardly have been stated more succinctly. And a few lines later Shaftesbury actually uses the word 'romantic'. "Why is it," he asks, "that the only people who seek the woods, the Rivers and the Seashores are your poor vulgar LOVERS?" And his antagonist in the dialogue replies, "It is the same with POETS." Shaftesbury continues, " 'However,' said I, 'all those who are deep in this *romantick* way are look'd upon, you know, as People either plainly out of their wits, or over-run with Melancholy and ENTHUSIASM.' "[41] That

[40] Shaftesbury, *Characteristicks*, ii, 313.
[41] ib., ii, 394.

would seem to mean, persons in a labile emotional state, and these are precisely the sort of people we should expect to develop a feeling for Romantic scenery even in a Classical age.

To clinch the argument that the psychological forces at work in Shaftesbury were similar to those at work in the Romantics, it next seemed necessary to inquire whether the Shaftesburean poets also advocated the wild garden. I found that they did, most specifically Warton in his *Pleasures of Melancholy* (1745).

The patrist attitude to æsthetic matters is also beautifully demonstrated in the field of architecture—especially the new movement in church architecture associated with the Camden Society and with the name of A. W. Pugin.

This group dismissed eighteenth-century architecture on moral rather than æsthetic grounds—façades, blind windows, the use of stucco were "unworthy deception" or "abominable sham".[42] Indeed the Camden Society even condemned taste and proportion as principles "pernicious in themselves and most derogatory of God's glory".[43] They looked instead for the "true Christian architecture" and found it in what we now call Gothic, and of all the Gothic the most Christian was the Decorated.

In imitating Decorated Gothic extreme accuracy was essential, for inaccuracy would be a lie and the fanciful use of the Gothic detail, such as Wyatt employed, immoral. Pugin condemned Wyatt as "vile, cunning and rascally". It was held that only good men could build good buildings; they declared "the worldliness, dissipation and patronage of our own architects issued in unvarying and hopeless failure". (Even the value of church bells was affected by the morality of the ringers.)[44] This is a magical belief: and magic is even more clearly present in the belief that only by reviving the true Christian architecture could one hope to revive religion.

Aided by our new understanding of the nature of Romanticism and its relation to Classicism, it becomes possible to fit a number of

---

[42] Clark, *Gothic Revival*, pp. 201–2, citing Pugin's *Contrasts*.

[43] *Ecclesiologist*, i, 78.

[44] "How very sinful any levity in the performance of their duties!" *Ecclesiologist*, 1854, i, 151.

additional pieces into the jig-saw, and to extend our understanding of patrism-matrism generally.

For instance, it seems that it is a characteristic of the Romantic to synthesise and unify, where it is a characteristic of the patrist to analyse and classify. Schlegel makes the point clearly when he says, "The ancient art and poetry rigorously separates things which are dissimilar; the romantic delights in indissoluble mixtures. . . . The former is more simple, clear and like to nature in the self-existent perfection of her separate works; the latter, notwithstanding its fragmentary appearance, approaches more to the secret of the universe. For Conception can only comprise each object separately, but nothing in truth can ever exist separately and by itself; Feeling perceives all in all at one and the same time."[45]

These opposing tendencies are evidently the product of the degree of ego-definition. The Romantic capacity to perceive "all in all at one and the same time" is obviously only a variant of the sense of unity with all life of which I have already spoken. The Puritan's sense of separation, similarly, gives rise to a sense of the world as being composed of separate objects, which can be placed in distinct categories. The differences strike him as far more important than the similarities; with the Romantic the reverse is true.

It was for this reason that the more thick-walled personality felt that tragedy and comedy should not be commingled, the *genres* should be kept distinct. The Romantic felt that life comprised both tragic and comic elements, and so a playwright might, indeed should, show them in juxtaposition.

Nowhere is the difference of viewpoint between these two types of person more apparent than in the field of moral judgment. The two types base their judgments on two contrasting sets of moral assumptions. For the Romantic, what is beautiful is necessarily good: hence moral virtue becomes merely the perfect expression of æsthetic sensibility. This view is explicit in Shaftesbury. The ideas of beauty and goodness are conjoined when he apostrophises Nature as "supremely fair and good", but the point is made even more clearly when he writes, " 'So that BEAUTY,' said I, 'and GOOD, with you, THEOCLES, I

[45] Schlegel, *Dramatic Art and Literature*, Lecture xxii.

perceive are still *one and the same.*' ' 'Tis so,' said he."[46] The Deistic poets agreed: Akenside declares, "For Truth and Good are one."[47]

Recognition of this fact enables us to understand how Renan could say, "Be beautiful, and then do at each moment whatever your heart inspires you to do. This is the whole of morality."[48]

In contrast, the patrist considers that what is good is automatically beautiful—a notion which found repeated expression in the nineteenth century, when the expression "moral beauty" became popular. Conversely, that which is immoral cannot in the eyes of the patrist be beautiful. Thus it is that he cannot admit æsthetic value in literary or graphic works which depict behaviour of which he disapproves. This is an outlook so often manifested, even to-day, that no examples need be cited here.

Appreciation of this contrast in assumptions suggested to me that, if the moralist is the type-figure for the Puritan, the artist is the type-figure for the Romantic. It had already occurred to me that the field of art was especially important for gaining an insight into the Romantic personality, if only because he less often leaves behind him tracts and polemics which reveal his views, in the way that the Puritan does. But I now realised that art was not merely a useful avenue of approach, it was precisely the one appropriate avenue of approach to the Romantic, since it is through the imagination rather than the intellect that he expresses his views. Even when he wishes to state his philosophy in words, he will tend to choose the imaginative medium of poetry, as did Wordsworth, Shelley and others.

It may also be noted that just as the Puritan's views on art are value-less, since they are in fact moral judgments, not æsthetic ones, so also the Romantic's views on morals are valueless, for the corresponding reason.

If the patrist thinks that the Good is Beautiful, we must next ask what he thinks is the Good. As we have already seen, his conception of goodness is based on the idea of restraining impulse. The Romantic, in contrast, believes in giving way to impulse, for impulse is good. Thus

---

[46] *Characteristicks*, ii, 399.
[47] *Pleasures of the Imagination*, i, 374.
[48] *Avenir de la Science*, p. 179.

Renan says, "Morality has been conceived up to the present in a very narrow spirit, as obedience to a law, as an inner struggle between two opposite laws. As for me, I declare that when I do good, I fight no battle and win no victory. The cultivated man has only to follow the delicious decline of his own inner impulses."[49] Blake carried this doctrine to its extreme when he declared, "Sooner murder an infant in its cradle than nurse unacted desires."[50] (Notice, however, that Renan says "the cultivated man"—for he recognises that man's talent for goodness must be fostered before it becomes effective.)

So vast is this difference of viewpoint that each side finds it impossible to understand the other. As one educationist asks, "Education's great business must necessarily be the counteracting of the natural bent of the mind to evil. . . . How can this be effected under the plan of Rousseau or his followers?"

Because of his ironbound assumption that impulse is bad, the Puritan can only regard those who urge obedience to impulse as advocating immorality.[51] As a rule, he supposes that the Romantic is consciously and deliberately advocating immorality; he fails to realise that he is advocating morality, but of a kind differing from his own. The idea that his assumptions might be open to question scarcely occurs to him. Thus one writer remarks, shrewdly enough, that the Romantic's desire for less trimness in the garden only reflects his desire for less trimness in human behaviour:[52] he evidently feels that in making this remark he has exposed the underlying defect in this Romantic preference. The possibility that less trimness in human nature (and hence in the garden) might be a good thing simply does not occur to him.

In short, between these two outlooks a great gulf yawns. To emphasise this fact, I have considered only the extreme cases. In a more extensive treatment one would have to recognise intermediate

---

[49] ib., p. 354.

[50] Blake, 'Marriage of Heaven and Hell,' in Poetry and Prose, p. 185.

[51] Cf. Burke: "They [the Philosophers] explode or render odious or contemptible the class of virtues which restrain the appetite. These are at least nine out of ten virtues. In the place of these they substitute a virtue which they call humanity or benevolence. By this means their morality has no idea of restraint." Correspondence, iii, 213 (June 1791).

[52] Babbitt, Rousseau and Romanticism.

forms, particularly that corresponding to the Classical position. Outside the Puritan persuasion, the dominating moral ideas were decorum and propriety. What is decorous is to observe convention: good behaviour is to be achieved by imitating approved models, and rules exist by which the propriety of all behaviour can be objectively assessed. The moral scheme is indistinguishable from the æsthetic one.

The discovery that there are two moralities, not one, is of some importance, since both these points of view are extant to-day. In the concluding chapter, I shall consider the wider implications of this fact. At this stage I am only concerned to interpret Romanticism in terms of the general analysis of the period which I am trying to make.

Unfortunately, this difference of viewpoint extends not only to Romantics and Puritans living in the eighteenth century, but also to historians and literary critics living to-day. As a result, much confusion is created. Historical study and literary criticism frequently attract persons of predominantly patrist type: naturally enough, since the man of impulse is constitutionally ill-equipped for scholarship. These patrist critics are ill-at-ease when dealing with matrist phenomena, and fail to preserve the requisite critical detachment. The strictures which they make, while ostensibly literary, are in reality moral. The assertion may be illustrated by reference to Professor Babbitt, who became widely known for his polemic attacks on what he termed 'Rousseauism', written in his capacity as a Professor of English Literature.[53] Thus of Shaftesbury, he writes, "He insidiously undermines decorum, the central doctrine of the classicist, at the very time that he seems to be defending it. . . . Shaftesbury is actually engaged in rehabilitating 'nature', and insinuating that it does not need any control."

Such writing, and his works consist of a continuous sequence of such self-revealing passages, betrays its lack of critical detachment by its unblushing use of 'loaded' terminology. Shaftesbury 'insinuates' he 'insidiously undermines', he 'actually' seeks to rehabilitate Nature. But

[53] His patrism may be illustrated by the following passage, "The very heart of the classical message, one cannot repeat too often, is that one should aim first of all not to be original, but to be human, and that to be human one needs to look up to a sound model and imitate it." (*Rousseau and Romanticism*, p. 64.)

in fact Shaftesbury did not insinuate, he put his view most clearly. The very word 'rehabilitate', which to-day we associate with the restoration to respectability of those who have committed some crime, implies that Nature has some fault which Shaftesbury wishes us to overlook.

Rousseau naturally comes off even worse than Shaftesbury: his programme amounts in practice "to the indulgence of infinite indeterminate desire".[54] The objection to self-indulgence is of course characteristically Puritan. It would be possible to expose the defects of Babbitt's analyses in some detail, but it is unnecessary for our present purpose.

When we recognise the nature of this fundamental difference of viewpoint we can understand why, throughout the period we are considering, Romanticism was considered actively anti-religious. Warburton said that "to his knowledge the *Characteristicks* had done more harm to revealed religion than all the works of infidelity put together".[55] (Warburton's objection was that they provided a scheme of virtue which did not depend on revealed religion.) Shaftesbury was only saved by his rank and the interposition of Lord Somers from prosecution under the heresy laws. Rousseau, who went so much further, had to flee the country, and his books were publicly burnt.

So pervasive are these two attitudes that the holders tend to develop moral judgments on matters which one might have thought quite outside the sphere of morality. Thus the patrist condemns the changeability of mood of the matrist, and feels no need to explain why he assumes that this is deplorable. Conversely, the matrist objects to the patrist's rigid consistency.

I have already mentioned the Romantic's tendency to unify and synthesise, as against the patrist tendency to classify and analyse. Both are valid processes, but the patrist invariably sees the unifying process as undesirable and even immoral. Thus Babbitt complains that the 'Rousseauist' breaks down the barriers between the arts in terms which suggest that he also breaks down the barrier between good and evil.

[54] ib., p. 79.
[55] *Chalmers' Biog. Dict.* art. 'John Brown.' As early as 1698, however, we find Heidigger attacking Romanticism on moral grounds in his *Mythoscopia Romantica*, saying that the only resource against it was religion.

"The breaking down by the emotional romanticist of the barriers that separate not merely the different literary genres but the different arts is only another aspect of his readiness to follow the lure of the infinite. . . . The Rousseauist . . . does not hesitate to pursue his ever-receding dream across all frontiers, not merely those that separate art from art, but those that divide flesh from spirit, and even good from evil, until he finally arrives like Blake at a sort of Marriage of Heaven and Hell."[56] To the patrist the stressing of similarities appears as a wilful obscuring of differences; the Romantic, of course, finds the patrist equally perverse in exaggerating differences.[57]

But while in many respects the Puritan and the Romantic are at opposite poles, there are certain respects, in which they are singularly alike, and some of the accusations which they make display, in consequence, a curious air of paradox.

The patrist accuses the Romantic of 'individualism', and this is odd because, in the economic sense, it is the patrist who is an individualist. The nineteenth century, a patrist period, is the prime exemplar of economic individualism. Clearly the word is being used in two different senses. In the light of our theory we can see that the thick-wall patrist is an individualist in the sense that he feels a sense of isolation from his fellow men, and is therefore enabled to operate an economic system which is based on the assumption that men are isolated units, responding only to market forces and uninfluenced by sympathies, traditions or irrational impulses. In contrast, the Romantic has a strong feeling of kinship with others, and rejects competitive economic schemes in favour of co-operative ones. But the Romantic is an individualist in the sense that he admires individual uniqueness, where the patrist wishes all people to conform to an ideal type. We may say that the thick-wall patrist is an economic individualist, but a moral conformist.

[56] *Rousseau and Romanticism*, p. 94.

[57] This fact may be applied to explain the attitude of each type to class distinctions. The thick-wall type accentuates class distinctions, because he is acutely aware of the differences between social groups: the thin-wall type tends to dissolve class differences because he feels that the differences are less significant than the similarities.

Again, the Puritan sometimes accuses the Romantic of idealising reality, and sometimes of presenting it with a disgusting and unnecessary degree of 'realism', as in the case of Zola. If such things exist, the Puritan says in effect, it would be much better to pass over them in silence. Now it is true that the Romantic does these things because his approach is subjective, and sometimes his sympathies drive him to depict the blacker sides of life in the hope that this may shock people into remedial action; sometimes, in contrast, he prefers to set a target by describing things as they might be. In both actions his purpose is ethical.

But what the Puritan forgets is that his own approach is equally subjective; he, too, sees man's sins as blacker than they are, and at the same time holds out an impossibly high ideal of behaviour. The fiction he writes is moralised: it is also untrue to life.

What the Puritan really objects to is the fact that the Romantic works in such a way as to arouse his emotions, his sympathies, and it is precisely this which he has striven to repress. Conversely, the Romantic complains that the Puritan makes his claims in a dry and abstract way, devoid of sympathetic feeling. He produces intellectual reasons for right action where the Romantic attempts to stir a sympathetic impulse.

In short, both approach the problem *subjectively*: we might say that the matrist uses art-forms to convey his æsthetic feelings where the patrist uses them to convey his moral feelings. It is only the Classicist, balanced between these extremes, who can turn his eyes outward and observe nature objectively for its own sake.

This is not the only point of similarity between these two positions. For instance, the patrist accuses the matrist of an excessive preoccupation with his own ego, and of an unduly subjective approach. But it is most noticeable that the Puritan also broods on the state of his own soul—I have already quoted Schuecking's phrase "moral hypochondria"—and he sees the world strongly coloured by his preconceptions. Again, the patrist accuses the matrist of selfishness, declaring that though the matrist may claim to be interested in the good of humanity, his policy of indulging his impulses actually causes only distress. Babbitt goes even further and speaks bitterly of the 'hypocrisy' of the matrist or Rousseauist. But it is equally true that the patrist, while also professing love of his fellow men, treats them harshly: even if we ignore the persecutions which have marred the history of Puritanism, we must recognise that the Puritan is generally intolerant and uncharitable. As has been said, it is difficult to be stern towards one's own faults without being at least as stern to the faults of others. Thus the Puritan too is often accused of hypocrisy. It seems paradoxical to find the patrist, himself an individualist, accusing the matrist of individualism. (The word is, of course, used in different senses, but these ambiguities are a general source of confusion.)

In the same way, the patrist accuses the matrist of anti-intellectualism, and once again the accusation is perfectly justified. The matrist prefers to follow his emotions rather than his intellect. But on a close analysis we see that the patrist's claim to operate by the light of reason is unjustified. If he uses logical argument, it is only in order to justify attitudes already arrived at and determined by irrational forces.

To take one last example, the patrist accuses the matrist of idealism or perfectionism, that is, the desire to remake the world according to some ideal pattern: but this above all is what the Puritan himself seeks to do. And if it is true that the matrist reacts from his idealism into cynicism and depicts the world in gloomy colours, it is equally true that the patrist overestimates the degree of vice in society at large because he contrasts actuality with his own conception of how men ought to behave. Each nurses in his heart the image of Arcadia or Paradise.

All these attitudes are pathognomonic of a particular form of psychological disorder—trauma caused by emotional disappointment: the results are similar because the cause is similar. The patterns are related as closely as object and image, they correspond at every point, but the sense is reversed.

PART FOUR

INTERPRETATIONS

CHAPTER 13

THE AGE OF IMPULSE

HAVING INVESTIGATED how, in the eighteenth century, unconscious factors affected the development of taste, I next attempted to study more briefly how the same factors influenced attitudes and behaviour in various other fields. My ultimate purpose in so doing was to see whether I was justified in claiming that the whole field of social attitudes has some kind of internal coherence. For if this could be shown, we should have taken a decisive step towards uncovering some kind of pattern in the process of history. History, though it may certainly include random elements, could no longer be considered wholly random. For this purpose I passed rapidly over a number of topics.

It struck me that it would be an interesting exercise to apply the psychological criteria I had been using to the whole field of intellectual thought, though it would require more space than can be allotted here. Take, for example, economic theory. Adam Smith condemns prodigality as misconduct, just as Baxter and Watts did. Parsimony is a virtue because it leads to the formation of capital; and capital formation is good, not simply, as one might think, because it leads to a higher standard of living, but because it provides an opportunity for the meritorious act of saving. "Every prodigal appears to be a public enemy, every frugal man a public benefactor."[1]

The eighteenth-century economists, Smith and Ricardo, distinguished two main theories of value: utility and exchange. According to utility theories, objects are to be valued in proportion as they are capable of satisfying human wants—this is clearly a matrist theory. Water has high utility value. Diamonds, in contrast, have a low utility

[1] Smith, *Wealth of Nations*, p. 323.

value but a high exchange value. Now it is curious that Smith and Ricardo, having made the distinction, devote all their space to exchange value: the satisfaction of human needs evidently doesn't strike them as important. Moreover they proceed to justify exchange theories of value by reference to the amount of labour expended in producing the goods: labour seems to them a real source of value. This is an anal view, and it is clear that the illogical preference for one theory as against the other is unconsciously determined.

Weisskopf has shown in some detail that these attitudes can be related directly to parental identifications.[2] Land, the earth, he argues, is invariably a mother-symbol. The land is made fruitful by the efforts of men, who plough it, and the whole process is a well-known symbol of intercourse. (Cf. Shakespeare, "An she were thornier ground than that she should be ploughed.") Now Ricardo not only exalts the importance of labour but minimises that of land, which is to say that he exalts the male part of the productive process and disparages the female part. Malthus and Marx do the same. It is interesting to note that Locke employs this conception as part of his argument that man has property rights in the object which results from the application of his labour to land: "Whatsoever then he removes out of that state that Nature has provided and left it in, he has mixed his labour with it and joined it to something that is his own, and thereby makes it his property."[3] Since property is an anal concept, this displays the anal element linked with the patrist element.[4] Similarly, in Malthus we find the view that male moral restraint is needed to lessen the damaging effects of female fecundity.

I have reproduced only the gist of Weisskopf's argument, in the most condensed possible form: no doubt it appears speculative, if not far-fetched. If it were presented as an isolated proposition, I should probably be a bit dubious myself. When it is seen as simply one more instance in a long sequence of cases in which unconscious attitudes are

[2] *Psychol. of Economics*, Part IV, 'Male and Female Symbolism in Ricardo, Malthus, Engels and Marx'.

[3] Locke, *Civil Govt.*, ii, 5.

[4] This also accounts for the fact that patrists often display a sense of property in their wives.

found to be influencing conscious behaviour, the weight of probability is on its side.

The analogy can be worked out a good deal more fully, as a matter of fact. Thus the whole conception of economic activity as determined by *competition* presupposes that men are quite uninfluenced by emotional factors, such as a preference for buying from people they like or from those who are civil, and that they cold-bloodedly act from motives of self-interest—and here the very phrase 'self-interest' conceals an assumption that the accumulation of property is in some way more truly in one's interest than the satisfying of emotional demands, loyalties or preferences. It is of course the Puritan, not the Romantic, who acts thus. The concept of competition also implies that each individual is socially isolated from the community and from those with whom he trades, and thus expresses the Puritan feeling of human isolation. Conversely, as we see in the proposals of various Romantic writers, the matrist thinks naturally in terms of co-operation.

Similar trains of thought can be developed in the field of ethics. I have already made the point that matrists assume that men are actuated by altruism, or original virtue, while patrists assume they are actuated by self-interest or original sin. Furthermore, the Utilitarians (such as Bentham) regard as good the satisfaction of needs: Bentham, I fancy, can be regarded as a matrist of the thick-walled ego type, as against the thin-walled matrism of Shaftesbury and his followers. Shaftesbury's morality is a morality of intentions; that of Bentham, and his predecessors, a morality of consequences.[5] Against both of these we can set the absolute morality, and its variant, the morality of self-evident principles, which are of patrist type, the former more extreme than the latter, since the latter makes some appeal to reason, the former none.

[5] In ethical theory, these types of morality are distinguished: (1) The morality of principle—certain acts are bad, regardless of their consequences in any given case: such acts are either specified by God as bad, or are self-evidently so; (2) The morality of consequences—an act is bad if it produces bad consequences; (3) The morality of intentions—arguing that a man who seeks to commit an act which normally has undesirable results cannot be absolved from blame because these consequences happen to be averted, many writers substitute for a morality of consequences a morality of intentions—an act is bad if the doer intends, or has reason to suppose, that it will have bad results.

Thus ethical theories, like economic theories, may be of patrist or of matrist type.

About religion it is not necessary to say much, since we have seen in detail how closely the Puritan view reflects the father-image combined with the thick-walled type of ego, while the Romantic provides the contrasting viewpoint. As argued in Chapter Eleven, the Cambridge Platonists, like the Christian mystics of an earlier period, seem to represent the thin-walled patrist; as do many of the evanescent sects of the seventeenth and early eighteenth century, such as the Family of Love. The Quakers seem to have been thin-walled patrists with strong anal elements in addition.

An analysis of this kind enables us to avoid some of the errors into which commentators are apt to fall. Thus the rationalists, if by this term we mean those who felt that the nature of the universe could be rationally inferred, are those who were balanced between matrism and patrism. Some of them would be thin-walled, and so would approach the pantheist position, which is why Toland describes the pantheists as disputing calmly on philosophical topics and as never punishing or disgracing a man for his opinions.[6] Those, however, who display a more thick-walled attitude can properly be termed Deists. Shaftesbury is usually described as a Deist, but, as the quotations already given show, he was probably somewhere between Deism and pantheism. When these distinctions are clear, it becomes impossible to make such an assertion as that of Benn, when he describes Schleiermacher as the extreme point of eighteenth-century rationalism.[7] Schleiermacher, the Romantic who has been called the founder of modern scientific theology, was unquestionably a thin-walled matrist of the most clear-cut type: to link him with rationalism is completely to misunderstand the position.

As an example of the way in which this approach seemed to throw light on what had before been puzzling, we may take the idea of progress. Of this I knew little when I started the inquiry, except that it was widely held to be a belief of the Victorians, now generally abandoned in Europe, but not in the United States.

[6] *Pantheisticon*, p. 101.
[7] Benn, *History Eng. Rationalism*, i, 392.

It soon occurred to me, however, that the belief that things were getting better was characteristic of the manic-matrist; and at once I realised that this was the counterpart of the belief, which we have already noted among patrists, that things were getting worse.

Now if my general conception of the period as embodying two contrary movements, patrist and matrist, is correct, it should be possible to find the steady growth of a notion of progress throughout the eighteenth century, and this notion should be in eclipse in the first half of the nineteenth century. Rousseau was the obvious starting-point. Rousseau preached the doctrine of *'perfectibilité'*. He did not, it is true, believe that progress was universal or inevitable; far from it. Man's desire to place himself *'au dessus des autres'* leads to political inequality and injustice. But potentially man is perfectible, and we "must draw from the very evil from which we suffer the remedy which shall cure it", i.e. the social contract.

Characteristically, while it is *moral* decline in which the patrist is interested, it is a gain in *welfare* which preoccupies the matrist. Between these extremes lies the belief that the social order is fixed and un-changeable. Rousseau, at least, believed in both the desirability and the possibility of change.[8]

In England, ideas of progress naturally emerged among the matrist upper class rather than elsewhere. Lord Monboddo (1714–99), though best known for his insight that men are akin to the apes, held that the higher faculties were gradually unfolded, and hence that man's progress was upwards not downwards. In less intellectual circles, the belief in perfectibility found expression in the doctrine and practice of agricultural 'improvement', so popular with landowners.

While one would expect the belief in progress to be general in upper-class circles in the eighteenth century, one would not expect to hear much of it from 1800 until some time after the accession of Victoria, when it might be expected to emerge in academic circles. In point of fact, it can be found emerging in Buckle and Lecky, but does not seem

[8] The doctrine of progress, fully fledged, was proclaimed at the Sorbonne almost simultaneously by Turgot (1750), and was elaborated later in the century by Condorcet. It is worth noting that the word *'optimisme'*, first used in 1732, was admitted to the Dictionnaire of the Academic Française in 1767.

to have been popular in the interim. On the other hand, in the early nineteenth century one would expect to find the depressive outlook spreading from the specifically religious reformers and affecting political and social comment generally. Thus it seems to be confirmatory when we find Greville writing soon after Victoria's accession, "The political world is all out of joint. . . . The whole country is full of distress, disquiet and alarm. Religious feuds are rife . . . everybody says it is all very alarming, and God knows what will happen. . . . Somehow or other, it does seem very strange, that after thirty years of peace, a thing unprecedented, during which time all the elements of public prosperity have been in full activity . . . we find ourselves to all appearance in as bad a condition, with as much difficulty for the present and alarm for the future, as we have often been in. This is a great problem."[9]

An important phenomenon in the eighteenth century was the emergence into popularity of the notion of sensibility, or, in modern terminology, sensitiveness. Not only women, but men too, felt deeply affected by tragic events or by their portrayal in fiction, and wept freely. Fox cried at the theatre, and it was Mrs. Siddons' pride that she received "the copious tribute of tears". The Duke of Newcastle howled when he was presented to the King. Even the harsh Lord Chancellor, Thurlow, turned them on.[10] Mr. Crawfurd testily complained when told of a man who cried, at the death of a friend, saying, "If *I* hear of the death of a friend, *I* burst into tears."[11]

This is often regarded as an affectation, and no doubt it became one, but I think we must treat it primarily as a genuine increase in the capacity to feel, together with a decrease in the inhibition which prevents the expression of feeling. Excessive sensibility is the natural counterpart of the Puritan's impaired emotional response. It is worth

[9] *Memoirs*, Part 2, i, 161–2.

[10] See White, *Age of Scandal*, Chapter 13, for these and other instances.

[11] ib. When Jane Austen ridiculed sentimentality in *Sense and Sensibility*, she intended Marianne to exemplify this kind of behaviour. To-day, however, Marianne seems merely pleasantly spontaneous, if young and foolish, as is natural at her age. Elinor seems less sensible than stilted. Thus the work is not, in reality, the satire on sentimentality that was intended so much as advocacy of an inhibited decorum.

noting that sensibility was not confined to grief: intense pleasure was also felt in happy events, including those fictional happy events known as 'happy endings', and sensibility also embraced the capacity to feel horrified by cruelty or to respond to the sublimity of great beauty. Boswell's response to music was almost hysterical: certain tunes "agitated his nerves painfully", so that he was ready either to shed tears or to rush into a fight.

Evidently, we must regard this as a matrist, and to some extent a Romantic, phenomenon. It is confirmatory of this that patrists condemned it: that Dr. Johnson hated "the fashionable whine of sensibility" and roughly told Boswell that he for his part would never listen to music "if it made him such a fool".[12]

The image which was found especially poignant was a child deserted by its parents, which is understandable enough on the basis of the present analysis.

Until the middle of the century, the word sensibility is rarely found, and then usually used to mean physical sensitivity. Johnson gives a characteristically patrist definition: "quickness of perception, delicacy"; Sterne a typically matrist one: "an exaltation of the feelings based on imagination". That is, Johnson defines it as either a physical endowment or a moral attitude, while Sterne treats it in terms of emotion and fantasy, essentially matrist concepts.

Almost simultaneously the word 'sentimental' emerged: it was introduced by Sterne in 1741 and made widely popular by his *Sentimental Journey* in 1768. For him it denoted the state of being full of emotion—the state which the gift of sensibility was liable to produce. Thus in Richardson's *Grandison* (1753) we read, "My dear girl, take the pen, I am too sentimental." John Wesley could not conceive that the word could have a meaning. "I casually took a volume of what is called *A Sentimental Journey Through France and Italy*," he writes. "Sentimental! What is that? It is not English; he might as well say *Continental*. It is not sense. It conveys no determinate idea."[13] But long before Sterne's work was published the term and the attitude had become a vogue. Mrs. Balfour (Lady Bradshaigh), writing to Richard-

[12] Cited Vulliamy, *Ursa Major*, p. 86.
[13] Wesley *Journal*, v. 445.

son in 1749, asked what was the meaning of this word "so much in vogue among the polite, both in town and country. . . . Everything clever and agreeable is comprehended in that word; but [I] am convinced a wrong interpretation is given, because it is impossible that everything clever and agreeable can be so common as this word."[14]

But gradually genuine sensitivity was replaced by a deliberate wallowing in emotion. Richardson admits that he contrived for Grandison to be tortured by distress "to make sport for the tender-hearted".[15] Colman neatly summarised the sentimental novel as

> Plot and elopement, passion, rape and rapture
> The total sum of ev'ry dear, dear chapter.[16]

While the moralists criticised sentimentality at all periods, we can detect the victory of middle-class conceptions by the end of the century. Though still described as 'fashionable' in 1775, Sheridan had ridiculed it in 1774.[17] In the nineteenth century the satires became numerous: Mrs. Edgeworth in 1801, *Sense and Sensibility* in 1811, Barrett's parody, *The Heroine*, in 1813. As early as 1806 we find a girl saying, "Sentiment is now considered completely Gothic and canaillish" —i.e. barbaric and lower-class.[18] Cunnington observes that the women's magazines of 1800–10 were interested in ideas, not feelings.[19]

But the rejection of emotion applied much more strongly in the case of men than of women. In the nineteenth-century conception, men were assigned the function of thinking, women of feeling. Hence women, though not expected to wallow in emotion, were still allowed, if not expected, to feel strong emotions in the appropriate real-life situations, whereas men were expected to remain stoical. But even for the women this sensitivity was a defect, one which their weaker nature

[14] Richardson, *Correspondence*, iv, 282–3.

[15] ib., iv, 12.

[16] Prologue to *Polly Honeycombe*, 1760.

[17] Prologue to *The Rivals*.

[18] Cunnington, *Feminine Attitudes*, p. 30. 'Gothic' of course, still carried the connotation 'barbaric, uncivilised,' from the Goths. Medieval architecture was not called Gothic until later.

[19] ib., pp. 28 f.

could not be expected to conquer. In Catherine Ward's *The Mysterious Marriage* (1824), the heroine endeavours to "check that excess of sensibility which on some occasions she had strongly indulged in, the only fault (if it be a fault) she was possessed of".

In eighteenth-century drama, the vogue for sensibility became interfused with another element of quite a different psychological origin, and this seems to have confused the majority of commentators. It was a curious feature of the moral doctrine that plays and novels should indicate clearly who were the virtuous characters and who the villains, and that the former should triumph over the latter. Thus *Biographia Dramatica*, reviewing *The Virgin of the Sun* (1799), complains bitterly, "Yet, in contempt of every principle of morality, these characters are made happy, and that without their having shown the most trifling marks of contrition!" The formula of the happy ending could thus be made to meet the demand of the matrists for a pleasurable emotion, and the demands of the patrists for moralistic one. Failing to perceive this distinction, some commentators have (as it seems to me) classed as sentimental plays which were properly moralistic, and vice versa.

The attitude of sensibility also appeared in other guises. Blended with aggression, it produced the Gothic novel; blended with escapism, the tale of far away and long ago.

Perhaps someone with more time and better resources will one day analyse the broad field of the Gothic novel in the kind of terms developed in this book. The unblushing sadism and desire to humiliate women in *The Monk*, the obvious Œdipal elements in the *Castle of Otranto*, in which a tyrannical father plots to marry his son's bride, the frequency of the theme of the imprisoned woman (e.g. *The Sicilian Romance*) fairly invite psychological interpretation.[20] And it is significant that the public which enjoyed this last theme was feminine.

At first there seemed to be some difficulty in fitting into the analysis the concept of benevolence. In many works the idea is put forward that benevolence was an invention of the Evangelical movement, and on the whole a nineteenth-century phenomenon. In general, however, one would expect benevolence to be a matrist phenomenon, and thus

[20] See Birkhead, *Tale of Terror*, Chapter 2, for further instances.

characteristic of the eighteenth century, and closely associated with sensibility.

In elucidating this problem one must distinguish benevolence as a spontaneous impulse motivated by pity or sympathy with some actual victim of misfortune concretely present, and benevolence in the sense of organised charity, in which the giver puts aside money as a moral duty for charitable purposes, never knowing the specific individual on whom it will be bestowed; such a giver characteristically remains unmoved by scenes of actual distress. (Note how the very word charity, which originally indicated an emotion, has come to mean a cold and mechanical system of aid.)

The impassivity of the early nineteenth century in the face of suffering is well known. The Evangelicals are often praised for their humanity, and even regarded as founders of the humanitarian movement; but it is significant that they took up the remote issue of slavery, while remaining unmoved by the no less serious cruelties before their eyes. Hannah More pressed tracts on the starving peasants of Mendip, but did not think it necessary to offer them food. Newman (originally Evangelical in outlook) could hardly bear to think of the poor, and Simeon, the great Evangelical preacher, maintained that, as the Bible declared that the poor were always with us, nothing could be done. Thus the great system of organised charity which the nineteenth century created must be regarded psychologically as an elaborate device to prevent the giver needing to feel any emotion of pity, or the recipient any emotion of gratitude. It is thus also a form of social barrier.

At the other extreme, we find a sensitivity to suffering which can justifiably be criticised as too capricious to do much good. The misfortune which falls before the matrist eye is handsomely relieved, but the much worse or more widespread misfortune which is out of sight is ignored.

The distinction between the two attitudes is expressed with great clarity by Hannah More, who declares that benevolence is "the reigning virtue of the present age". But, she says, "mere casual benevolence" is no good—charity does not deserve the name if it is done from impulse and not from a sense of duty.[21] In fact, the im-

[21] More, *Estimate of Religion*, Chapter 2.

portant thing, it would seem, is to be charitable when you *don't* feel like it.

It is also often alleged that only in the nineteenth century was consideration given to animals.[22] But, as one would predict, it can be found in Shaftesbury, who deplored bull-baiting and praised the humanitarian views put forward in the *Essays* of Montaigne. (He also supported a bill for giving right of counsel to the accused.) The Shaftesbury poets were strong on benevolence: Blacklock wrote a *Hymn to Benevolence* (1746) and John Armstrong wrote *On Benevolence* in 1751. Thomson pleaded in *The Seasons*:

> "But let not on thy hook the tortur'd worm
> Convulsive twist in agonising folds;
> Which, by rapacious hunger swallowed deep,
> Gives, as you tear it from the bleeding breast
> Of the weak helpless uncomplaining wretch,
> Harsh pain and horror to the tender hand."

By 1756 we find an advertisement in the *Gloucester Journal* complaining of the Whitsun cock-fighting, which will be greatly approved by "such as have no reverence for the Deity nor benevolence for his creatures".[23]

Richard Gough pastured his old horses and set up tablets to immortalise a sparrow, a monkey and a tortoiseshell cat. As Allen declares, "Implicit in all these epitaphs is the sentimental fallacy of attributing to animals virtues equal if not actually superior to those of men." He instances the well-known inscription to Fido at Stowe; and might have mentioned, even more aptly, the seventh Earl of Bridgewater's habit of dressing his pets as humans and having them sit at the dining-table with him and drive out in his carriage. More cynically, Byron addressed verses to Boatswain, the dog who possessed "all the virtues of man without his vices".

Actually, Allen exaggerates. Day could not bear to crush a spider, but never suggested that animals were better than men; and the same

---

[22] No satisfactory account of the development of consideration for animals seems to exist. See, however, Harwood, *Love for Animals*.

[23] Kindness to animals is inculcated in Day's *History of Sandford and Merton*, 1783–9.

might be said of those who objected to such sports as cock-fighting. To believe animals better than men is to sentimentalise them, i.e. to invest them with emotion. Not all who displayed sensibility proceeded to the extreme of sentimentality.

Casting about the period for phenomena which call for some kind of explanation, we find, naturally enough, a number which are not the result of the particular processes I have been stressing, but which can, nevertheless, be understood fairly readily in psychological terms.

One of these is the peculiar attitude known as dandyism. This is constantly confused with the tendency of the behaviour of the two sexes to assimilate in a matrist age, to which I shall refer again in the next chapter. The term 'dandy' is seen as a synonym for beau, fop, macaroni, and so forth. Or it is thought to be based on neatness of attire. But Bulwer Lytton, a dandy himself, said, "A sloven can be a dandy."

Actually, the essential feature of dandyism is a refusal to betray suffering. Baudelaire said, "A dandy may be bored, he may even be ill and in pain. But he will keep smiling all the time with Spartan serenity. It will be seen that in some respects dandyism resembles both religious faith and stoicism."[24] Margaret Blessington once said, "There are so few before whom one would condescend to appear otherwise than happy," a remark which Bulwer called "a grand and true saying". This is the attitude, not quite identical with stoicism, of one who has been made to suffer sadistically: he refuses to give his tormentor the satisfaction of betraying his suffering. It seems a logical product of a certain type of parental treatment. Evidently it was not uncommon in England: Rousseau portrayed something of the sort in Lord Bomston. His instructions to the engraver were to depict him with "*un maintien grave et stoique sous lequel il cache avec peine une extrême sensibilité*". Again, Lamington says of d'Orsay, whom he knew personally, that he possessed "that great quality, as I say, of self-command; this enabled him to bear his own burden in life without inflicting the history of his sorrows on others".[25]

[24] Cited Sadleir, *Blessington d'Orsay*, pp. 50–1, from Baudelaire, *Le Peintre de la Vie Moderne*, whence also the remark of Lady Blessington which follows.
[25] Lamington, *In the Days of the Dandies*, pp. 27–8.

In so far as the term 'dandy' also implies elegance, no doubt we may detect narcissism, the admiration of self. To make oneself one's love object is the recourse of those from whom all external love objects have been removed. One would expect to find in the childhood of dandies such as Bulwer and d'Orsay not only unsatisfactory relationships with both parents, but perhaps lack of alternatives—grandparents, aunts and uncles, or even other children—with the aid of whom the habit of forming emotional relations could have been built up.

The dandy is not, of course, a pure type. In Brummell we can see dandyism fused with anal elements, to judge from his preoccupation with cleanliness and 'delicacy'; in Sir Lumley Skeffington, something between the dandy and the Romantic. To the satirists, of course, it was the clothing which mattered most, and the cosmetics. The dandies were going strong by the opening years of the nineteenth century. Thus Captain Adon in *Six Weeks at Longs* (1811) is depicted as not only rougeing and plucking his eyebrows, but as tingeing the palms of his hands with vermilion and whitening the backs with enamel.[26] But when *The English Spy* attacked Lord Petersham (afterwards fourth Earl of Harrington) it was not only for rougeing and corseting, but for his "mincing step, gooseberry eyes and ghastly grin", phrases which seem to suggest a degree of physical inhibition.[27]

By 1841 Mrs. Gore declared "the thing is obsolete" and attributes this to the Prince Regent becoming middle-aged, and preferring superciliousness to noise, wit to humour.[28] Pausing only to observe that superciliousness is here presented as a virtue, one may add that Mrs. Gore has, as usual, got things muddled, for wit and superciliousness are far more the dandy's qualities than are noise and humour.

The nineteenth-century dandy was suspected of effeminacy: and this, according to Rosa, caused them to engage in duels and violence to prove their masculinity.[29] It is true that in the *Annals of Sporting and Fancy Gazette* (1822) we find a correspondent complaining of the "Corinthian affrays now become so very frequent and fashionable"

26 Op. cit., p. 61.
27 Cited Melville, *The Beaux of the Regency*, ii, 108.
28 In *Cecil*, i, 233 ff.
29 Rosa, *Silver Fork School*, p. 26.

and describing how he had to go to the help of a man whom he found being "attacked by myriads of effeminates".[30] While evidence of aggressive violence is common, there is little to indicate that it was a habit of dandies as such, and much to make such a conclusion unlikely. The duel, and the upper-class conception of honour which lay behind it, is a feature of this period. As I have argued elsewhere, the duel is not only an institution for the expression of aggression, but also reflects fears of impotence.[31] (It also represents what, in Chapter Seven, I called a situation of no escape.) Fears of impotence are frequently associated with mother-identification, as can be shown more easily on a historical scale, though the fact is confirmed in the consulting-room of the psychiatrist. We can all laugh off a slur which could not possibly be true: the suggestion that he could not "stand up for himself" was, it would seem, a slur which the eighteenth-century gallant could not afford to treat with contempt.

While it would of course take a lifetime to survey every aspect of eighteenth-century life in detail, I felt that a good *prima facie* case had been made out for the view that eighteenth-century attitudes over a broad range show signs of being determined, in part, by unconscious patterns derived from the father and mother, and modified by the degree of ego-definition present. On this showing alone, then, it is possible to introduce some degree of systematisation into the study of history. But to complete the argument it seemed necessary to deal, even if only briefly, with the two questions which I had so far studied only from the Puritan aspect: spontaneity and anal-restrictive attitudes.

I was greatly struck by the absolutely uninhibited and guilt-free attitude of the upper class to sexual pleasure in the eighteenth century. The evidence at divorce and 'crim. con.' trials reveals sexual adventure being conducted in an atmosphere of laughter and practical joking quite foreign to such adventures in the Victorian period. For example, Lord Augustus Fitzroy, having arranged an assignation with Lady

[30] *Annals*, i, 209. Apparently the term Corinthian, originally applied to any man of fashion or pleasure, without inference of effeminacy, had now changed its meaning.
[31] *Sex in History*, pp. 184–5.

Morrice, on his arrival in her room found the maid warming her mistress's shift at the fire. He sends her away, saying that he would "shift her himself". A few hours later, the maid, alarmed by a loud crash, hurries back to the bedroom to find that the bed-curtains have collapsed. They tell her to fix them up, with various broad jokes about how they came to fall down, and then pack her off with the hope that she is having as much fun with his Lordship's valet as his Lordship is having with her mistress.[32]

The interest in sex does not seem, in most cases, to have had the obsessive quality it had for, say, Casanova. Hickey, wishing to pass a sunny afternoon, calls at a brothel, and takes a couple of the girls down to Turnham Green, where they light-heartedly spend their time on a seesaw in the garden of a pub.[33] Lord Denbigh, writing to David Hume in 1776, mentions quite casually how he, Lord Sandwich, Lord Mulgrave, Mr. Banks and "two or three Ladies of Pleasure" have just passed five or six days at the inn at Spine Hill, near Newbury, adding that they "intend to pass all this week and the next".[34] Indeed, to maintain a mistress actually became something of a social obligation; thus the Duke of Dorset, when he parted from Nancy Parsons, took Mrs. Armistead as his *maîtresse-en-titre*, thinking it improper to maintain an establishment without such an adornment.[35]

Boswell's *Journal*, I think, does show some sense of uncertainty; we seem to see a Scotsman, anxious to shake off his Presbyterian background and ape the manners of the English aristocracy, tentatively putting his foot in the water and finding it rather warm. There is nothing of this in the memoirs of Hickey, for instance, which are remarkably spontaneous and unstudied.

As we have already noted, there is not the slightest trace of inhibition about anal matters.

The prodigality and extravagance which so often characterised the upper class was, of course, the complement of the tight-fistedness of the Puritan group; and as the latter reflects the restrictive and retentive

---

[32] Plowden, *Crim. Con. Biography*, i, 84–5.

[33] Hickey, *Memoirs*, ii, 344.

[34] David Hume to Strahan, in Hume's *Letters*, ii, 319.

[35] Falk, *Royal Fitzroys*.

attitude resulting from severe anal control, so the former reflects the relaxed and expulsive attitude which complements it.

Upper-class attitudes—as we may term them, despite the existence of some exceptional cases—thus present the obverse of middle-class manners in a remarkably precise way.

In the sexual life of the eighteenth century there are, of course, signs of neurosis among the matrist upper class, just as there are among the patrist trading group. Homosexuality existed, just as it did in the nineteenth century. At the beginning of the century Dudley Ryder was told that it was prevalent at Oxford, where "among the chief men in some of the colleges sodomy is very usual", and that "it is dangerous sending a young man who is beautiful to Oxford".[36] As the Puritan pressures built up, it became either more common, or more commented upon, as I have noted in Chapter Five. The *Annual Register* records a series of convictions from 1763 onwards, as well as several cases of the blackmail of homosexuals. Those convicted were sent to the pillory—where some of them died, which indicates the resentment of the crowd—but not until 1807 do we find convicted homosexuals being condemned to death. (There were death sentences in 1807, 1808, 1810 and 1811.) The authorities seem to have launched a drive against homosexuality in the 1780s (which, as mentioned earlier, was a period of intensified Puritan pressure in many fields) and a number of striking cases occurred, culminating in the uncovering of an alleged sodomitical group in Exeter in 1788; about the same time, a similar group in London was exposed.

Since it is human to resent in others the enjoyment of vices to which we are ourselves tempted, this campaign against homosexuality indicates the increasing homosexual components in the Puritan group, for homosexuality is always the preoccupation of the father-identifier. Archenholtz comments on the exceptional sensitivity of the English to this phenomenon. "The English women are so beautiful, the desire of being agreeable to them so ardent, and general, that unnatural pleasures are held in great abhorrence with the men. In no country are such infamous pleasures spoken of with greater detestation."[37]

[36] Ryder, *Diary*, p. 143 (December 1st, 1715).
[37] *Picture of England*, p. 309.

The neurotic nature of this fear is revealed when he continues, "The custom of embracing each other, so common among the men in other European countries, is for this same reason displeasing to the English. A foreigner who did so would be in risk of insult from the populace." This last remark shows that it was the middle or lower classes which felt so strongly.

No corresponding fear of incest was displayed: it was condemned, of course, but it was not hunted down, and the fairly numerous cases which figure in the assizes are reported in a much more casual and objective manner.

Impotence of psychic origin was not uncommon: this is frequently found in matrists, who have had to repress their infantile sexual wishes towards the mother.[38] In such cases, as already noted, it is often found that the person concerned is only potent with a person from a lower class, who need not be idealised and does not resemble his mother. This may explain the very numerous marriages between members of the aristocracy and females of the lower class, upon which many foreign visitors commented; marriages between upper-class females and lower-class men were also not unheard of.[39]

The other striking sexual phenomenon of the period was the preference in some groups for virgins, which was general enough to induce Bloch to speak of a "defloration mania".[40] This I interpret as an attitude peculiar to father-rejectors, who, as a result of their unconscious Œdipal resentments of their mother's interest in their father, wish to prove that all women are really whores. It seems certain that those who had this peculiarity were a limited group, for foreign visitors, such as Shebbeare, particularly note that most men, on the contrary, are surprisingly uninterested in virginity. Thus Shebbeare, "I do not wonder that they indulge themselves with taking girls from the lower classes, which are extremely beautiful, provided they had yet been unpolluted; but such is the indelicate taste of many of the nobility and

[38] See *Sex in History*, p. 184.
[39] See, for instance, Shebbeare, ". . . men of the highest rank marry women of infamy even, not to say of extreme low birth, and ladies of noble family wed their footmen, players and singers . . ." *Letters*, i, 162–3.
[40] Bloch, *Sexual Life in England, Past and Present*, pp. 176 f.

gentry of this nation, they keep expensively women as well known, and as much hackney'd, as the Appian Way in Italy."[41]

The motivation of a certain type of rake is vividly brought out in a story which Johnstone inserts in *Chrysal*, a novel which is known to be based largely on fact.[42] A certain peer, overhearing his kennel boy making an assignation with a girl to meet in the dog-kennels half an hour later, sends the boy on an errand and takes his place. "As he was about the dog-boy's size, and the place was quite dark, she never perceived the change put upon her, but lavished her caresses upon him with the greatest tenderness, vowing never more to have any correspondence with the pantry-boy, or scullion, who it seems were the dog-boy's formidable rivals, but always to be constant to him alone; and took her leave of him, with a promise to meet him there, at the same time next evening."

The peer could not ask any questions, as this would reveal his identity, and bring on an explanation he did not desire "as his greatest pleasure was in the cheat". The author adds, "Disgusting as every circumstance of this affair should have been, the oddity of it, with *the pleasure of supplanting another*, even so mean a person and so unworthy an object, made him determine to be punctual to her appointment." The Œdipal origins are too obvious for further comment.

At this stage, I paused to take stock. I had, I felt, achieved the first of my aims. I had surveyed all the principal features of the eighteenth-century scene, and had demonstrated the fact that the personality elements under consideration, and particularly parental identifications, could be found to have coloured all of them. In doing so, some confusing topics had, for me at least, gained a much greater degree of clarity.

I had begun to see, too, that once this approach was adopted, it would be possible to develop the narrative of history in a novel way. Thus in the eighteenth century, the significance of the French Revolution would appear to be that it activated the unconscious anxieties of patrists in the upper class, driving them into alliance with middle-class patrists of a much more anal type, from whom they normally felt

---

[41] *Letters on the Eng. Nation*, i, 162.
[42] Op. cit., ii, 236–7.

themselves separated by barriers of class and outlook. At the same time, the desire of the middle class for political reform, which was an essential step in its march to social dominance, drove it into alliance with liberals, that is, matrists, many of whom were free-thinkers or atheists. Once that obstacle had been surmounted, the alliance broke up. It was the creation of this ill-assorted triple alliance which carried the middle class to its goal. At the same time, the failure of the matrist lower class to ally itself with its natural sympathisers, the matrist upper class, ensured that no victory of the proletariat could take place in England. For it was from the upper class alone that it could have drawn the intellectual leadership and organising power which might have brought it victory.

Now let us attempt to analyse the psychological features of the early nineteenth century in a similar way.

CHAPTER 14

THE AGE OF FANTASY

TAINE noted that in English railway stations Bibles were provided free for the benefit of intending passengers, but that they were chained to the desks.[1] It is an observation which epitomises the period.

At first sight, the pattern of the nineteenth century seems clear enough. I have already presented material which demonstrates the pre-eminence accorded to the father, the stress on obedience, the belief in a fixed order of society, the preoccupation with the chastity of women, the widening of the distinction in sex-roles, the conservatism and fear of innovation, together with the stress on a father-religion, which are the positive earmarks of father-identification.

We can also employ the æsthetic criteria developed in Chapter Twelve to establish this point: as we should expect, the moralistic middle class feared the use of colour. Knight records how in his youth (he was born in 1791) the Corporation marched to church "in solemn procession of red gowns and blue, with the mace bearer in front and the beadle in the rear". But now (i.e. 1854) "all this glory is departed from the land. Elective corporators now go to church in frock coats".[2] And that the use of colour was felt to be actually sinful in tendency is shown by the writer who, in 1831, considered that it was permissible for parsons to hunt, provided that they did not wear scarlet.[3]

Another patrist characteristic is a deep suspicion of original inquiry. This was also displayed by the moralists. Thus Dean Milman deprecated "deep researches into philosophy of any kind". Hugh James Rose, preaching at Cambridge in 1826, deprecated the enthusiasm for physical science, and Lyell in his letters constantly bewails the opposition

[1] *Notes on England*, p. 15.
[2] Knight, *Once Upon a Time*, ii, 242.
[3] Mathieson, *English Church Reform*, p. 7.

to scientific inquiry, declaring that "the Puseyites have driven physical science from Oxford". He felt obliged to suppress his view that the earth was more than 5,000 years old. Archbishop Howley went so far as to declare that the diffusion of knowledge, disjoined from religious instruction, was "a positive evil" and said that what was needed was "prostration of the understanding and the will".[4]

The patrist substitutes for inquiry rote-learning. Its function is disclosed by Vicesimus Knox when he declares that unless the mind is filled with rote-learning it will fill itself with harmful ideas.[5] The question-and-answer books so popular at this period may be seen as a device to achieve this end, while forestalling awkward inquiries: by providing the learner with ready-made questions they made it more difficult for him to formulate his own.

Freud declares that the father-identifier's distrust of inquiry springs, in the last analysis, from a fear of discovering the real nature of the relationship between his parents—that is, it reflects Œdipal conflicts. Certainly the moralists condemned curiosity in quite general terms; popular compendiums frequently attacked it, and the same theme occurs all through Puritan teaching. Thus in the seventeenth century Taylor rules "avoid curiosity".

The idea that the early nineteenth century was a period in which inquiry was discouraged may come as a surprise to those who think of the nineteenth century as the age of such intellectual giants as Darwin and Huxley. But these did not propound their views until the pendulum was already swinging back. As I have sought to show, the period of most extreme patrism was from about 1800 to 1837; by 1850 the pressure had considerably relaxed. No doubt it was the early nineteenth-century eclipse of reason which accounted for the long gap between Monboddo's first intimations of a theory of evolution (also foreshadowed in Erasmus Darwin's *Botanic Garden*, 1791) and Charles Darwin's statement in 1858.[6]

Similarly, the higher criticism, so often thought of as a nineteenth-

---

[4] These four instances from Benn, *Hist. of English Rationalism.*
[5] Cited Dressler, *Gesch. Eng. Erziehung*, Chapter 9.
[6] Monboddo may be called the first British evolutionist, though his concept of the gradual unfolding of the higher faculties is foreshadowed by Warton.

century development, had actually been developed in the eighteenth century: Hume's *Essay on Miracles* appeared in 1748 and was followed by other works.[7] The textual criticism offered in the later nineteenth century signalised the re-emergence of reason after a period of relapse.

The moralists' preference for chopping learning up into discrete facts by question-and-answer techniques, instead of presenting it as a cohesive system, may also be seen as a product of the divisive nature of the Puritan ego. It is not difficult to detect this factor at work in other fields. The numerous social barriers and the tendency for each family to form a cohesive unit, excluding the stranger, exemplify it. We may even detect it in the numerous sections—often as many as seven, and each of a distinct social character—into which the Victorian public-house was divided. The high panels, like the thick curtains and obscured glass, reflect the fear of being spied upon or 'super-vised'. In a world of censorious public opinion, one could only relax in privacy.

The numerous conventions and social regulations evolved in the nineteenth century may be regarded not only as devices to restrict spontaneity but also as a consequence of the general lack of spontaneity. For, whereas an uninhibited person will treat a social situation as the spirit moves him, an inhibited one will feel unable to act unless a behaviour pattern is laid down for him. The way in which the spontaneity was taken out of ordinary actions is well illustrated by *Hints on Sea Bathing* (1838): by the time the intending bather had observed all the rules, made all the preparations, equipped himself with the impedimenta recommended in this work (including a 'flesh brush') practically all desire to bathe must have vanished. Indeed, at no point is it suggested that the experience is one to enjoy: it is recommended purely as advantageous to health.

But despite the evident existence of father-fixation, the 'Victorian' (or, more accurately, pre-Victorian) attitude to women was not entirely as predicted. It is true that women's liberty was restricted, and this chiefly with the object of preserving their chastity, just as the theory

[7] Its origins can be traced back to Simon in 1678. Dean Milman's *History of the Jews* appeared in 1828: though it accepted the genuineness of many of the miracles, it treated the Jews as objects of historical study. It was met with a storm of abuse.

foresees: and their intellectual attainments were undervalued. But this was not accompanied, as it was in some earlier patrist periods, by a general depreciation of women. On the contary, this was made a reason for admiring them. To the moralists and the early Church women were the source of all evil, the temptresses to whom man's fall from purity was due. To the pre-Victorians, in contrast, women were the repositories of all the nobler emotions, and a powerful influence for good.[8] As *Female Tuition* said in 1786, "All virtues, all vices and all characters are intimately connected with manners, principles and dispositions of our women."[9] Thus the pre-Victorian male in this sphere places women upon a pedestal in a way strongly recalling certain groups of matrists, such as the Troubadours. Indeed, women, far from being regarded as sexual temptresses, were, as we have seen in Chapter Six, regarded as pure and even as totally uninterested in sex.

Thus, when the pre-Victorians saw the mother as 'pure', by 'pure' or 'like an angel' we may understand 'desexualised'. The "five and twenty breadths of petticoat" within which the woman lay "entombed like a mummy" (as Mrs. Gore said) may perhaps be seen as an effort to blot out the existence of the genital parts, while the simultaneous acceptance of low décolletés shows that no such alarm was felt about the secondary sexual characteristics, i.e., about the woman in her aspect of nourisher and mother.[10] The advertisements of the period, when they show female undergarments, almost always show them folded, so that the nether part is invisible; it has been said that the Victorian woman hardly existed below the waist.

But while some women, and especially one's own mother, were conceived as 'pure', there was also another race of women who were conceived as devoted wholly to sex, and these, in a phrase curiously reminiscent of the fall of Adam and of Lucifer, were known as "fallen women". In other words they had lost their original divine purity. It

---

[8] Thus Mrs. Sandford says, "The character of women, though inferior, is not less interesting than that of men . . . her very defects make her an object of solicitude." *Woman in her Soc. and Dom. Character*, Chapter 6.

[9] Op. cit., p. 30.

[10] Décolletés low enough to show the cleavage of the breasts appear in *Punch* about 1858. (See p. 69.)

was held that prostitutes were "devoid of moral feeling" and hence incapable of any form of virtue. When, as often happened, evidence was given to government commissions or other bodies that prostitutes were honest, or showed gratitude, or were sober, or were conscientious mothers, this was always regarded as astonishing, if not incredible. Another tacit assumption was that the prostitute, being 'bad', would necessarily spend her whole life as a prostitute, unless perhaps redeemed by the ministrations of kindly philanthropists who would re-educate her. When Acton demonstrated that prostitution was often simply a phase through which women passed, after which they married and settled down to respectability, this was thought incredible.[11] In short the pre-Victorian divided women into two groups, the angelically pure and the irredeemably impure.

This process of separating good and bad elements is known as 'decomposition'. Its psychological origins are approximately as follows. The child feels for its parents both love—because they support it—and hate—because they frustrate it. (That is to say, its feelings are *ambivalent*.) As it grows more mature, it learns to reconcile these extremes to an increasing extent. But if the emotions felt are very powerful, it may be unable to make this reconciliation. Yet to feel conflicting emotions is painful and biologically unsatisfactory, since mixed motives lead to inconsistent behaviour. It simplifies matters to separate them, directing all the good feelings to one woman, all the bad feelings to others.

It is easy to imagine that the pre-Victorian mother, who combined great tenderness for her children with an extremely frustrating series of prohibitions, may well have created an ambivalence too powerful to resolve.[12] When to this decomposition we add the notion of sexual

[11] Acton, *Prostitution considered*, pp. 72 f.

[12] A lesser, but still considerable, degree of ambivalence was also felt in respect of the father, as shown by the fact that males, too, were divided fairly clearly into 'black sheep' and white ones. *The Lady's Magazine* in 1818 commented approvingly on a suggestion that all immoral persons be segregated in an island or city set aside for the purpose, a proposal which illustrates the tendency to decompose very vividly. The Fascist treatment of Jews provides a contemporary instance, and segregation in a ghetto or special district is a natural product of such outlook.

guilt, we at once arrive at the 'good' mother, who is desexualised (a postulate which also goes some way towards taking the sting out of the Œdipus situation), and the 'bad' woman, who is pre-eminently concerned with sex, i.e., the prostitute—and, in an earlier age, the witch.

Decomposition is of course a sign of immaturity, and betrays an unrealistic attitude to life; it may also be seen as a sign of regression to an earlier development stage—or a failure ever to emerge from it—for children commonly divide the world into heroes and villains, into mothers and witches. (As we shall see in a moment, this is not the only sign of immaturity the Victorians displayed.)

Though decomposition emerged most strongly in the attitude of men to women, it can also be found, to some extent, in women's attitude to men, and even to events. There was a tendency to take a decisive position, to approve or condemn; a man was socially acceptable or not, he was a good risk or a bad risk, a gentleman or a cad. Children, too, were told that they must be on one side of the moral fence or the other.[13] Political issues were also judged in this all-or-nothing way, perhaps more frequently than to-day, when the view that 'there's not much to choose' is often expressed. Above all, this applied in religion: one was either saved or damned. The fact that 'good' women were the severest condemners of prostitutes is easily explicable, of course, by the fact that they resented (at the unconscious level) others having unrestricted right to the sexual and social freedom which they were denied: this of course is a common mechanism—if I can't have it, you must not either. And no doubt they feared the rivalry of the 'bad' woman who had so much to offer which they had not.

In the last analysis, decomposition may be seen as a means of resolving a particularly severe Œdipal struggle. The mother's 'wickedness' is felt to be so intolerable that it must be denied: she must not only be seen as pure, but as constitutionally incapable of unchastity—an angel, in short.

The sphere in which we can most readily confirm the occurrence of decomposition is the theatre: from early in the eighteenth century we

[13] Thus Mrs. Chapone opens her *Letters on the Improvement of the Mind* by emphasising that "you must either become one of the glorious children of God . . . or a child of destruction . . ." p. 4.

find a growing tendency to distinguish protagonists of a play into hero and heroine on the one side and villain or villains on the other. Restoration comedy, in contrast, had attempted to present people realistically, though cynically.[14]

The new middle-class drama was less realistic, for it concentrated all the evil in one character, and imputed an incredible degree of virtue to others.

By idealising and desexualising the mother-image the Victorian was enabled, I suggest, to introject it at the same time as the father-image; if so, this would account for the presence of certain non-patrist items in the Victorian make-up, such as the tendency to advocate humane treatment for animals.

To check this rather tentative diagnosis, I thought it might be instructive to look at the Victorian conception of the garden. While extreme patrists would, of course, be interested in it only for utilitarian reasons or for purposes of ostentation, those who treated it as an æsthetic form might be expected (if the foregoing argument were correct) to take a fundamentally Classical view, yet with a restricted infusion of softened picturesque elements. Sure enough, I found that the Classical ideas of symmetry and subordination to a plan had been reinstated, while the more jagged Romantic features were to be strictly avoided. Thus Hibberd, a leading Victorian authority, says in 1859 that he "would have every garden symmetrically arranged; the paths should never diverge at sharp angles". No attempts at the picturesque should be be made, "as far as the eye could reach from terrace or window, all should be artistic, and every separate feature subordinate to the whole."[15] He likes "the idea of order which prevails in such a scene" and again he stresses that detail must be "subordinated to a complete effect". Rockwork too must "ever have symmetry about it".[16]

---

[14] Such plays appear early in the eighteenth century, as the theatre begins to cater for the new middle class. (See Bernhaum, *Drama of Sensibility*.) Dryden, echoing Aristotle, had said, "All reasonable men have long since concluded that the hero of the poem ought not to be a character of perfect virtue." (Preface to, *All for Love*, 1678.)

[15] *Rustic Adornment*, p. 340.

[16] ib., p. 405.

Where the Romantic sees the garden as a continuation of the land-scape, Hibberd (apparently unaware that he is reverting to an earlier thesis) explains that a garden is "a continuation of the house" and "not a patch of wild nature". Though he pays lip-service to the picturesque, the context shows that this term no longer signifies wild, untrammelled Nature as it did for Uvedale Price. "While we delight in some amount of picturesqueness, we are to consider art rather than nature as the basis of every arrangement".[17] In fact the picturesque can display its possi-bilities within a narrowly defined frame or order, just as the Victorian woman herself could only display her female nature within a rigid man-made frame. Finally, Hibberd makes the revealing remark: "Nature is to be robed, dressed, beautified and made to conform to our own ideas of form and colour."[18] This, too, is exactly the role reserved for women, and children. The notion of an order imposed on chaos, as against the revelation of a natural order, is characteristically anal-patrist.

As we might expect, moral judgments replace æsthetic, "The house itself is a pattern of chastity," while in the garden it is not only the idea of order but the "refined tone of plastic embellishments" which appeals. From the wreckage of Romanticism is rescued the only notion which can be fitted to the Victorian pattern—the notion that Nature has a moralising effect—and even this undergoes a sea-change in the process. "Without the help of a garden it is impossible to cultivate chaste ideas and refined feelings."[19] Pan himself is made to bear witness to chastity!

Another feature of middle-class behaviour in the early nineteenth century which may seem to call for explanation is the extreme readiness of the moralistic group of the pre-Victorians to accept as real

---

[17] ib., pp. 330 f. Very similar views are expressed by Mrs. Foster, at a rather later date (1879). A "landscape garden" can never give "profitable delight". . . . "Ornament, to be correct, should be based upon geometrical construction." "The best gardens have always been rectangular." A lawn "is not improved by having patches of colour spotted about it." She regrets the absence of fountains and warns us on no account to imitate Nature in building them (*On the Art of Gardening*, pp. 8, 13, 16, 85).

[18] *Rustic Adornment*, p. 331.

[19] ib., p. 326. Naturally grottoes were unacceptable, as "disagreeable and injurious to health." See Kemp, *How to Lay Out a Garden*, p. 337.

what were actually fantasies, a phenomenon usually termed super-stition. In this wave of superstition, which mounted to a peak in the 1820s, three overt themes can be described. First, there is a belief in God's daily, detailed, intervention in human affairs, in the sense of his rewarding and punishing people immediately for their actions. Secondly, there is a disposition to believe in miraculous events, that is, in divine interventions or demonstrations of the suspending of natural law. Thirdly, there is a sense of impending doom. These three themes are often closely interwoven.

The belief that God directly punishes human behaviour was clearly stated in 1798 in Bowdler's *Reform or Ruin*, which attributed the bad crops not to the mischance of bad weather but to divine punishment for immorality.[20] Going still further, some claimed that each act is punished as it occurs: Evangelical magazines were full of stories of how clergymen had been struck dead when playing cards, and the like. There was even a man who, when stung by a bee, swore so horribly that the bee promptly stung him again on the tongue.[21] This was a convenient view for the middle class, since it implied that those who made money were only receiving their deserts, while those who remained poor did so because God recognised their worthlessness. As Arthur Young said after unexpectedly making £221 17s. 6. in the Funds, "I find it comfortable to attribute everything to God."[22] It justified harshness to the poor, who were obviously poor because they deserved to be. And it could even be acceptable to those who did not prosper, if they had a sufficient sense of guilt: their misfortune was not due to lack of business acumen but to God's punishing them for their sins.

[20] Palmerston was accused of blasphemy when he proposed improving the system of drains as a measure against cholera, since cholera was clearly a visitation of God. (See Kellett, *As I Remember*, p. 42.)

[21] See Quinlan, *Victorian Prelude*, p. 188. In 1717–18 Thomlinson, for instance, had told his congregation just the opposite. "Preached on Luke xiii, 1–5, and proved that calamities happen alike to all, good and sinners, etc." (Hodgson, *Six North Country Diaries*, p. 141 (October 5th).

[22] *Autobiography*, p. 380. When two of the Bishops who censured Tract 90 died before delivering their charges, Newman and Pusey thought God had performed this miracle for their benefit. (See Kellett, *As I Remember*, p. 41.)

But the adoption of this view cannot be explained simply on grounds of convenience. *Reform or Ruin*, which prophesied a general doom, went through eight editions in the first year of publication—which suggests that an appreciable number of people were oppressed by a sense of guilt.

The belief in God's direct intervention was definitely a middle-class belief. Edmund Gosse tells how, whenever he was ill, his father used to come and question him closely as to whether he had committed any sin which might have caused it; and when the senior Gosse's book *Omphalos* was greeted with ridicule, he searched his conscience for some sin which he must have committed to provoke this.[23] Nor was this belief confined to extreme Calvinists, like the Gosses. No less a figure than Professor T. H. Huxley wrote to Charles Kingsley in 1860, "I have the firmest belief that the divine government (if we may use such a phrase to express the sum of the 'customs of matter') is wholly just. The more I know intimately of the lives of other men (to say nothing of my own), the more obvious it is to me that the wicked does not flourish, nor is the righteous punished. . . . The ledger of the Almighty is strictly kept, and every one of us has the balance of his operations paid over to him at the end of every moment of his existence."[24] (It is interesting that, in the saner atmosphere of 1893, he abandoned this superstitious view.)[25]

The belief that everyone is punished and rewarded in this life on a day-to-day basis is quite foreign to the normal doctrine of the Christian Church, so much insisted on by early Puritans, that it is in the next world that accounts will be paid, and is therefore especially significant. Only powerful feelings could have modified such strongly received doctrine.

Since it is completely unrealistic, its adoption represents a retreat into fantasy. If one believes that God watches every deed and punishes or rewards at once as a parent would, then clearly the world is "under control" and one knows where one is. The authoritarian is made

[23] *Father and Son*, pp., 108, 293–4.
[24] Cited R. Mortimer, *Sun. Times*, August 7th, 1955.
[25] *Vide* letter from Sir L. Collier, *Sun. Times*, August 14th, 1955.

deeply anxious by events which are not ordered, or which seem out of control—we have already seen that control is his key preoccupation; this belief constitutes a device for reducing such tension. It is, of course, a neurotic device; and since it implies an inability to accept the world as it is, it is a sign of psychological immaturity.

In the 'thirties and 'forties a wave of millenarianism swept over the middle classes. The translation of Lacunza's *Coming of the Messiah* in 1827 seemed to crystallise an emotional need which had been increasingly felt. Miracles were reported—such as the supernatural cure of Miss Fancourt in 1830—and were widely credited. Henry Drummond, the banker, cancelled his tour to the Orient and hastened to advise the Archbishop of York that the day of judgment was at hand. He called a meeting on Unfulfilled Prophecies; prayers were offered for the gift of tongues. "Send us apostles, send us apostles!" the meeting cried. Irving addressed crowds of up to 13,000; at his meetings many were seized with glossolaly.[26] Fire burned in their bones.[27] The outbreak of glossolaly at Port Glasgow, when a number of women were apparently seized with the gift of tongues, was interpreted by many as a sign that the day of the Lord was at hand, and other events, which we should regard as random, were interpreted as signs and portents. Arnold entered in his diary, following the Port Glasgow incidents, "Whether this be a real sign or no, I believe that the 'day of the Lord' is coming, i.e., the termination of one of the great αἰῶνες of the human race."[28]

Augustus Hare tells us that the motive of many of those who were working for the establishment of a diocese of Jerusalem was that there might be a suitable reception committee for Christ at His second coming.[29] Gosse's father believed in the second coming to the end of his life, and repeatedly calculated the date of the event. It seemed so "absolutely imminent" that he would often bid his son good-night, saying with "sparkling rapture in his eyes", "Who knows? We may

[26] That is, confused utterances, supposed to be the gift of tongues.

[27] This curious phrase, used at one of Irving's meetings (see Drummond, *Irving and his Circle*, p. 282), was also used by an ecstatic observed by Wesley. (Tyerman, i, 262.)

[28] Stanley, *Life of Arnold*, i, 273.

[29] *Years with Mother*, p. 37.

next meet in the air, with all the cohorts of God's saints!" "This conviction," Gosse adds, "I shared without a doubt."[30]

For Gosse this event was to be expected eagerly, since the elect (of whom he was one) would be swept up to heaven, leaving the rest of the world's population to stew in their own juice; but for many it was suffused with a sense of disaster. Arnold equated the "great day of the Lord" with the calamities, wars and tumults promised by *Revelation*. He wrote in a letter in October 1831, "All in the moral and physical world appears so exactly to announce the coming of the 'great day of the Lord', i.e., a period of fearful visitation to terminate the existing state of things, whether to terminate the whole existence of the human race, neither man nor angel knows. . . ."[31] Here presumably we can detect an unconscious preoccupation with the idea of a punishing father always liable to descend upon one. But in the general tendency to see random events as mysteriously significant I perceive a factor more obscure and interesting. For an exaggerated sense of the significance of events which are really fortuitous is a common feature of paranoid states; thus in persecution mania quite chance actions of others are interpreted as part of a deep-laid plot against the patient. The latter is so preoccupied by his inner tensions, so comparatively uninterested in the external world, except in relation to himself, that he has little difficulty in fitting external phenomena into his internally motivated fantasies. In effect, he projects on the real world events occurring within himself. As Arnold's and Drummond's cases show, superstition was not the peculiarity of an uneducated lower class.

I have dwelt only on the religious aspects of superstition; but it may be added that there was during the first half of the nineteenth century a great revival of belief in astrology, which had dropped into disrepute during the previous century.[32] Intense interest was also manifested in ghosts and spiritualism, and the medium Home aroused tremendous interest in the 'fifties.[33]

---

[30] *Father and Son*, p. 305.
[31] Stanley, *Life of Arnold*, i, 252.
[32] Moody, *Complete Refutation*, p. v.
[33] See, for instance, Lewald, *England und Schottland*, i, 307-8.

If I am correct in regarding superstition as a result of the immaturity of the moralistic personality, then there should also be limited evidence of its existence in similar circles during the eighteenth century. This seemed to provide a useful opportunity for a check on this hypothesis. Examples are in fact not difficult to find. Not only do we find a belief in God's intervention—see, for instance, a tract which gleefully notes the death of forty people in an explosion, while watching a Punch and Judy show, as evidence of God's disapproval of the theatre[34]—but we also find belief in miracles, as in Doctor Latham of Firdeane's carefully authenticated account of the events at his church in 1745: "Several Hundreds of Bodies rose out of the Grave in the open day in that Church [i.e. Heafield, 3 miles from Chapel-en-le-Frith] to the great astonishment and Terror of several spectators. They deserted the Coffins, and arising out of the graves, immediately ascended directly towards Heaven, singing in Concert all along as they mounted thro' the Air; they had no winding sheets about them, yet did not appear quite naked, their Vesture seemed streaked with gold, interlaced with sable, skirted with white, yet thought to be exceeding light, by the agility of their motions, and the swiftness of their ascent; they left a most fragrant and delicious Odour behind them, but were quickly out of sight." And with proper caution he adds, "I can assure from eye-witnesses of the Truth of every particular."[35]

In the same period we can also find actual millenarianism. Neglecting the sect of Millenaires, which consisted of poor and uneducated persons, let us take the case of the learned Doctor Whiston, who, about 1748, proved by "99 infallible signs" that the day of the Lord was at hand. The storms foretold by the scriptures are certainly those of November 27th, 1703, the great earthquakes are those of 1749–50 and earlier, and the great city, one-tenth of which is to be destroyed by an earthquake, is undoubtedly London. It cannot be Rome, the other likely candidate for divine displeasure, since we know from other prophecies that the Lord is going to destroy Rome in 1866. "It is true," he adds, with scrupulous fairness, "that the moon has not yet been turned to blood,

---

[34] *The Explosion* (1772).
[35] Clegg, *Diary*, p. 14.

but this sequel, cannot, I think, be long future."[36] (It is in the light of this that we must interpret the general panic which followed the Lisbon earthquake, and the announcement of the end of the world in 1750, when so many people fled London.)

The realisation that patrists are given to superstition, and that they also retreat in various other ways into fantasy, comes as a surprise to many people who imagine that patrists are always hard-headed and realistic, and that fantasy is the prerogative of the Romantic, or matrist, with his readier access to the unconscious. In point of fact, it seems to be the person who has balanced introjections who is least prone to fantasy: it is almost as if the two sorts of fantasy cancel one another out.

For patrist and matrist fantasies are certainly of very different kinds. The patrist organises his fantasies in an apparently logical form—as does the paranoiac who believes he is being persecuted. Furthermore his fantasies are, I think, less often visual than those of the matrist. The nature of fantasy is something which seems never to have been exhaustively analysed; and it may be that we use the word to describe a number of distinct processes. For instance, we describe the patrist's sense of impending doom as a fantasy, especially when it emerges in a concrete prophecy like Whiston's, but it is primarily a matter of emotion. Similarly Hoffmann's fantasies about identity are merely symptoms of an underlying sense of loss of identity. Such emotions may be described visually or may be described in terms of ideas. They seem to emerge just as freely whether the individual concerned is inhibited or not. The patrist fits them into an intellectually elaborated structure, the matrist into an imaginatively elaborated one, that is all.

The matrist, because less dominated by 'cerebral' considerations of rational consistency, is more open to those non-rational voices we call intuition. But this is evidently another story altogether, and intuition would seem to spring from some quite other layer of consciousness than fantasy.

Perhaps it is the fact that the moralist in the period we are considering

[36] Whiston, *Memoirs*. The whole of Vol. iii is devoted to these predictions. Similarly Bishop Horne thought the Lisbon earthquake foretold in *Amos*. See Kellett, *Religion and Life*, p. 138, for a general impression.

appealed so frequently to reason which has established the idea that the patrist group was rational. The phraseology which was almost invariably used was that men should use their 'reason' to restrain their 'emotions'. Francis Place congratulates himself that the Sunday crowds now behave more 'rationally' than they did, when he means more inhibitedly. In reality, the force which inhibits spontaneity is not the reason, but the super-ego, a thing which is frequently far from reasonable. And it may be added that what it inhibits are not, except incidentally, the emotions, but the basic drives of the id. This whole terminology is fallacious. No doubt an appeal was made to reason because, in the eighteenth century, reason—in the correct sense of the power of ratiocination—had already been enthroned as the means by which man could detect God's presence in the universe and infer his characteristics. To the rationalist, however, it was reasonable to indulge both one's appetites and emotions up to a point ('within reason'). In adopting reason and declaring that its function was to inhibit emotion, the moralist performed a kind of philosophical feat of ju-jitsu, in which one part of rationalism was employed to defeat the other.

Because of his advocacy of 'reason', it is often imagined that the patrist values dispassionate inquiry and research. But, as we have seen, the patrist accepts learning in the sense of mere erudition and the exegetic study of works and doctrines laid down by our forebears, but deeply distrusts all original inquiry. It is true that the immediate reason for fearing science was that it would imperil the fundamentalist interpretation of the Bible. But this fear was only a particular instance of a general fear of anything which might imperil the tenability of the patrist system of attitudes, and patrist opposition to inquiry in other fields was just as strong whenever this danger arose. Mill, for instance, abandoned his plan to write a history of the French Revolution for fear of public disapproval. Faced with a choice between his fantasies and cold facts, the patrist (like the matrist) chooses to preserve his fantasies, as Sedgwick betrayed when he exclaimed that if science interfered with religion he would "dash it to the ground".[37]

It is also part of this story that numerous prosecutions for blasphemy

[37] Caroline Fox, *Memories*, i, 41.

were brought against those who denied the historicity of the Bible, or even the existence of God—for to deny the existence of the Father is not merely to defy authority but to deny the reality of the father-figure altogether.

Parallel with this went a recrudescence of 'fundamentalism'. This is a phenomenon of some interest. What the fundamentalists believed was not only that the Bible was the directly-inspired word of God, but that it was the sole source of doctrine and belief, containing full and complete guidance for every eventuality as well as an authoritative account of the past and future of human history. Given the Bible, one needed no other guidance; the religious exercises of the fundamentalists were confined, apart from Communion and baptism, to prayer and Bible exegesis. But the Bible was not merely inspired as a whole: each word was also to be regarded as separately inspired, so that whole sermons were preached on texts consisting of the single word 'How' or 'Notwithstanding' or 'Therefore'. Kellett recalls hearing a sermon preached on the word *Selah*, which is a Hebrew word, supposedly a musical direction, of which the meaning remains unknown to this day.[38] Fractions of sentences were also inspired, so that one could preach on the paradox "This is that" by lifting the first three words from the sentence, "This is that man". Even when Paul said, "In this speak I, not the Lord" he was inspired to say that he was not inspired.

Many could repeat the genealogy of Christ from Adam, and all the kings of Israel and Judah with their dates: and this was not merely industrious but actively virtuous, since these lists were inspired. Were we to come across such behaviour in a primitive tribe, we should describe it as demonstrating magical belief in the power of words; and we are entitled to infer that those that so behaved were in a comparably primitive mental state.[39]

I could see, in a general way, that this extreme preoccupation with words represented the anal components, because this association is well established, as I have noted in Chapter Nine. And I could see that to turn to the Bible was also to turn to the past, to adhere to tradition.

[38] Kellett, *Religion and Life*, Chapter 5.
[39] It is against this background that one can begin to understand the terrified opposition offered to the Revised Version in 1881.

But this did not seem quite enough to account for the extraordinary *literalness* with which the words of the Bible were taken. It was only while I was re-reading Gosse's *Father and Son* that I achieved a moment of insight into the problem. Gosse comments on his pious and fundamentalist father's total lack of imagination. I suddenly realised that where the Romantic lets his imagination play freely, the extreme patrist inhibits it from all action whatever: literalism is a total—I had almost written, pathological—lack of imagination.

A puzzling feature of nineteenth-century society is the stress laid on social reputation, and hence on appearances, and on conformity to custom. In order to explain why I found this puzzling, I must refer to a recent psychological theory, according to which societies tend to be regulated either by shame or by guilt.[40] (Shame may be defined as a reaction to loss of *social* approval; in contrast with guilt, which arises from failure to live up to an *internalised* standard, or, in ordinary language, to the demands of conscience.)[41] The individual who is motivated only by shame is quite prepared to commit a sin if no one will know; and if he moves into a society with different standards, he conforms to these and cheerfully performs acts which were forbidden in his first environment but which are permitted in the new. In contrast the guilt-ridden person is always worried by a breach of the code, and if necessary defies the customs of his society in order to conform to his private conception of what is right.

Now if it is true that societies are either shame-ridden or guilt-ridden, into which category does the nineteenth-century society fall? Since the Puritan is guilt-ridden, we should expect it to be a guilt-culture. But the stress on social conformity is characteristic of a shame-culture.

The contradiction is, I think, only apparent. The fact is, while the Puritan middle-class group was guilt-ridden, the upper-class group

[40] Piers and Singer, *Shame and Guilt*.

[41] The ideal to which people seek to conform is borrowed, in the first instance, from parental figures and other models, and then 'internalised' or made part of oneself. The word 'conscience' usually covers both the ideal and the forces which impel one to adhere to it.

(and perhaps a part of the middle-class) was shame-ridden. This is clear enough in the eighteenth century: the concept of honour—though it has other psychological undertones—is fundamentally a shame concept, it concerns one's reputation with others.[42]

Recognition of this fact enables us to explain both the general licentiousness of the upper class in the eighteenth century and the way in which it swung round to sober behaviour in the nineteenth. For in a period, and a social group, in which 'immorality'—meaning wenching, gambling, drinking, and the like—is "the done thing", the social and psychological pressures towards conformity will drive many with little taste for such activities into them, and so will tend to increase the impression of general immorality. But once 'moral' behaviour has become "the done thing" the same pressures will tend to drive the undecided into morality.

Thus, as soon as the middle class had become sufficiently dominant to make a moral code more general than an immoral one, we find the upper class swinging round to conform. The shame-pressures which formerly impelled this group to immorality now have the reverse effect. A reading of upper-class diaries for the period of change-over suggests strongly that this is what occurred.

The point is clearly made by Hodgson, who declares, "In the final analysis public opinion was the real enforcing agency. And so strongly in favour of a strict Sabbath was public opinion that even royalty was forced to accede to it. A demonstration of this fact occurred in 1809, when old Bishop Porteus, the friend of the Evangelicals, heard that a club, of which the Prince of Wales was a member, customarily held its meetings on Sundays. Having secured an audience with the Prince, the Bishop remonstrated with him, and before he left secured a promise that thereafter the club would meet on Saturdays."[43]

The evidence from novels also confirms this diagnosis. In *The Semi-Attached Couple* we observe in the upper class a conformity to moral

---

[42] It is significant that moralists attacked the concept of honour, and disliked the theatre partly because it exhibited this conception. Hannah More acutely described honour as "the religion of the drama".

[43] Hodgson, *Life of Porteus*, i, 249.

standards which is completely superficial, and based on no feeling of guilt or religious conviction. Thus, in this book, although Lady Eskdale feels it important to go to church, she arrives after the first lesson and leaves after the sermon.[44] And the life which she and her compeers lead is entirely vapid and self-centred. At the same time, when a man at a house-party suggests walking to the end of the garden with a girl in order to look for another guest, it is hastily recollected that they will need a chaperone. It is quite clear that no one really feels that any danger is involved: the whole thing comes as an afterthought.

Again, when Mrs. Birkett, the apothecary's wife, passes a young man watching his fiancée painting in the garden of the castle, she is shocked at their not being chaperoned, and takes the gossip back to the village; in retailing it she adds, "But I fancy in high life there is a great deal more ease than we should think right. But I can't say I approve of young engaged people being left so much to themselves."

No doubt the process was aided by the fact that many members of the middle class were created peers, and then proceeded to intermarry with the aristocracy; while the gradual capture of the public-school system by the middle class must have tended to bring the upper class into line.

I am inclined to think that in this interaction of shame and guilt is an important mechanism for understanding social process on the historical scale.

At this point it becomes possible to analyse the 'hypocrisy' of which the Victorians are so often accused.[45] They evidently felt quite strongly that appearances were extremely important. Thus Malcolm remarks, "But we have now the consolation to reflect that Vice is compelled to hide her fascinating visage, and though it is impossible to dive into all her haunts, we do not find them blazoned with large characters in the public ways, where her votaries, however, contrive intimations which

---

[44] By Emily Eden: as sister of Lord Auckland she speaks with authority on upper-class behaviour.

[45] Hypocrisy was being satirised in 1811: all those who keep mistresses or seduce servants and shop girls "talk morality, ore rotundo, and descant unmercifully on the depravity of the age". London, or a Month at Steven's, ii, 11.

are passed unobserved by the virtuous." The importance of public opinion was stressed even more explicitly by the *Morning Chronicle* in 1827: "Our men of rank may occasionally assume a virtue which they have not, they may sometimes be greater hypocrites than their forefathers were, but hypocrisy is, at all events, an homage offered to public opinion, and supposes the existence of a fear of the people."[46]

How this view was adopted even by the middle-class moralists is shown by Burder's sermon on *Lawful Amusements*,[47] in which, after listing all the actual sins, he devotes a chapter to saying that one should also avoid all activities which are "not of good report"—even when they are entirely harmless.

Finally we reach the point at which appearances are explicitly stated to be more important than the reality, when *The Lady's Magazine* says, "A woman without delicacy is a beast; a woman without the *appearance* of delicacy is a *monster*."[48]

Obviously, if we are chiefly concerned with reputation, appearances are what matter most. But mingled with this aspect of hypocrisy there is another, which seems to me to be etiologically different. In the eighteenth century it was customary to make no pretences. Coyer says, "*Il est du moins un vice presqu'inconnu ici, l'hypocrisie. Chacun se montre comme il est, sans excepter les Ecclésiastiques.*"[49] And as late as the 1790s Archenholtz says, "The English consider dissimulation the worst of vices."[50]

From showing oneself as one is, it is but a short step to speaking one's mind—showing one's thoughts as they are. The upper class in the

---

[46] *Morning Chron.*, October 1st, 1827. Cf. also Scott's remark in the same year, "We are not, perhaps, more moral in conduct than men fifty years ago, but modern vice pays a tax to appearances, and is contented to wear a mask of decorum." (*Misc. Prose Works*, iii, 516.)

[47] Op. cit., Chapter 3.

[48] Op. cit., September 1818, p. 408. But as early as 1762 Gausenna Minor declared, "Women must not only be but seem decent." (*Gentleman's Mag.*, Vol. 32, i, 69.)

[49] *Nouvelles Observations*, p. 281.

[50] *Picture of England*, p. 42.

eighteenth century were often outspoken enough, or expressed themselves clearly in other ways, but a century later things had changed. "We still constantly hear . . . remarks concerning the honour, the virtue, the cleverness, the ability, the beauty, the accomplishments of our friends. But it is behind their backs. We no longer try to put the truth openly before them. We stab in the back; but the back is a portion of the frame which feels nothing. So far the change is a distinct gain."[51] The eighteenth century regarded frankness as a virtue: Lucy Aikin, in contrast, said, "Few characters repel me more. . . . Frankness means freeness."[52] In this we may see, perhaps, the desire not to lose approval by unwanted frankness, but also a reduced ability to stand up to aggression. And in the nineteenth century the approved reaction to an insult was to turn haughtily away, not deigning (as it was put) to reply. Where all impulses are controlled, and overt expression of aggression is taboo, the situation allows of no other response.

Hypocrisy may also result from lack of moral courage. Newman and Ward used pitiful sophistries to justify retaining their posts as Protestant ministers while accepting Roman doctrine. Arnold used his whole influence to make a young friend take orders under a pledge to repeat as true what both believed to be false.[53] Stanley publicly rebuked Rowland Williams for declining to say, what he knew to be a fact, that the *Book of Daniel* is a Maccabean forgery.[54]

While nineteenth-century hypocrisy can be analysed in terms of public approval, it is worth pointing out that it also indicates a retreat from reality.[55] If it makes one feel better that prostitution is out of

[51] Besant, *Fifty Years Ago*, p. 114.

[52] *Memoirs*, p. 56. If frankness means freeness, then lack of frankness means inhibition and self-control. A century before, his editor had thought to praise Hammond by saying, "he wrote to his Mistresses as he spoke to his Friends, nothing but the true, genuine sentiments of his heart." (Preface to Hammond's *Love Elegies*.)

[53] Stanley, *Life of Arnold*. Keble advised Arnold, "Settle your doubts about the Trinity once for all by taking orders." Bohler gave identical advice to Wesley.

[54] See Benn, *Hist. Eng. Rat.*, Chapter 9, for further examples, and contrast the behaviour of Bray, George Eliot and others of the non-Puritanical sort.

[55] Colman, so severe as a censor of plays, was living with Mrs. Gibbs, the actress, in Brompton Square at the time. (Collier, *Old Man's Diary*, i, 71–2.)

sight, it must be because this enables one to pretend that it doesn't exist. When a moralist actually sees a prostitute, painful emotions are aroused, and he feels an obligation to take action. In short, the early Victorian attempt to thrust the unpleasant side of life out of sight represents another facet of the retreat into fantasy. The attempt to deny the sexuality of the normal woman shows this process in its most extreme form.

The term hypocrisy may also be applied to the finding of moral justifications for selfish actions, at which the Victorians were adept. Thus, while declaring that one should always make justice and morality the criterion for settling political problems, Bright justified the repeal of the Corn Laws by the text, "The Earth is the Lord's" and was ingenious in showing by Biblical quotations that God had indicated His preference for Free Trade. Strangely enough, Free Trade was in Bright's commercial interest. It recommended itself to his conscience as just and moral to oppose the seventh Lord Shaftesbury's efforts to protest against factory labour, and to resist all public health measures. Here again we have a retreat from reality into fantasy.

While the genuinely moral members of the middle class no doubt enjoyed the moralisation of every possible aspect of life, insincere conformists doubtless hastened to dress everything in moral trimmings for purely commercial reasons.

But the subject of hypocrisy is not adequately covered until it has been stressed that it was often quite unconscious. Gosse's father was in many ways a sincere man: he rejected worldly reward rather than imperil his religious position. Yet he could kneel down with his son and pray that God should reveal to him whether he might go to a child's party; as Gosse observed, it was not fair in him to remind the Lord of the disadvantages of the proposal; and when Gosse announced that the Lord had said he might go, it was bad politics for his father to slam the door. Gosse calls his father's prayer a form of incantation, but dishonest moral pressure would seem a nearer description.

My rummage among the attitudes of the pre-Victorians also produced evidence of a number of other neurotic manifestations, which might be mentioned, but which would not throw any further light upon my theme. One of the more amusing was the irrational fear which many women developed of being spied upon, culminating in the 'Judas Hole' scare of the 'fifties. It was alleged that in continental hotels Englishwomen were put in a bedroom equipped with a concealed spy-hole, through which foreigners would watch them undressing. This might no doubt be interpreted equally well as a fear of being overlooked (since fantasies so often embody an extraordinary felicity of verbal expression) and as a fear of supervision, which is of course the same thing etymologically. What the pre-Victorians had described as the all-seeing eye of God had now become an all-too-human eye, and the change marks the existence of a retreat from patrism.

To sum up, however, I felt that the survey had certainly confirmed the existence of parental introjections in the period, and, in particular, the existence of father-introjections in precisely that moralistic group which was creating the ethos of the day. Realisation of the force of social pressures had served to explain why the many who did not accept these extreme views nevertheless felt obliged to pay lip service to them—like Robert Owen, who scoffed at geology in public while studying it in private. To be sure, the patrist attitudes were modified and supplemented in various ways, but these were all of predictable type.

I emerged deeply impressed by the immense cost in neurosis of these patrist attitudes, and I do not think it would be too difficult (except in a methodological sense) to show that the severer the sexual inhibition, the severer the neurosis. The pages of Augustus Hare's diary are peopled with more or less unbalanced figures, some of them undoubtedly psychotic. There is Leicester Lyne, who brought up a foundling never to speak to a woman in his life; Lady Ruthven, walking through the dark ante-rooms after dinner in her turquoise tiara, playing the concertina; Mrs. Bowes, in her bath of 'coal black acid', with her black-painted finger-nails and the "underlids of her eyes" painted with belladonna; Mrs. Grote, who wore a man's hat and a coachman's cloak, and expatiated on rat hunts; Mr. Dormer, who always insisted he was a Roman Catholic in disguise, to torment his wife; Georgiana Shipley, who spoke Greek, always wore white, and went to church accompanied by a white doe; Landor, with his spitz

'Pomero' sitting on top of his bald head; Mrs. Trafford, who raised a coachman's daughter from the dead; Miss Salt, whose cat often tore her face; the Duke of Hamilton, with Pauline Borghese's feet inside his waistcoat; and last but not least Hare's mother, with her cataleptic trances lasting (in one case) 196 hours.

Even the ostensibly normal people act strangely, such as the Reverend Mr. Chetwode, who combs his hair only with a leaden comb, and the kindly Bulwer Lytton, who throws his food out of the window.

The eighteenth century has gained a reputation for eccentricity, but the nineteenth is every whit as strange. I have already mentioned Henry Drummond—"a man so able and eccentric as to be treading on the very edge of the partition which divides wit from madness." Mrs. Woodham-Smith has recently depicted the eccentricities of the Binghams and the Brudenells, among whom must not be forgotten Lady Augusta, whom we are shown being rowed round Portsmouth Harbour playing the mandoline and smoking a cigar. Others can be found in Edith Sitwell's *English Eccentrics*.

I stress this point partly because of the persistent tendency to regard patrism as a norm from which matrism is a departure, when the evidence is decisive that both are equally neurotic departures from normal balance; partly because of the tendency to dismiss certain kinds of unbalanced behaviour as a kind of amiable eccentricity of no social importance and in any case impossible to-day. The Bible fundamentalists who preached sermons on the word *Selah* thought themselves supremely rational, precisely at the moment when they were most irrational. Yet man's belief in his rationality dies hard, and to suggest that in our own day much social behaviour which passes for rational is also unbalanced is to invite both disbelief and resentment from any but a specialist audience.

The most extreme examples of these attitudes received criticism and even ridicule in their own time, it is perfectly true, but this was only for their extremity. The psychological make-up which in them appears in an extreme form was present only rather less strongly in an influential segment of the population, as one may judge from such things as the frenzied opposition to the use of anæsthetics in childbirth, or the prolonged refusal to open public parks on Sundays, to say nothing of the now well-known cruelties of the Industrial Revolution.[56]

We have completed our survey of the main psychological features of the period. Enough has now been said, I think, to show that among the upper class during the eighteenth century there was a constellation of attitudes—in religion, art, morals, politics, and other fields—all derived from mother-identification. A similar consistency of outlook has also been revealed among the father-identifying group. The social change which took place represents the gradual rise to dominance of the ideas of the latter group, and the eclipse of the former.

We have seen how these patterns were masked, to some extent, by other psychological factors, notably anal preoccupations and variations in ego-definition. We have noted the high level of aggression, some-times turned outward, sometimes turned against the self. As the nine-teenth century advanced, while the guilt and aggressiveness declined, the anal-retentive element lingered on.

Though necessarily not exhaustive, the analysis has, at least, accounted satisfactorily for the salient features of the period. It remains to ask whether any light can be thrown on why such changes should have been taking place.

---

[56] It is about 1840 that we first find the press beginning to protest about such matters as the harshness with which paupers were treated—they were reduced to gnawing human bones. (*Times,* 14.8.1845.) Thus it was precisely when moral pressure was beginning to relax that humanitarianism, properly so called, began to re-emerge.

CHAPTER 15

PSYCHOLOGICAL WARFARE

THE PRESSURES AND DISCIPLINES applied to children and infants are obviously of central importance, since they both reflect the attitudes of one generation and help to mould the next.

In the field of educational theory, two views, corresponding to the Puritan and Romantic attitudes, can be seen with the greatest clarity. The Puritan view is based on the assumption that the child is naturally wicked, and hence that the function of education is to teach him to modify and control his natural proclivities. As Mrs. Sherwood said, "All children are by nature evil. . . . Pious and prudent parents must check their naughty passions in any way they have in their power, and force them into decent and proper behaviour and what are called good habits."[1] Hannah More said it was a "fundamental error to consider children as innocent beings, whose little weaknesses may perhaps want some correction, rather than as beings who bring into the world a corrupt nature and evil dispositions, which it should be the great end of education to rectify."[2] Education was therefore based on the idea of restraint: all spontaneity was to be checked: children were not to speak unless spoken to, were not to laugh or jest: even exclamations such as, 'Mercy!' or 'Gracious!' were forbidden.[3] At Bobbin's school,

[1] Cited Darton, *Children's Books*, p. 174 (from *The Fairchild Family*).

[2] More, *Strictures*, p. 44.

[3] Caprice was taboo: "fancy and humour should never on any occasion be indulged." *The Management . . . of Children* (Anon), p. 206. The *Polite Academy* condemns whistling, singing, loud discourse, etc. in 1765.

for instance, "all running and swift motion" were prohibited.[4] In contrast, the children of upper-class parents and of followers of Rousseau during the eighteenth century were either indulged by their parents or were allowed to run wild. Even before the seventeenth century opened, Misson had observed with astonishment, "They have an extraordinary Regard in England for young Children, always flattering, always caressing, always applauding what they do; at least it seems so to us French Folks, who correct our Children as soon as they are capable of reasoning; being of Opinion, that to keep them in Awe is the best way to give them a good Turn in their Youth."[5]

Ned Ward, in 1707, complains of the way fashionable mothers treat their children as pets, spoiling them with sweetmeats and showing them off to friends. Too much feminine influence in childhood, he thinks, is responsible for effeminacy in adult years.[6] The indulgent treatment C. J. Fox received from his father is well-known. When Charles told his father he was going to smash his watch, he replied, "Well, if you must, I suppose you must."[7] Fox's father referred to him in his letters as "a little animal" and, when Lady Holland complained of his behaviour, said nothing must be done to break his spirit, he would learn to cure himself. Grosley comments that the English do not understand that the proper function of education is to temper the natural disposition. In England the object of education was "not to put any constraint upon the tempers of children, nor any bias upon the operation of nature, in unfolding the faculties either of the body or

---

[4] Young, *Autobiog. of Arthur Young*, p. 263. Cf. also Wollstonecraft, *Vindication . . . Rights of Women*. Patrist writers also held that it was the explicit function of education to uphold authority (cf. Sheridan, *Brit. Education*, 1756; Brown, *Thoughts on Civil Liberty*, 1765), while matrist writers took a contrary view (cf. Priestley, *Essay on the First Principles of Govt.*, 1768). For a general review, see Adamson, *Eng. Education*.

[5] *Memoirs and Observations*, p. 33.

[6] *London Terraefilius.*

[7] Drinkwater, *C. J. Fox*, p. 15. Muriel Jaeger says Fox's upbringing was exceptional (*Before Victoria*, p. 56), but there is much evidence to the contrary: the tendency of the upper classes to spoil their children was the constant theme of moralists. Often they were allowed to run wild.

mind: this is conformable to the principles laid down by Aristotle, in the last book of his Politics."[8]

In the last phase he refers to the "appeal to experience". Children were not to be punished, but to learn from the results of their own actions: thus a child who over-ate would learn from being sick. This was the view espoused by Rousseau.

In short, the matrist educator seeks to provide an optimum environment for the child's natural development, but does not attempt to influence it to be other than its nature prompts. The child, as is sometimes said, is to be allowed to 'express itself'. The Puritan policy, in contrast, might be described as teaching the child to *repress* itself.

The view, derived from Locke, that the child is neither good nor bad, but is a *tabula rasa* upon which anything may be written, clearly represents a 'Classical' position, poised between the two extremes. It is striking how many of the educational writers of the period fall squarely into either the Puritan or Romantic category; Lockean ideas were at a discount. Some of the lay writers, such as Mrs. Cartwright, attempt a *mélange* of patrist and matrist views: though distinctly Puritan in general outlook, she was opposed to novel-reading and practical joking and thought children should attend church from the age of three. She nevertheless held that children should "have free liberty to express their sentiments", and believed that encouragement was preferable to fear as a method of training. Such attempts to have the best of both worlds are few, and vanish as the eighteenth century closes.

Because of his belief in the child's original sin, education was seen by the Puritan as nothing less than a desperate struggle to reconstruct the child's personality, in which all means, however terrible, were justified. Significant changes in technique took place during the period, and these doubtless played a key role in the process by which changes in the social pattern were produced.

Initially, the child was to be conditioned to good behaviour by physical violence. For the Puritan, flogging was not just *a* method of discipline, it was *the* method which God had appointed. Batty rhapsodises on God's wisdom and foresight in providing children with bottoms, so that they can be beaten repeatedly without permanent

[8] *Tour to London,* i, 167.

damage.[9] Flogging was gradually developed into a ceremony as humiliating as painful. The flogger should first pray and explain that the flogging was for the glory of God.[10] The child must next read from the Bible the passage for ignoring which he was being beaten. The wife then "bares the child's bottom with delight for the flogging".[11] Finally the child must *ask* to be beaten, thus relieving the parent from any lingering sense of guilt.[12]

In the upper classes, family flogging had been abandoned by the time of George I [13] (except in the royal family, who retained it from their German experience) but it persisted in the Puritan group; Henry Longden recalls how his father, before beating him or his brothers for any offence, would pray and ask God's blessing on the flogging.[14] But as the century drew to a close, flogging ceased to be the approved form of punishment: instead was substituted isolation and restraint. When Charlotte Charke ran away from home, she was punished by being tied to a table leg.[15] When Fanny Kemble did so, she was imprisoned in the tool-house for a week to "meditate on her sins".[16] *A Practical View of Christian Education*, which went through many editions in the opening years of the nineteenth century, advises parents to avoid whipping on the grounds that this 'brutalises' the children; it urges that, instead, the child should be locked in his room, which will lead him to think.[17] There was, in fact, a general feeling that flogging had failed to prove effective, and often seemed to drive the child into revolt.

The writer of the work named gives us a further clue to the nature of the change when he says that the objection to whipping is not only that it brutalises the child, but that it 'discomposes' the mind of the parent. This is a fairly plain statement that the repressed sadism of parents had

[9] Batty, *Christian Man's Closet*, p. 26.
[10] Griffith, *Bethel, or Form for Families*, p. 407.
[11] Rogers, *Matrimoniall Honour*, p. 299.
[12] Baxter, *Christian Directory*, ii, 10, 11.
[13] It continued, of course, in the public and many private schools.
[14] Longden, *Life*.
[15] Charke, *Narrative of the Life*, p. 22.
[16] Kemble, *Record of Girlhood*, p. 72.
[17] Op. cit., Ch. 6.

reached a level at which an act of violence produced a painful internal conflict and some danger of loss of self-control.

The Puritan principle that a child should also have as few friends as possible, because these might lead him astray, also comprises an attempt to isolate the child.

Since various other punishments are available (e.g. deprivation of food) the choice of isolation is significant, and becomes perfectly intelligible when we recall that the Puritan is one who feels acutely isolated himself, and finds this isolation painful. It is noticeable that in reforming prisons the Puritans also substituted isolation of each prisoner for the eighteenth-century system in which prisoners were herded together.

But the general assumption that reconstruction was to be achieved by methods based on compulsion remained untouched: nail-biting, for instance, was to be cured by tying the hands into gloves.[18] How deeply embedded this attitude was is shown by the way in which it also influenced ideas about physical growth. Many mothers conceived the idea that their children were growing up physically misshapen, in the sense that they were not erect.[19] To counteract this, children were slung up by the neck with weights attached to the feet. Mrs. Hartford recalls, "There were backboards, iron collars, stocks for the feet, and a frightful kind of neck swing, in which we were suspended every morning whilst one of the teachers were lacing our stays . . . I wonder any of us kept our health: we had very little exercise of any kind, were tight-laced in very stiff stays, not sufficiently warmed in winter, and both coarsely and sparsely fed." This refers to life in school, about 1790.[20] Similarly, Mrs. Sherwood, who was educated at home, recalls wearing collar and backboard from the age of six, being

---

[18] It is noticeable how the Edgeworths, while claiming to follow Locke, who regarded rewards and punishments as equally important, actually, in developing their system of education, stress punishment to the virtual exclusion of reward. "Associate pain with certain habits . . . *immediately, repeatedly, uniformly.*" (*Practical Education*, 229–324.) Though often described as followers of Rousseau, they were actually engaged in distorting his teaching into patrist forms.

[19] See *Semi-Attached Couple*: the parallel between physical erectness and moral uprightness is evident.

[20] Aikin, *Memoirs*, p. 14.

made to translate fifty lines of Virgil a day while in the stocks at the age of twelve, i.e. from 1781 and in 1787.[21]

Another curious Puritan assumption is that a person is most able to resist evil if he knows nothing about it. Lord Holland took Charles James Fox to Paris and carefully chose his mistress for him. Mrs. Sherwood, quarter of a century later, was "preserved during all my childhood in an ignorance of vice such as I would hardly have believed to be possible".[22]

The assumption implied in such a view is that any knowledge gained is more likely to be harmful than helpful, and is thus a depressive view, but stems even more directly from the general fear of knowledge which I have noted in Chapter One.[23] Maria Edgeworth goes so far as to say that ideally the child should learn about life entirely from books, because in this way its experience can be censored, and it can be kept in ignorance of its true nature.[24] Believing that almost everyone is ideally virtuous, and that the few who are not are invariably punished, it will be more likely to behave well. Here the theme of isolation is neatly conjoined with that of ignorance. Augustus Hare was in fact deprived of all playmates, as was Edmund Gosse until quite a late age. It was also part of the theory that the child should be deprived of all books of adventure, indeed of all fictional narratives, and confined to books of factual instruction. Fairy tales were especially reprobated: John Marshall advertised that his books were "entirely divested of that prejudicial Nonsense (to young Minds), the talk of Hobgoblins, Witches, Fairies, Lore, Gallantry, etc". That is to say, there was to be no exercise of fantasy or imagination.[25] Charles Lamb was one who regretted the substitution of the new books for "the beautiful and wild tales which made a child a man" while Hugh Miller rejoiced that "those intolerable nuisances, the useful knowledge books, had not yet arisen

---

[21] Darton, *Life of Mrs. Sherwood*, p. 34.

[22] ib., p. 33.

[23] *The Polite Academy*, 1765, describes curiosity as "a dangerous enemy which lurks within their own Breasts." It warns children against "Earnest or loud Discourse" and prohibits laughing, whistling, singing, etc. in accents which seem characteristically 'Victorian' (pp. vii, xii, 22, etc.).

[24] *Practical Education*, p. 325.

[25] Darton, *Children's Books in England*, p. 164.

to darken the world and shed their blighting influence on the opening intellect of youthhood".[26]

Sir Walter Scott shrewdly recognised the parallel between the methods of physical and of mental education when he said, "The minds of children are, as it were, put into stocks, like their feet at the dancing school, and the moral always consists in good conduct being crowned by success."[27]

Some teachers were quite clear that the object of education was to "break the will". By this they meant, to destroy the capacity to make autonomous decisions. But what most educators sought to achieve was not the destruction of the will, but its investment in another by a process of identification. This is the psychological process upon which popular dictators, such as Hitler, rely. The real object of such teachers was, in fact, to strengthen the identification of children on their parents in order to set up just such an authoritarian pattern.

Throughout the period, great stress was laid by the Puritan group on the formative influence of the family. Baxter says, for instance, "It is an open fact that almost all the unhappiness we now see in the world arises from wrong conduct of the family, or touches it."[28] Schuecking has shown that the Puritan code was based on the influence of the family rather than that of the Church.[29] Books on domestic conduct were circulated, and the practice of reading them aloud to the family became general: the preface to Baxter's *A Christian Directory* specifically orders this to be done. Richardson's *Familiar Letters* derive directly from these books, as Hornbeak has shown.[30]

Stress continued to be laid upon the importance of the home environment throughout the period. Mrs. Chapone, for instance, urged that children should be confined to the home and that they should be allowed few friends, so that they should be wholly subject to domestic influence. The middle-class group became increasingly critical of the practice, originally an upper-class one, of sending

---

[26] Miller, *My Schools and Schoolmasters*, pp. 28–9.
[27] Cited Godfrey, *Children in the Olden Times*, p. 307.
[28] *Christian Directory*, ii, 5.
[29] *Die Familie im Puritanismus*, Chapter 3.
[30] Hornbeak, *Richardson's Familiar Letters*.

children away to boarding-school, where they could choose their own friends and might learn undesirable habits.[31] During the eighteenth century, schools for the newly emerging middle class were springing up everywhere; but by 1831 a writer claimed that the plan of "domestic education" for females had been "universally adopted". Thus it was that the governess emerged as a new social type.

But within the home the emphasis began to change, and these changes are quite instructive. In the sixteenth and seventeenth centuries the father was the dominating figure in the family circle, and he was an awe-inspiring figure, who made no attempt to win his children's love or to meet them on terms of friendliness. "Laugh not with your son," said Becon. "Give him no liberty in his youth and excuse not his folly. Bow down his neck . . . hit him on the sides while he is yet but a child."[32] In this set-up the mother plays no significant role; the emphasis is entirely on the father. But during the eighteenth century this began to change. More and more, we find that it is at the mother's knee that the child learns: Schuecking thinks that this is particularly characteristic of the generation born in 1725-40.[33] John Newton, who was born in 1725, certainly describes the influence of his mother, who taught him prayers and hymns, while he rarely saw his sea-captain father. Cumberland, the dramatist, who was born in 1732, tells in his memoirs how his mother not only watched his spiritual interests, but, like Goethe's mother, stimulated the first flights of his imagination and helped to develop his taste.[34] Many other examples can be found.

This change was made possible by the increasing literacy of women, for it became the task of the women to read aloud to the family circle from the numerous "conduct books" provided for this purpose, but it was the growing belief in the power of woman as a civilising influence, and the special role created for her, which provided the real motive power.

[31] By undesirable habits was meant, at this stage, not bullying and drunkenness but sexual interests. Cf. Lackington's *Confessions*.

[32] Becon, *Catechism*, pp. 323-4.

[33] *Die Familie*, pp. 201-2.

[34] Cumberland, *Memoirs*, pp. 18, 39.

At the same time, there was a gradual change in the role of the father. Whereas Erasmus Darwin said that his father kept his children "at an awful kind of distance", the father of Thomas Bowdler, the expurgator and moralist (b. 1767), hoped to be a friend to him. The change is well illustrated by Richardson. For Lady Bradshaigh's benefit, he drafted a letter from a father to a daughter about to get married, as it might be in life as opposed to fiction. "My children's reverence seems to have exceeded their love for me. . . . If anything disagreeable, stiff, distant be imagined by you, in my temper or behaviour; if you find, in your own heart, more awe of me than love for me; and if to get out of my power, be one of your motives; I will endeavour wholly to change this my outward behaviour. I will, if possible, overcome your fear and engage your love. I will make you my companion, my friend. . . . You shall contract friendships, preserve friendships, visit, receive visits at your pleasure. . . ." etc.[35] These promises have the air of a last-minute repentance, when severity has become ineffective, and the reference to the mother betrays how little freedom she had been accorded. But we can at least see here the desire to receive love, a desire which the more Calvinistic Puritan of a previous century could not even admit.

The point which I believe is not generally appreciated, is that these Puritan families were not simply strict and restrictive; they exerted on the children a sustained psychological pressure of almost fantastic intensity.

Religious instruction started at the earliest possible age. It was thought desirable that the first word the child uttered should be God. The first sentence it should learn to say was "Christ save me!" This was still true in 1702, when Thomas White exclaimed, "Oh, how precious a thing it is to hear a little child pray, as soon as, nay sooner than, it can speak plain!"[36] As Defoe said, one must get a march on the devil.

Education on these lines was still customary in Puritan circles in the mid-eighteenth century.

Henry Longden reports of his childhood—he was born in 1754—

[35] *Correspondence*, No. 26.
[36] White, *Little Book for Little Children*, p. 3.

that lessons in obedience to his parents began at the age of twelve months. He and his brothers were taught "implicit obedience to their parents, without reference to reward". Next came instruction in the nature of filial obligation and gratitude. At the age of five years their father began to explain to them the omnipresence, omniscience and omnipotence of God; at seven, their duty to subject themselves to their superiors, and to abhor falsehood. "After this, he would explain the nature of our moral depravity; our total helplessness, and insufficiency to save ourselves; and the everlasting punishment which is prepared for the wicked. He would then unfold the plan for our recovery and salvation by Jesus Christ. . . . These instructions were accompanied with fervent prayer."[37]

Longden recalls that his father was always careful never to display any lightness or jesting when with his children. He adds, in an understatement that savours of irony, that his father's conversation "tended to the edifying".

All behaviour was referred to the religious sanction. While eighteenth-century writers like Mrs. Chapone make suitable reference to the key role of religion, and in particular the importance of referring to the scriptures, by the nineteenth century the stress has become far stronger. There are no venial offences. "I endeavour," says Christian Observer, "to make every fault of our children to be felt by them as an offence against God, and as a sin to be repented of, and upon repentance to be pardoned through our Saviour and in prayer."[38]

Not only are the most trifling of infantile slips to be treated as mortal sins which call for the intervention of Jesus Christ to forgive, but God Himself will punish the sinner, in addition to anything the child's parents may do. "Tell of God's power as making it impossible to escape the punishment or lose the blessings which He appoints," urges another writer.[39]

Children were taught that God's eye was continually upon them, so that their most secret fault was known; but, as if unconvinced that God's determination to punish their charges equalled their own,

[37] Longden, *Life*, pp. 152–5.
[38] Appendix to *A Practical View of Christian Education* (Anon).
[39] ib., p. 140.

parents attempted to exercise an equally rigorous supervision.[40] Margaret Gardiner (Lady Blessington) describes how Mary Howard's parents never allowed her a secret, nor to read any letter which had not been previously inspected, right up to the time of her marriage. (The conception of the all-seeing eye seems to have had peculiar significance for many pre-Victorians: for instance, Bentham's Panopticon, in which prisoners were isolated in separate cells, the cells being disposed radially so that a warder could keep every one continuously under observation, curiously combines the principle of isolation with the principle of the all-seeing eye.)

Everything possible was done to activate the fear of death. In the eighteenth century, when the power of example was still considered important, children were taken to see men executed. Grosley reported in 1765 that the custom of taking children to public executions, and, on returning home, of whipping them to make them remember the example, was then being abandoned; but as late as 1816 the seven-year-old Fanny Kemble was taken to see a man guillotined "in order that she might know to what evil courses lead". Looking back on this experience, as an old woman, she thought it "so foolish in its cruelty, that the only amazement is, how anybody entrusted with the care of children could dream of any good results from such a method".[41] Fictional representations of this did not go out, however; in *The Fairchild Family*, which was one of the most popular children's books of the early nineteenth century, the children are taken on three occasions to see dead or dying individuals—on one occasion to inspect the corpse, hanging from a gibbet, of a man who had murdered his brother. Kellett says that the fear of death became so intense that "some, from fear of dying, prayed to die"; and he illustrates the ruthlessness of the pressure by saying that when a child said to its father, "I'm five years old to-day, papa," the father replied, "Five years nearer your grave." In a still more terrible anecdote, he describes how a father asked his

---

[40] Thus Mrs. Cartwright in 1777 said, "Teach them that an all-seeing eye is witness even to their most private faults" (*Female Education*), and cf. *Saturday Mag.*, 1835, p. 99, for an example fifty years later.

[41] Kemble, *Record of Girlhood*, pp. 214–16. Grosley, i, 172–3.

son, "Why aren't you happy?" The boy, too frightened even to admit that he was not happy, replied, "I am—in my sleep."[42]

And these tremendous pressures are to be directed on to the child, full force, from birth. At the same time a tremendous standard of achievement is demanded. Jane Treffry's child had read "the greater part of the Bible before he was four years old". By the time he was eight Richard Wright had read the Old and New Testaments, "and was well acquainted with every remarkable story to be found there, and in the Apocrypha". The diaries of Hannah Ball, Mary Tatham, Mary Bosanquet and others reveal a similar picture.

Children were admitted as church members (in the case of Methodists) as early as nine or ten; at the Methodist school started at the Foundry in London, children were admitted from six years, and had to be present at morning service at five a.m.

Not surprisingly, they wilted under such pressure. Joseph Pearson says the "alarming sermons" which he heard caused him to become so 'intent' that as a small boy he listened to 149 sermons in a year. His lessons and tasks were taken out of Janeway's *Tokens*—two horrifying early eighteenth-century books designed to produce a conviction of sin. Full of excruciating accounts of martyrdoms, they emphasised that hell was a thousand times worse than a beating. When Pearson gave his rabbits a little extra clover on Sunday, he was not surprised to find that they were all dead on Monday. He "felt the admonition in his conscience; he had done wrong and reaped his reward".[43]

The Rev. William Jones exhorted his children to be serious, to such good effect that all were reduced to tears. "I have never spent a more happy evening," he adds.[44]

The effect of these fantastic pressures in demoralising children, and even sometimes driving them into the grave, is clearly shown in the tragic case of Margaret Gray.[45] She was subjected to the usual intensive Puritan upbringing: for instance, from the age of four she had to commit the Gospel for the day to memory every day and already knew

[42] Kellett, *Religion and Life*, p. 35.
[43] Pearson, *Memoirs*, pp. 1–17.
[44] W. Jones, *Diary*, pp. 106–7.
[45] Gray, *Papers and Diaries*, Ch. 14.

her Catechism. Every evening, when left alone, she used to employ her time in writing painful notes of self-reproach to her mother; some faint impression of this child's agony of mind can be given by a few extracts, but it is necessary to read the whole diary to gain the full flavour. A typical entry, written at the age of eleven, runs, "I often think how shocking it would be to go to hell. I can't bear the thought of it; and I think sometimes, suppose I was to die, where should I go to? But, my dear mother, I will pray to God. He will hear my prayers. If I pray to him through Jesus Christ, he will hear me. 'Whatsoever ye ask the father in my name, he will give it you.' But I must do it earnestly. Oh! mother, pray for me: and I will pray earnestly, with God's grace, that he will take me to heaven when I die."

Or again, "I think nothing but the fear of hell would make me religious. I fear I shall never get to heaven. But if I believe in the Lord Jesus Christ, I shall be saved. Oh! Lord, increase my faith! . . . When I survey the sins of my past life, I feel almost inclined to despair."

We can get some idea of the sins over which this unhappy child worried from the entry, "I am obliged to confess that too great love for music is one of my besetting sins . . . I can only pray to God to keep me by his Grace from being tainted with the evil of it." On the first of January, 1826, she began to make use of the Biometer—a sort of chart prescribing every thought and activity throughout the day; after twelve days of this discipline she began to feel giddy, by the end of the month she was dead. The cause was given as "inflammation of the brain". But she had already entered in her pocket-book, "This year thou mayest die."

Psychological warfare in its most highly developed form was practised at Kingswood School, where a remarkable wave of conversions so gratified John Wesley in 1770.[46] Most of the schoolchildren had been taken to see the corpse of a neighbour; that evening one of the masters 'exhorted' them, and announced as the hymn, 'Am I born to die?' This "increased their concern; so that it was with great difficulty that they contained themselves until he began to pray. Then Alexander Mather and Richard Noble cried aloud for mercy, and

[46] *Journals*, v, 389–92.

quickly another and another, till all but two or three were constrained
to do the same, and as long as he continued to pray, they continued the
same loud and bitter cry". Fifteen of them, at the master's invitation,
"continued wrestling with God, with strong cries and tears", till about
nine o'clock.

This was on the Tuesday; on the subsequent days their concern
greatly increased and they spent all their spare time in prayer. On
Sunday, Wesley personally gave them "a strong exhortation . . . their
very countenances were entirely changed". On the following Wednesday a master found three of these children praying continuously in a
room; three more then came in, so he improved the occasion by praying with them. Next morning, at his suggestion, nine children
followed him upstairs, saying that they wanted "to flee from the wrath
to come". He then exhorted them further, with the result that "the
power of God came down in so wonderful a manner that my voice was
drowned by their cries". One of them burst into extempore prayer in a
manner which astonished him, and "a peculiar spirit of seriousness"
rested on the children all day. He then (on Friday) concentrated on
those children who had not already caved in, individually, with such
success that "in a few minutes, my voice could not be heard amidst
their cries and groans". When he goes out into the grounds, children
flock round him asking what they must do to be saved, and he cannot
get rid of them. After further pressure that evening, three of the
children decide not to sleep until the Lord has revealed Himself to
them. Richard Piercy is in "such agony of soul" that he cannot be
persuaded to rise from his knees. The children who have gone up to
bed, hearing the praying, come down again and continue "wrestling
with increasing cries and tears" until three more "find peace with
God". He then insists on their going to bed, but before long the
terrified children are out of bed again, praying. He notes that they
appear "cut to the heart".

The master now begins to have some misgivings that they may
injure themselves, and sends for a maid, but she too gets caught up in
the hysteria, and all cry and pray till past eleven, the other maids
joining in. At four a.m. Wesley is awakened by the children's crying;
the maids have been up all night "praying as in an agony". The boys

continue praying and weeping for several hours, without thought of food. Richard Piercy "took no food all the day, but remained, in words or groans, calling upon God". One of the maids sinks down in a coma and appears to be about to die. By evening everyone is so worn out and hoarse that they can hardly speak, but all have been "brought into the fold".

While the primary motive in setting up this extraordinary ideal of child-upbringing was clearly a fundamental belief in the rightness of authoritarian methods, coupled with an equally profound belief in the inherent wickedness of human nature, there are also other factors at work. For one thing, it is impossible to overlook the convenience to parents of completely subdued children, and to husbands of completely submissive wives. (Convenience is perhaps too neutral a word: one should rather say, the extreme self-indulgence of expecting others to inhibit themselves so completely that one will never be challenged oneself.) This is sometimes almost overtly stated. For example, Mrs. Chapone says one should not marry without one's parents' consent, because such a marriage is automatically without God's blessing and cannot be productive of anything but misery; then she adds, rather testily, that in any case one should not put one's parents in such an awkward dilemma.[47]

Then, again, there are signs of a tremendous manipulative urge. Mothers plunge into the task of remoulding the unruly nature of their children without any sense of hesitancy. The rules expressed so drily and flatly can only be applied in actual situations in which emotions are deeply involved. It requires to-day some effort of the imagination to visualise the terrifying battles of will which must have occurred. But it is not difficult to appreciate that women deprived of almost every other outlet for constructive and manipulative activity, and themselves dominated by their husbands, must have found in the domination of their children an outlet for their pent-up frustration. Here, I suspect, is an important social mechanism, by which the frustrations of one generation are, as it were, amplified in the course of being transmitted to the next.

In many cases this desire to dominate took on a genuinely neurotic

[47] Chapone, *Letters on the Improvement*, p. 73.

character: a desire to revenge oneself for one's own unhappiness by depriving the child of pleasure. Sometimes it verged on sadism. Augustus Hare's account of his childhood provides the best insight into such relationships.[48] For instance, his mother allowed him in infancy no toys whatever, saying he would develop better without them; a few years later his cousins were encouraged to steal his things, but when Augustus retaliated, he was shut up for two days on bread and water "to break his spirit". His mother said that if he asked the reason for any instruction, she made a rule to give none but that it was her will he should do it. At the age of three he was whipped for breaking the branch of a tree. At every moment he was subjected to education, learning the topography of Jerusalem (among other things) at the age of five.

He could never express a wish to his mother, as she would have thought it her duty to refuse it. "The will is the thing that needs to be brought into subjection," she said. When he asked whether he could have some children to tea on the anniversary of his adoption, he was punished so severely for merely making the request that he "never dared to express a wish to play with any child again". When the curate's wife gave him a sweet, he was forcibly dosed with rhubarb. To break his will, his mother invented ingenious techniques, such as showing him appetising puddings, and then at the last moment telling him he could have none. When he slept in a bare unheated room, in which the washing water froze overnight, the candlestick which he used to break the ice was removed, so that he should have to break it with his bare hands.

The catalogue of physical and mental cruelties imposed on him is so long that one can only pick a few instances. He was left in the dark every evening from five till seven, when the evening meal began; after it, he was not allowed to read, speak, or engage in any activity. On his birthday he was given a book, but in order that this should not be productive of too much pleasure, he was given the same book every year (a history of architecture). Perhaps the most appalling of all the incidents was that in which his mother, finding him much attached to a

[48] *Years with Mother.*

household cat, ceremoniously hanged the cat in the garden, so that he should have no object but her to love. Little wonder that he thought Harrow, where he was flogged till the blood ran, fun in comparison.

This sort of treatment was supplemented by psychological warfare of the approved kind. He was given Foxe's *Book of Martyrs* to read, and was "continually talked to about death and hell".

So powerful were the death-wishes of his adoptive mother and aunt that when he was ill no steps were taken to cure him, the reason given being that pain was sent to be endured. These extraordinary, Mauriac-like characters were really clinical cases. His mother withdrew into prolonged catatonic stupors. His aunt died as a result of lying for hours in the pouring rain on the grave of her husband.

They represent, to be sure, extreme instances; and I mention them not to suggest that they were typical but simply because the extreme case shows the trend more clearly. They were, furthermore, Calvinists, and the Calvinistic groups always attained a greater degree of severity than the Methodists and others who, to some degree, introjected the mother-figure.

These Puritanical parents were not only severe, but, what may be psychologically more important, they were extremely demanding. They not only demanded a high moral standard, but a high rate of educational progress. Mrs. Wesley gave each of her children a single day to learn the alphabet, at the age of four. I have already noted a number of cases of children able to read the Bible by four, and obliged to memorise long and no doubt largely unintelligible passages daily. To set tasks impossible of achievement and to punish failure is one of the commonest devices of the sadist. But the pattern is also significant for the formation of personality. Demanding supervision tends to create the schizophrenic (or 'split') type of personality, as against the hysteric: that is, the child constructs a screen-personality which satisfies the parents' demands, while continuing to live its own life in fantasy behind the screen. This fact may well explain the only important attitude-system which we have not yet related to the general picture— that is, the 'hypocrisy' of which the early Victorians were accused. As I have shown, this consisted primarily in a tendency to regard the surface appearance as supremely important, and a tendency to push tabooed behaviour out of sight rather than to eliminate it. This corresponds exactly to the schizophrenic reaction.

Correspondingly, the neglectful treatment afforded by many upper-class parents to their children satisfactorily accounts for the more hysterical pattern (I use the word in the technical sense) shown by many upper-class children.[49]

It is also relevant that special pressure was brought to bear on girls, and I have already given some explanation of why this was so.[50] But it is also fair to relate it to the special psychological difficulties faced by the female sex. Thus Hannah More said that girls should be taught that life was dull and tragic and that girls must resign themselves to doing what men prefer. This may seem odd, coming from a woman who wrote plays and books, was admitted to some of the most interesting intellectual society of her day, and attained national fame. But it becomes intelligible when we remember that Hannah More was twice jilted by the man she expected to marry. In a period in which women out-numbered men by three to two, to be ignored by men was no doubt the experience of many women, though the traumatic nature of the experience doubtless depends on a failure of the basic relationship with the male parent.

It is clear enough, then, that the way parents behaved accurately reflected their own personality-structures. Can we conclude from this that parents succeeded in modelling their children in their own image— or did they, perhaps, succeed in making children a little nearer their ideal than they themselves had attained?

In asking such questions, one raises the much more far-reaching issue of how changes in the mode of personality take place, on the historical scale. For if the answer to the first question is yes, Puritans will tend to breed Puritans, and Romantics, Romantics, and the situation will be stable, unless one of these groups is reproducing itself more numerously than the other. Alternatively, if Puritans grow ever more Puritan, and Romantics ever more impulsive, the split between the two groups will widen, until finally no further intensification is possible and some kind of reversal or reaction will presumably take place.

[49] See Campbell, *Manic Depressive Disease.*
[50] See p. 281.

It seemed to me, therefore, that the next step would be to consider what I had learned about the way in which the change of outlook took place. But at the same time I was conscious of the fact that the aspects of child-upbringing so far considered did not go to the heart of the problem. In the psychoanalytic view, personality is broadly determined in the first two or three years of life. Subsequent experiences are only formative to the extent that they reanimate primitive conflicts and reinforce patterns already laid down. I had already gathered such data as I could on these basic experiences, and it will be convenient to consider the two topics in conjunction.

PART FIVE

CONCLUSION

CHAPTER 16

THE CHILD AND THE MAN

CAN WE DEMONSTRATE the existence during the eighteenth century
of methods of treating the infant which would plausibly account for the
constellations of adult traits which we have explored? Were these
practices capable of accounting for the abnormally heavy load of guilt
and the emotional impoverishment of the Puritan, or the mother-
preoccupations and defective ego-definition of the Romantic?

The clue which I followed first was that of emotional impoverishment. Ernest Jones has drawn attention to the serious results which
arise when a child is left to "cry itself out". This, he considers, results
in an emotional exhaustion (which he calls aphanisis) and ultimately in
a permanent impairment of the capacity to feel emotion at all.[1] But he
goes further. He declares that the prospect of such aphanisis arouses
intense anxiety, and that the super-ego is instituted primarily to deal
with it.[2] It also appears, in modern clinical experience, to be associated
with death-wishes, no doubt because the frustration engendered creates
powerful aggressions, which may be turned against the self. Hence if
we could establish the existence in the eighteenth century of a practice
of letting children "cry themselves out", we should have gone a long
way towards explaining three of the psychological attitudes we have
noted in the Puritan—his preoccupation with death, his severe morality
and his emotional impairment.

At an early stage, I came across a specific instance of this practice.
John Howard, the prison reformer, was accustomed, when his infant
son cried, to place him on his lap and leave him there "till fatigued with

[1] Jones, *Papers on Psychoanalysis*, especially Chapter 14. See also pp. 196–200,
where he discusses the process whereby a loving attitude towards others is replaced by one of moral judgment.
[2] ib., p. 152.

crying, he became still: this process a few times repeated had such an effect that the child, if crying ever so violently, was rendered quiet the instant his father took him."[3]

However, this was but an isolated instance, and Howard's son did not become a Puritan, quite the reverse. (This was perhaps due to his losing his mother in infancy, which, as we have seen, seems to conduce to a matrist attitude.) Information concerning child-rearing is hard to come by and it was only when revising the manuscript that I found an unequivocal statement that this practice was general. Dr. Gregory, who was Professor of Medicine at Aberdeen from 1749, strongly criticises this universal practice in his *Comparative View*. And he shrewdly adds, "When a Child's first sensations partake so much of pain and distress, and when the turbulent passions are so early awakened and exercised, there is some reason to suspect that they may have an influence on the subsequent temper."[4]

While this practice alone must have generated powerful aggressions, Dr. Gregory also records another which must have contributed to them—the custom of swaddling infants "as tightly as possible".[5] Weeden Butler speaks of the frustration of swaddling bands—which he declined to use on his children—and in a poem (1812) on the birth of his fifth child observes:

"Prison'd and truss'd, swath'd, manacled and drest,
Hard is the lot of infant weak and dumb."[6]

[3] Aikin, *A View of Howard's Character*, p. 44. Howard was a very characteristic anal-patrist. Even his admiring biographer, Field, thinks his idea of the authority due to a head of a family was exaggerated; he was "a very Mussulman in his ablutions." He prayed daily for "restraining grace" and, according to Aikin, died from the excessive use of James' Powder, a proprietary laxative, which he took every two or four hours. Field, *Life of John Howard*, pp. 55, 223, 470.

[4] Op. cit., pp. 52–3. Similarly Buchan says, "Children are often hurt by nurses suffering them to cry long and vehemently" (*Domestic Medicine*, edns. 1749 to 1813).

[5] Op. cit., p. 45. Buchan names a similar complaint (*Domestic Medicine*, 1749 to 1813).

[6] Cited Stuart, *Roundabout*, p. 105. In 1827 "the barbarous custom of swathing is not yet universally exploded" (*A Letter on the Management*, Anon, p. 219), but by 1843 *The Magazine of Domestic Economy* speaks of the practice as one "not long since abandoned" (p. 148).

Anthropological studies have given support to the idea that the cold-blooded savagery and the self-control of many Red Indian tribes is due, in part, to their use of the practice of confining the infant in a birch-bark tube, and the existence of an analogous practice in Europe is probably significant.

However, frustration may be emotional as well as physical. The child needs caresses, and (as a modern research has shown) needs to be fondled and rocked if the myelinisation of the nerves is to proceed normally. Dr. Cadogan condemned rocking in 1748, and in 1811 even the relatively enlightened *Female Instructor* still condemned it.[7] Dr. Gregory devotes several pages to attacking it; there is evidence that it was uncommon in the middle class throughout the eighteenth century. More generally, frustration can be inferred from the amount of crying, which was so common that sedatives were widely given.[8] Buchan declared in 1769 that half the children who died annually in London did so from being given laudanum, spirits or proprietary sedatives.[9]

Thirdly, there is the crushing nature of the Puritan's sense of guilt to explain. The sense of guilt is the product of fear of a punishing parent coupled with performance of a forbidden act which might evoke parental wrath. We have already seen that fathers were in fact often severe, and that aggressions were generated against the parents which, in accordance with the usual psychological law, have the effect of making the parents seem more alarming, for we suspect that those we hate, hate us also. It remains to identify the forbidden act. In the simple pattern of the Œdipus situation the forbidden act is the possession of the parent of opposite sex. The boy desires his mother and fears the father's revenge; and the prohibition tends to be seen as a general prohibition of sexual desire.

In actual practice the first genuine sexual act is that of self-gratification. When parents forbid infantile masturbation, the prohibition is significant, at the unconscious level, because the taboo expresses the general

---

[7] Cadogan, *An Essay on Nursing*, 1748.

[8] A writer of 1827 says that "continual crying" of infants is so common that it is "erroneously supposed natural to them" but is really due to bad management. (*A Letter on the Management*, p. 203.)

[9] Buchan, *Domestic Medicine*, p. 1.

sexual taboo. To-day psychiatrists regard infantile auto-erotism as not only a normal but actually a necessary step in development. By discovering that he has the power to give himself pleasure, instead of relying on his mother for all satisfactions, the child takes a step towards independence and maturity. It is therefore in the highest degree significant that—as I discovered—there was built up during the eighteenth century an enormous literature condemning masturbation.[10] The first work known to bibliographers on this topic is *Onania*, of which the first edition is believed to have been in 1716 and the fifteenth in 1730. Thereafter there was a stream of works on the topic, until by the end of the century the quack doctors, such as Brodum and Solomon, were selling tracts which claimed to have run through sixty or seventy editions. These last, it is true, were not inspired by moralistic considerations but by the desire to sell nostrums: thus Brodum's *Guide to Old Age*, after stressing the appalling consequences of masturbation—impotence, insanity and almost everything else was alleged to follow—ends by explaining that a tablespoonful of Brodum's Balm of Gilead, beaten up with an egg and taken three times a day, will put everything right in no time: two guineas a bottle. The first editions of these works are small and tentative; they obviously met with instant success, and successive editions are progressively larger and more confident, and are padded out with letters received from readers. It therefore seems beyond question that there was a very widespread preoccupation with the subject. An increasing number of foreign works on the topic was translated, and it is noticeable that masturbation in the female sex (which was alleged to lead to nymphomania, as well as to the routine

[10] See Spitz, 'Authority and Masturbation' in *Psychoanal. Qtly*, Vol. xxl, 490–527 (1952), for a list of 314 titles between 1700 and the present day. However, Spitz's list omits many of the most important references. See under Acton; de Bienville; Brodum; Culverwell; Farrer; Hodson; Onania; R. C.; Ryan; Philo-Castitatis; Secret Sin; Solomon; Varley, in bibliographical list to this book, for further titles of English provenance. There was also in the early nineteenth century an extensive literature concerned with spermatorrhea, Milton's work of this name running through twelve editions by 1887. Circumcision and even clitoridectomy were recommended as preventive measures, the surgeon being advised to leave as much scar tissue as possible, in order to reduce the temptation to normal intercourse also. (Acton, *Functions and Disorders*, p. 24.)

consequences, such as insanity and paralysis) is mentioned about as frequently as masturbation in the male.[11] In the nineteenth century handbills on the topic were distributed and public lectures held.[12]

The discovery of this vast and terrifying literature provided the missing evidence required to explain the excessive burden of Puritan guilt, which had puzzled me from an early stage in the investigation. It explains, equally, the general fear of pleasure in this group, and was no doubt a factor in the common fear of impotence. And it is a legitimate guess that a child, denied genital expression, is forced back to earlier modes of libidinal experience: this might help to explain the preponderance of anal erotism in the period.

Presumably the immediate cause of the anal fixation was a severe toilet-training. On this topic I have been unable to find any evidence whatever, unfortunately. The omission is in itself somewhat significant, however. Apparently the topic was felt to be too delicate even for doctors and the writers of mothers' manuals to deal with. Certainly there was an extensive use of purges, which provides good indirect evidence.[13]

Oral frustrations seem particularly relevant to the subject of this book, for Ernest Jones has argued that they tend to lead to an identification with the parent of opposite sex.[14] (The analysis is extremely complex and cannot be given here.) Hence it is certainly significant that the upper-class group of self-indulgent parents tended to farm children out to wet-nurses, while the Puritan group pressed emphatically for breast-feeding. For instance, Susan Ferrier's father (b. 1744) was "sent out to be nursed, according to the custom of those

[11] De Bienville's *Nymphomanie*, translated into English in 1775 by Wilmot, is almost entirely concerned with female masturbation. Tissot's *L'Onanisme*, Lausanne 1760, was repeatedly issued in English translation.

[12] See British Museum Miscellaneous Tracts for the specimen hand-bill, and under Varley and Dyer for reprints of lectures.

[13] Since severe toilet-training produces constipation. The case of Howard, who died from excessive purging, has been mentioned. Buchan complains of the numerous nurses who rely on Godfrey's Cordial, Daffy's Elixir, Dalby's Carminative, etc. (*Domestic Medicine*, p. 32).

[14] Jones, *Papers on Psychoanalysis*, p. 461.

days"[15], but by 1789 Lady Craven reported a change: "You will find in every station of life mothers of families who would shrink with horror at the thought of putting a child from them to nurse: a *French* custom with people of every degree, which I have been shocked at a thousand times."[16] "Farming out" might well be expected to create the sort of disturbance in relations with the mother which we have inferred lies behind the Romantic personality. Equally important, perhaps, is the period for which the child was allowed to breast-feed, and the degree of suddenness and finality with which weaning took place. There are some indications that weaning was early and abrupt. Thus *The Female Instructor* (1811) speaks of a strong prejudice against the use of mother's milk, based on vanity. "Believe it not," exclaims the writer, "when it is insinuated that your bosoms are less charming, for having a dear little cherub at your breast!"[17] And since he stresses the need to wean gradually, we may infer that this was not generally understood.[18] Abrupt weaning may have been usual in the Puritan group, in conformity with the general tendency to deal with children by abrupt and disciplinary methods, and perhaps for subtler reasons. Thus Stukeley records of his mother, "I suckt of my Mor. about a week & then was brought up by the Spoon, & was the only child she indulged so far, for tho' she was the fondest Parent in the world yet she had that peculiarity that she could not show in the common tenderness [sic] so that she scarce in her life ever kisst any of her children, & I remember perfectly well that even at the age of 16 I was a perfect stranger to giving a common salute to a woman." (He says, however, that she was tender to her children and adored by all of her own sex.)[19] Stukeley was a doctor, and seems to have sensed the significance of these facts, which makes his evidence valuable. Apparently many other mothers suffered

---

[15] Ferrier, *Memoirs*, pp. 5–6.

[16] In Meister, *Letters*, p. 85.

[17] Op. cit, p. 208.

[18] As Cadogan complains (op. cit., p. 14), children were crammed with food other than milk from birth, and were even given "roast pig, to cure it of mother's longings". According to Buchan "wines are universally mixed with the first food of the children" (op. cit., p. 15).

[19] Stukeley, *Family Memoirs*, p. 6 n.

similar inhibitions in the expression of affection. D'Hausset, for instance, comments, "Instead of an interchange of caresses . . . maternal affection is limited to attentions on the one part and respect on the other."[20] It may well be that such mothers felt a corresponding inhibition in respect of breast-feeding.

It seems that forcible cramming with pap was so common that infants were constantly sick, and that this was accepted as inevitable. *The Female Instructor* regarded this as also the cause of infants continually crying: "Surely it is wrong to put a large boat full of pap into their little mouths, suffering them to swallow the whole of it in the space of a minute; and then, perhaps, from their cries, to ply them with a second which is no sooner down than thrown up again." The writer adds that this ridiculous practice has been "rendered universal by custom".[21] To overfeed her child is the natural reaction of a parent who has suffered an oral frustration herself.

Further evidence of oral frustration may perhaps be found in the number of voracious eaters. Dr. Fordyce would eat one and a half pounds of steak every day, with half a chicken or some fish as *hors d'œuvres*, and a pint of port or brandy to wash it down. Uvedale Price and Payne Knight were also gigantic eaters; so were Porson, Paley and Herbert Spencer.[22]

Evidently oral frustrations may have existed even in the guilt-ridden, father-identifying group, and this particular constellation of traits is, in fact, illustrated by the Evangelicals, who allied to a particularly narrow and arid doctrine a quite unexpected capacity for gastronomic indulgence. Baring-Gould, who saw a good deal of them as a boy, was "somewhat amused to see how every degree of indulgence was tolerated in meat and drinks, but music, literature, the theatre, and games were tabooed. They had strawberries out of season,

[20] D'Hausset, *Britain in 1833*, i, 84. In 1807 Goede noticed "nor do they fondle and caress their children . . . the least token of depravity is most severely punished" (*Stranger in England*, i, 180). See *Recollections of a Maiden Aunt* (1858), p. 15, for her mother's "manner of habitual constraint".

[21] Op. cit., p. 209.

[22] Farington, *Diary*, VIII, 112, 154. The fact that Victorian meals were large was made clear in Chapter 3. The light breakfast of the eighteenth century was replaced by the heavier meat breakfast of the nineteenth.

when they cost something like sixpence apiece, but we young folk were not suffered to play Puss in the Corner. From the library, Sir Walter Scott's novels were excluded, as were also those of Jane Austen."[23] In a more guilt-ridden group the tendency to asceticism would, no doubt, have over-ridden these oral desires; but the Evangelicals had compounded their guilt by conversion. This instance also demonstrates that the fear of spontaneity springs from different roots from the fear of pleasure, since the former attitude remained unimpaired.

However, the main significance of weaning and feeding disturbances is not the amount of frustration immediately produced, but the total effect on the child's relationship with its mother. A mother who continually frustrates, however loving she may be in reality, seems to the infant to be unloving. I have already noted how often the child whose mother dies in childbirth suffers a profound disturbance: obviously the mother who vanishes completely is seen as unloving and rejecting in the highest possible degree. Thus, feeding disturbances reproduce in milder form the same trauma, and in the adult the same search for the loving mother who will supply all needs.

The consequent fixation upon the mother has profound indirect results, and serves to explain such apparently unrelated phenomena as the 'effeminacy' of clothing in the eighteenth century. As Ernest Jones has said, the child must either renounce his sex or his incest.[24] In less lapidary form: the male child can either renounce his Œdipal desire for his mother, in which case he can safely remain a male, or, if he declines to renounce the desire, he must renounce his sex; that is, identify with the mother. Thus, the matrist is one whose loss of the mother has come too early or too abruptly for him to rise above it; he chooses identification rather than renunciation. He seeks to restore the lost mother by impersonating her himself, i.e. by 'identification'—hence, the 'effeminacy' of a section of society in the eighteenth century. Conversely, the Puritan is one who has retained his sex at the price of renouncing his desire for the mother and his admiration of the things she (normally) stands for, such as compassion, softness, love. Since he

23 Gould, *Church Revival*, p. 103.
24 Jones, op. cit., p. 445.

fears identification with her, he regards effeminacy of clothing or behaviour as immoral, and urges a maximum differentiation of the sexes. There is reason to suppose that the fear of aphanisis intensifies this whole situation.

In the conversion histories of the Methodists, the pattern of severe parent, early preoccupation with death and an unsuccessful revolt is constantly repeated. (The early age at which the preoccupation with death occurs shows that some factor operating in the first years of life must be involved.)[25] The combination of mild father and loss of, or disappointment in, the mother occurs with equal frequency in the matrist. It seems reasonable to say that the Puritan, being more afraid of the father, chooses to renounce his desire for the mother and is the more able to do so because his relationship with the mother is good; while the Romantic, disturbed by a broken relationship with the mother, spends his life in trying to recover her even at the cost of sacrificing his sex, and is the more able to do so because he does not unduly fear the father.

Finally, it is necessary to account, if possible, for the disturbance of the ego: the rigid ego-delimitation of the Puritan and the weak delimitation of the Romantic. The pantheist, or Romantic, sense of kinship with the rest of creation has been interpreted as a regression to the infantile stage in which the child has not learned to distinguish I from not I, and lives in blissful dependence on the maternal breast. If so, it becomes a possible simplification to treat Romanticism as regression to the oral, Puritanism as regression to the anal. The taboo on the genital, imposed by the prohibiting attitude to infantile masturbation, might therefore be seen as forcing people to regress to either of these stages. But it is clear that the Puritan is preoccupied with his relationship with a father-figure, the Romantic with his relationship with a mother-figure. These cannot be regarded as simple alternatives, because for every child, irrespective of sex, the initial relationship is with the mother; the relationship with the father is laid down, as it were, on top of it. Hence, it may perhaps be the case that only when a

[25] The early occurrence of "serious feelings" and death preoccupations is a constant feature of the Methodist diaries. See Bourne (ed. Walford, J.), Pawson, Longden, Treffry, etc., and the *Lives of the Early Meth. Preachers*, passim.

reasonably satisfactory relationship with the mother has been established can a child proceed to a relationship with the father. If the mother is already seen as rejecting before the father enters the scene, the father cannot be regarded as the interloper who has taken the mother away. (This is, of course, an over-simplification because, however rejecting the mother may be, the need for her still exists.) Hence, for such a child, the Œdipus complex still develops, but the emphases are different. If this is so, we might expect any child which never knew its mother (because she died while the child was an infant, for instance) to become a matrist, for it would start life with a disturbance of the mother-relationship. The rule would not be invariable, for in some cases an adequate substitute might be found in a nurse or near relative. Casting one's eye over the eighteenth century, one at once perceives a number of prominent instances, such as Rousseau; and this theory would serve to explain, for instance, why Howard's son did not take after his severe father, although exposed continuously to his influence, but became a very distinct matrist.

The view that Romanticism represents a regression to the oral receives confirmation from the prevalence of manic-depression in the eighteenth century. Thus Abraham, as long ago as 1912, stated that manic-depression was derived from oral erotism consequent upon a severe disappointment with the mother before the Œdipus conflict had been resolved.[26]

I have suggested earlier that the fear of death is a phenomenon apparently connected with the delimitation of the ego: the Puritan fears death, while the pantheistically-inclined regard death with some equanimity. The fact that children are much preoccupied with the topic between three and five years may therefore be connected with the fact that at this time they are becoming fully aware of their own individuality and separateness. But it is also a phenomenon connected with death-wishes, i.e. with aggression. The technique of deliberately activating death-fears precisely in this period must certainly have been traumatic.

I make these suggestions for what they are worth, but I regard the question of the integrity of the ego, and the infantile experiences

[26] Abraham, cited Bellak, *Manic Depressive Psychosis*, p. 54.

affecting it, as still basically unsolved, and I hope at some future date to investigate the point further in another book.

From this short survey of infant-training methods a remarkably coherent picture has emerged. I cannot claim to have demonstrated the whole mechanism connecting such methods and adult personality, since there may well be further factors which I have overlooked. But available information, while not perhaps full enough to be conclusive, is entirely consistent with the analysis of personality-structures which I have offered.

Though I have treated them somewhat schematically, for simplicity of exposition, it will be seen that the various factors act so as to reinforce one another. The genital taboos probably help to create the anal fixation. The anal insistence on restraint motivates the use of swaddling bands; these contribute to the fund of aggression. The aggression strengthens the death-wishes, and these strengthen the guilt. The guilt in turn ensures the transmission of the genital taboos, and so the circle is completed. Other links will suggest themselves: thus, the emotional impairment resulting from aphanisis is what enables the parent to be so severe, while the various frustrations create the situation in which aphanisis can be evoked. It is striking, for instance, how the Puritan group not only practised just those actions, such as letting the child cry itself out, most calculated to produce the desired effect, but also attacked precisely those actions of the upper class, such as farming children out, which were most likely to create the opposite effect. This is no accident. For instance, it is just because the Puritan values restraint that he employs swaddling bands, and it is because he is emotionally inhibited that he can, unmoved, watch a child cry itself into exhaustion, where a more responsive person would feel driven to intervene. Conversely, an over-sensitive person would intervene too readily and thus 'spoil' the child.[27]

It would seem to follow from such considerations that the patterns

---

[27] Howard's biographer, Field, "cannot forbear expressing" admiration at the wisdom of Divine Providence in killing off Howard's mother, since he might have been spoiled by her. "And then lest the affection of the bereaved father should be too much lavished on the surviving child, sickness is sent upon him and a separation effected . . ." *Life of Howard*, p. 5.

tend to be self-perpetuating. The Puritan must tend to produce Puritans, and the indulgent matrist parent uninhibited matrist children, if not indeed Romantics. This, of course, is what we normally assume, even when we take a less Freudian view of the process by which the transmission occurs.

Such a mechanism is consistent with the conclusion reached in Chapter Five concerning the nature of the social change we have been studying. I suggested there that the change consisted not so much in the spreading of a stricter moral attitude through society as a whole, as in the passing of economic and social power out of the hands of a lax (and, as it happened, upper-class) group into the hands of a strict (and, as it happened, middle-class) group. As a result of this shift of power, the lax group was compelled to pay lip-service to the middle-class ethical ideal. Such a statement, it will be evident, expresses merely the general character of the change. I do not mean to claim that members of the laxer group were not influenced to some extent towards an actual acceptance of stricter ideals. Quite certainly they were, in degrees which differed widely from individual to individual. But this, it seemed to me, was a secondary effect, a by-product of the main socio-economic change. This had been, for me, a quite unexpected conclusion, for I had started the study expecting to find psychological rather than economic factors to be paramount.

But further consideration suggested that the matter was not quite so simple. For it is much harder to account for the increasing matrism of the middle class in the nineteenth century in economic terms. They lost none of their economic power. Why, then, did the middle-class group become progressively less afraid of pleasure, as the nineteenth century progressed? Why did the pietists of Exeter Hall come to be regarded as bigots? It would seem that some psychological factors were indeed at work; and, if so, presumably contrary forces had helped to intensify Puritanism during the eighteenth century.

The hypothesis which first occurred to me was that the moralising tendency might tend to grow like a snowball. The severe parent would tend to produce an even severer child, for the child would react with excessive force to the pressures put upon it. Such a process seemed to be illustrated in the case of Margaret Gray, for instance. But such a mechanism seems quite unable to account for the gradual reduction in severity during the nineteenth century. One can imagine that severity might become so severe that the child would rebel and reject the whole code—as in the case of Howard's son—but it is harder to see how a more gradual relaxation could occur—as it did in the case of Hare.

Moreover, on closer inspection it looks as if it is the child which does not suffer under too extreme pressure which has the courage to rebel. When the pressure is really severe, resistance collapses completely.

It seems to me more likely, if any such self-reversing mechanism exists, that it functions in a different manner. It is conceivable, for instance, that inhibition may reach a point at which the individual concerned becomes unable to carry on life effectively. He may be so handicapped in his relations with others that he cannot maintain himself economically; he may fail to achieve marriage and to propagate children, or he may even die, as Margaret Gray apparently did, from loss of the will to live. Conversely, the completely uninhibited matrist may also be unable to maintain himself, or to bring up a family and so perpetuate himself. Such factors, however, would merely limit the trend: it does not follow that they would reverse it.

I suspect that the answer must be sought, not at this overt level, but in changes in methods of child-rearing, which affect the personality of the adults of the next generation. For instance, it seems perfectly reasonable to regard the reduction in the use of swaddling which was occurring towards the end of the eighteenth century as a main cause of the disappearance of that frenzied violence which was achieved round about 1830, when the children who were brought up without such trammels became adult. (It was, for instance, about this date that the duel died out.) It is equally reasonable to suppose that such factors as the campaign in favour of breast-feeding children, bringing an improved relation with the mother, may have borne fruit in the mid-nineteenth century in the form of the re-emergence of matrist elements. (Unfortunately, we lack sufficiently precise knowledge of the extent to which breast-feeding and other relevant practices were employed, to make any but a speculative statement.)

But since it is part of my fundamental hypothesis, that people only adopt such methods when psychologically disposed towards the attitude they represent, even if we assume the existence of some such mechanism we are left with the problem of why such changes of method should have gained ground.

While we cannot give a positive answer, it is not difficult to think of factors, so complex that we may call them fortuitous, which would help to bring such changes about. For instance, the middle class, growing richer, may have made an increasing use of nurses, and these, being drawn from a matrist class, may have indulged children more than a middle-class parent would have. Similarly, in larger houses, with more servants, and a more elaborate social life, children may have seen less of their father; punishment became, almost certainly, a thing which, except in extreme cases, the mother inflicted. This, in turn, was probably a causative factor in the dropping of corporal punishment in favour of isolation and other disciplinary methods.

Again, one has to reckon with the fact that certain individuals changed from matrism to patrism in the course of their lives. Thus Coleridge and Southey changed from a pantheist Romanticism to Christian conservatism in the course of a couple of decades. Such cases probably represent a re-introjection of the father-figure, and I suspect that this re-introjection becomes much easier to achieve after the actual father has died. A tendency for such changes to occur might therefore be created by an increase in the expectancy of life, or by a tendency for people to marry and bear children at, or until, a higher age than formerly.

While it is possible to think of numerous factors of this fortuitous kind which might well act so as to modify the basic personality-structure, I have not been able to discover any mechanism as a result of which such changes would tend to recur in a regular cyclic manner. In other words, there seems to be no natural inherent tendency for society to pass regularly from phases of matrist dominance to phases of patrist dominance and back again. The analogy of the swing of the pendulum may in fact be inappropriate.

Furthermore, it seems that the mechanism of social process cannot be regarded either as primarily economic or as primarily psychological. Socio-economic and psychological factors interact in an exceedingly intimate way, and while the personality forms a nodal point through which all the forces pass, the process cannot be explained without giving full weight to both aspects.

These conclusions, I needly hardly emphasise, are derived from a single case-study and are therefore quite tentative. Other such studies will have to be made before they can be confirmed or rejected. If such studies confirm my general conception of the way in which social process occurs, it will be necessary to attempt the larger task of exploring more precisely the forces at work. In our present state of ignorance, it has been possible to do no more than make suggestions. My purpose has been rather to erect a model showing the *sort* of way in which social process may be explained, than to attempt a precise account of how it actually functions.

CHAPTER 17

CONCLUSIONS

HAVING REACHED the end of the inquiry, let us look back at the subject as a whole and take stock.

We have been concerned, as it turns out, almost entirely with the relationship between the middle and upper class. The growing discontent of the lower class, especially in the agricultural areas, and its connection with father-rejection, as evidenced by atheism, has not concerned us. The story of the efforts made to moralise this father-rejecting group in the latter part of the nineteenth century is subject-matter for another inquiry. But this is of no importance, for the object of the exercise was not to give a complete social history of the period, but to investigate a theory.

The test of a theory is sometimes said to be its effectiveness in accounting for matters other than those it was originally devised to explain. By this criterion, it seemed to me when I had reached this point, the inquiry had proved fertile. Numerous isolated facts which I had noted in passing could, I perceived, be fitted readily into the general structure, and proved not to be isolated at all. For instance, so small a thing as the popularity of the urn in eighteenth-century decoration can be explained by the universality of interest in death, for urns are intended to contain the ashes of the dead. We can understand why, by the end of the eighteenth century, the castrato singer had come to be thought repulsive; and why the graceful Italic script gave place to the rigidly formalised copperplate about the same date. History reveals a new coherence when we note that the abolition of the practice of physically restraining lunatics coincides in time with the abolition of the swaddling of infants and the vanishing of restraint as an ideal. Again, when Mrs. Sherwood tells us, with horror, of a lady she knew in her youth who took an emetic in preparation for a good meal so that

340

she could eat a maximum amount, we evidently have the polar opposite of the idea that "the luxury of eating is beyond words indelicate and disgusting".[1]

The attempt to align what is known with the pattern thus established is useful in exposing misconceptions. Thus I had ignorantly imagined that eighteenth-century public schools were run in an authoritarian manner, and supposed that the introduction of prefects represented a step towards democracy. Theory evidently required, however, that they should have grown more authoritarian, not less so, as they came under middle-class influence. Investigating this point, I found that, in point of fact, in the eighteenth century discipline was left almost entirely to committees of the boys. It was Arnold and his successors who abolished these in favour of an authoritarian system. The institution of prefects created a more hierarchical structure, as was happening in society as a whole. We realise, too, that the change is not so much administrative or political as moral. Mrs. Sherwood comments on a country ball (about 1793) at which both the gentry and the servants danced, that her parents saw not the 'evil' which lurked under this "confusion of ranks".[2]

Again, if poetry is Romantic it must seem objectionable and even immoral to the patrist. As the *Quarterly Review* observed in 1812, "We admit that the temperament which disposes the soul to take fire at the beauties of poetry must, in every state, be limited to a very small number; and we suspect that even these, considered as a body, are not the most moral class of the community. The warmth which makes them so feelingly alive to the charms of verse, is apt to lead them to the indulgence of less innocent emotions; and though they may be capable of a sudden exertion of virtue, yet that very propensity which disposes them to receive impressions so readily, occasions these to be as readily effaced." And since Romanticism is based on the mother-introjection, it comes (as a result of decomposition) to be seen as peculiarly feminine.

By the same token, we can now understand how Johnson, though himself a novelist, could say, "The rejection and contempt of fiction is rational and manly," or how moralists could refer regretfully to the

[1] Darton, *Life of Mrs. Sherwood*, p. 25.
[2] ib., p. 56.

passing of the "manly noble orders" in architecture. Classical rectilinearity seemed more masculine than the curvilinear, rococo Romantic designs.

To take a final example, we can understand why the theatre should have turned increasingly to realism and spectacle in presentation as the eighteenth century closed. For the patrist both lacks the imagination to build a picture from a few dramatic hints, and supposes that the function of art is a mere reproduction of reality as distinct from the provision of a specialised æsthetic stimulus.

Arguing in this kind of way, one comes to see that the real significance of the French Revolution, as an historical influence, is that it represented a threat to authority, and thus to the father-figure. This threat was probably the only thing capable of forging an alliance between the guilt-ridden middle-class patrists and non-guilt-ridden upper-class patrists, who were in every obvious social respect poles asunder. The anxieties aroused were stronger and more irrational in character than would have resulted from a purely rational appreciation of the situation, and the measures adopted—such as the suppression of debating clubs—were characteristically patrist.

History, it may be said, has been written too largely in rationalistic terms, as if the actions of social leaders at least—however impulsive the mob might be—were determined almost entirely by judgments intellectually arrived at.

But while the inquiry had thrown some light on the historical process in the period selected for study, it had also, I felt, illuminated a number of issues of a more general character, and it may be appropriate in this concluding chapter to discuss these wider issues. The fields in question are psychological theory, historiography and the nature of moral judgment.

The most obvious achievement is some clarification in the specialised field of psychological dynamics. My immediate purpose in undertaking the inquiry was to test in detail the validity of the concepts of matrism and patrism put forward in more general terms in *Sex in History*. It seems to me that these have proved useful tools, with the aid of which much that before seemed arbitrary and unintelligible has been rendered serviceable. Nothing has emerged to imperil the validity of these concepts, though they have had to be elaborated; and it has also become clear that it is only in a specialised sense that one is justified in speaking of a period as being matrist or patrist.

A second achievement in this field was an unexpected one: the emergence of the concept of ego-definition as a primary personality variable. This may be considered as a novel contribution, for, while psychoanalysis offers a number of rather scattered observations on the integration of the ego, this has never been treated as a major determinant of overt personality. The biographical material here adduced suggests that it is, nevertheless. (This illustrates the value of cross-fertilisation between history and psychology—or what today is called the "interdisciplinary approach".) It is evident that this concept calls for closer study: in particular, it would be valuable to know whether there are any childhood experiences which determine it or, if not, what other causative factors are at work. I would hazard the guess that the answer will be found to be closely bound up with the question of narcissism, a matter which is still little understood.

This is not the only new line of development which has been opened up. The inquiry has, unexpectedly, provided the basis for a novel scheme for the analysis of personality under six headings: aggression, guilt, parental identification, and so on. Pursuing this lead, it might be asked whether there are still other factors, additional to the six listed in Chapter Eleven, which are crucial for the understanding of social development. Psychologists have developed many schemes for personality-analysis; none is wholly satisfactory. The one used here has been developed in a different way; and while it derives some justification from its practical usefulness, its acceptance will depend, in the end, on whether it can be incorporated in the whole body of psychological thinking. The testing of numbers of persons now living is an obvious step, but one which could only be satisfactorily undertaken by a team with adequate financial and academic support.

Again, I have been struck by the fact that when a balance is achieved between father- and mother-identification in a single individual, the balance seems to be achieved in a variety of different ways, so that several distinctive personality types result. This question I hope, one day, to explore further.

The present study may have been of value not only to psychologists but to historians. If nothing else, it has made it possible to bring a greater degree of precision to the use of such terms as 'Romanticism' and 'individualism'. Hitherto, writers on these topics have passed as precise if they gave their definition, whatever it might be, and every definition was based on arbitrary and subjective judgments. Now that fairly precise referents for such terms can be given in psychological language, the problem is seen to have changed in character. A genuinely novel alternative definition can only be proposed if an alternative psychological explanation is simultaneously offered.[3]

The kind of approach here employed discloses the unsatisfactory way in which literary critics and social historians tend to employ terms descriptive of social phenomena. To take an instance, Professor Moore, normally a clear-sighted writer, attributes the rise of 'sentimentalism' to 'benevolence'.[4] But, from the psychological viewpoint, it is obvious that what comes first is a change of attitude—an increased sensitiveness to the plight of others. Benevolence is the result of such sensitivity; sentimentalism a specialised development of it. Thus to explain sentimentalism by reference to benevolence is to explain an effect by an effect, and to ignore the cause of both.

Sentimentalism and benevolence are, when it comes to the point, names given to particular kinds of behaviour. Ultimately, behaviour can only be explained in psychological terms. Hence, in all such cases, an explanation of the cause-and-effect type can only be offered on the basis of some general psychological hypotheses about behaviour. In all such explanations a hypothesis is implied even when none is stated.

In practice, the tacit psychological assumptions on which many such explanations are based are extremely naïve. Thus one writer attributes the increasing prudery of language to the increasing literacy of women. The unstated assumption here is that women are *necessarily* opposed to

---

[3] Thus Kitson Clark argues for an extension of Romanticism into the nineteenth century, by adducing evidence of the death wish. But, as I have shown, the death wish alone is no proof of Romanticism, the central feature of which is matrism. (Plumb, *Studies in Soc. Hist.*, Ch. 7.)

[4] Moore, *Backgrounds of Eng. Lit.* (p. 51). He also thinks the growth of altruism, at least in poetry, to be due largely to Shaftesbury's *Characteristicks*.

frank language, which even a superficial examination of social history would at once show to be untrue.

The ambiguity of much historical comment is quite extraordinary. Thus one writer declares that the eighteenth-century spirit of criticism gave way to the nineteenth-century spirit of creation. But it would be at least equally fair to speak of the eighteenth century as creative and the nineteenth century as critical. For this writer, 'critical' evidently implies "critical of established ideas" but not "critical of morals and behaviour", while creation implies "commercial production" rather than artistic and philosophical creativeness.

Another writer, comparing the nineteenth century with the eighteenth, says that "the individualism of the eighteenth century broke down". But, for most writers, the eighteenth is the period of classical order; the nineteenth the period of economic individualism. Evidently such writers are using the word 'individualism' in different senses, but they offer no satisfactory definition. On the basis of an analysis of individualism, such as is offered in Chapter Twelve, it is possible to resolve such confusions.

The fact is, historians stand revealed as subject, much more than they realise, to the unconscious prejudices of their period and their personality. Thus when Vulliamy says of Boswell's sensitivity to music, and Johnson's brusque comment on it, "Of course, one would here prefer to resemble Boswell rather than Johnson," there is no "of course" about it, for whether one sympathises with Boswell's view or not depends entirely on whether one is inclined to matrism or to patrism.[5] Conversely, Allen makes an unconscious patrist assumption when he refers scathingly to the unrealistic scenery and clothing of the late eighteenth-century theatre: the belief that plays should necessarily be presented realistically is a patrist belief.

But much more important than such clarifications of detail is the demonstration of a remarkable degree of coherence between social attitudes in different fields, such as art, religion and politics, and to have shown their relationship to the structure of personality. By so doing, it has been possible to make some small inroad on the assumption that history is a random process.

[5] Vulliamy, *Ursa Major*, p. 86.

History is not so random that moral, political and religious views can be regarded as uncorrelated; moreover the changes which occur in these views follow a predictable pattern. Many of the factors at work may be random from the viewpoint of the individual, yet when society as a whole is considered they are found to conform to laws of probability. So far, however, we have found no law which would enable us to predict when a swing from matrism to patrism (or vice versa) would take place, how far it would go, and when it would reverse. Of course, even this degree of historical determinism is a limited one, for it seems probable that individuals vary in their capacity to withstand psychological blows, and that this capacity is inherited. Hence the chance factors in the transmission of inherited characteristics make it certain that no wholly reliable prediction of how society would develop (as between matrist and patrist forms) can be made.

However, even this limited achievement—the demonstration of coherence—has, I think, important implications for historiography. It gives some precision to the concept, to which historians often resort, of "the spirit of the times". But, while there certainly is such a pre-disposition, at least within specific groups or classes, the sphere in which it can be appealed to as a causative factor is limited. It can account for the success of an idea, but it cannot be regarded as a decisive influence on individuals. Indeed, historians will have to think carefully in future before employing the idea of influence. Influence still has a role, but it appears to be no more than the detonator which fires a charge which has long been laid. Thus people may be influenced by, let us say, a book, in the sense that it may confirm and make more explicit the prejudices to which they are already prone, but they cannot be influenced in a contrary direction. Philip Gosse, for example, read *The Lady of the Lake* in his youth, and other Romantic works: they did not make him a Romantic. But when he read Habershon's *Dissertations on the Prophetic Books*, it at once made him into an apocalypticist, because he was already set for such a development.[6] No more classically pure instance can be found than that of Edmund Gosse, who was screened from Romantic influences—and exposed to Puritan ones—perhaps more thoroughly than anyone of whom we

[6] Gosse, *Life of P. Gosse.*

have precise knowledge. No fiction was admitted to the house; he was allowed no friends. Yet so great was his natural bent towards Romanticism that he constructed for himself Romantic images out of the few scraps available to him—a second-rate ballad and the sight of the sea. He even twisted the Bible to his purpose until, as he says, "I was at one momently devoutly pious, at the next haunted by visions of material beauty and longing for sensuous impressions. In my hot and silly brain, Jesus and Pan held sway together."[7]

On the historical scale, it is often remarkable how little effect even the most drastic events have on basic attitudes. It took more than a hundred years of inter-marriage and interpenetration before even an event so far-reaching as the Norman Conquest appreciably affected the national ethos. By the same token, little value would seem to attach to the concept of reaction: thus statements such as the assertion, so often made, that Romanticism represents a reaction from rationalism appear to have no basis in reality.

It is sometimes said that the test of a theory is whether it enables one to make predictions. While we cannot foresee how the balance will shift between matrism and patrism, the present theory nevertheless has a certain predictive power: thus, when we detect one aspect of matrism in a man, we can, with some degree of assurance, expect to find all the others. For instance, from the fact that Edward Young praised originality we can predict that he would prefer Romantic scenery, as in fact he did.[8] I qualify this statement by saying, "with some degree of assurance," because special factors may introduce apparent anomalies in some cases, and other elements of personality may mask or modify the patrist-matrist pattern. But even with this qualification the assertion has implications of considerable philosophical significance. It implies that freedom of the individual to choose his own course of life is greatly restricted.

Many people dislike the idea that the individual does not have a free choice of behaviour, and resent the assertion that because their per-

[7] Gosse, *Father and Son*, pp. 301–7.
[8] See his *Conjectures*. He also considered "children as the next order of beings to the blessed angels", and spoke of their "spotless innocence". Cited from Bath MSS, i, 255, by Shelley, *Edward Young*, p. 119.

sonality has been moulded in a particular way, they are 'obliged' to take a particular view in politics or in art. To some extent, this feeling is due to a semantic confusion. The theory does not say that Young was *obliged* to like Romantic scenery, whether he would or no, because the question of his not wanting to does not arise: it is just this failure of the issue to arise that we are talking about. Anthropologists have already taught us to what extent our views are derived from our cultural environment, and how restricted our choice is by this fact.

In surveying a large mass of material written in the period 1700–1850, for the purposes of this study, I was greatly struck by a particular application of this determinist tendency: the realisation dawned that the great bulk of what passes for rational writing and discussion actually has a strongly irrational character, in the sense that it consists in finding reasons to justify tenets which are already held. In short the process is one of rationalisation. For instance, Edward Young did not, as I believe, arrive at his advocacy of originality in art because he had considered the pros and cons and found that they necessitated this point of view: he started from the point of view and sought for reasons to support it. This tendency to rationalise would matter less if the writers realised that this was what they were doing, but in most cases the work is presented as logical and unbiased inquiry. This is true not only of obvious polemicists such as the moralistic writers, but equally of philosophers such as Hume or Ricardo, and even of doctors and scientists. It leads in extreme cases to fantastic claims: thus Victorian doctors claimed to have observed insanity as the frequent consequence of Sunday work.[9]

I do not go so far as to suggest that no rational factors enter into the formation of a belief. I suspect that there is a continuous interplay between rational processes and emotionally based prejudices, in which the mind searches for items which are consistent both with what is known to be demonstrably true and with its prejudices. In pursuing the rationalising processes a first-class brain will find reasons of a highly logical character; an inferior one will be satisfied with feeble ones. This is very obvious in the writings of the moralist, whose reasons are often feeble in the extreme.

[9] See, e.g., Osborn, *Evils of Sabbath Desecration*, p. 7.

348

Full realisation of this fact leaves one with a tremendous sense of wasted effort. With the great bulk of philosophical writing (using the adjective in its broadest sense) one need only ask what views the author holds and how they differ from the norm; the reasons he advances for the belief are of minor interest, and even the identification of the author's views usually reveals them to represent one stereotype or another. Thus Young's advocacy of originality tells us something about Young but virtually nothing about originality. The same is true of, say, Wilberforce's views on original sin.

To the extent that the proposition which a man defends contains an element of truth, his arguments concerning it may, if he has a sufficiently good intelligence, be completely valid ones. In such cases the arguments become of greater interest, but this does not make his behaviour less irrational in the sense here intended. But, as we can now see, in many cases the question is not so much whether a writer is correct or incorrect in his thesis, as whether he is stressing one aspect of a dichotomy at the expense of its counterpart. Thus it is perfectly true that originality must be disciplined. Or again, in the moral field, it is perfectly true that self-control is of value, but it is also true that spontaneity is of value and must not be wholly suppressed.

The art of existence consists in finding an appropriate balance between such alternatives in every relevant field. Hence arguments which stress one half of the equation at the expense of the other are at best half-truths, than which nothing is more misleading.

Unawareness of this fact makes much advocacy nugatory, and this is still entirely true to-day. For instance, there are some who prefer to attribute criminal or delinquent behaviour to a "lack of moral fibre" while others blame unsatisfactory home life. That is, some blame internal forces, some external, environmental ones. It is noticeable that the first type of comment often comes from judges, army officers and others whom we might expect to be patrists, while the second comes from reformers and persons who betray that preoccupation with social welfare which marks the matrist. Both are irrational.

It seems to me that if this proposition is true, the history of thought requires fresh examination.

Looking back on the biographical material which I had examined in the course of this study, I find myself left with a strong impression, yet one which I find it difficult to put into words which will convey it effectively. It arises from the conjunction of two preliminary impressions: first, an enhanced awareness of the great variety of patterns into which the elements of personality can fall, producing types as different as the ascetic and the businessman: second, the realisation that, in a given period, society arbitrarily selects one of these patterns and assumes that it is 'normal' in the sense of healthy and natural, and that all other forms are deviants which are to be regarded as increasingly abnormal and unhealthy the further they depart from the preferred type. A Romantic like Byron was no more and no less abnormal than an anal-patrist like Arthur Young: the religious fanatic, Richard Brothers, was just as much abnormal as the manic-depressive George III.

We can see what the criteria for a true functional normality must be: for instance, a balance between father- and mother-identification, a balance between excessive and insufficient ego-definition, and so on. We have no reliable information as to how common, at any given period, persons answering to such a description may be.

It follows not only that we should avoid the mistake of treating the dominant type of a given era—or of our own—as normal; but also that we should not dismiss with some such label as 'eccentric' those individuals whose personality-pattern is unusual, as if they were biological 'sports' or freaks. The probability is that in a sufficiently long view of society they are no more and no less 'normal' than the types we regard as 'normal' to-day. Indeed, since the standard with which we compare them is generally off-centre, we may even fall into the error of dismissing the functionally normal and psychologically healthy individual as 'abnormal'.

Realisation of this fact, while useful to the historian, seems essential to the biographer: at present biography is written almost entirely from an ethnocentric viewpoint. But it is also important for all those who venture to assess human behaviour in comparative terms: and this is a category which includes not only historians, moralists and leader-writers, but almost all of us at one time or another.

There is one application of this proposition which is of especial interest. In this study, the Puritanical moralist emerges as a psychologically abnormal and functionally unhealthy type. Perhaps for some people this will seem to imply that moral feeling as a whole is to be regarded as abnormal; alternatively, if the moral standards of moralists are rejected as the product of personality-distortions, the question may be raised: are there any standards upon which one can rely? To-day, indeed, there seem to be many who believe that psychiatry has undermined the basis of moral judgment completely. It seems advisable, therefore, to make clear just what the implications really are.

In declaring the moralist to be a neurotic, the analysis does not imply that his standards are valueless; it suggests that his mistake is to lay too much stress on one particular set of values and too little on the complementary set. He sees the value of self-control, but fails to see the value of spontaneity. The analysis justifies the Classic ideal of moderation, and it adds that the moralist has not arrived at his views because he has (as he so often thinks) examined the position and has arrived by calm reflection at a balanced conclusion, but for unconscious reasons; and that he holds these views with excessive force and rigidity.

As I pointed out in Chapter Twelve, there are, in fact, not one but two 'moralities', the Puritan and the Romantic, and each is a pseudo-morality: each is the product of psychological abnormality. The bases of moral judgment lie between these two extremes. This is a fact which it is easy enough to recognise intellectually, but difficult to apply in practice. So strong is the Puritan tradition that we tend to measure behaviour against a standard of repression rather than one of balance. Even when we disagree with him, we find it difficult to see that the unduly severe judge or military martinet is just as much a psychological 'case' as the delinquent whom he sentences. We see the need for some kind of remedial treatment for the one, but do not demand it for the other.

Another conclusion which seems frequently to be drawn from such arguments is that moral blame can never be attributed: the wrong-doer, it is assumed, was foredoomed by his childhood experiences to behave as he did. This is a special instance of the problem of determinism which we have already discussed earlier in the chapter.

This conclusion is due, I believe, to a misapprehension, as one can see by considering an analogy from physical medicine. The child who is habitually undernourished may, as an adult, have a small frame and a poor musculature. This may make it impossible for him to become a great athlete, and to this extent his future is irrevocably determined. But a considerable degree of freedom still remains: he may train his muscles as best he can, and seek to make up by skill for what he lacks in strength, or he may abandon the attempt to attain physical fitness altogether. Equally, the victim of psychological mismanagement will be handicapped. In some fields, he may be well advised to avoid competing with more favoured individuals, just as one might advise a physical weakling to take up some less strenuous activity than putting the weight or rowing. But in areas where effort is definitely desirable on social grounds, scope for considerable self-improvement always exists. The potential delinquent may be unable to become a saint, but that does not mean that he cannot, still less that he should not, struggle against his anti-social impulses.

The analogy also indicates that he is most likely to struggle successfully if he is provided with an alternative and more constructive outlet for such impulses. Many of those who devise and administer the judicial system still operate upon an assumption that 'good' behaviour is achieved by repression of 'bad' instincts, although it has long been abundantly clear that the problem is one of finding 'good' channels of expression for instincts which are ethically neutral.

More generally still, I hope that the survey may have done something to demonstrate how inadequate are the factual bases of many contemporary moral judgments. It is often simple ignorance of historical fact which enables people to accept the assertion, so often made in every age, that moral standards have declined. Investigation usually reveals that the standards of the past were no better; certainly they did not seem so at the time. A good many such judgments have been quoted already. Here is one from an earlier period: "The world is passing through troubled times. The young people of to-day think of nothing but themselves. They have no reverence for parents or old people. They are impatient of all restraint. They talk as if they alone knew anything, and what passes for wisdom with us is foolishness to them. As for girls, they are forward, immodest, and unwomanly in speech, behaviour and dress." These words were written by Peter the Hermit in 1274.

In Britain and America in recent years there has been much concern at a supposed increase in the amount of homosexuality. Some speakers have treated it as an unprecedented development. They are evidently quite unaware that homosexuality was practised continuously throughout the eighteenth and nineteenth centuries, to say nothing of earlier periods.

Not only are the judgments of such critics based on historical ignorance; so, too often, are their proposals for mending matters. The survey we have made has demonstrated in historical terms what had already been learned by psychological investigation, that moral reform is not to be achieved by imposing external or even internal prohibitions—nor, as some who go to other extremes appear to think, by removing all such prohibitions. It is to be achieved, in so far as it is possible at all, by building well-balanced personalities and setting them in a social environment which offers adequate opportunity for the expression of basic human impulses. To do so is a prodigious but not altogether an impossible task. It is a far more complex undertaking than the old-style, self-appointed reformer conceived, and calls for higher qualities. In it condemnation plays little part, a genuine desire to understand and help occupy the leading roles. If this inquiry has done anything to demonstrate that fact, it will not have been in vain.

THE THEORY OF PARENTAL
IDENTIFICATIONS

THE THEORY OF PARENTAL IMAGES is based on two related propositions. First, it suggests that the attitudes of individuals differ in certain important respects, according as they model themselves on their father or on their mother—or, to be more exact, according as they introject a father- or a mother-figure. While most people will introject elements from both parental figures, it indicates the possibility of two extreme cases, and for these I have suggested the terms 'patrist' and 'matrist'. From a consideration of psychological theory I inferred what these attitudes would be and then tested these inferences by reference to specific cases. The patrist tends to be authoritarian in politics, to be restrictive in sexual matters, to give a low status to women and to worship a father deity. The matrist is just the reverse. Thus the attitudes resulting are crucial for the three important fields of politics, religion and morals, and for the equally important, though less carefully studied, field of the relationship between the sexes. These were only the principal attitudes emerging, and, as we see in the present volume, it is also possible to detect patrist and matrist attitudes to art, scientific inquiry and other matters.

The roots of the analysis lie in the Œdipus complex; as most people now know, this term refers to the choice which the child, in its infancy, feels impelled to make between its parents. Loving its mother, it sees its father as an interloper; but equally it tends, in the infantile recesses of the unconscious, to conceive the mother as having betrayed its love with another person, the father. Thus, if it finally identifies itself with the father and his interest, it regards women as constitutionally unfaithful, and is concerned to prevent their being so. Thus it is that the father-identifier stands for authority and sets a high value on the chastity of women, where—since the mother is the source of food and support—the mother-identifier sets a higher value on welfare than on matters of morality.

Again, the property of the father must not be interfered with: thus the father-identifier is a conservative, a traditionalist, who feels that one should not interfere with the works of one's forefathers; the mother-identifier is an innovator.

From the Œdipus complex was also derived the theoretical prediction that the father-identifier will be preoccupied by the question of homosexuality, the mother-identifier by the question of incest—a prediction abundantly verified by the historic facts. It was also predicted that the father-identifier would tend to make a sharp distinction between the clothes of the two sexes, as if unwilling to be confused in any way with the female sex; while in matrist periods the clothes of the two sexes will tend to become similar.

A second group of characteristics derives from the idea of inhibition. The father-identifier will tend to be inhibited in his movements, and to fear drink, dancing and anything which tends to remove inhibition. Conversely the matrist will be uninhibited; the orgiastic dancing and drunkenness associated with the worship of Artemis is a well-known Classical instance. The patrist also fears colour, as we see when we recall the sober costume on which the Puritans insisted, and the way in which they took the colour out of church decoration, and indeed out of life.

These aspects are connected with the first group by the fact that it is the super-ego which performs the function of inhibiting impulse, and the super-ego is formed by the introjection of parental and especially paternal images. Introjection of the father, who seems a figure of supreme authority, naturally produces a much severer super-ego than introjection of the supportive and comforting mother.

Finally, we may note asceticism, or fear of pleasure, in many (but not, I now realise, all) patrists; and a fear of inquiry; this last was deduced from the Freudian tenet that the child fears and wants to inquire into the nature of the relationship between its parents, and that all subsequent curiosity is a sublimation of this primitive urge. These attitudes, too, the previous inquiry proved to exist.

The second proposition was of a more controversial character. In the history of western society, phases may be distinguished in which patrist attitudes and values were dominant and other phases in which matrist attitudes and values were dominant. As one phase changes into another, society seems to pass through a phase of balance, and it is in these periods of balanced or mixed parental influence that the greatest achievements in art and culture are made. It was not asserted that this change was inevitable, nor that it had some cyclic character: an attempt was simply made to trace it over some two thousand years of western history. This investigation seemed to confirm the suggestion, which had originally been made on the basis of anthropological and archæological data.

This discovery, assuming it to be valid, had various implications, of which two seemed to me to be especially interesting. First, it suggested that the institutions of society normally exhibit a certain coherence: if we find a society with a sky-father religion we can expect to find that it will be authoritarian, restrictive in sexual matters, and give a low status to women. It follows that if, in our own time, we wish to bring about a certain reform we cannot expect to do so without simultaneously effecting changes in many fields as well: moreover, we shall only achieve the change in proportion as we are able to alter the personality of the people constituting our society, in respect of parental identification. Second, it suggests that the usual theories which are employed to explain literary and even social changes—theories by which people borrow from or are influenced by other societies—are of marginal validity. For instance, to explain the fact that the twelfth-century Troubadours developed a new form of poetry quite unlike any that had gone before in Christian Europe, it is suggested that they borrowed from or were influenced by the Arabs, via Spain; and much ingenuity has been exerted to find parallels. Now, according to the present theory, the Troubadours were matrists and developed their type of poetry on lines which matrists always follow; in contrast Christian Europe was patrist. And in fact the Troubadours proved to have the matrist outlook on politics, women, etc., and their poetry paralleled that of other matrist groups, such as the early Celts, in the critical respects.

Hence, according to my theory, the Troubadours would still have produced this kind of poetry (assuming they produced poetry at all) even if they had been hermetically insulated from all extraneous influences. This is not to say that they did not, in fact, borrow from the Arabs; it is to say that if they borrowed from another matrist group it was because they were already predisposed by their personalities to look for this kind of material, and were equally impervious to 'influences' of a patrist kind. Thus, in my view, the theory of influences or borrowing accounts for the appearance of specific items within a general range and hence may account for the speed and elaboration with which an art form develops, but it in no way accounts for the choice of the range or determines the direction in which development takes place.

Sometimes we see cases where a group has decisively rejected a particular influence; no whit dismayed, the orthodox critic or historian declares that the group has *reacted* from the influence, without explaining why it should sometimes react from and sometimes follow a particular lead. By a skilful use of the concepts of influence and reaction, almost any development can be 'explained', but it is fairly obvious that, in the absence of any guiding principle to determine when reaction is appropriate and when influence, such explanations only serve *post hoc*, and a theory which has no predictive value can scarcely claim to be scientific.

While in *Sex in History* the theory had worked out well on the whole, each period displaying just the characteristics predicted, yet I was aware that there were certain features which did not conform exactly as they should. For these discrepancies I had suggested explanations, but not, I feared, completely adequate ones. Chief of these difficulties was the fact that the Victorians gave a high status to woman, even though they restricted her freedom, and not a low status as the theory predicted. And whereas earlier patrist periods had consistently seen the woman as the sexual temptress and the cause of man's fall from grace, the Victorians saw woman as angelically pure and as a refining influence upon man.

Most of these difficulties, I am happy to say, it has been possible to resolve in the course of the present more detailed inquiry, in which there has been an opportunity to consider a number of factors in personality, over and above those due to parental identifications.

357

LIST OF SOURCES

References in the notes are given in abbreviated form. Following is a list of the necessary bibliographical details of nearly all works mentioned as sources of material, either in the notes or the text. Works merely mentioned in passing are not included: neither are novels. Periodicals and manuscript sources appear separately at the end.

ABBEY, C. J. and OVERTON, J. H. *The English Church in the Eighteenth Century*. London, 1878.

ACLAND, A. *Caroline Norton*. London, 1948.

ACTON, W. *Functions and Disorders of the Reproductive Organs*. London, 1857.

ACTON, W. *Prostitution considered in its Moral, Social and Sanitary Aspects*. London, 1857.

ADAMSON, J. W. *English Education, 1789–1902*. Cambridge, 1930.

AIKIN, J. *View of the Character and Public Services of John Howard*. London, 1792.

AIKIN, L. *Memoirs, Miscellanies and Letters of the late Lucy Aikin*. London, 1864.

AINSWORTH, E. G. and NOYES, C. E. *Christopher Smart: A Biographical and Critical Study* (Univ. of Missouri. Studies, Vol. 18, No. 4). Columbia, Miss., 1943.

ALEXANDER, W. *History of Women from the Earliest Antiquity*. London, 1779.

ALLEN, B. S. *Tides in English Taste, 1619–1800*. Cambridge, Mass., 1937.

[ANCILLON, C.] *Eunuchism Displayed*. London, 1718.

ARBUTHNOT, A. *Memoirs of the Remarkable Life and Surprizing Adventures of Miss Jenny Cameron*. London, 1746.

ARCHENHOLTZ, J. W. *The British Mercury, 1790–1800*, (17 vols.) Hamburg.

ARCHENHOLTZ, J. W. *A Picture of England*. London, 1797.

ASHTON, J. *Eighteenth Century Waifs*. London, 1887.

ASHTON, J. *Social England under the Regency*. London, 1890.

ASHTON, J. *Social Life in the Reign of Queen Anne*. London, 1882.

AYTON, R. *A Voyage Round Great Britain*. London, 1814–15.

BABBITT, I. *Rousseau and Romanticism*. Boston, 1919.

BARBAULD, A. L. *Correspondence of Samuel Richardson*, etc. London, 1804.

BARBER, J. T. *A Tour throughout South Wales and Monmouthshire*. London, 1803.

BARING-GOULD, S. *The Church Revival*. London, 1914.

BARRETT, E. S. *Six Weeks at Longs* (by a late Resident). London, 1817.

BARRINGTON, J. *Personal Sketches of his own Times*. London, 1827–32.

BATH CITY MISSION. *Reports, 1837–47*. Bath, 1838–48.

BATTY, B. *The Christian Man's Closet*. London, 1581.

BAXTER, R. *A Christian Directory.* . . . London, 1673.

BAYNE-POWELL, R. *Travellers in Eighteenth Century England.* London, 1951.

BEBB, E. D. *Nonconformity and Social and Economic Life, 1660–1800.* London, 1935.

BECON, T. *A Catechism.* London, 1844.

BEERS, H. A. *History of English Romanticism in the Eighteenth Century.* London, 1899.

BELLAK, L. *Manic Depressive Psychosis and Allied Conditions.* New York, 1952.

BELLASIS, E. *Memorials of Mr. Serjeant Bellasis, 1800–1873.* London, 1893.

BENN, A. W. *History of English Rationalism in the Nineteenth Century.* London, 1906.

BERNHAUM, E. *The Drama of Sensibility, 1696–1780.* Cambridge, Mass., 1925.

BESANT, W. *Fifty Years Ago.* London, 1888.

BIRKHEAD, E. *The Tale of Terror.* London, 1921.

BLAKE, W. *Poetry and Prose of William Blake.* London, 1941.

BLOCH, I. *Sexual Life in England, Past and Present.* London, 1938.

BOSWELL, J. *Journal of a Tour to the Hebrides with Samuel Johnson.* London, 1852.

BOWDLER, T. *Reform or Ruin: Take Your Choice.* London, 1797.

BOWEN, M. *Wrestling Jacob: a Study of the Life of John Wesley.* London, 1937.

BRANDES, G. *Main Currents in Nineteenth Century Literature*: Vol. 2, *The Romantic School in Germany.* London, 1902.

BRAYSHAW, A. N. *The Personality of George Fox.* London, 1933.

BRIFFAULT, R. *The Mothers: A Study of the Origins of Sentiments and Institutions.* London, 1927.

BRIGGS, A. *Victorian People: Some Reassessment of People, Institutions, Ideas and Events, 1851–1867.* London, 1954.

BRODUM, DR. *A Guide to Old Age and A Cure for the Indiscretions of Youth.* London, 1795.

[BROWN, J.] *Thoughts on Civil Liberty and Licentiousness.* Newcastle, 1765.

BROWNRIGG, W. *Literary Life of William Brownrigg.* London, 1801.

BUCHAN, W. *Domestic Medicine: A Treatise.* London, 1813.

BUCKE, R. M. *Cosmic Consciousness: A Study in the Evolution of the Human Mind.* Philadelphia, 1901.

BULWER, E. G. (Lord Lytton). *England and the English.* London, 1833.

BURDER, G. *Lawful Amusements: A Sermon.* London, 1805.

BURNET, T. *The Sacred Theory of the Earth.* London, 1681.

BYROM, J. *Private Journal and Literary Remains of John Byrom.* Manchester, 1855–6.

[CADOGAN, W.] *An Essay upon Nursing* (by a Physician). London, 1748.

CAMPBELL, J. D. *Manic Depressive Disease.* New York, 1953.

CAPEL, LADY C. *The Capel Letters* (ed. Marquess of Anglesey). London, 1955.

CARTWRIGHT, H. *Letters on Female Education.* London, 1777.

CARUS, W. *Memoirs of the Life of the Rev. Charles Simeon.* London, 1847.

CHALMERS, A. *Works of the English Poets.* London, 1810.

CHAMBERLAYNE, E. *Magnae Britanniae Notitia: or, the Present State of England.* London, 1718.

CHAMBERS, J. D. *Nottinghamshire in the Eighteenth Century.* London, 1932.

CHAPONE, H. *Works.* London, 1807.

CHARKE, C. *A Narrative of the Life of Mrs. Charlotte Charke.* London, 1755.

CHARLTON, B. *Recollections of a Northumbrian Lady, 1815–1866.* London, 1949.

CHEYNE, G. *The English Malady, or A Treatise of Nervous Diseases of All Kinds.* London, 1733.

CHURCH, L. F. *The Early Methodist People.* London, 1949.

CLARK, K. *The Gothic Revival.* London, 1928 and 1950.

CLARKE, A. *A Letter to a Methodist Preacher.* London, 1800.

CLARKE, C. P. S. *The Oxford Movement and After.* London, 1932.

CLEGG, J. *Extracts from the Diary and Autobiography of the Rev. James Clegg, 1679–1755.* London, 1899.

COCKLE, MRS. *Important Studies for the Female Sex.* London, 1809.

COETLOGON, C. DE. *Sermon on the Nature, Necessity and Advantages of the Religious Observation of the Lord's Day, to which is added a Brief Account of the Society for the Prevention of the Profanation of Sunday.* London, 1776.

COLE, W. *A Journal of my Journey to Paris in the Year 1765.* London, 1931.

COLERIDGE, S. T. *Poetical Works* (ed. J. D. Campbell). London, 1898.

COLLIER, J. P. *An Old Man's Diary.* London, 1871.

COWPER, W. *Memoir of the Early Life of William Cowper, Esq. written by himself.* London, 1816.

COYER, G. F. (L'Abbé). *Nouvelles Observations sur l'Angleterre par un Voyageur.* Paris, 1779.

CRAGG, G. G. *Grimshaw of Haworth.* London, 1947.

CREEVY, T. *The Creevey Papers.* London, 1904.

CULVERWELL, R. J. *Lecture to a Young Man on Chastity.* London, 1847.

CULY, D. *The Works of David Culy, etc.* London, 1726.

CUMBERLAND, R. *Memoirs of Richard Cumberland written by himself.* London, 1816.

CUNNINGTON, C. W. *Feminine Attitudes in the Nineteenth Century.* London, 1935.

DALTON, J. *A Genuine Narrative of all the Street Robberies, etc.* London, 1728.

DARTON, F. J. H. *Children's Books in England*; in *Cambr. Hist. Mod. Lit.* Cambridge, 1932.

DARTON, F. J. H. *The Life and Times of Mrs. Sherwood.* London, 1910.

DARWIN, E. *The Botanic Garden: A Poem.* London, 1799.

[DEFOE, D.] *A Tour thro' the Whole Island of Great Britain, etc., by a Gentleman.* London, 1742.

DERRICK, S. *Letters written from Leverpoole, Chester, Corke, the Lake of Killarney, etc.* Dublin, 1767.

DIMOND, S. G. *The Psychology of the Methodist Revival.* London, 1926.

DODDRIDGE, P. *The Rise and Progress of Religion in the Soul.* London, 1743.

DOWDELL, E. G. *A Hundred Years of Middlesex Quarter Sessions.* Cambridge, 1932.

DRESSLER, B. *Geschichte der Englischen Erziehung.* Leipzig, Berlin, 1928.

DRINKWATER, J. *Charles James Fox.* London, 1928.

DRUMMOND, A. L. *Edward Irving and his Circle.* London, 1937.

DUNTON, J. *The Life and Errors of John Dunton.* London, 1818.

DUNTON, J. *The Pilgrim's Guide from the Cradle to his Death-bed.* London, 1684.

DYER, A. *Lecture to Men, delivered at Exeter Hall.* London, 1884.

EDGEWORTH, M. and EDGEWORTH, R. L. *Practical Education.* London, 1798.

EDWARDS, H. L. R. (ed.) 'Stendhal in London (1817).' *The London Magazine,* Vol. 2, No. 3. (March, 1955.)

EDWARDS, J. *The Distinguishing Marks of a Work of the Spirit of God.* Boston, 1741.

EDWARDS, J. *Sinners in the Hands of an Angry God.* Boston, 1772.

EDWARDS, J. *Some Account of the Conversation and Experiences of . . . Jonathan Edwards,* etc. (By Himself.) [Boston, 1760?]

ELIOT, G. *George Eliot's Life* (ed. J. W. Cross). Edinburgh, 1885.

EMDEN, P. H. *Quakers in Commerce: A Record of Business Achievement.* London, [1940].

EMDEN, P. H. *Regency Pageant.* London, 1936.

EVANS, A. B. *The Cutter.* London, 1808.

EVERETT, J. *Wesleyan Methodism in Sheffield.* Sheffield, 1823.

FALK, B. *The Royal Fitzroys.* London, 1950.

FARINGTON, J. *The Farington Diary* (ed. J. Greig). London, 1922-8.

FARINGTON, J. *Memoirs of the Life of Sir Joshua Reynolds.* London, 1819.

FAUJAS DE ST. FOND, B. *A Journey Through England and Scotland to the Hebrides in 1784* (ed. Sir Archibald Geikie). Glasgow, 1907.

FAUSSET, H. I' A. *Samuel Taylor Coleridge.* London, 1926.

FERRIER, S. *Memoir and Correspondence of Susan Ferrier, 1782-1854* (ed. J. A. Doyle). London, 1929.

FIELD, J. *The Life of John Howard.* London, 1850.

FITZBALL, E. *Thirty-Five Years of a Dramatic Author's Life.* London, 1859.

FOSTER, J. F. *On the Art of Gardening.* London, 1881.

FRAXI, P. [i.e. H. S. ASHBEE]. *Catena Librorum Tacendorum.* London, 1885.

FRAXI, P. [i.e. H. S. ASHBEE]. *Index Librorum Prohibitorum.* London, 1877.

FREUD, S. *Civilisation and its Discontents.* London, 1930.

FROE, A. DE. *Laurence Sterne and his Novels in the light of Psychology.* Groningen, 1925.

FYFE, J. G. (ed.) *Scottish Diaries and Memoirs, 1746-1843.* Stirling, 1942.

GASKELL, P. *The Manufacturing Population.* London, 1833.

GEIJER, E. G. *Impressions of England, 1809-10.* London, 1932.

GILDON, C. *The Complete Art of Poetry*. London, 1718.

GISBORNE, T. *An Enquiry into the Duties of the Female Sex*. London, 1797.

GLENBERVIE, LORD (Douglas, S.) *The Diaries of Sylvester Douglas, Lord Glenbervie* (ed. F. Bickley). London, Boston, 1928.

GODFREY, E. *English Children in the Olden Time*. London, 1907.

GOEDE, G. A. C. *A Stranger in England*. London, 1807.

GOSSE, E. *Father and Son: A Study of two Temperaments*. London, 1930.

GOSSE, E. *The Life of Philip Henry Gosse*. London, 1890.

GOTHEIN, M. L. *A History of Garden Art*. London, 1938.

GOUGE, W. *Of Domesticall Duties*. London, 1622.

GRANVILLE, H. *Letters of Harriet, Countess Granville, 1810–1845* (ed. F. Leveson Gower). London, New York, 1894.

GRAY, E. *Papers and Diaries of a York Family, 1764–1839*. London, 1927.

GREGORY, J. *A Comparative View of the State and Faculties of Man with those of the Animal World*. Edinburgh, 1788.

GREGORY, J. *A Father's Legacy to his Daughters*. London, 1774.

GREVILLE, H. W. *The Greville Diary* (ed. P. W. Wilson). London, 1927.

GRIFFITH, M. *Bethel, or a Form for Families*. London, 1633.

GROETHUYSEN, B. *Origines de l'Esprit Bourgeois en France*. Paris, 1927.

GRONOW, R. H. *Reminiscences of Capt. Gronow, etc., by Himself*. London, 1862.

GROSLEY, P. J. *A Tour to London, or, New Observations on England and its Inhabitants*. London, 1772.

GUEST, R. *A Compendious History of the Cotton Manufacture*. Manchester, 1823.

GUIZOT, F. *An Embassy to the Court of St. James in 1840*. London, 1863.

GUTTMACHER, M. S. *America's Last King: An Interpretation of the Madness of George III*. New York, 1941.

HABERSHON, M. H. *Chapeltown Researches*. London, 1893.

HALÉVY, E. *A History of the English People, 1815–30*. London, 1926.

HALÉVY, E. 'La Naissance du Methodisme en Angleterre.' In *Revue de Paris* (1906), pp. 519 ff.

HAMMOND, J. *Love Elegies*. London, 1757.

HAMMOND, J. L. and HAMMOND, B. *The Bleak Age*. London, 1947.

HAMPDEN, J. (ed.). *An Eighteenth Century Journal, 1774–6*. London, 1940.

HAMPSON, J. *Memoirs of the late John Wesley*. Sunderland, 1791.

HARDMAN, W. *A Mid-Victorian Pepys: the Letters and Memoirs of Sir William Hardman, M.A., F.R.G.S.* (ed. S. M. Ellis). London, 1923.

HARE, A. J. C. *The Years with Mother* (ed. M. Barnes). London, 1952.

HARWOOD, D. *Love for Animals and how it developed in Great Britain*. New York, 1928.

HAUSER, A. *The Social History of Art*. London, 1951.

HAUSSET, BARON D'. *Great Britain in 1833*. London, 1833.

HAVENS, R. D. *The Mind of a Poet: A Study of Wordsworth's Thought*, etc. Baltimore, 1941.

HEIDIGGER, G. *Mythoscopia Romantica, oder Discours von der so-benannten Romans*, etc. Zurich, 1698.

HERVEY, J. *Meditations among the Tombs, in a Letter to a Lady*. London, 1746.

HIBBERD, S. *Rustic Adornment for Homes of Taste*. London, 1857.

HICKEY, W. *Memoirs of William Hickey* (ed. A. Spencer). London, 1948.

HILL, T. W. *The Remains of Thomas Wright Hill*. London, 1859.

[HOARE, L.] *Hints for the Improvement of Early Education and Nursery Discipline*. London, 1819.

HODGSON, J. C. (ed.) *Six North Country Diaries*. Surtees Society, Vol. 65. 1877.

HODGSON, R. *The Life of the Rt. Rev. Beilby Porteus, Bishop of London*. London, 1811.

HODSON, J. *Nature's Assistant*. London, 1794.

HOGARTH, W. *The Analysis of Beauty*. London, 1791.

HOGARTH, W. *Frolic: the Five Days Peregrination around the Isle of Sheppey*, etc. London, 1732.

HOLLAND, LADY E. *Elizabeth, Lady Holland to Her Son, 1821–1845* (ed. Earl of Ilchester). London, 1946.

HORNBEAK, K. *Richardson's Familiar Letters and the Domestic Conduct Books*. Northampton, Mass., 1938. (Smith College Studies in Modern Langs., Vol. 19, No. 2.)

HUDSON, D. *Thomas Barnes of The Times*. Cambridge, 1943.

HUET, P. D. *Huetiana, ou Pensées Diverses*. Paris, 1722.

HUGHES, J. SMITH. *Six Ventures in Villainy*. London, 1955.

HUME, D. *The Letters of David Hume* (ed. J. Greig). Oxford, 1932.

HURD, R. *Letters on Chivalry and Romance*. Dublin, 1762.

INGRAM, T. and NEWTON, D. *Hymns as Poetry*. London, 1956.

JACKSON, T. (ed.) *The Lives of Early Methodist Preachers*. London, 1865.

JAEGER, M. *Before Victoria*. London, 1956.

JAMES, W. *Varieties of Religious Experience*. London, 1903.

JANION, J. *Some Account of the Introduction of Methodism into the City . . . of Chester*, etc. Chester, 1833.

JONES, B. *Follies and Grottoes*. London, 1953.

JONES, E. *Papers on Psychoanalysis*. London, 1950.

JONES, L. C. *The Clubs of the Georgian Rakes* (Col. Univ. Studies in Eng. and Compara. Lit., No. 157). New York, 1942.

JONES, R. F. *Mysticism and Democracy in the English Commonwealth* (W. B. Noble Lectures, 1930–1). Cambridge, Mass., 1932.

JONES, W. *The Diary of the Rev. William Jones, 1777–1821* (ed. O. F. Christie). London, 1929.

KAMES, LORD (Home, H.) *Elements of Criticism*. Edinburgh, 1816.

KAY, J. *The Social Condition and Education of the People in England and Europe.* London, 1850.

KELLETT, E. E. *As I Remember.* London, 1936.

KELLETT, E. E. *Religion and Life in the Early Victorian Age.* London, 1938.

KEMBLE, F. *Record of a Girlhood.* London, 1878.

KEMP, E. *How to Lay Out a Small Garden.* London, 1864.

KETTLEWELL, J. *The Great Evil and Danger of Prophaneness and Prodigality.* London, 1705.

KEYSERLING, COUNT H. (ed.) *The Book of Marriage.* London, 1927.

KIND, A. and FUCHS, E. *Die Weiberherrschaft in der Geschichte der Menschheit.* Munich, 1914.

KING, W. *An Essay on the Origin of Evil.* London, 1731.

KIRK, H. *Mother of the Wesleys.* London, 1876.

KLUCKHOHN, P. *Die Auffassung der Liebe in der 18e. Jahrhundert und in die Romantik.* Halle-a-S, 1922.

KNIGHT, C. *Passages of a Working Life.* London, 1864.

KNIGHT, C. *Once Upon a Time.* London, 1854.

KNIGHT, R. PAYNE. *The Landscape: A Didactic Poem.* London, 1794.

LACKINGTON, J. *The Confessions of J. Lackington, late bookseller, etc.* London, 1804.

LA COMBE, F. *Tableau de Londres.* London, 1784.

LAKER, J. *History of Deal.* Deal, 1917.

LAMINGTON, LORD A. *In the Days of the Dandies.* London, 1906.

LA MOTRAYE, A. DE. *Travels through Europe, Asia and into Part of Africa.* London, 1732.

LANGLEY, B. *New Principles of Gardening, or the Laying Out and Planting of Parterres, etc.* London, 1728.

LAW, W. *A Practical Treatise upon Christian Perfection.* London, 1759.

LAW, W. *A Serious Call to a Devout and Holy Life.* London, New York, 1920.

[LE BLANC, J. B.] *Letters on the English and French Nations.* London, 1747.

LECKY, W. H. *A History of England in the Eighteenth Century.* London, 1887.

LENNOX, LADY S. *The Life and Letters of Lady Sarah Lennox, 1745-1826* (ed. Countess of Ilchester and Lord Stavordale). London, 1901.

LEWALD, F. *England und Schottland: Reisetagebuch.* Braunschweig, 1851.

LEWIN, B. D. *The Psychoanalysis of Elation.* London, 1951.

LICHTENBERG, G. C. *Lichtenberg's Visits to England as described in his Letters and Diaries* (ed. M. L. Mare and W. H. Quarrell). Oxford, 1938. (Oxford Studies in Mod. Lang. and Lit.)

LOCKE, W. *Two Treatises of Government: on Civil Government; in Works,* Vol. 5. London, 1812.

LONGDEN, H. *The Life of Mr. Henry Longden, late of Sheffield, etc.* Liverpool, 1813.

LOUDON, A. *The Wonderful Magazine and Extraordinary Museum.* Carlisle (U.S.), 1804.

LOVEJOY, A. O. *Essays in the History of Ideas*. Baltimore, 1948.

LYELL, SIR C. *The Life, Letters and Journals of Sir Charles Lyell* (ed. Mrs. Lyell). London, 1881.

LYNTON, L. *The Girl of the Period*. London, 1883.

MACAULAY, LORD. *A History of England*. London, 1849.

MALCOLM, J. P. *Anecdotes of the Manners and Customs of London during the Eighteenth Century*, etc. London, 1808.

MARTIN, B. *John Newton*. London, 1950.

MARTINEAU, H. *A History of the Thirty Years' Peace*. London, 1846.

MASSEY, W. N. *A History of England during the Reign of George III*. London, 1865.

MATHER, I. *Angelographia: or a Discourse concerning the Nature and Power of the Holy Angels*, etc. Boston, 1696.

MATHER, I. *An Arrow against Profane and Promiscuous Dancing*. Boston, 1864.

MATHIESON, W. L. *English Church Reform, 1815–1840*. London, 1923.

M--X--LL, K. *The History of Miss Katty N——, by Herself*. London, 1757.

MAYHEW, H. *London Labour and the London Poor*. London, 1861-2.

MEISTER, H. *Letters written during a Residence in England*. London, 1799.

MELVILLE, L. *The Beaux of the Regency*. London, 1908.

MIDDLETON, E. *Biographia Evangelica*. London, 1779–86.

[MIÈGE, G.] *The New State of England under . . . King William and Queen Mary*. London, 1693.

MILLER, H. *My Schools and Schoolmasters: or the Story of my Education*. Edinburgh, 1854.

MILLER, P. and JOHNSON, T. H. *The Puritans*. New York, 1938.

MISSON, F. M. *Memoirs and Observations in his Travels over England*, etc. London, 1719.

MOODY, T. H. *A Complete Refutation of Astrology*. London, 1838.

MOORE, C. A. *Backgrounds of English Literature, 1700–1760*. Minneapolis, 1953.

MOORE, T. *Life of Richard Brinsley Sheridan*. London, 1825.

MORE, H. *An Estimate of the Religion of the Fashionable World*. London, 1798.

MORE, H. *Strictures on the Modern System of Female Education*. London, 1799.

MORE, H. *Thoughts on the Importance of the Manners of the Great to General Society*. London, 1799.

MORITZ, C. P. *Travels in England in 1782*. London, 1886.

MORRIS, C. *The Diary of a West Country Physician, A.D. 1684–1726* (Claver Morris) (ed. E. Hobhouse). London, 1934.

MUELLER, G. *The Autobiography of George Mueller, or A Million and a Half in answer to Prayer* (ed. G. F. Bergin). London, Bristol, 1914.

MURALT, B. L. de. *Lettres sur les Anglois et les Francois et sur les Voiages* (ed. C. Gould and C. Oldham). Paris, 1933.

MUSKAU, PRINCE P. H. L. VON PUECKLER-.—*A Tour in England, Ireland and France in 1826–9*. London, 1832.

NEEDHAM, H. A. *Taste and Criticism in the Eighteenth Century.* London, 1952.

NELSON, R. *An Address to Persons of Quality and Estate.* London, 1715.

NEWMAN, J. H. *Apologia pro Vita Sua.* London, 1864.

NEWTE, T. *A Tour in England and Scotland.* London, 1785.

NEWTON, J. *Life of the Rev. William Grimshaw.* London, 1833.

NICOLL, A. *A History of Early Nineteenth Century Drama, 1800–1850.* Cambridge, 1930.

NICOLL, A. *A History of Late Eighteenth Century Drama, 1750–1800.* Cambridge, 1927.

NICOLSON, H. *Good Behaviour.* London, 1955.

NOKES, G. D. *A History of the Crime of Blasphemy.* London, 1928.

ORTON, J. *The Practical Works of the Rev. Job Orton.* Shrewsbury, 1842.

OSBORN, W. *The Moral and Physical Evils of Sabbath Desecration Considered, and a Legislative Remedy Suggested.* Brighton, 1875.

OVERTON, J. H. *The English Church in the Nineteenth Century.* London.

OVERTON, J. H. *Life in the English Church, 1660–1714.* London, 1885.

OVERTON, J. H. *William Law: Mystic and Non-Juror.* London, 1881.

PARKER, G. *A View of Society and Manners in High and Low Life, being the Adventures of . . . Mr. G. Parker.* London, 1781.

PASCAL, R. *The German Sturm und Drang.* Manchester, 1953.

PASTON, G. *Social Caricature in the Eighteenth Century.* London, 1905.

PAWSON, J. *A Short Account of the Lord's Gracious Dealings with J. Pawson,* etc. Leeds, 1801.

PEARL, C. *The Girl with the Swansdown Seat.* London, 1955.

PEARSON, J. *Memoirs of Joseph Pearson.* London, 1849.

PIERS, G. and SINGER, M. B. *Shame and Guilt.* Springfield, Illinois, 1953.

PILLET, MARECHAL-DE-CAMP. *L'Angleterre vue à Londres et dans les Provinces.* Paris, 1815.

PLOWDEN, F. *Crim. Con. Biography.* London, 1830.

PLUMB, J. H. (ed.) *Studies in Social History.* London, 1955.

POLLNITZ, C. L. *Memoirs de Charles Lewis, Baron de Pollnitz.* London, 1747.

[POLWHELE, R.] *The Unsex'd Females: A Poem.* London, 1798.

PONSONBY, A. (ed.) *English Diaries.* London, 1923.

POWICKE, F. J. *The Cambridge Platonists.* London, 1926.

PRAZ, M. *The Romantic Agony.* London, 1933.

PREEDY, G. *This Shining Woman: Mary Wollstonecraft.* London, 1937.

PRICE, SIR U. *On the Picturesque.* London, 1794.

PUGIN, A. W. *Contrasts, or a parallel between the noble edifices of the fourteenth and fifteenth centuries and similar buildings of the present day showing the present decay of taste.* London, 1836.

PURCELL, J. *A Treatise of Vapours and Hysteric Fits.* London, 1702.

QUINLAN, M. J. *Victorian Prelude: A History of English Manners, 1700–1830.* New York, 1941 and 1949.

RANULF, S. *Moral Indignation and Middle Class Psychology.* Copenhagen, 1938.

RATTENBURY, J. E. *The Conversion of the Wesleys: a Critical Study.* London, 1938.

RAUMER, F. VON. *England in 1835.* London, 1836.

READE, R. S. *Registrum Librorum Eroticorum.* London, 1936.

REDDING, C. *Memoirs of Remarkable Misers.* London, 1863.

REED, A. L. *The Background of Gray's Elegy.* New York, 1924.

REEVE, H. *Journal of a Residence at Vienna and Berlin in 1805-6.* London, 1877.

REITH, C. *The Police Idea.* London, 1938.

RENAN, J. E. *L'Avenir de la Science: Pensées de 1848.* Paris, 1890.

REYNOLDS, F. *The Life and Times of Frederick Reynolds, written by himself.* London, 1826.

REYNOLDS, J. *The Discourses of Sir Joshua Reynolds* (ed. E. Gosse). London, 1884.

REYNOLDS, M. *The Treatment of Nature in English Poetry between Pope and Wordsworth.* Chicago, 1909.

RITCHIE, J. E. *The Night Side of London.* London, 1857.

ROBERTS, B. D. *Mr. Bulkeley and the Pirate.* London, 1936.

ROBERTS, W. *Memoirs of the Life and Correspondence of Hannah More.* London, 1834.

ROCHEFOUCAULD, F. DE LA. *A Frenchman in England 1784.* Cambridge, 1933.

ROGERS, D. *Matrimoniall Honour,* etc. London, 1650.

ROSA, M. W. *The Silver Fork School.* New York, 1936.

ROUSSEAU, J. J. *Confessions.* Italy, 1904.

ROUSSEAU, J. J. *Emile, ou de l'Education.* Paris, 1921.

RUSSELL, B. *History of Western Philosophy.* London, 1947.

RUSSELL, G. W. E. *Collections and Recollections.* London, n.d.

RYAN, M. *Prostitution in London, with a comparative view of that in Paris, New York,* etc. London, 1839.

RYDER, D. *The Diary of Dudley Ryder* (ed. W. Matthews). London, 1939.

SACKVILLE-WEST, V. *Knole and the Sackvilles.* London, 1922.

SADLEIR, M. *Blessington-D'Orsay: A Masquerade.* London, 1933.

SANDFORD, E. *Woman in her Social and Domestic Character.* London, 1831.

SCHLEGEL, A. W. *A Course of Lectures on Dramatic Art and Literature.* London, 1815.

SCHNEIDER, H. W. *The Puritan Mind.*

SCHUECKING, L. L. *Die Familie im Puritanismus.* Leipzig and Berlin, 1929.

SCHUETZ, F. W. VON. *Briefe ueber London.* Hamburg, 1792.

SCOTT, SIR S. H. *The Exemplary Mr. Day, 1748-1789.* London, 1935.

SCOTT, SIR W. *The Visionary, No. 1, 2, 3.* Edinburgh and London, 1819.

SEILLIERE, E. *Les Etapes du Mysticisme Passionel, de St. Preux à Manfred.* Paris, 1919.

SHAFTESBURY, 3RD EARL (A. A. Cooper). *Characteristicks.* London, 1732.

SHARP, T. *The Life of John Sharp . . . Archbishop of York*. London, 1825.

SHEBBEARE, J. *Letters on the English Nation*. London, 1756.

SHELLEY, H. C. *Life and Letters of Edward Young*. London, 1914.

SHENSTONE, W. *The Works of William Shenstone* (ed. Dodsley). London, 1773.

SILLIMAN, B. *A Journal of Travels in England, Holland and Scotland, etc. in 1805 and 1806*. London, 1820.

[SIMOND, L.] *Journal of a Tour and Residence in Great Britain during the Years 1810 and 1811*. Edinburgh, 1815.

SITWELL, E. *The English Eccentrics*. London, 1933.

SKINNER, J. *Journal of a Somerset Rector: John Skinner, 1772–1839* (ed. H. Coombs and A. N. Bax). London, 1930.

SMITH, A. *An Inquiry into the Nature and Causes of the Wealth of Nations*. London. 1904.

SMITH, E. *Foreign Visitors in England*. London, 1889.

SOLOMON, S. *A Guide to Health*. London, 1796.

SOUTHEY, J. *Letters from England*. London, 1807.

SOUTHEY, J. *Life and Correspondence* (ed. C. C. Southey). London, 1849–50.

SPITZ, R. A. 'Authority and Masturbation: some remarks on a bibliographical Investigation.' *Psychoanalytic Quarterly*, XXI, 490–527 (1952.)

STANLEY, A. (ed). *The Life and Correspondence of Thomas Arnold, D.D.* London 1844.

STEEGMAN, J. *The Rule of Taste*. London, 1936.

STUART, D. M. *Regency Roundabout*. London, 1943.

STUKELEY, W. *The Family Memoirs of the Rev. William Stukeley, M.D.*, etc. London, Durham and Edinburgh, 1882.

STUKELEY, W. *Of the Spleen, its Description and History*, etc. London, 1723.

STYLES, J. *An Essay on the Character, Immorality and Anti-Christian Tendency of the Stage*. Isle-of-Wight, 1806.

SUTTIE, I. D. *The Origins of Love and Hate*. London, 1935.

SWITZER, S. *Ichnographia Rustica: or the Nobleman, Gentleman and Gardener's Recreation*, etc. London, 1718.

SYKES, N. *Church and State in England in the Eighteenth Century*. Cambridge, 1934.

TAINE, H. A. *De l'Intelligence*. Paris, 1870.

TAINE, H. A. *Notes on England*. London, 1872.

TAINE, H. A. *A History of English Literature*. Edinburgh, 1871.

TALON, H. *John Bunyan, the Man and his Works*. London, 1951.

TAWNEY, R. H. *Religion and the Rise of Capitalism*. London, 1937.

TAYLOR, G. R. *Sex in History*. London, 1953.

TAYLOR, J. *The Rules and Exercises of Holy Living*. London, 1864.

THOMSON, J. *The Seasons*. London, 1796.

THURSTON, H. H. C. *The Physical Phenomena of Mysticism*. London, 1952.

TOLAND, J. *Pantheisticon*. London, 1751.

TREFFRY, M. A. C. *Heavenward: Memorials of Mrs. M. A. C. Treffry of Maiden-head* (ed. J. A. MacDonald). London, 1866.

TROELTSCH, E. *Protestantism and Progress.* London, 1912.

TRUSLER, J. *Hogarth Moralised.* London, 1768.

TRUSLER, J. *A System of Etiquette.* Bath, 1805.

TURNER, E. S. *A History of Courting.* London, 1954.

TURNER, T. *The Diary of Thomas Turner of East Hoathly* (ed. F. M. Turner). London, 1925.

TYERMAN, L. *The Life and Times of John Wesley.* London, 1870.

UFFENBACH, Z. C. *London in 1710.* London, 1934.

UTTER, R. P. and NEEDHAM, G. B. *Pamela's Daughters.* New York, 1936.

VARLEY, H. *A Private Lecture in Exeter Hall, January 18, 1883.* London, 1883.

VENN, H. *The Complete Duty of Man: or a System of Doctrinal and Practical Christianity.* London, 1836.

VULLIAMY, C. E. *Ursa Major; a Study of Dr. Johnson.* London, 1947.

W. J. *The Necessary Duty of Family Prayer and the Deplorable Condition of Prayerless Families Consider'd.* London, 1704.

WALFORD, J. *Memoirs of the Life and Labours of the late Venerable Hugh Bourne* (e. W. Antliff). London, 1855.

WALPOLE, HORACE. *An Essay on Modern Gardening.* London, 1785.

WARD, E. *The London Terraefilius.* London, 1707.

WARD, R. *Life of the Learned and Pious Dr. Henry More,* etc. London, 1710.

WARNER, W. J. *The Wesleyan Movement in the Industrial Revolution.* London, 1930.

WATTS, I. *A Preservative from the Sins and Follies of Childhood and Youth.* London, 1734.

WEARMOUTH, R. F. *Methodism and the Common People of the Eighteenth Century.* London, 1945.

WEBB, S. and B. *The History of Liquor Licensing in England, principally from 1700–1830.* London, 1903.

WEBER, F. P. *Aspects of Death in Art.* London, 1910.

WEBSTER, W. *Two Sermons upon the Sabbath.* London, 1751.

WEISSKOPF, W. A. *The Psychology of Economics.* London, 1955.

WENDEBORN, F. A. *A View of England towards the Close of the Eighteenth Century.* London, 1791.

WESLEY, J. *An Earnest Appeal to Men of Reason and Religion.* Bristol, 1743.

WESLEY, J. and C. *Funeral Hymns.* London, 1817.

WESLEY, J. *The Journal of John Wesley* (ed. N. Curnock). London, 1909–16.

WESLEY, J. *Letters of the Rev. John Wesley* (ed. J. Telford). London, 1931.

WHISTON, W. *Memoirs of the Life and Writings of William Whiston . . written by himself.* London, 1753.

WHITAKER, W. B. *The Eighteenth Century English Sunday.* London, 1940.

WHITE, T. *A Little Book for Little Children.* London, 1702.

WHITE, T. H. *The Age of Scandal.* London, 1950.

WHITE, T. H. *The Scandalmonger.* London, 1952.

WHITEHOUSE, F. R. B. *Table Games of Georgian and Victorian Days.* London, 1951.

WHITWELL, J. R. *Analecta Psychiatrica.* London, 1946.

WILBERFORCE, W. *A Practical View of the Prevailing Religious System of Professed Christians.* London, 1797.

WILLOUGHBY, L. A. *The Romantic Movement in Germany.* London, 1930.

WITHERS, P. *A History of the Royal Malady.* London, 1789.

WOLLSTONECRAFT, M. *Vindication of the Rights of Women.* London, 1792.

WOODFORDE, J. W. *The Diary of a Country Parson, the Rev. James Woodforde, 1758–1802* (ed. J. Beresford). London, 1924.

WOODHAM-SMITH, C. *The Reason Why.* London, 1953.

WOODWARD, J. *An Account of the Rise and Progress of the Religious Societies in the City of London.* London, 1701.

WOOLSTON, T. *The Life of Mr. Woolston, with an Impartial Account,* etc. London, 1733.

WORDSWORTH, W. *Poems of William Wordsworth* (ed. N. C. Smith). London, 1908.

WORDSWORTH, W. *Prose Works of William Wordsworth* (ed. A. B. Grosart). London, 1876.

WRIGHT, T. *The Autobiography of Thomas Wright of Birkenshaw* (ed. by his Grandson). London, 1864.

YOUNG, A. *The Autobiography of Arthur Young with Selections from his Correspondence* (ed. M. Betham-Edwards). London, 1898.

YOUNG, A. *An Enquiry into the State of the Public Mind,* etc. *In a Letter to William Wilberforce, M.P.* London, 1798.

YOUNG, E. *Conjectures on Original Composition in a Letter to the Author of Sir Charles Grandison.* London, 1759.

Z.C. *Hymns Composed for the Use of the Brethren.* London, 1749.

ZETZNER, J. E. *Londres et l'Angleterre,* A.D. *1700* (ed. R. Reuss). Strasbourg, 1905.

ZOUCH, J. *Hints respecting the Public Police.* London, 1786.

ANONYMOUS WORKS

ANON. *An Account of the Progress of the Reformation of Manners in England, Scotland and Ireland, &c.* London, 1703.

An American in England. New York, 1835.

The Book of Elegance.

The Book of Gentility (by a member of the Beefsteak Club). London.

The Christian Visitor's Handbook. London, 1851.

A Congratulatory Epistle from a Reformed Rake to John F———g, Esq., upon the New Scheme of Reclaiming Prostitutes. London, 1750.

Considerations on Parochial Evils. London, 1788.

Dens of London Exposed. London, 1835.

Doings in London. London, 1840.

Errors of Pronunciation and Improper Expressions Frequently and Chiefly Used by the Inhabitants of London. London, 1817.

The Explosion: or an Alarming Providential Check to Immorality (by a citizen of Chester). London, 1772.

Fashionable Amusements. London, 1827.

The Female Husband named James Allen Married for over 21 Years. Universal Pamphleteer Series of Popular Tracts (pub. by G. Smeeton) c. 1829-30.

The Female Instructor, or Young Woman's Companion. Liverpool, 1811.

The Female Jockey Club: A Sketch of the Manners of the Age. Dublin, 1794.

Females of the Present Day Considered as to their Influence on Society. London, 1831.

Female Tuition: an Address to Mothers. London, 1786.

The Heaven Drivers: A Poem. London, 1701.

Hell Upon Earth: or The Town in an Uproar. London, 1729.

The Hermit in Edinburgh. London, 1824.

The Hermit in London: Sketches of English Manners. London, 1822.

Hints on Etiquette (by Agogos). London, 1834.

Hints to the Public and the Legislature on the Prevalence of Vice and the Dangerous Effects of Seduction. London, 1811.

Hints on Sea Bathing. London, 1838.

How to Woo, When and to Whom. London, 1855.

How to Woo; How to Win and How to get Married. Glasgow, 1856.

A Letter on the Management and Education of Infant Children. London, 1827. (in Chapone, H., and others: *Letters on the Improvement of the Mind,* etc.)

371

The Life and Times of Selina Countess of Huntingdon (by a member of the Houses of Shirley and Hastings). London, 1844.

The Life of Mr. Woolston. London, 1733.

London and all its Dangers. London, 1835.

London by Moonlight: A Series of Tracts (by a Secretary of a Female Temporary Home). London, 1853 and 1854.

London in the Sixties (by One of the Old Brigade). London, 1914.

London, or A Month at Steven's (by a late Resident). London, 1811.

The Metropolitan Pulpit. London, 1819.

The New Whole Duty of Man. London, 1744.

The Noble Funeral of that Renowned Champion the Duke of Grafton. London, 1690.

Onania Examin'd and Detected (by Philo-Castitatis). [London, 1724.]

The Phoenix of Sodom, or the Vere St. Coterie. London, 1813.

The Polite Academy, or School of Behaviour for Young Gentlemen and Ladies. London, 1765.

A Practical View of Christian Education in its Early Stages. London, 1817.

Recollections of a Maiden Aunt. London, 1858.

Sacred Meditations and Devotional Hymns, with some Essays in Prose. London, 1813.

Satan's Harvest Home: or the present state of Whorecraft, Adultery, Fornication, Procuring, Pimping, Sodomy and the Game at Flatts. London, 1749.

Les Serails de Londres, ou les Amusements Nocturnes. Paris, 1801.

Sinks of London Laid Open: to which is Added a Pocket Flash Dictionary, etc. London, 1848.

Six Weeks at Long's. London, 1817.

Statement Respecting the Prevalence of Certain Immoral Practices in H.M. Navy. London, 1821.

The Swell's Night Guide through the Metropolis (by the Hon. F.L.G.). London, 1841.

Travels in Town. London, 1839.

The Vices of the Cities of London and Westminster. Dublin, 1751.

The Whole Duty of Man. London, 1806.

The Yokel's Preceptor, or More Sprees in London. London, c. 1850–60.

MANUSCRIPTS CONSULTED

JACKSON, E., MS *Diary*, 1702.
VINEY, R., MS *Diary*, 1744.
MARRIOTT, MS *Diary*.
BESWICK, MS *Diary*

LUTTRELL, N., MS *Diary*, 1725.
Hist. MSS Commn. Astley MS.
Bath MS.
Francis Place Collection.

PERIODICALS

The Annual Register.
The Annals of Sporting and Fancy Gazette.
The Architect's Yearbook.
The Arminian Magazine.
The Athenian Oracle.
The Bristol Journal.
The British Mercury.
The Connoisseur.
The Covent Garden Magazine.
The Ecclesiologist.
The Edinburgh Review.
The Englishwomen's Domestic Magazine.
The Evangelical Magazine.
The Exquisite.
Fog's Journal.
The Gentleman's Magazine.
The Gospel Magazine.
The Guardian of Education.
Harris' List of Covent Garden Ladies.
The Ladies' Newspaper.

The Lady's Magazine.
The Leeds Intelligencer.
The London Chronicle.
The London Magazine.
Magazine of Domestic Economy.
The Methodist Magazine.
The Psychoanalytic Quarterly.
Punch.
The Rambler.
The Recreative Review.
The Repository of Arts, Literature, Commerce, Manufactures, Fashions and Politics, 1809–29.
La Revue Historique.
La Revue de Paris.
The Saturday Magazine.
The Scourge.
The Spectator.
The Sunday Times.
The Times.
The Town and Country Magazine.

INDEX

INDEX